FOOTPRINTS ON A BRAIN
The Inspector Allhoff Stories

D. L. Champion

Edited and Introductions
by Alfred Jan
Bill Blackbeard

A Dime Detective Magazine™ Masterpiece
as published by Adventure House

AT THE STROKE OF MIDNIGHT by John K. Butler

Other Adventure House Pulp Reprints Include:

HIGH ADVENTURE a bimonthly pulp reprint anthology series

FOOTPRINTS ON A BRAIN

The Inspector Allhoff Stories

D. L. CHAMPION

**Edited and Introductions
by Alfred Jan
Bill Blackbeard**

Adventure House, 914 Laredo Road, Silver Spring, MD 20901 - sales@adventurehouse.com
www.adventurehouse.com

Printed in the United States of America
First Trade Paperback Printing: July 2001
10 9 8 7 6 5 4 3 2 1

ISBN: 1-886937-52-4

C

Contents

IT'S ALLHOFF FOR NOW: Notes on D. L. Champion's Ultimate Odd Detective

By William Blackbeard

The name D. L. Champion gave the dark hero of his unique Dime Detective Magazine series of the 1940s, sounds to some very much like a black joke in view of the police inspector's brutally truncated legs, "all off," you see. The recent discovery, however, of an earlier Dime Detective Magazine writer in Jim Traylor's index to the magazine actually named Allhoff—Fred Allhoff, author of just one story, "The Midas Curse," in 1934 — seems to scuttle this notion handily. Or perhaps not: after all, Champion did name Inspector Allhoff's permanent police department victim — the detective responsible for his reduced height — Battersly. In the pulps, more often than not, nomenclature ruled (as old pros like Champion and Bill Pronzini — a might-have-been pulpster who launched a nameless detective — well knew).

Allhoff, certainly, is a peak accomplishment in the multitudinous ranks of oddly endowed detectives that first swarmed off the pages of turn-of-the-century from the 1890s on, posturing adroitly in their varied novelty to capture the eager attention of a public already enraptured by the melodramatic escapades and brilliant crime elucidations of A. Conan Doyle's very odd private detective in The Strand Magazine and Collier's month after month. By and large, the popular fiction readers savored them all, immersing themselves in an addicted orgy of crime reading which has not let up yet, welcoming the sight of a regularly renewed array of bizarre sleuths (together with a plethora of ordinary detectives crafted as security blankets for mundane readers) year in and year out. (Who could resist such great creations as I KLIK 4 U, the robot detective, or Manmangler McCanvasback, the wrestler detective? Or "I-Beam" Turntable, the lighthouse keeper detective? Or Kate Sutureself, the slaughterhouse detective? And think of the sleuths that might have been — if only Robert Heinlein had thought to have Joe-Jim pursue some detectival activity in "Universe," we could have rejoiced in the world's first two-headed detective. But we must be content with the bounty we have.

Allhoff, I think, can be said to surpass most of his blind, dwarfed, pseudo-Belgian brethren, and to equal the handful remaining of the very best in sheer cussed brutality of concept and a deep character appeal sustained devilishly well in spite of foul behavior and vengeful rant. He is truly unique, non-pariel, a once in a lifetime experience for anyone who encounters him in these pages. Vulgar, boisterous, savagely canny, never to be put down, he is the Popeye of pulp.

Try him out if you have the nerve.

"Footprints on a Brain" awaits . . .

Santa Cruz
California
Copyright © Bill Blackbeard, January 2001

Biographical Note

Bill Blackbeard researches, writes, and edits books on popular art and fiction for the San Francisco Academy of Comic Art, which he founded in 1967. Faced with expanding collections, he moved the Academy to nearby Santa Cruz, California, in 1997, where questions about its non-profit activities and research files can be answered at 813-427-1737, or billblackbeard@webtv.net

Inspector Allhoff: Armchair-Hardboiled Hybrid

By Alfred Jan

By the late 1930s, American detective pulp fiction was in full swing, evolving many directions away from classical European armchair characters. An earlier American counterpart, S. S. Van Dine's Philo Vance had already fallen out of favor. Great Detective, the only pulp magazine to include stories by Dorothy L. Sayers in every issue ended its original run in late 1933. One evolutionary result was Rex Stout's Nero Wolfe and Archie Goodwin, a team representing the armchair and hardboiled types, respectively. However, the obese, orchid-growing gourmand Wolfe was too eccentric, untrue-to-life, and Goodwin was too polite to be hardboiled. Not surprisingly, they never appeared in the pulp glory days, only in the short-lived Nero Wolfe Mystery Magazine of 1954.

D. L. Champion's original contribution consisted of incorporating both armchair and hardboiled genres in one character, Inspector Allhoff, who is true-to-life, because losing one's legs from gun fire is a believable occupational hazard. While he worked for the New York Police Department, rather than as a loner P. I., and lived in a slum tenement, his hardboildness derived not from the sociological, but the psychopathological. On Death and Dying author and psychiatrist Elizabeth Kübler-Ross' sequence of mourning the loss of a loved one, or major body part, includes denial and isolation, anger, bargaining, depression, and acceptance. After Allhoff's wounded, gangrenous legs were amputated above the knees, his mourning stalled at the anger stage, resulting in narrator Simmonds identifying three main hatreds emanating from "shriveled heart and twisted soul": 1) the world in general, 2) the rookie cop Battersly who ran from his job and failed to prevent Allhoff from getting his legs shot to pieces, and 3) the idea of Homicide or anyone else solving a murder before he did. Perversely, this overarching anger fueled his existence, just as the viscous black coffee he slurped down every morning.

The interpersonal dynamics among Battersly, Allhoff, and Simmonds was extremely warped. The "bargaining" in Kübler-Ross' sequence usually refers to victims, upon hearing they would die, making a deal with Cod to extend their lives in exchange for doing good deeds; but Allhoff bargained the Police Commissioner into giving Battersly to him as assistant and psychological punching bag in exchange for remaining on the Force - Simmonds was assigned by the Commissioner to mediate between the two, and because his pension was at stake, he could not have refused. Add to this volatile mix an outsider making a quip about dancing or cripples, and the fireworks began. Simmond's description of Allhoff's intensifying infuriation, culminating in a crescendo of expletives is disturbing and sickly comical. The weak-willed Battersly regularly submitted to verbal abuse, and any attempt to atone for his cowardly failure to kill the machine gunner was met with brutal contempt. Thus the Inspector, in addition to a physical handicap, also acquired a personality disorder from not satisfactorily working through the grief process.

Armchair aspects of Allhoff compared favorably with tradition. Most of the time, he sat in his apartment, but occasionally visited crime scenes. His ability to interpret clues keeps readers riveted to the story, and Champion sets up seemingly impossible crimes to stimulate our curiosity but does not reveal enough for us to solve the mystery ahead of time. Allhoff's knowledge of obscure word origins and language subtleties puts him on par with the best scholarly sleuth. In several stories, he gathered suspects around his desk, and deceived the murderer into exposing himself or herself. Although he may have bent the rules according to today's standards, Allhoff rarely fired a gun or beat confessions out of suspects. In addition, the narrator did not crudely describe women's bodies, and Champion did not use obnoxious racial caricatures, especially of Asians, a refreshing change from many other detective pulp story authors.

Do armchair and hardboiled conventions cohere in one character? I say they do in Champion's Inspector Allhoff novelettes, which portrayed a very functional yet dysfunctional police unit, a paradoxical tension which drove the stories forward. The first Allhoff story's title, "Footprints on a Brain", from the July 1938 Dime Detective Magazine depicts the duality of hardboiled action (taking steps) and armchair deduction using the brain, but a grimmer interpretation sees Battersly fleeing footsteps trampling on his sanity. Significantly, Champion's titles reflect specific story content except the first, setting the stage for the next 28. To my knowledge, only two Allhoff stories have been anthologized, so Bill and I wanted to bring almost half of them out of obscurity for contemporary mystery lovers to enjoy.

Santa Clara
California
Copyright © Alfred January 2001

Biographical Note

A practicing optometrist, Alfred Jan has published freelance art criticism nationally and internationally, and has served as Adjunct Professor of Humanities at De Anza College. He holds an M.A. in Philosophy, specializing in Aesthetics.

FOOTPRINTS ON A BRAIN

"I was at the head of my men—and got twenty bullets in my legs."

CHAPTER ONE

Three Men and a Half

I was halfway down the hall when the commissioner came out of his office. On general principles I decided to keep out of the way and began a fast detour down the corridor that runs parallel to Centre Street—but he nailed me anyway.

"Simmonds," he yelled. "Just the man I want. Come here."

I sighed, swung around and saluted.

The commissioner indicated a burly Irishman at his side. The man held a thick manila envelope under his arm.

"This is Detective-sergeant Carrigan of Chicago," said my chief. "Take him over to see Allhoff. Carrigan thinks he's got something."

The commissioner's tone implied that he, personally, didn't think Carrigan had anything at all. I saluted again.

"Yes, sir," I said. "This way, Sergeant."

Carrigan followed me out of the building into Centre Street. As I led the way to the ramshackle frame tenement opposite, he looked at me inquiringly.

"Who's this Allhoff?" he asked. "Why ain't he got his office in Headquarters?"

"Well," I told him, "Allhoff's not exactly a member of the department."

"For God's sake," said Carrigan, mildly resentful. "What the hell's the chief sending me to him for? I got a murder case."

I didn't say anything to that. If Carrigan's murder case was so weak that it failed to interest the commissioner, Allhoff would make short shrift of it. If the commissioner, for reasons of politics or diplomacy, had refrained from telling this Irishman he had no case, Allhoff would certainly have no qualms about doing so. It was one of Allhoff's bad days, too. He'd been raising hell since breakfast.

I led the way up the rickety flight of stairs that ascended to Allhoff's tiny two-room combination office and living quarters. Carrigan followed me, his wonder increasing at every step. By the time we reached the door, he was completely bewildered.

The room, as usual, was in depressing disorder. A dressing-gown and a soiled pajama-coat were flung carelessly over the back of a chair. My battered old desk near the window was covered with disarrayed morning papers. Allhoff sat close up to the other desk, his narrow chest pressed against the wood. At his left a blackened coffee pot perked sullenly on an electric plate. Through the open door on his right, the unmade bed in the next room was evident.

The place looked like a fifteen-dollar-a-month slum tenement flat—which, as a matter of fact, it was.

Across the room, young Battersly, in uniform, stood by the window staring moodily into the street. His dark eyes smoldered. A single glance at him convinced me that Allhoff was in prime condition this morning.

"Inspector," I said to Allhoff, "this is Detective-sergeant Carrigan of Chicago.

The commissioner told me to bring him over."

Carrigan, still somewhat confused by the layout, extended a meaty hand. "Glad to meet you, Inspector," he said.

Allhoff grunted. He poured some hellishly black coffee into a chipped, stained cup. He sipped it, and regarded Carrigan hostilely over the cup's edge. Carrigan stood there like a fool with his hand held out. A slow resentful flush came over his honest face. He dropped his hand and shifted his bulk uncomfortably beneath Allhoff's scrutiny.

It wasn't pleasant to have Allhoff stare at you. I knew that. His little seamed face was yellow as if it reflected the bad temper within him. His eyes held a savage bitterness, a dark brooding which had their roots deep down inside him.

Over at the window, young Battersly lifted his gaze from its unseeing contemplation of Centre Street and stared at the back of Allhoff's neck. His face was dark, his eyes sullen. I sighed, shook my head futilely and sat down at my desk. This was one hell of a place to work. Between Battersly and Allhoff I was going quietly nuts. Three times I'd asked the commissioner for a transfer. Three times I'd been told: "We need you

there, Simmonds. We need an old clear head to watch those two. You're the oil on the troubled waters." Well, damn it, let them change the oil. I was getting fed up.

Allhoff drained the cup and put it down. "Sit down, Carrigan," he said. "There—in that chair."

Carrigan removed the worn shirt from the indicated chair. He sat down, still clutching the manila envelope under his arm. It was apparent that he still resented Allhoff's manner. The amiability had left his face. There was a definite antagonism about him.

"Before you begin," said Allhoff, "you, Simmonds, get me a scratch pad. Battersly, find my fountain pen."

His tone, as was customary, was dictatorial and insolent. Carrigan stared at him strangely. I took a pad from my desk and gave it to him. Battersly opened a closet door and rummaged in the pocket of a hanging vest for Allhoff's pen. Carrigan viewed these proceedings sourly.

"All right," said Allhoff. "Now what is it, Carrigan?"

Carrigan opened his mouth to speak when Allhoff interrupted him. "Here," he snapped with curling arrogance in his voice, "before you get going, hand me those cigarettes over there."

Carrigan looked around. An opened package lay on a typewriter stand less than three feet away from Allhoff's right arm. It was more than twice that distance from Carrigan over on the other side of the desk. Carrigan looked from the cigarettes back to Allhoff. Slowly his face became red as the Russian flag. The Irish in him which had been quietly seething since Allhoff had ignored his hand, boiled over now.

He got out of his chair and towered over Allhoff's anemic frame like a giant.

"Damn it, Inspector!" he roared, "Get your own cigarettes! They're nearer to you than they are to me. You've been playing God ever since I came in here. You've treated me and these other two men like we were dirt. Maybe they'll stand for it. I won't. Get your own damn cigarettes. You're no cripple."

I nearly died at that. I heard the sharp intake of Battersly's breath behind me. I saw the little gleam of unholy joy that flashed in Allhoff's eyes. Battersly lit a cigarette with fingers that trembled. On Allhoff's face was an awful grimace that he meant to be a smile. His ugly teeth showed through his parted lips. His eyes were the eyes of a fanatic. Carrigan did not notice these things. He remained standing over Allhoff, glowering.

"Well," he bellowed again, "why don't you make a move? Why don't you get your own butts. You ain't a cripple. Are you?"

Allhoff's ghastly smile grew broader, more horrible. Slowly he pushed his chair away from the desk. When he spoke, his voice was frozen honey.

"You have come to the crux of the matter, Sergeant," he said softly. "And I'm afraid I must correct you. I am a cripple."

Carrigan stared down at the chair in which Allhoff sat. He looked foolishly at the two stumps which ended Allhoff's body where his legs should have begun. I shot a swift glance at Battersly. His lips were compressed. His eyes were hot and tortured. Allhoff looked about the room, grinning like a fiend. Carrigan's wrath fell from him. Covered with confusion, he took the cigarettes from the stand and handed them to Allhoff.

"I'm sorry, Inspector," he blurted. "Sorry—er, I, er—I didn't know. I had no idea. I—"

Allhoff lifted a deprecating hand and waved him to silence. "We all make mistakes, Sergeant," he said. "Not your fault. No one's fault, excepting of course, the yellow rat who left me facing a machine gun three years ago. It's an interesting story, Sergeant. Very interesting. It happened just three years ago next month. I was—"

Something cracked inside me. I couldn't stand any more of this. "Shut up, Allhoff!" I shouted. "Damn you, man! Shut up!"

Allhoff swivelled around in his chair and glared at me. "Simmonds," he said, "I'll thank you to remember that you're a sergeant attached to the Nineteenth Precinct. My rank is that of deputy inspector."

That got me sore. "Deputy inspector of what?" I yelled. "You're not even a member of the department. What the hell right've you got to give me orders?"

That got him. His little eyes smoldered. For a tense silent moment, he fought his temper. Young Battersly looked on nervously. Carrigan sat quietly in his chair, a puzzled expression on his face.

"Listen," said Allhoff to me, and I knew his calm tone cost him an effort, "if you think you're not under my orders, ask the commissioner. If there's any doubt about it, I'll call him now." He reached for the telephone.

I threw up my hands. The commissioner would back him to the hilt, and I knew it. I could hear Battersly's knuckles drumming on my desk-top. I felt suddenly weary and despairing.

"All right, Allhoff," I told him. "I'll shut up. Go ahead. Have your psychopathic fling."

He swung around again and faced Carrigan. "Now, Sergeant," he said, "I was going to tell you how I lost my legs. Wasn't I?"

"Er—yeah," said Carrigan, obviously uncomfortable. "But I got a murder case, Inspector. I got a—"

Allhoff ignored him. He breathed deeply and sat back in his chair. A strange expression of feline pleasure was in his eyes.

"It was three years ago, Sergeant," he said again. "First week in August it was, and just as hot a day as today. You'll probably remember the Roseman mob. Well, it was the night we got Roseman and Kaylor."

Battersly's desk-drumming had stopped abruptly. I looked up to see him snatch his cap and jam it down over his eyes. He walked rapidly toward the door. Allhoff spoke to him as his hand was on the knob.

"Where are you going, Battersly?"

Battersly glared at him. He stood on the threshold like an animal in a trap. His lips moved convulsively. For a moment, I thought he was going to explode. Then his eyes fell on Carrigan. He took hold of himself again.

"Cigarettes," he said hoarsely. "I'm going down for cigarettes. I'll be right back."

"I've got plenty of cigarettes here," said Allhoff. "You can smoke mine. I want you to stay. I may need you."

You'll need him all right, I thought to myself. In about three minutes now you'll need him like a hophead needs a shot.

Silently Battersly recrossed the room. Allhoff turned again to Carrigan.

"We had a tip," he resumed. "Roseman and Kaylor, his right-hand man, were holed up in a rooming-house on the West Side. We knew further, that they had a Tommy-gun trained on the front door. They were taking no chances."

Allhoff paused and refilled his cup from the blackened coffee pot. Battersly's eyes were riveted on his scrawny neck. A low feral growl came from Battersly's throat. He took a half-step forward. I put a hand on his arm.

"Steady, son," I said. But I was feeling sick myself.

Uneasily, Carrigan moved his bulk in the chair. "I remember Roseman, Inspector," he said. "He burned, a couple of years back. Now, listen, Inspector, I got a murder case here."

Allhoff sipped his coffee for a moment, then continued as if Carrigan had not spoken.

"We arranged a zero hour," he said and his voice was high with suppressed emotion. "We sent a man up the rear fire-escape. His job was to affect an entrance through a window and, at any cost, to get the man behind the Tommy-gun before we broke in the front door. Get that, Carrigan, *at any cost!*"

Allhoff made a nasty gurgling sound as he drained the coffee cup. His little eyes were glowing now. I watched him, fascinated. I had heard this damned story a hundred times, yet there was something repulsively attractive listening to him wallow in the slime of his own insane emotions.

"Well, Sergeant," said Allhoff, "to make it brief, the man we sent up the back way was yellow. Someone saw him, fired at him. He went to pieces. Instead of fighting it out and blasting the Tommy operator, he ran up the stairs. At zero we broke down the door and charged in. I was at the head of my men, Carrigan—at the head, where I belonged. I got twenty bullets in my legs. Gangrene set in. They cut 'em off, Carrigan."

There was sweat on Allhoff's brow, there was a hellish glow on his face and madness in his eyes.

Carrigan, ill at ease, murmured something inadequate. "That's too bad, Inspector. Now about this murder case—"

"Wait a minute," snapped Allhoff. I tightened up. Now it was coming. Allhoff had said he might need Battersly. Well, this was the time. He needed him now. Needed him badly—to work off some of the accumulated bitterness that had seethed within him for three searing years.

He swung around in his chair, raised a trembling finger in Battersly's direction. His lips twitched. Now his crazy passion had reached its peak. Now he would shoot the works. I shuddered as I looked at him.

But this time it didn't quite go off according to schedule. For once Battersly took the play away from him. I heard him inhale with a sound like a rasping saw. He leaned forward over my desk.

"All right, damn you!" he screamed in a voice that broke just two points this side of hysteria. "All right, tell him I did it! Tell him I went crazy for a minute and ran up the stairs leaving a machine-gun to cut off your legs. Go ahead and tell him! Tell him as you've told everyone else who ever came into this office."

He broke off to catch his breath. Then, before I could restrain him, he raced across the room and stood over Allhoff.

"But, tell him, too," he shrieked, "that if I was crazy for a minute that night, you've been insane ever since. Tell him that you've put me through hell for three years that you're making me lose my mind and spirit as surely as I made you lose your legs. Tell him that, you grinning madman! God, I'll—"

He lifted his hand. I dashed across the room and grabbed him. Allhoff looked like a sneering skull.

"You're running true to type," he said bitterly. "After you cripple a man you find enough courage to lift your fist to him."

I felt the tenseness go out of Battersly's body. His muscles were limp beneath my fingers. Then he brushed me aside and walked out of the room. Allhoff made no attempt to stop him now.

As the door slammed Allhoff uttered a little feline sigh—almost the sigh of a woman surfeited with love. He turned to the dazed Carrigan. When he spoke all the passion had gone from his voice. His tone was crisp and businesslike.

"Now, Sergeant," he said evenly. "What was this you said about a murder case?"

CHAPTER TWO

End of a Chapter

Carrigan began to talk. I didn't listen to him. I was savagely wishing that I was pounding a nice quiet beat out on Staten Island. At least three times a week since I had drawn this assignment, I had been forced to witness this same ghastly scene. At every opportunity, Allhoff forced Battersly to pay for his lost legs.

It was inhuman and, if I knew anything about the minds of men, it was insane. Frankly, I believed that three years of hate and brooding had driven Allhoff, literally, crazy.

Officially, Allhoff no longer belonged on the force. After all, you couldn't have a deputy inspector minus a pair of legs. But Allhoff's brain was of more value to the commissioner than his body had ever been. He wasn't carried on the departmental roster, but through some circuitous bookkeeping the city paid him an inspector's salary.

The single condition Allhoff had laid down as the terms of his employment was that Battersly should be assigned as his assistant. With grim poetic justice the commissioner had acceded to his request.

Allhoff had rented this slum flat because it was close to headquarters. He rarely left it. He lived and worked here with his hate and bitterness. He, who had once been the Brummel of the department no longer cared about appearance. His clothes were soiled and dirty. The tenement in which he dwelt was always filthy.

I had been dragged down from a good desk job on the Heights to take care of his paper work. At least that was the ostensible reason. Actually, I was supposed to see that Allhoff and Battersly didn't kill each other. I had come up as a rookie with Allhoff and was one of the few men on the force who wasn't daunted by his superior attitude. That's why I was elected—and I'd been regretting it ever since.

It was a ghastly thing to sit here day after day, to watch Allhoff's cunning mind devise new methods of torturing the younger man. It was sickening. I'd rather stand in the basement of a precinct house and watch a couple of strong-arm dicks rubber-hose a murder suspect any day.

Besides, I'd never liked Allhoff, even in the old days. He was too damned smug and superior. He had a Sherlock Holmes complex. Granting his good mind, it annoyed me when he cloaked his simplest activity in unnecessary mystery merely to impress the rest of us. I suppose, too, that I resented his promotion over my head.

I was straightening up the papers on my desk, when I became aware of the fact that Allhoff was barking at me.

"Simmonds," he snapped, "it's part of your job to clip all-important police news for me each morning."

I swung around in my chair. "What's the squawk," I asked. "They were clipped and on your desk before you'd finished breakfast."

"Sure," he said sarcastically. "You just overlooked a little routine item that made the front page of every paper in town. Richard B. Hadley was found dead out on Long Island, early this morning. I suppose even you know who Hadley is?"

"Oh, that," I said. "What the hell do you want that for? It was cold suicide. Spectacular but cold. Both the papers and the Bayside cops agree on that."

"Carrigan doesn't," said Allhoff.

I looked up. So it was the Hadley affair that Carrigan had on his mind. No wonder the commissioner hadn't seemed particularly interested.

"Well," I said, "Carrigan knows more about it than Hadley himself, then. Hell, Hadley left a message saying he was killing himself. I got the whole story here."

I picked up the *Bulletin.*

"Hold it for a minute," said Allhoff. "Let's have it from the beginning, Carrigan. Tell me what you're doing here from Chicago."

"A couple of years ago I was assigned as Hadley's bodyguard in Chicago," said Carrigan. "He was in some trouble out there."

"You're damned right he was," I put in. "The plant of his only competitor in the whole middle west was bombed and fired. Five guys were killed. Hadley beat the rap, but every cop and newspaperman in the country is sure he was back of it."

"Shut up," said Allhoff. "Keep talking, Carrigan."

"Well," said Carrigan, "five months ago the medicos told Hadley he was a pretty sick man. He gave up all active management of his interests and moved out to a quiet place in Bayside to write his autobiography. Said he wanted to finish it before he died. He wanted me to come along with him. He was still-leery about that guy whose plant was bombed. He had a lot of drag in Chi. So they let me come."

Allhoff wrote something down on his little pad. "See?" he said to me. "Get that?"

"So what?" I said impatiently. "It's still suicide. Hadley was a sick man—cancer. He came down to

Long Island to write his book. That done, he shot himself. He always was a spectacular guy. All his life he'd made sensational gestures. If you doubt that, read the obits here. He'd promised his publishers something sensational in his book. All right, he gave it to them. That's the angle all the papers play up. In the last paragraph of the final chapter of his autobiography, he wrote this—" I picked up the *Bulletin* again and quoted:

"I have lived my life as I have written of it. I shall not wait for Death to come upon me slowly; to drag me through a vale of pain. Rather, I shall go forth to meet him. This is the end, Deus Vult!"

Allhoff grunted. "What's that last business?" he asked.

"I don't know," I told him. "Looks like Latin to me. Maybe it means: Dear Inspector Allhoff, the butler killed me."

"Keep those smart cracks for the precinct house," said Allhoff. "Go on, Carrigan."

"Well," said Carrigan. "We all left Chi and went out to the Long Island house."

"All?" said Allhoff. "Who?"

"Well, there was Nina Autrey. That's Hadley's daughter. Paul Autrey, her husband. And—"

"Wait a minute," said Allhoff. "This Paul Autrey was Hadley's partner as well as son-in-law, wasn't he?"

"Yeah," said Carrigan. "For the past ten years they worked together. Autrey is a ruthless, fighting, red-headed tough guy. Hadley cottoned to him right away. He's more like the old man's son than son-in-law."

"All right," said Allhoff. "Who else?"

"There was Rutledge, Hadley's secretary. A quiet little guy who's been his right hand for twenty years. And Parks—that's his valet—a nut on religion but otherwise O. K."

Allhoff was still scribbling on his pad. "Was that all?" he asked.

"Yeah," said Carrigan. "Except Weldon."

"Weldon?" said Allhoff. "I know that name. Utilities guy, isn't he? Worth dough."

"That's right. He's a fat baldheaded guy. Lousy with millions. I think he financed some of Hadley's deals."

"Why did he come along?"

"Just for the ride, I guess," said Carrigan. "Said he needed a rest. Wanted to get away from business."

Allhoff grunted again and proceeded to mark more hieroglyphics on his little pad. His manner irritated me.

"For Heaven's sake, Allhoff," I said. "What are you masterminding? Hadley was just that sort of a guy. He killed himself in a blaze of glory. Here, read the damned paper. It's obvious enough."

"Will you shut up," said Allhoff. "Go ahead, Carrigan. Tell me about last night."

I shrugged futilely. Allhoff was going moving-picture detective on me again.

"Well," said Carrigan, "a little after midnight everyone had gone to bed but Hadley and me. He told me to take the car and drive to town. Said he was going to work late on the book."

"What did he want in town?" asked Allhoff.

"A stamp and a package of razor blades."

"All right. What then?"

"I got a whole book of stamps out of a slot machine," said Carrigan slowly. "I got the razor blades. Then I went back. Hadley was typing like hell. He told me to go to bed. Said he'd have his book finished by morning. He seemed very pleased about it."

"So," said Allhoff, "you went to bed."

"I went to bed," said Carrigan. "Then the shot woke me. I jumped up, put on my bathrobe and raced into the library. Hadley had a hole in his skull and a gun in his hand."

"And the manuscript?"

"Was on the desk in front of him. The last chapter was written. Apparently, he had completed the book."

"Where is it now?"

Carrigan plucked the large manila envelope from under his arm. "Here," he said.

llhoff took it and placed it on the desk. He nodded his head slowly and assumed an expression that he'd swiped from Warner Oland in the movies. I grinned at him.

"All right, Inspector," I said. "Who do I arrest?"

He didn't even yell at me, just held the pose of the master detective lost in thought.

"Listen," I said, nettled, to Carrigan. "Have you the slightest, foggiest reason for believing Hadley was murdered?"

Carrigan scratched his head. "Well I'll tell you," he said slowly. "This may sound screwy to you, but I laid out my own dough for those stamps, for those razor blades. Hadley said he'd give it to me in the morning. He was awful fussy about little things like that. Whenever I laid out anything for him, he'd repay it to the penny. He never forgot. No matter how little it was."

I laughed in his face at that. "Screwy is the word," I said. "Old man Hadley, unofficially known as one of the biggest unindicted crooks that ever ran up a million bucks, postpones the most magnificent gesture of his life because he owes a big flatfoot a lousy thirty cents. Even you ought to get a laugh out of that, Allhoff."

Allhoff was staring at Carrigan. His little eyes gleamed as if there was a thought behind them that was forcing them out of their sockets. His thin nostrils quivered as he spoke.

"You're not as bright as you'd like to be, Simmonds," he said. "Carrigan's right. Of course, he's got the wrong reason."

"If you're so damned superior," I snapped, "what's the right reason?"

"The razor blades," said Allhoff explosively. "Why in hell should a potential suicide be worrying about his beard?"

Carrigan sat upright in his chair. "Geez," he said. "I never thought of that."

"Listen," said Allhoff. "Did Hadley shave himself?"

"Yes," said Carrigan. "Either first thing in the morning or just before he went to bed at night."

Allhoff turned to me and bowed like Barrymore. "You see?" he said.

For a moment, I'd been startled. After a second's thought it seemed pretty thin.

"Wait a minute," I said. "Maybe he didn't want them for himself. Maybe he ordered them when he didn't know he was going to finish the book that night. Maybe—"

"Maybe you're a damned fool," said Allhoff. "Anyway, get out to that Bayside house. See what you can see. Talk to everyone in the house. Look over Hadley's study carefully. Find me that stamp book. Look for that package of razor blades. See if one's missing. In the meantime, I'll look over this manuscript and ask Carrigan some questions."

"Listen," I said. "This is crazy. I—"

"Shut up," said Allhoff. "I'm thinking. Take Battersly with you."

I got up and walked to the door. "I don't know where Battersly is," I said testily.

"You know damned well where he is," said Allhoff. "He's downstairs in the corner saloon, drinking fifteen-cent rye and wishing to God that I had two legs."

I stood in the doorway and looked him in the eye. "Do you know what you are?" I said.

He grinned his mirthless, unholy grin at me. "Say it," he said. "Say it, and I'll have you fined a month's pay. Now what am I?"

I turned around and walked out of the room. I didn't say it until I was halfway down the stairs.

Allhoff was right again. Young Battersly was sitting at a table in Noonan's drinking straight rye. His black eyes were gloomy and morose. He paid no attention to me as I sat opposite him. He drained the drink and banged the empty glass on the tabletop in signal for another.

I was looking at a beaten man. There was an air of utter hopelessness about him that gave me a vacant feeling at the pit of my stomach. The bartender brought him another drink. He gulped it like a man who was actually thirsty.

"Listen, kid," I said. "Why don't you quit?"

He shook his head miserably. "I can't quit," he said. "I can't."

"Why not?" I asked him. "I know it's a damn good job. Three thousand a year with a guaranteed pension's not bad at your age. But, hell, you're young. You can drive a truck or something. I wouldn't take the beating you take for ten times the money."

He lifted his head and looked at me with the eyes of an old man. "It's not the money, Sergeant," he said.

"My God!" I said. "What is it? Love?"

He shook his head again. "I'd quit in a minute if it was just the job," he said. "But it's not. It's more than that. I can't quit. See?" His expression was appealing—as if it were important that I understand him. "No matter what he does, no matter what he says, I got to take it. He's not altogether wrong. After all, what happened up there on West End Avenue was my fault. I got to pay for it. I got to stick with him till I can square it up."

"That's screwy," I told him. "How can you square up a thing like that?"

"You see?" he said. "I can't. That's just it. So I got to stay and take my beating."

He banged the empty glass on the table again.

"No," I said. "That's enough. We're going to Long Island. Allhoff's orders. Come on."

He sighed. "All right," he said. "Let's go."

He didn't ask where we were going or why. He didn't give a damn. He didn't give a damn about anything. He was completely licked. The trip to Bayside was like taking a train ride with a dead man.

CHAPTER THREE

Allhoff Sets the Stage

It was a little before two o'clock when Battersly and I got back to Allhoff's place. Carrigan drowsed in the chair where we had left him. Allhoff's dirty coffee pot was gurgling unenthusiastically, while Allhoff himself, still wearing his Charlie Chan expression, pored over the typewritten sheets of Hadley's biography. He had a pencil in his hand, and I noticed two pages that he had put to one side were annotated. He looked up when we came in.

"Well?" he said.

"Suicide," I said. "Cold."

"I don't want an opinion," he snapped. "Give me some facts."

"All right," I said. "I talked to everyone. They all swore that they were in bed when the shot was fired. I found out nothing that you probably haven't dug out of Carrigan by now. And if you're looking for a money motive, there isn't any."

"How do you know?"

"I talked to Rutledge, the secretary. He told me that Hadley's will provides him and Parks—that's the valet—with annuities. Autrey gets nothing. Apparently, he's got-enough. Weldon gets nothing. The girl gets nothing. A Methodist charity gets it all. Maybe they killed him."

Allhoff ignored the last crack. He nodded his head slowly. "That's right enough about the will," he said. "I've already checked it with Hadley's lawyer. Had him on the phone. Where's that stamp book?"

I took it out of my pocket and handed it to him. "One stamp gone," I said. "He must have mailed a letter before he died— between the time Carrigan went to bed and when he shot himself."

"All right," said Allhoff. "What about the razor blades?"

"Well," I admitted, "the package had been opened. One blade had been used."

Allhoff pounded the desk. "I knew it he said explosively.

"I admit that's a point," I said. "But there are at least fifty things that might explain that. You can't go yelling murder just on that razor blade."

Footprints On A Brain

llhoff waved his hand in the air like a hypnotist. "Shut up," he said. "I'm thinking. There's something screwy about this case. I can't just put my finger on it—but I feel it."

My God, he *felt* it! "Do you figure your psychic vibrations will name names?" I asked him.

He didn't even look at me. "Battersly," he said, "come here."

I threw up my hands and went to my desk. Battersly stood before Allhoff, avoiding his eyes.

"Now," said Allhoff, "what were you doing while Simmonds was talking to all these people?"

"Well," said Battersly uneasily, "I was looking around. I—"

"What did you see?"

"Nothing much. When we got to the study, I found—"

"Wait a minute," said Allhoff. "Begin at the beginning. You're coming through the garden gate. There is a garden, isn't there? All right, you're coming through the gate. Start there. Tell me everything you saw and talk slowly."

I shook my head. Allhoff was getting positively infantile. I was certain he didn't have an idea in his head. He was simply trying to impress Carrigan.

Battersly screwed up his brow and concentrated.

"Well," he said at last, "there was the trees, and a car parked in the driveway. Then there was the birds. The birds squawking on the roof. Then there was—"

"What sort of birds?" asked Allhoff.

Battersly looked puzzled. "They was black," he said. "With sort of fan tails. They was making a hell of a noise."

"Chimney swallows," I said. "Maybe they killed Hadley."

Allhoff swung around in his chair and fixed me with his agate eyes. "Simmonds," he said, "how'd you like to get back into uniform again and pound a beat in Staten Island?"

"It's been the dream of my life for more than two years," I said. "I'd love it. When do I start?"

He looked at me for a long time. Then that ugly smile split his lips. "I guess maybe you would," he said slowly. "So I suppose I'd better keep you here."

Battersly cleared his throat nervously. "Then," he went on, "we got to the porch—" He mumbled a lot more inconsequential detail, until at last Allhoff waved him to silence.

"That'll do," he said. "Now everybody keep quiet. I want to read some more."

Battersly crossed the room and sat down next to the window. Carrigan drowsed in his chair. I just sat there and got more and more irritated at Allhoff. I knew that he had an exaggerated opinion of his own mentality that he delighted in acting the aloof and superior sleuth. But I'd never seen him go this far. He was playing it to the hilt today.

He made another mark on the manuscript with his pencil, lifted his head. "Carrigan," he said, "I want you to go out to Long Island. Stop in at the precinct house in Bayside and get a couple of men. I'll have the commissioner O.K. it. Bring everyone in the Hadley house here to me. Now how long will it take you?"

Carrigan looked at his watch. "About two hours."

"All right. Get going."

Carrigan dragged his bulk out of the chair and waddled through the door.

"Allhoff," I said, "what are you trying to do? Hadley killed himself. You're arguing that he didn't merely because he happened to shave himself first. That'd be fine in a movie but it won't sound so good in the Grand Jury Room."

Allhoff picked up two pages of Hadley's book. "Look," he said. "I've picked out two very interesting spots in Hadley's life. Undoubtedly there are others."

"So what?" I said.

"First," said Allhoff, "it seems that years ago when Hadley was living on a ranch out West, he had a buggy accident. It broke his arm in two places. His right arm was shorter than his left all his life. The accident occurred while he was driving with a girl out in the country. The horse bolted when the whiffletree broke, releasing the surcingle."

"Allhoff," I said. "Why don't you stop? You've got no case and you know it. You're going to look like an awful fool when those people get here."

He ignored me. "The other item," he went on blandly, "was that Hadley went to the Senate once—in Nineteen Eight."

"Everybody knows that," I told him. "It's in all the papers this morning."

"He was elected by a plurality of the voters," said Allhoff. "That's what it says here."

"Well," I said, "how do you think a guy gets into the Senate. By buying a ticket?"

Allhoff looked at me and there was mockery in his gaze. He poured himself another cup of coffee.

"I suppose your mentality is typical of that in the Detective Bureau," he said, "so I shouldn't complain. You and Battersly go down and get some lunch. Hurry back. I'll need you."

"Delighted to get away even for a half-hour," I said. "Come on, kid."

Battersly and I walked to the door.

"You want us to bring you back a sandwich?" I called to Allhoff.

"Well," he said, deliberating, "I guess you'd better. Combination on rye. I don't feel like walking down the stairs myself. I don't—"

"All right," I said hastily. "All right. Come on, Battersly."

I took his arm and got him out of the room before Allhoff could elaborate on that theme.

When Battersly and I got back from lunch, we found Allhoff squinting through the barrel of a thirty-eight. He paid no attention to us. He lowered it and ran an oily rag over its blue steel. Battersly, as usual, did not speak. He walked across the room and stared with dark miserable eyes into Centre Street. I stared at Allhoff.

"What the hell are you doing there?" I asked.

He put the gun down and smiled unpleasantly. He unwrapped the sandwich I had laid on his desk and poured out some coffee.

"I'm strolling down the Boardwalk at Atlantic City," he said bitterly. "Occasionally, I'm breaking into a run. Sometimes, I skip gayly. Then—"

"Damn you!" I said. "Will you stop that?"

He glared up at me. "Well, what the hell do you think I'm doing? I'm cleaning a gun."

"For what?"

Allhoff bit into the sandwich, sipped the foul black brew from the chipped cup. That unholy gloating smile that I hated crawled over his face. He put down the cup.

"For two reasons," he said. "The first is that I expect to meet up with a murderer."

"You're pretty smug about it," I told him. "What's the other reason?"

"Stick around," said Allhoff. "You might find out."

I shrugged my shoulders and went over to my desk, Battersly still stared out the window. His lips were compressed and white. He hadn't missed that crack about the Boardwalk.

"Say," said Allhoff. "Got any carbon paper?"

I opened the desk drawer and took out a fresh package. Allhoff shook his head.

"Not that," he said. "I mean some that's been used."

"What sort of a tangent are you off on now?" I asked. "There's some in the waste basket if you want that."

"I want that," said Allhoff. "Give me all you've got."

I took a handful of smudged carbon paper from the basket and dropped it on his desk. I stood there, looking inquiringly at him for a moment. He didn't say anything. He opened the top drawer of his desk and took out the stamp book I had found at Hadley's place. Deliberately, he tore all the stamps from the book and thrust them in his vest pocket. He placed the empty book on the desk near the carbon paper.

Now he opened another drawer and took from it Hadley's manuscript. This, he also laid on the desk-top.

"That's one hell of an imposing array for the customers," I said. "All the exhibits of the case, plus a nicely cleaned thirty-eight and a diseased coffee pot."

I thought he'd growl at that, but he didn't.

"Battersly," he said. "Come here."

Battersly left the window, crossed the room and stood at my side. Allhoff looked at his watch.

"That mob'll be here with Carrigan any minute now," said Allhoff. "Now get this, both of you. I want you two guys in the bedroom there. Close the door and stay there. If curiosity overcomes your discretion, there are enough cracks in that panel for you to peep through. But no matter what happens, stay in there until I call you. Understand?"

"Yes, sir," said Battersly stiffly.

I grunted. Allhoff was being spectacular, superior and mysterious.

"What sort of voodoo is this?" I said. "Shut up," he snapped. "If you had my brains, you might have my rank. I got where I am with my head. Despite the fact I have no—"

My God, here it was again. "All right," I said. "Anything you say. Come on, Battersly."

We went into the disreputable bedroom. I closed the door, selected a slanting crack that split the upper panel. I glued my eye to it.

In the other room, Allhoff carefully arranged the display on his desk. He pushed the thirty-eight to its edge and grouped the other exhibits in front of him. He drained the coffee cup again, and refilled it. It seemed to me that he looked even smugger than usual. There was a nasty sardonic glitter in his little eyes.

I had no idea what he was up to, but frankly, I considered that he was overplaying the hand. Whatever suspicion had crawled into his hateful mind, it was certain he had no evidence. If he had, he would order an arrest and dispense with all this mumbo-jumbo.

Battersly moved up beside me and put his face against the door. From below I heard the sound of scuffling footsteps on the creaking stairs.

"They're coming," I whispered. "I'd like to know what in hell he's going to say to them."

Battersly made a bitter sneering sound in his throat. "Probably going to tell 'em how he lost his legs," he said.

CHAPTER FOUR

"A Bird Told Me"

wo plainclothesmen ushered in the menage from Bayside. Paul Autrey, tall, slim and redheaded, entered first with Hadley's daughter, Nina, on his arm. Nina was thirty and brunette. Her face was pale, and her dark eyes sunken deep into her white cheeks. Rutledge and Parks came next. They wore the worried furtive air peculiar to the white-collar class when trouble arrives. Weldon, fat and well-to-do, brought up the rear with Carrigan.

Carrigan nodded to Allhoff who paid no attention to him. Carrigan's neck didn't get red this time. He was getting used to Allhoff. Weldon; on the other hand, was frankly hostile. He stood before Allhoff's desk and stared wonderingly around the shabby room. When his eyes fell on that filthy coffee pot he turned to one of the plainclothesmen.

"What's this?" he demanded testily. "Why have we been brought here? I understood that we were to go to headquarters. I—"

"Shut up," said Allhoff.

Weldon stared at him in utter amazement. Probably no one had told him to shut up for forty years. He made a little hissing sound as he exhaled. At the moment he was beyond speech.

"Sit down," said Allhoff. "Sit down, all of you. Carrigan, drag up some chairs."

Carrigan gathered up the furniture. They all sat down save Weldon who still stood there, his blue eyes blinking. He hadn't quite recovered yet. Allhoff waved a dismissing hand at the two dicks.

"You guys get out."

The dicks exchanged a dubious glance.

"But, Inspector," said one of them, "we ought to stay here. Our orders were—"

"Get out," said Allhoff. "Get out or I'll kick you out." He grinned ghoulishly and raised his voice. He wanted to be sure Battersly heard him on our side of the door. "That's a hot one. Isn't it? I'll kick you out."

I heard a crazy choking sob in Battersly's throat. On the other side of the door, Weldon had recovered.

"See here," he said angrily. "Why have we been brought here? Who are you? I'm damned if I see why all this fuss is being made, anyway. Hadley was a clear suicide. It was a grandiloquent gesture characteristic of the man. My God, he made that lucid enough in his manuscript."

Allhoff gave him his grade-A, first-class, nasty look. "Sit down," he said. "Sit down and shut up. That's all I'm asking of you for the moment."

But Weldon didn't sit down. He flushed and glowered at Allhoff. "I refuse to stay here. I refuse to be insulted. I'm leaving."

Allhoff grinned unpleasantly. "The hell you are," he said. "Try it and I'll have you held as a material witness."

Weldon sniffed and remained standing. Autrey frowned. But it was Nina Autrey who spoke.

"A material witness to what?" she asked in a thin tremulous tone.

"Murder," said Allhoff quietly.

Weldon sat down. Rutledge and Parks exchanged a nervous look. Nina Autrey clutched her husband's arm more tightly. There was a taut dramatic silence in the room, and I knew from Allhoff's expression he was loving it. But it still baffled me. I knew damned well he didn't have anything. Yet there was an inexplicable confidence about him.

"May I say something," said Autrey politely. "It seems apparent to everyone, including the Bayside police, that my father-in-law killed himself. Why do you say it was murder?"

Allhoff showed his teeth. "A little bird told me," he said.

"Will you stop clowning?" snapped Weldon.

"I'm not clowning," said Allhoff. "I repeat, a bird told me. And I'll know more when my messenger arrives from Buckley and Nunn."

"Buckley and Nunn," repeated Weldon. "You mean the publishers?"

"Hadley's publishers," said Allhoff. "And while we're waiting, I'd like to check on one point. Sergeant Carrigan told me this afternoon that none of you has ever read Hadley's manuscript that he even refused to show it to his secretary. Is that right?"

I screwed up my brow and pushed my eyes closer to the crack in the door. In the other room, Allhoff's inquiring gaze swept the faces of the visitors. Each of them in turn denied ever having seen the contents of Hadley's manuscript.

"Wait a minute," said Autrey. "What about this messenger from Buckley and Nunn?"

"What about that damned bird?" said Weldon. "What did you mean when you said a bird told you Hadley had been murdered?"

Allhoff sighed. "Well," he said, "while we're waiting, I may as well tell you about it."

"Tell me anything you like," snapped Weldon. "You'll never convince me Hadley was killed."

"No?" said Allhoff quietly. "The best authorities hold to the belief that beards are practically *de rigueur* in Heaven."

De rigueur? Well, I thought, he certainly is hitting on all six now, and where in hell did he ever pick that up?

"And yet," he went on leaning forward and glowering at Weldon, "Hadley shaved within an hour of his death."

"He'd been shaving himself at night regularly for years," put in Autrey. "Probably habit, that's all. There was no reason for anyone to kill him."

"What about the dough Rutledge and Parks get under his will?" asked Allhoff.

Parks squirmed in his chair. Rutledge opened his mouth and said nervously: "Mr. Hadley always shaved himself, Inspector. I assure you that Parks and myself—"

"Never mind," said Allhoff. "That's just a reason. It isn't the real reason."

"You needn't be so damned mysterious about it," said Weldon. "What the devil are you driving at?"

"This," said Allhoff. He lifted up the empty stamp book and the crumpled carbon paper. "See this?"

"What about it?" said Autrey.

"In a few minutes we'll know very definitely," said Allhoff. "As soon as Hadley's manuscript gets here from the publisher."

Nina Autrey uttered a little gasp. Carrigan stirred uneasily in his chair, then came out of his lethargy.

"What's it all about, Inspector?" he asked plaintively. "That's the Hadley script on your desk there."

"The hell it is," said Allhoff.

I moved back from my peep-hole and wiped my head with a handkerchief. "What, in the name of God," I demanded of Battersly, "is he doing now? He's had that script all day. What does he mean, it's not Hadley's?"

Battersly shrugged his shoulders. "I don't know what he's doing," he said. "But whatever it is, I hope he falls flat on his ugly face before he's through." That was a sentiment I shared, but I kept my mouth shut and returned to my peep-hole.

"Now look here," Allhoff was saying. "I'll tell you why Hadley was killed. He was killed because of the sensational disclosures in his book—disclosures which would harm someone else." He picked up the thick manuscript from his desk. "This thing's as phoney as a Tammany magistrate."

"But—" Carrigan began, frowning.

"Shut up," said Allhoff. "I'm telling you what happened. The killer knew what was in that manuscript. He walked into Hadley's study last night. He shot Hadley through the head. He thrust the gun into the dead man's hand. He snatched the genuine manuscript from Hadley's desk and left this one in its place. He got back to bed before Carrigan arrived from his room on the lower floor."

It seemed to me that Nina Autrey's face was whiter than before. Parks shifted nervously in his seat.

Weldon cleared his throat. "How do you know that?" he asked in a matter-of-fact tone.

"First," said Allhoff, "there were the birds. Four chimney swallows were fluttering around on the roof of the Bayside house this morning. They were chattering frantically. That's an act chimney swallows usually resort to, when their nest has been destroyed."

A little light began to seep into my brain. Apparently Weldon hadn't seen it yet.

"What's that got to do with it?" he asked.

"Well," said Allhoff, "it started me to thinking. The simplest explanation of anything that destroys the nest of a chimney swallow is that a fire has been lighted in the furnace. And if someone lit a fire in mid-July, it argues he was burning something."

Autrey laughed at that. It sounded as weak as the razor blades to me personally

"So," said Autrey, and it seemed to me that there was an undercurrent of relief in his tone, "someone was burning the original script, eh? That smoked out the birds. What are you going to do, Inspector? Put the swallows on the stand? The D. A.'ll have hysterics when you hand him this case."

I expected Allhoff to blow up then. He didn't like people who used mocking tones with him. He considered sarcasm strictly his own prerogative. However, he remained amazingly calm.

"Yes," he said with suspicious amiability, "I dare say he would if that was all I had to give him. But it isn't." He looked benignly around the room. "Whichever one of you mugs killed Hadley." he went on, "overlooked something that was right under your nose."

There was an aching silence then. I could hear Battersly's stertorous breathing in my ear, feel him tense beside me.

"Yeah," continued Allhoff, "You overlooked this." He lifted the empty stamp book and the carbon paper again. "You burned the original of Hadley's book all right. But it didn't occur to you that he had made a carbon copy. Carrigan bought Hadley a book of stamps early in the evening. This is the book and it's empty. My men salvaged this used carbon paper out of the basket in the study. After that it was a cinch. Undoubtedly, there was a copy, I reasoned from the carbon paper. Then the missing stamps indicated that Hadley had probably mailed it late on the night that he was killed. I phoned the publishers. The script had arrived in the afternoon mail, They hadn't even opened it. It's on its way over here now."

"And what," said Weldon, "do you expect to demonstrate with it?"

"Murder," said Allhoff. "The killer planned it all very neatly. He had some hack writer knock out this innocuous purported biography of Hadley. He stuck in that ingenious suicide paragraph at the end. What Hadley had written in the genuine script will undoubtedly incriminate the man who killed him. After that it should be easy enough to ferret out the hack who wrote it. His testimony'll clinch it."

"And," said Weldon, "suppose the script that the publishers send over is an exact copy of the one on your desk now."

Allhoff smiled thinly. "Then I shall feel like a damn fool," he said.

Again brooding silence fell over the room, What Allhoff had said sounded glib enough to me—too damn glib. It was smooth, logical, but still it seemed that there was something screwy about it somewhere.

"Say," whispered Battersly, "what's he talking about? He tore those stamps out of the book himself, didn't he? There was only one missing when we picked it."

"Yeah. And that carbon paper came out of my own waste-paper basket, only half an hour ago."

"He's pulling a crazy bluff," said Battersly. "I don't know what it's all about, but he's going to look like an awful, fool before it's over."

It certainly looked that way to me, too.

CHAPTER FIVE

Without A Leg to Stand on

I peeped through the crack again. Allhoff was calmly pouring himself a cup of coffee. The others stared at him expectantly.

Knuckles cracked against the outer door. "Come in," said Allhoff.

A messenger boy walked in, carrying a thick brown envelope. "Inspector Allhoff?" he asked.

"Right," said Allhoff. "Give it to me."

He signed for the package, waved the kid away without tipping him. The kid slammed the door angrily and clattered down the stairs. Allhoff sighed and opened the envelope.

"This is the genuine manuscript," he announced. "You people will have to wait here while I read it."

There was a crackling silence for a moment, then Paul Autrey said: "Put up your hands!"

He had leaped from his chair as if catapulted by a steel spring. He snatched the blue thirty-eight that lay on Allhoff's desk, put his back against the wall and faced them all. The gun's sights drew a bead in the general direction of Allhoff's heart.

"God!" said Battersly. His hand jerked out to the knob of the door.

I remembered Allhoff's instructions. "Wait a minute," I whispered. "I don't think he's finished yet."

Battersly relaxed.

From the other room came the sound of Autrey's voice, tremulous, but determined. "I'm getting out of here, Inspector," he said. "Give me the key to this door. I'll lock it on the outside. That'll give me a five-minute start."

"Paul!" cried Nina Autrey. "For heaven's sake, Paul—" A sob shattered the words in her throat. She covered her face with her hands.

Allhoff unleashed one of his ghastly grins. "Changed your mind about the case I'll hand the D. A., Autrey?" he said mockingly.

Autrey, pale and grim, nodded. His calm, however, was the calm of utter desperation.

"I've changed it," he said. "You'll find it in the script. The complete story of how Hadley and I put the Juggers Company out of business four years ago. There's a murder rap attached to it. Hadley didn't care. He wouldn't have lived a year. Cancer. But I was damned if I was going to let him kill me, too. You called it right, Inspector. I had that phoney book written from facts that I supplied. But I'm not done yet. Give me that key."

Battersly strained beneath my grip. "We got to go in now," he said.

"Wait a minute," I told him.

"Give me that key," said Autrey again. Allhoff shook his head. "I'm a policeman, Autrey," he said. "I'll give you no key. Instead, I'll give you—"

He jerked open his desk drawer with swift movement, Autrey saw the revolver there.

"Stop that!" he yelled. "Stop it, damn you I'll—"

The thirty-eight in his hand jerked convulsively. Battersly swore as I let go his arm. He burst through the door like a battering ram, hurled himself across the room and flung his arms around Autrey's legs. The pair of them fell to the floor together.

I heard Nina Autrey scream. I saw her keel over in her chair in a dead faint. Weldon shouted an alarm. Carrigan sprang from his chair and groped for his gun. I raced across the room to Allhoff, but even as I did so, even with all this crazed excitement about me, I felt there was something wrong somewhere.

I put my hand on Allhoff's shoulder. "Are you all right?" I asked him. "Are you hurt?"

Allhoff reached for the coffee pot. "I'm O. K.," he said. I noticed that there was a little tremor of excitement in his voice.

Battersly was on his feet now. He had wrenched the thirty-eight from Autrey's fingers. He held the collar of Autrey's suit with his left hand. Rutledge and Parks had risen, were standing white-faced by their chairs. Weldon knelt at Nina Autrey's side, fanning her futilely with a handkerchief.

"Carrigan," said Allhoff, "take Autrey across the street. Have him booked for murder. I'll sign the complaint later."

"My God," said Carrigan slowly. He crossed the room and touched Autrey's arm. "Come along, Mr. Autrey."

He took his prisoner out the door. I lit a cigar and tried to think. I still had that damnable sensation of trying to recall something which had registered on my brain during that crazy ten seconds of bedlam.

Allhoff lifted his coffee cup and looked around the room.

"Get those people out of here," he said to Battersly. "Get 'em out."

Weldon, with the aid of Rutledge, dragged Nina Autrey to her feet. Battersly ushered them, with Parks, toward the door. I looked at Allhoff. He was beaming like a stock-company juvenile.

"Well," he said, sneeringly triumphant, "what did you think of that? I swung it, didn't I? Brains is what it took. Brains and cast-iron nerve. I—"

"I still don't get it," I said.

"It was simple enough," said Allhoff with a smirk that indicated it wasn't simple at all. "Those damned chimney swallows did give me the idea. Then, while reading this phoney script, I noticed those boners about the breaking surcingle and the Senatorial election."

"Listen," I said. "I admit you have a great mind. I grant you're God's own personal gift to the police department. And now will you come down to earth. Talk in one-syllable words and try to remember that I'm only mortal."

If I thought that would puncture him, I was wrong. His beam grew broader.

"All right," he said as if he really believed me. "First, take the surcingle. A surcingle is the girth strap that holds on the saddle. This hack writer of Autrey's had it confused with the trace. Hadley, who'd been born on a farm, would never have made a mistake like that. Of course, the error about the Senate was even worse than that."

"How so?" I asked.

"Hadley was senator in Nineteen Eight," said Allhoff. "Well, they didn't elect senators then. They were appointed by the State Legislatures. So that little paragraph about the popular vote and the electorate was ridiculous. Hadley never could have written that."

"All right," I said. "Keep talking."

"So," said Allhoff, "first, I decided the script was phoney. Then those birds gave me the idea that Hadley had been murdered, a switch made, and later the original manuscript had been destroyed. I thought if I could convince the killer that the publishers already had a copy of the book, he'd crack. I called Buckley and Nunn. As a matter of fact they had received a letter from Hadley—that's what he used that single stamp for. He told them he'd send the book along in a day or so. Then I arranged with them to send me over an envelope filled with blank paper by messenger. It arrived at a critical moment. And by God did I put it over? Boy, this'll kill the commissioner. It's a great day for me, Simmonds."

"It's a great day for me, too," said Battersly.

I looked up at him surprised. There was a buoyant note in his voice that had never been there before. Allhoff's beam fell from him like a plummet. He scowled as he met Battersly's eye.

"What are you grinning about?" he demanded. "Anyone'd think you solved this murder."

Battersly laughed. I gave a little start. Then I realized that it was because I had never, in two long years, heard Battersly laugh before.

"In five minutes," said Battersly happily. "I'm writing out my resignation from the Police Department. I can do it now."

What do you mean you can do it now?" asked Allhoff.

"I'm free," said Battersly simply. "You sent a man to prison today, Inspector. But you also let me out of a darker cell— one that I've been in for three damnable years."

Allhoff's death's-head grin spread itself over his thin lips. His little eyes glowed red.

"Do you mind telling me what in God's name you're talking about?"

"Sure," said Battersly. "Once I cost you your legs. I swore to myself I'd stick with you here until I squared it up. It didn't seem possible until today. But I did it. I just saved your life, Inspector. Autrey would have drilled you cold. We're even now and I'm through."

I was aware of a sudden elation. In the excitement of a moment ago, both Allhoff and myself had overlooked this point.

"Sure," I said. "Sure, Allhoff. The kid's right. He just saved your life. Autrey would have got you sure."

Allhoff nodded. "Sure," he said. "Sure."

I should have noticed his tone then. I should have remembered he was still wearing that grin that he retained that wicked little flash in his eyes. But I wasn't paying much attention to Allhoff. I was too happy about Battersly. Besides I was still troubled about that crazy undefined stirring at the back of my memory.

I shook Battersly's hand. The brooding misery had gone out of his face. His eyes sparkled.

"I'm quitting tonight," he said. Then he added in a lower tone: "Thank God! Thank God!"

Allhoff laughed harshly. "Save your pious gratitude," he said. "You're not quitting."

We both looked at him. He wore that bitter sadistic expression which invariably accompanied his recital of the West End Avenue raid of three years ago.

"Now listen," said Allhoff, "you guys hate my guts. But that's no reason why you should think I'm a complete idiot." Battersly stared at him. For some reason, I felt suddenly afraid.

"What now?" I said.

Now all his benignancy had completely vanished. There was frank hatred in his eyes as he glared at us.

"Do you think I'm fool enough to leave a loaded gun where a murderer could snatch it A murderer that I had just sent to the chair? Do you think I'm fool enough to let a guy like Autrey blow my brains out?"

Then I got it. Then I knew what it was that had been bothering me. It was the sound of those shots Autrey had fired. They had made a flat crackling noise like a wet firecracker. It had not been the sharp staccato report of a thirty-eight.

My stomach was abruptly empty. I saw Battersly's hand tremble as he wiped it across his forehead.

"Wha—what do you mean?" he said.

"I put that gun there for Autrey to snatch. If he did it, it was a dead giveaway. It meant he'd actually read the original script when all of them had denied reading it. Furthermore, I figured he'd talk a trifle more freely, when he thought he could make a break for it. That thirty-eight was loaded with blanks. Are you such a lousy copper you can't tell the difference in sound between blank and ball ammunition? Hell, he fired two shots point-blank at me. Do you think I'm wearing bulletproof underwear?"

Battersly's face was a dirty muddy gray. "You're lying," he said without conviction. "You're just saying that because I saved your life."

"All right," said Allhoff. "Have it your way. The gun was loaded with dumdums.

He fired point-blank at my chest and I'm now in the morgue while the commissioner consults the records to see where the body goes."

Battersly's face was almost green now. There was moisture in his eyes. Allhoff took up the thirty-eight and swung the cylinder out. He took out three cartridge cases. There were no bullets in them.

Battersly stared at him for a moment. His facial muscles twitched palely. His eyes were blank and empty. In that instant I saw a man die as surely as if a bullet had pierced his heart. His lips moved slowly and a single short ugly word fell from them. He turned abruptly and walked out the door. Allhoff's savage laughter echoed in his ears.

I felt suddenly sick. I turned to Allhoff. Hateful words welled up inside me. I met his hard gaze, saw his bitter brittle lips. Then I knew that there were no words in all the world that could ever change him. I swung around and headed out for Noonan's.

Halfway down the stairs, I saw Battersly standing by the little window on the second landing. His back was toward me and his face was buried in his arms, against the windowsill. His shoulders moved convulsively, and I heard the horrible sound of a grown man sobbing. I raised my hand to touch his shoulder. I wanted to talk to him, to offer him what comfort I could.

But I forebore. I turned quietly and went on down to Centre Street. I felt like a weak-kneed coward, but I knew I never could have borne the look in his eyes had he turned around.

I'LL BE GLAD WHEN YOU'RE DEAD

I flung open the bedroom door and my stomach turned over.

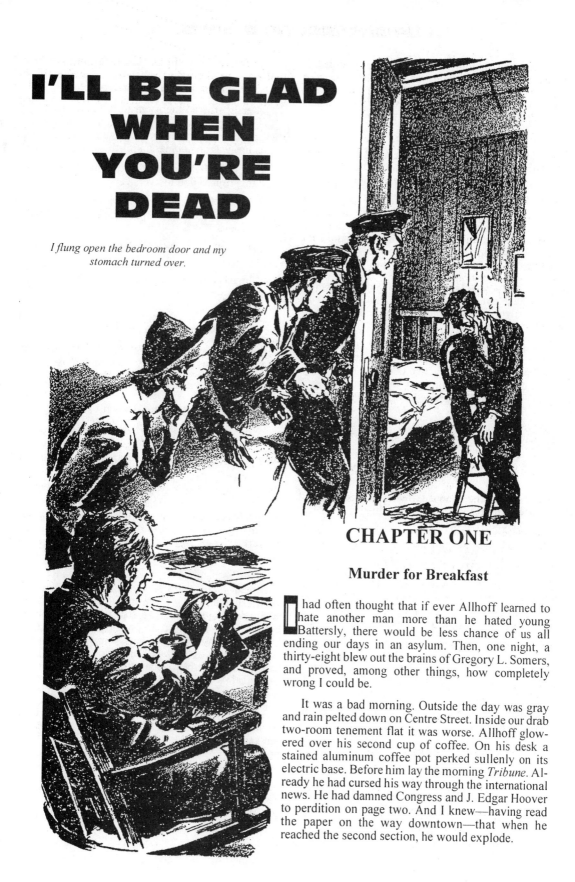

CHAPTER ONE

Murder for Breakfast

I had often thought that if ever Allhoff learned to hate another man more than he hated young Battersly, there would be less chance of us all ending our days in an asylum. Then, one night, a thirty-eight blew out the brains of Gregory L. Somers, and proved, among other things, how completely wrong I could be.

It was a bad morning. Outside the day was gray and rain pelted down on Centre Street. Inside our drab two-room tenement flat it was worse. Allhoff glowered over his second cup of coffee. On his desk a stained aluminum coffee pot perked sullenly on its electric base. Before him lay the morning *Tribune*. Already he had cursed his way through the international news. He had damned Congress and J. Edgar Hoover to perdition on page two. And I knew—having read the paper on the way downtown—that when he reached the second section, he would explode.

Originally Published - September 1938

Furthermore, it was ten-twenty now and young Battersly had not come in.

I decided it would save a lot of headache if I diverted his attention.

"Hey," I said, "what about Somers?"

Allhoff put down his coffee cup, swung around in his swivel chair and fixed me with his little brooding eyes. There was a distorted smile on his thin lips.

"There's not a functioning brain-cell across the street," he said bitterly. "Headquarters hands me a case that's three days old. A case without a lead, without a clue. What the hell do they expect me to do on a cold trail? If they dug up nothing six hours after the murder, what can I do now?"

"They're paying you tribute," I said ironically. "You've told 'em often enough that you're the only copper in town with a mind. They're asking you to prove it."

He glared at me. "For God's sake," he said, "I'm no mystic. They find an ace corporation lawyer dead in his own office. They find no motive that'll hold up. They discover cast-iron alibis for every one connected with the case. What am I supposed to do? Buy a crystal ball?"

"You mean you're licked and you're squawking about it," I said maliciously.

A hint of red came into his lined and yellow face. There was anger in his beady eyes.

"Damn you," he snapped, "what do you expect? There's nothing there. Absolutely nothing. But they'll make me take the rap for it."

He turned back to the paper, muttering under his breath. He turned the pages, working steadily toward the second section. Then, as I was trying to think up some more sprightly conversation, young Battersly walked in.

Allhoff glanced ostentatiously at his wrist watch. Then he looked up. "Well," he said with phoney affability. "Good-morning, good-morning."

Battersly shuffled his feet uneasily before Allhoff's desk. "Sorry, Inspector," he mumbled. "Sorry I'm late. Sorry if I inconvenienced you."

I bit my lip. That was a damn-fool thing to say and the crazy little flicker in Allhoff's eyes told me he was going to take advantage of it.

"Cause *me* inconvenience?" he said with elaborate mockery. "Why, of course not, Officer Battersly. There's nothing to do in this place anyway. Sergeant Simmonds and I have just been sitting here, whistling merrily and gayly swinging our legs from our chairs."

My heart sank at that. The pair of them were starting early this morning. Battersly dropped his eyes. His youthful face was drawn and pale. Allhoff reached for the coffee pot with one hand and savagely turned the

page of the *Tribune* with the other. I heard him inhale deeply as his eyes caught the headline of the left-hand-column story in the second section.

Battersly crossed the room to his desk. I watched Allhoff apprehensively as he read. Then he looked up and there was a familiar insane fire in his eyes. On his lips was an unpleasant mirthless smile.

"Battersly," he said in a thick strained tone, "what was it that caused you to oversleep?"

Battersly blinked nervously. "Why," he said slowly, "I don't know, Inspector. Just one of those things, I guess."

"Perhaps," said Allhoff silkily, "you didn't get to bed until late?"

"Well," stammered Battersly, "I—I— guess it was pretty late, sir."

"Ah," said Allhoff, "burning the midnight oil, eh? Studying for your promotion, undoubtedly."

Battersly squirmed in his chair like a butterfly on a pin. Allhoff grinned horribly like an Inquisition torturer. "Well?" he said sharply as Battersly didn't answer.

"Why, no. No, Inspector, I wasn't studying?"

"No?" said Allhoff. "What kept you up so late then?"

Battersly sat silent and miserable. Deliberately he avoided Allhoff's eyes. His face was ashen and his fingers drummed nervously on the desk-top. Allhoff picked up the *Tribune*. He leaned over to the side of his desk and his face took on a terrible intensity. Gone now was his pretense of patronizing amiability. His eyes glittered like angry diamonds, His voice was high-pitched and there was a hint of hysteria in it.

"You're damned right you weren't studying." he screamed. "You were at the Patrolman's Ball. You were dancing. You were winning a stinking little tin cup to put on your mantel-piece. You treacherous yellow rat! You dare keep me waiting while you dance. Dancing on my legs! The legs your rotten cowardice deprived me of! Dancing! Dancing!" His voice soared and shrilled like beating wings. Obscene epithet shot from his lips. He pushed his chair away from his desk, revealing the two stumps of his legs and wiggled them horribly. "Dancing! Dancing!" he shrieked again.

Battersly, pale and breathing hard, stared resolutely out the window. Allhoff's crescendo of vilification poured on. I looked at his wriggling amputated thighs and felt suddenly sick.

"Damn you Allhoff!" I yelled. "Shut up. Shut up, you blasted madman! You'll talk us all into an asylum yet. And you'll lead the way, yourself—in a straight jacket."

Allhoff's stumps ceased their grotesque movement. He turned his head and stared at me. He was panting—physically and emotionally spent. Yet the inexhaustible fountain of hate within him, pumped on. I knew I should have kept my mouth shut, that I had merely diverted his invective from Battersly to myself.

"Simmonds," he began, enraged, "I—" To my relief, the jangling of the telephone bell interrupted him. I picked it up, said, "Hello," and listened for a long while. Then I put my hand over the mouthpiece and turned to Allhoff.

"It's the commissioner's office," I told him. "The Somers killing's been cleaned up."

Allhoff frowned. I knew this information would get him even sorer. He would never admit that another copper could accomplish something at which he had failed.

"I don't believe it," he snarled. "Who broke it?"

"Callahan," I told him. "Pat Callahan."

Allhoff threw back his head and laughed harshly. "That's a hot one," he said. "That's a departmental classic. Pat Callahan breaks a case that no one else can touch. I still don't believe it."

As a matter of cold hard fact, I didn't believe it myself. Callahan was a dumb flatfoot who had been thrown off the force two years ago for the sheerest sort of incompetence. Since then he had set up a private agency which specialized in divorces and strong-arm stuff. Callahan didn't have enough brain to solve a crossword puzzle in a tabloid.

"Well," I said, "what do you want to do? Callahan and Phillips—he was Somers' partner—are in the commissioner's office now."

"Tell 'em to come over here," said Allhoff. "I want to hear this story of Callahan's. It ought to be good."

I transmitted the message and hung up. Allhoff swung around again and poured himself another cup of coffee. Then he turned his eyes on Battersly.

"Get out of here, you," he snarled. "I'm sick of the sight of you. Go down to Noonan's and get yourself a drink. You can tell the boys how you won a tin cup dancing...Dancing!"

"Get out," I whispered to Battersly. "Get out before he goes off again."

Battersly got up and walked hastily out of the room. Allhoff glared after him and all the hate and bitterness that have accumulated since the beginning of time was in his gaze. I sighed, turned to the papers on my desk and heartily wished that I'd joined the Street Cleaning Department back when I was an ambitious youth.

Some twenty odd years ago, I had come up, a raw rookie, with Allhoff. We had worked our way up through the department together, but it seemed that Allhoff was always a couple of jumps ahead of me. He had reached the grade of deputy-inspector, while I had remained anchored at sergeant.

However, if I resented his superior rank, I was forced to concede that he deserved it. He had, even now, the finest mind in the department. More than once he had cracked a case wide open that the rest of us had abandoned as hopeless.

On the other hand he was the most friendless copper in all the city. His manner was brusk and contemptuous. His ego was prodigious. He was a misanthropic little man with a grudge against the world. Even in the old days he would have been meat for a psychiatrist, and now, since the West End Avenue affair, I firmly believed that he was literally insane fifty percent of the time.

Young Battersly had been on the force for less than six months at the time of the West End Avenue raid. He had been assigned to affect an entrance through a rear window and, at any cost, plug the killer who sat on the staircase with a machine gun trained on the door. At the last moment his nerve had gone back on him. So when Allhoff led the squad through the front door, his legs absorbed nearly two dozen machine-gun bullets. Gangrene set in within the week and Allhoff lost his legs. And, if you ask me, he lost his mind as well.

He hated Battersly with an all-consuming hatred. His life was dedicated to a deliberate sadism, to ruthless, brutal persecution of the man who was responsible for his deformity. He lived and worked in this dirty tenement flat opposite headquarters, and fed his hate on Battersly's suffering.

Naturally, he was no longer carried on the departmental rolls. But the commissioner needed him badly enough to see to it that the city, through devious bookkeeping devices, paid him an inspector's salary each month. And in spite of the fact that he had no official status, his word carried more weight than that of anyone, save the commissioner himself.

It had been Allhoff's diabolical demand that Battersly be assigned as his assistant.

It had been the commissioner's idea that I join this outfit, ostensibly to do Allhoff's paper work. Actually, I acted as a buffer between Allhoff's viciousness and young Battersly. All in all, the three of us led one hell of a life.

CHAPTER TWO

Coffee for a Copper

I looked up from my desk as Callahan and Phillips entered the room. Callahan, red of face, grinned inanely. His stupid little eyes held a triumphant gleam. Behind him, Phillips represented everything Callahan was not.

Phillips was tall, thin and dark. His face was gaunt and sharp, and his wits were even sharper than his features. He enjoyed a reputation as the top criminal lawyer of the state. He had defended twenty-three first-degree murder raps. Not one of his clients had ever burned. There were two schools of thought on Phillips. One claimed he bribed juries; the other that he bought judges. Whichever was right, he was eminently successful.

Allhoff waved the pair of them to chairs. Then he looked up and regarded Callahan hostilely.

"All right," he said. "Let's hear it. Let's hear the conclusions of the mighty Hibernian brain that has out thought the whole Police Department."

Callahan shifted uneasily in his chair. He was acquainted with the vitriolic qualities of Allhoff's tongue. Phillips looked annoyed. I lit a cigarette and sat back. With Callahan's lumbering mind pitted against Allhoff's wits, the slaughter promised to be good.

"Well," began Callahan, "just what do you know about the case? I got to know where to begin so that you understand my reasoning."

"Your what?" said Allhoff. Then he sighed. "All right, begin at the beginning. Three nights ago, Gregory Somers, eminent corporation lawyer was found dead on the floor of his office by Henry Hammond, his young law clerk. A bullet was in his skull and his brains were dribbling gently on the carpet. All right, go on from there."

"Right," said Callahan. "Now when I come on the case, Inspector, the cops hadn't found out nothing. When I come on the case—"

"Who asked you to come on the case?" snapped Allhoff.

"I called him in," said Phillips coldly. "Naturally, I was interested in getting to the bottom of this. Somers was more than my partner. He was my friend. He—"

Allhoff waved a weary hand. "All right," he said again. "Go on, Callahan."

"Well," said Callahan. "This was the set-up when I come in. First, I discovered that this law clerk, Hammond, had quarreled with Somers the day before the murder. Somers was sore as hell at him for screwing up some papers. Somers threatened to blackball him with the Bar Association. See, there's a motive."

"You're psychic," said Allhoff. "The police dug that up the first day. They threw it away the second."

"Which is damned silly, even though typical," said Phillips.

Allhoff swung around in his chair. "Will you keep your ugly mouth shut?" he said.

Phillips face grew purple. Phillips, who got a thousand-dollar fee every time he opened his mouth, was not accustomed to be told to shut it. He glared at Allhoff who calmly poured himself another cup of coffee. Callahan went on.

"Now," he said, "the offices of Somers and Phillips are in a three-story brownstone building. They occupy the entire house. There ain't another firm in it. It's all theirs."

"This is getting more and more ingenious," said Allhoff. "I bet you even know the address."

Callahan flushed uncomfortably, but said nothing. He knew Allhoff's temper too well to risk a retort. Phillips, however, got sore. He stood up.

"Damn it, Inspector," he roared, "neither Mr. Callahan nor myself came here to be insulted. If you want to hear us, all right. If not, we'll leave. But I demand courteous treatment."

Allhoff stared at the lawyer over the chipped rim of his cup. Then slowly he put it down. "Now get this, Phillips," he said stingingly, "you're not in a courtroom now, impressing a jury you've already bought. Neither are you talking to a judge, who's scared to death of you for political reasons. Hence, you'll sit down and shut up. Either here, or in a cell."

Phillips hovered for a moment, on the verge of apoplexy. "Cell?" he shouted. "Cell? Are you out of your head? You can't put me in a cell!"

"The hell I can't," said Allhoff.

"On what charge?"

"Vagrancy, disorderly conduct, or passing a red light. What does it matter? I can put you there. You might get out in ten minutes. But I'll have the pleasure of seeing you booked. Now shut up. Go on, Callahan."

Phillips sat down. His face was dark and the fingers that lit his cigar trembled with rage. Still, he shut up.

"Where was I?" said Callahan nervously. "Oh, yeah. The motive. See. Hammond was a bum lawyer. Three or four times he had messed up papers for Somers, cost him some big cases. Somers, a stickler for such things would actually have driven Hammond out of the profession. And Hammond, as I found out, had his heart set on being a lawyer.

Drove a cab to get through school and all that. So I established the motive."

"Sure," said Allhoff ironically, "you established the motive. But young Hammond went and established an even better alibi."

"That's just it," said Callahan, "I busted that alibi wide open. That's how I broke the case."

Allhoff looked mildly interested. He put down his cup and leaned forward over his desk.

"The night of the murder," went on Callahan, "Somers announced that he was going to work all night. Hammond left the office a little after nine o'clock. He went directly home and put his car in his private garage. He returned to the office very early in the morning, ostensibly to help Somers finish up. When he arrived at about five-thirty, he found Somers dead. Inasmuch as the medical examiner says Somers was killed a little after midnight, Hammond couldn't have done the murder."

"Then what the hell have you got him in jail for?" said Allhoff.

"If you had one tenth the brain Callahan has," snapped Phillips, "perhaps you'd see it."

I expected Allhoff to blow up again at that, but he didn't. He smiled quietly as if the idea of anyone not having one tenth Callahan's brain was too absurd even to bother to refute.

"Well," said Callahan, "it was that alibi that baffled everyone. But not me. I had a motive. All I had to do was break down the alibi. That was all I had to do. To break it down."

"Good God," said Allhoff impatiently, "did you break it down?"

"No," said Callahan.

"That's great," said Allhoff. "What've you got the guy in the can for? Soliciting?"

"Here's how it was," said Callahan. "Hammond planned a sweet murder. You'll notice he both left the office and returned to it under cover of darkness. Hammond slugged Somers in the office before he left at night. He made sure the coast was clear, then he carried Somers down to his car. He tied him up, threw him in the back seat and drove him home. He put his car, Somers still in it, in his garage. At midnight he came downstairs and blew Somers' brains out. Then, early in the morning, he drove the corpse back to the office. Then he called the cops. That's how it was done, Inspector."

llhoff didn't speak immediately. He was staring at Callahan with awesome interest, as a scientist might stare at a lunatic. Then he blinked his little eyes quickly and filled his cup with coffee.

"Do you mean to tell me, Callahan," he said, "that you've got a man in jail on the strength of that theory? Do you mean to tell me that the D. A. didn't have acute hysterics when you told him that tale? Do you mean to tell me that even you are dumb enough to think the screwiest grand jury in the country would indict on that Walt Disney fairy tale you've dug out of the murky recesses of your mind?"

"We can prove it," snapped Phillips. "And what the hell do you think of that?"

"We?" said Allhoff quickly.

"Well—Callahan."

"All right," said Allhoff. "Go ahead, Callahan. Prove it."

"First, I got hold of Hammond's car," said Callahan.

"Without a warrant?" said Allhoff. "Grand larceny."

Callahan smiled weakly. "*You* know how those things are, Inspector. I got hold of his car and searched it for fingerprints. I found 'em. Not only on the upholstery, but on a copy of the morning *Times* that had been left on the back seat. Hammond had used it to throw over the corpse. In some way Somers' hands must have touched it. Four prints are on it."

"So," said Allhoff. "Somers undoubtedly had been in the car sometime. That would account for the prints."

"But the *Times*—it was dated the day of the murder. It wasn't on sale until eleven-thirty that night. Half an hour before the medical examiner says Somers was shot."

I thought that over and decided that as far as I was concerned it was the clincher. Not only did that *Times* definitely pin it on Hammond, it was first-rate detective work as well.

"Well," said Phillips triumphantly, "what do you think of Callahan's theory now? Good, isn't it?"

"It's too damned good," said Allhoff. "It's so good, I don't believe it's his own."

"You're sore," said Phillips. "Sore because he's showed up the department. He's solved your crime. The girl's testimony clinches it."

"Girl?" said Allhoff.

"The stenographer in my office," said Phillips. "She was in love with Hammond. When we-that is, when Callahan put the screws on, she talked. She knew the whole story. Hammond had confided in her. He told her his heart was set on a legal career. He wasn't going to permit Somers to stand in his way. Besides he was sore as hell at the things Somers said to him in front of her. Now, Sherlock, what do you think of that?"

He was crowing a little and I didn't blame him for it. Knowing Callahan I was sure that Phillips had furnished a good deal of the brain power which had trapped Somers' killer. But I knew Allhoff, who couldn't bear to be beaten by anyone, wasn't going to like it at all.

Allhoff looked dreamily around the room. "I smell a smell," he said. "A vile malodorous stench. I'm wondering precisely where it comes from."

Phillips eyes flashed with anger. "Do you mean to tell me the D. A. can't get a conviction with what we've given him? Are you that dumb?"

Allhoff turned a hot ugly face to the lawyer. "Listen, Phillips," he said angrily. "I told you to shut up once before. I wanted to hear Callahan talk—not you. I've heard him and I reserve my opinion for the moment. Now you can get out. Take your thick-headed Irish flatfoot with you and remove your unsavory shyster presence from my apartment."

For an instant Phillips stood there in open-mouthed amazement. For fifteen years Phillips had been a political power. He had become accustomed to deference and respect. Not for a decade had anyone called him a shyster to his face. His reaction was natural, simple, and, as it developed, of awful consequence. He lost his temper.

He glared at Allhoff with bulging eyes. "You legless little devil," he exploded. "Your mind is as warped as your body. It's a shame those bullets didn't rip your heart out, instead of merely crippling you. You're an egotistical maniac. No one can be right save yourself. You stinking smug little gnome. Here, have some more coffee."

He snatched up Allhoff's half-filled cup and dashed the muddy liquid into that yellow, lined face. I sprang across the room and snatched the cup from his hand. Then I stood watching Allhoff, ready to pounce on him if he reached for a gun.

For there was murder, cold murder in Allhoff's feral eyes at that moment. For years there had existed an irrevocable unwritten law that Allhoff's affliction must never be mentioned. And his temper had been aroused to the point of fury for lesser reasons than this. But now he was actually beyond words. His bitter tongue was stilled. He stared up at Phillips with an awful iciness in his eyes. His lips contorted crazily. Little drops of coffee dribbled down his chin.

Then at last he spoke, softly and viciously—each word a globule of venom. "Phillips," he said in a strangled tone, "you're either a brave man or a heedless fool. In either case, those words will cost you more than you are willing to pay. Now, get out!"

Phillips was pale now. His wrath had left him, and he seemed to realize the enormity of his offense. He took a step backward.

"I'm—I'm sorry, Inspector," he blurted. "I—"

Allhoff's expression never changed. "Get out," he said again.

Callahan took Phillips' arm and the pair of them went down the stairs.

There was a long silence in the room after they had gone. Allhoff sat hunched over his desk, staring at the door. His malignant eyes were smoldering. Then slowly his lips moved and I heard him mumble more to himself than to me:

"God, if I could only pin it on him! If I could only burn him for it. Maybe. Maybe."

For an instant I was shocked. "Allhoff," I said sharply, "what the hell are you talking about?"

He swung around and faced me. "Phillips," he said. "That rat. Did it ever occur to you that perhaps he killed Somers?"

"No," I said flatly. "It didn't. And after what I heard Callahan say, I'm even more certain of it."

"You can be wrong," said Allhoff. "In fact it was what Callahan said that made me suspicious."

"In some circles." I told him, "that might be considered a brilliant paradox. To me it's crazy."

"Is it? Callahan's the dumbest copper that ever passed the exam. Isn't he?"

"At least he's in the bottom ten," I said. "What's that got to do with it?"

"Very well," said Allhoff. "How could a guy as dumb as Callahan work out the case he's built up against Hammond?"

"Well," I said, "Phillips undoubtedly helped him."

Undoubtedly," said Allhoff bitterly. Then he swung around to his coffee again and lapsed into thoughtful silence. He didn't even look up when Battersly came in.

Twenty minutes passed before anyone spoke. Then Allhoff said: "Undoubtedly they have a copper on duty up at Phillips' office. Battersly, you go up there. Snoop around. Bring me back canceled checks, the account books. It should be easy to get some of Phillips' stuff too. I want financial data and books. Bring 'em down in a truck if you have to. But bring 'em."

"Listen, Allhoff," I said. "You can't do that."

"The hell I can't. Who's going to stop me?"

"Well, what's your object?"

"I asked you a few moments ago if it had occurred to you that Phillips may have killed Somers. I want to make sure."

"For the love of heaven, Allhoff," I said. "Just because you're sore at the guy doesn't mean he's a murderer. Besides you can't knock down that theory of Callahan's."

"Maybe I can," said Allhoff. "I've got a hunch. And I'll back my intuition against Callahan's brains any time. You get going, Battersly. You, Simmonds, go and see that girl. Talk to her. Get what dope you can. Size her up."

I stood up and shrugged my shoulders. "All right," I said. "It's your rap. even if we have to do the dirty work for you. What are you going to do while we're out? Sit there and drink black coffee while you brood."

He shot me an angry glance. "Why, no," he said bitterly, as Battersly put on his cap. "I might go out for a little walk, give these old legs some exercise. I might—"

"For God's sake," I said, "don't start that again. Come on, kid, let's get going."

I could still hear Allhoff muttering about the benefits of hiking as we went out into Centre Street.

CHAPTER THREE

We Compound a Felony

Twenty-Four hours later Allhoff's tenement flat was even more untidy than usual. He squatted at his desk submerged by the books and papers that Battersly had purloined from the offices of Somers and Phillips. For three hours, Allhoff had not spoken. From time to time he would grunt enigmatically.

Personally, I believed he was headed for trouble. True, in the past he had showed a positive genius for getting out of a bad spot when things seemed darkest. But this time he was overplaying his hand. The black hate in his heart against Phillips was sending him overboard. I didn't know precisely what he was looking for in those documents, but I couldn't figure how he was going to pin something on Phillips that Hammond had so obviously done.

I had seen the girl, Ruth Murray, and I was certain her story was on the level. She seemed sincere enough, though there was a certain hard sullenness about her. I attributed that to the grilling she had been subjected to over at the D. A.'s office.

Allhoff interrupted my thoughts by pushing a huge ledger away from him and reaching for the coffee pot.

"Well." he remarked to Battersly and me, "I really believe we're getting somewhere."

"Sure," I said. "What have you found? A confession in Phillips' handwriting?"

He let that pass. "There are a number of checks here made out to cash, signed by Somers, cashed by him."

"So," I said, "what?"

"They're large checks," said Allhoff. "Some of them in five figures."

"Again," I said, "what?"

"What do you think Somers needed all that cash for?"

"Probably to pay Phillips to kill him," I said.

Allhoff didn't like that. He glared at me and for a moment I thought he was going to indulge in some fancy name-calling. But he checked himself and went on.

"You know what they say about Phillips in this town?"

"Sure," I said. "They say he's the smartest and crookedest lawyer that ever won a case. They say he's bought more juries than Jim Brady had diamonds. But," I added pointedly, "they don't say he's a murderer."

"Does it occur to you," said Allhoff, "that these checks were cashed, and the money used as bribes?"

"That occurs to me," I said. "But it doesn't advance your case."

Allhoff was silent for a moment. Then he said suddenly: "Ever hear of a Doctor Brainin?"

"No."

"He's a gynecologist," said Allhoff."

"Got a lot of dough. But not above something shady every now and then. Especially for an old customer."

"Allhoff," I said, "what the hell's going on in your mind?"

"There's another check here of Phillips," he said. "Made out for fifteen hundred dollars. To Doctor Brainin."

"Keep talking," I said. "It's still murky to me."

"Sure," said Allhoff. "Phillips has no living kin. No wife, no sisters, no mother. What the hell is he paying a gynecologist for?"

"Why don't you phone the doc and find out?"

"I have," said Allhoff grimly.

I was getting bored. The conversation was a masterpiece of pointlessness to me.

"Listen, Allhoff," I said, "at the risk of having you blast me with unprintable adjectives and nouns, may I call your attention to the fact that Phillips is going to miss that stuff any minute now. You had no right to take it. He'll be downtown raising hell."

"If I can pin a murder on him," said Allhoff, "he can't cause any trouble. As a matter of fact, I'm expecting him."

"Will you get that out of your head? Hammond's guilty and you know it. You're just sore at Phillips. Forget it and get out of this jam before it's too late."

He didn't answer that for just then footsteps charged up the rickety staircase. Phillips burst through the door without knocking. His face was flushed and he was in a blind fury.

"Who the hell do you think you are?" he roared as he stood confronting Allhoff.

"By what right did you steal those documents of mine? I'll break you for this Allhoff. I want that stuff sent back to my office immediately. Then I'm going to see the mayor."

Allhoff's yellow eyes gleamed. "You're going to a death cell, Phillips," he said. "That's where you're going.

"You're insane," said Phillips. "An utter madman, Allhoff. I'm seeing the mayor. You'll be under arrest for larceny within the hour."

Well, I'd been waiting for this. As far as I could see Allhoff was in the soup for fair. Phillips had something of a drag at City Hall, and Allhoff had left himself wide open. He had no more business taking that stuff from Phillips' office, than he had to take ten grand from the National City Bank.

Phillips turned and walked toward the door. Then Allhoff said: "Wait a minute, Mr. Phillips."

Phillips turned around, still fuming.

"It's no use, Allhoff," he said. "It's no use apologizing now. By God, you stuck your neck out too far this time. You're through."

Allhoff smiled unpleasantly. "I'm not apologizing," he said. "On the contrary. Battersly, Simmonds, hold this man."

Battersly, accustomed to spring to obey Allhoff's lightest command, strode across the room and seized Phillips' arm. Personally, I wasn't in such a hurry. Phillips struggled ineffectually and cursed like a trooper in Battersly's grasp. Allhoff poured himself a cup of coffee.

I stood up. "Allhoff," I said, "what are you going to do?"

"First," he said, "I want that guy securely tied and locked in the bedroom. Then I'll go ahead and break this case."

"What?" shrieked Phillips and his face was purple. "You can't—"

"Shut up," said Allhoff.

I went over to his desk and stood close to him. "You can't do it, Allhoff," I said. "You're crazy. It'll be the end of you if you try a thing like this. Phillips has you cold."

"You might shut up, too," said Allhoff. "Take him in there Battersly. I'll accept full responsibility."

"You're damn right you will," howled Phillips.

"Allhoff," I said again. "You—"

"Blast you Simmonds!" he yelled. "As long as the orders remain as they are, you're under my command, Do as I *say*. Take him in there. Tie him up."

I followed Battersly into the dirty bedroom, stood there as he put a pair of handcuffs over Phillips' wrists, bound his ankles to the bed with thick cord.

"Gag him too," Allhoff called in to us. Battersly stuffed a handkerchief into Phillips' spluttering mouth. Then we came out and closed the door.

"Well," I said. "I hope you're satisfied. What are you going to do now?"

"I had that Murray girl on the phone a little while ago," said Allhoff. "We're doing nothing until she gets here."

"And then?" I said.

"And then," said Allhoff and there was savagery in his tone, "then I'll burn Phillips in the chair."

I sat down at my desk and waited. This was the end, and I was damned glad of it. Allhoff could never get away with this. He was running down a blind alley. Obviously, he couldn't tie a killing on Phillips that another man had done. Those hot words that Phillips had thrown at him, had been his downfall.

When Phillips got out of that room, he would raise hell—hell which would result in the end of this crazy triumvirate of Allhoff, Battersly and myself. The only way that Allhoff could get out of this spot was to make the murder rap stick on Phillips—and that, I *was* willing to bet he couldn't do.

CHAPTER FOUR

Allhoff Can't Prove a Thing

My watch showed four-thirty when the girl came in. At the moment the room was particularly disorderly. A soiled shirt of Allhoff's was draped over the back of a chair. The papers from Phillips' office were strewn carelessly over the floor.

She looked about the room distastefully. Her nose wrinkled as she nodded to Allhoff. She was dark and pretty in a sallow sort of way. Her eyes were black and expressive. There was an air of strength, of defiance about her.

"Sit down, sit down," said Allhoff noting her expression of repugnance. "You'll contract no disease in here."

"I'm not too sure of that," she murmured.

Allhoff glared at her. However, she lost none of her self-possession. She opened her bag and took a cigarette from a silver case.

"Now," she said exhaling a stream of smoke through her nostrils, "do you mind telling me why I had to come down here?"

"I'll tell you," said Allhoff, and there was a little gloating note in his voice. "Between us, you and me, we're going to solve the Somers murder."

She raised her plucked eyebrows at that. "What?" she said. "Again? I thought it had been solved once."

"So did a number of people," said Allhoff. "But it hasn't. Now, first, what's your name?"

"My God," said the girl. "Are we starting all over again from there? I'm Ruth Murray. I've been employed by Somers and Phillips as a law stenographer for three years. I met Hammond six months ago when he first came to work there. I liked him—a lot. Maybe too much. Furthermore, I've said all this four times before and I don't see any sense in doing it all over again."

To my surprise Allhoff did not resent her manner. I attributed it to the fact that he was too worried about the weakness of his own position to be normal. He said quietly: "This Hammond—you still like him?"

She nodded her head. "Yes," she said slowly. "A woman can't turn her affections on and off at will. In spite of everything, I still care for him—a great deal."

"Yet," said Allhoff, "you're not particularly concerned at the fact of his being headed for the chair?"

She pushed her chair back and stood up, glaring at him like a tigress. "You damned dumb coppers," she said bitterly. "What am I supposed to do? Go around having hysterics? What do you know about what goes on inside me? What do you know of my sleepless nights? Of my misery?"

She sat down again, breathless. Allhoff smiled faintly. I watched him and wondered. What he was driving at was beyond me. And as far as I could see he was getting precisely nowhere.

"All right," he said soothingly. "Now would you mind answering one more question? Did you really love young Hammond a great deal?"

"Of course, I did," she said, and there was a little catch in her voice. "I still—do."

There was a moment's silence broken only by the sulky purring of the coffee pot, then Allhoff spoke in a bland conversational tone.

"Miss Murray, you're a damn liar."

The girl uttered a little gasp. Then she stood up again.

"*How* dare you talk to me like that?" she snapped. "I won't stand for it. I—"

Allhoff turned on her savagely. "Shut up," he said, "you little liar. I'll do the talking."

"See here, Inspector, I—"

"You'll sit in a cell next to Hammond if you don't do what I tell you," said Allhoff. "Now sit down."

There was iron in his tone and the girl sat down. An ugly smile had crawled across Allhoff's lips. His eyes held a crazy light. I suddenly decided that his mind must have gone at last. His bitterness at Phillips had snapped the attenuated thread that held it to sanity. I got up and walked over to him.

"Allhoff," I said, "don't you think you've done enough for one day? Don't you think perhaps—"

His eyes met mine and blazed. He understood quite well that I was trying to tell him he was mad.

"Simmonds," he said, "I'll thank you to remember there's a difference in our ranks. When I need your mighty brain, I'll ask for help. Now get back to your desk. I'll give you five seconds."

He spoke as he might have spoken to a dog. For three of those five seconds, I contemplated the idea of blowing up completely. I toyed with the idea of smashing my fist into his ugly face. Then I thought of a pension that would be due in two years, of my wife and two kids in the Bronx. I went back to my desk.

"Now," said Allhoff to the girl, "do you know a Doctor Brainin?"

He bent over his desk and watched her like a hawk. It seemed to me that her face paled slightly as she answered.

"Doctor Brainin? Why, yes. He attended me once or twice."

"For what?"

Their eyes met and clashed. "I don't have to answer that," she said steadily. "I know enough law to know that such things are privileged, confidential between doctor and patient."

"Let it go," said Allhoff. "Who paid the doctor?"

She inhaled deeply. "Who paid him?" she repeated.

"You heard me," said Allhoff. "Who paid him? Francis Phillips paid him. Didn't he?"

"Why, I—"

"Don't lie. I've got the canceled check right here."

"All right," she said. "Mr. Phillips paid him. And why not. He was my friend and my employer. He took a paternal interest in me."

Allhoff laughed coarsely. "Paternal is good," he said. "Very good."

She looked at him for a long time. Then she said slowly, challengingly: "You can't prove anything, Inspector."

For the first time, I began to believe that perhaps Allhoff had something, though I was eternally damned if I knew what. He leaned further over his desk, staring at her with hypnotic gaze.

"You listen," he said. "Listen to me. Do as I tell you and you'll get out of this clean, There's been a lot of brilliant theorizing about Somers' death. Now let me tell you exactly what happened."

The three of us, Battersly, the girl and myself sat tense and alert. There was a note of deadly seriousness in Allhoff's voice.

"Somers and Phillips had a bitter quarrel, a quarrel that was probably climaxed the day of the murder. Somers had uncovered the fact, which it seemed everyone else had always known, that his partner was winning his cases through jury-and judge-bribing. Somers, being a stuffed shirt, a blue-blood and a corporation lawyer of distinction, squawked to high heaven."

Allhoff paused and poured himself another cup of coffee. The girl's face was set hard now. There was an odd expression in her deep black eyes. Allhoff sipped his muddy brew with an unpleasant sucking sound, then resumed talking.

"To a man of Somers' ilk there was only one answer, and that answer meant the end of Phillips' career. Whereupon Phillips promptly blew out his partner's brains with a thirty-eight. After that little chore was attended to, he evolved that brilliant theory which he taught Callahan to parrot. He planted those fingerprints in Hammond's car. Then he gave Callahan a few thousand dollars to play Sherlock Holmes. To clinch it, he had you lie."

"Me?" said the girl. "Me? What— what's it got to do with me?"

"It's got everything to do with you," said Allhoff. "Every word of yours written in that statement the D. A. has is a downright damnable lie. You never were in love with Hammond. All that talk about civic duty overcoming your emotions, forcing you to testify for the State is the lousiest day's work I've seen in a muddy career. Phillips was your lover, Miss Murray. Was and is at this moment. Is that right?"

My teeth bit into the end of my cigar. Right? Of course it wasn't right. It was completely nuts. Allhoff had predicated his entire theory on the fact of half a dozen checks. It was impossible, unprovable, unindictable, and further proof that Allhoff should be mopping floors in the madhouse. Then, when I expected the girl to tell him he was a damned fool, to burst into laughter in his face, she said in a subdued but determined voice: "You can't prove it, Inspector."

"Listen," said Allhoff. "There's a guy sitting over there in the Tombs. He's an ordinary sort of guy, and a guy that you never gave a damn about. He's just another ten-dollar-a-week law clerk. He's a dime a dozen in this town. Middle class and ordinary." He leaned so close to her now that his corvine nose almost touched her. "But he's not a murderer."

The girl swallowed, her fingers twisted nervously. Allhoff took a long piece of foolscap from a desk drawer.

"I have a statement here," he said. "A statement detailing that true story of the killing. All it needs is your signature."

She shook her head. There was courage in her eyes. She repeated in a dull, dogged monotone: "You can't prove a thing, Inspector."

"Listen," said Allhoff, "they'll burn that kid down there. Phillips and Callahan have given the D. A. a cast-iron case. Thus far my theory's worthless. I've got to have your testimony as well. They'll burn that kid down there and it'll be your hand that pulls the switch. You'll never sleep again for the stench of burning flesh in your nostrils. You'll be nothing more or less than a cold-blooded murderess. And the waters of the flood'll never wash the stain off your hands. Damn it, now will you sign?"

Somehow it seemed to me that she had grown older in the past few moments. Her cheek bones protruded, her sallow face was gaunt. Yet her gaze was steady, unflinching. She pushed back her chair and stood up, looked at Allhoff, defiantly.

"Inspector," she repeated in a low husky voice, "you can't prove anything. Neither you or the whole Police Department can break me down. Even if what you say is true—and, mark you, I admit nothing—I wouldn't crack. If I really did love Phillips, I wouldn't let him down. I don't like to see a man die, guilty or innocent. But I wouldn't let the man I love die at any cost. She paused there for a moment and looked him squarely in the eye. "Do you understand what I mean, Inspector?"

Allhoff didn't shout. He didn't yell. It was if he had met, for the first time, an adversary whom he understood, whom he respected.

"I understand," he said quietly. "But I won't take that answer as final. I want you to think it over. Battersly, take Miss Murray down to Noonan's. Buy her lunch. Then bring her back here."

The girl flashed him an odd twisted smile, then turned and followed Battersly down the stairs. I sat at my desk in something of a daze. Now, at last, I knew that Allhoff had something. The girl's demeanor clinched that. Once again he had completely fooled me. Whenever I thought him at his maddest, he invariably pulled something out of his hat. Perhaps a guy *had* to be crazy to figure out the way Allhoff figured. From half a dozen canceled checks he had built up a case founded entirely on intuitive conjecture. And it began to appear that he had been right.

But now that he had something, what the devil was he going to do with it? He had nothing he could take into a courtroom, and he had the town's top criminal lawyer locked extralegally in his dirty bedroom. Furthermore, the very presence of the scattered papers on his desk had knocked several holes in the Bill of Rights.

"Well," I said at last, "what's the next move?"

He swung around and looked at me. His face was tired. His shoulders were more stooped than usual.

"Phillips killed him," he said. "I knew it. Phillips killed him, Simmonds. I figured it absolutely correctly all the way."

"I'm beginning to believe that myself," I told him. "But I don't see that it'll do much good. You're licked without that girl's testimony. Frankly, I don't think you'll ever get it."

He sighed heavily. "No," he said. "I don't think I will."

"If you grant that," I said, "can you see what's going to happen?"

His eyes met mine squarely and I shuddered. There was something terrible in his expression. Something beyond any definition of mine. But I knew instinctively it was evil. I knew that there was some ghastly thought in the recesses of his dark and tortured mind.

"Why," he said and there was an odd note in his voice, "I think things will go according to schedule. This is a contingency I had prepared for."

His tone nettled me.

"All right," I said, "if you can get out of this you're a master. Phillips is going to come out of the bedroom soon. You can't hold him there forever. He's going to come out with a squawk that'll be heard in Washington. You're violating the Constitution and heaven knows how many lesser laws, You'll be through, Allhoff, washed up. Lucky if you don't serve a short stretch. Furthermore, Phillips will thoroughly enjoy it all. It's his last laugh."

"Do you mind," said Allhoff with elaborate courtesy, "joining Battersly and that Murray girl in Noonan's. I'd like to he alone for a little while. I'd like to think.''

I got up and walked to the door. "Think your way out of this," I told him, "and you'll go down in history as Machiavelli, the second."

Then I went down to Noonan's.

CHAPTER FIVE

Dance, Little Copper!

Three quarters of an hour later the three of us returned. The first thing I noticed was that the bedroom door remained closed.

I wondered if Phillips was still in there, or if Allhoff had released him to rush over to City Hall yelling blue murder. Allhoff, I remarked, seemed calm and relaxed. The strange tenseness had left him.

Battersly, silent as usual, took his customary place at his own desk. Ruth Murray sat in the same chair she had occupied before. Allhoff pushed his coffee cup to one side, licked his lips slowly and picked up the sheet of foolscap again. He put it on the desk before her.

She shook her head grimly. "No, Inspector," she said, "it's no good. You can't get me to sign that with all the rubber hoses in the Police Department."

I looked at her—at her upright resolute figure, at the fanatical unyielding expression on her face, and I knew that he couldn't. I wondered why Allhoff, usually so keen in such matters, persisted.

"Listen," said Allhoff, "if you knew that your signature couldn't harm Phillips, if you knew your lying was utterly futile, would you sign to save an innocent man?"

"That's a trick question," she answered tensely.

"Whatever it is, answer it," said Allhoff. "If your telling the truth could not harm Phillips, would you sign this for Hammond's sake."

"But how—how could that be possible?"

Allhoff leaned closer to her. To my stark amazement he laid his gnarled bony hand softly upon hers. "Suppose," he said softly, "suppose, I told you that Phillips was dead?"

"Dead?" She stared at him with glazed eyes. Instinctively, I glanced toward the bedroom door. I began wondering where all this was leading.

"Listen," said Allhoff, "he was in my bedroom in there. All the while I was talking to you before. He took the only decent way out. Before I could reach him, he—"

"What are you saying?" she cried. "You mean he—he—"

"He killed himself," said Allhoff gravely. "He was in there. I heard a shot—went in. He was dead. You can save him no longer. Now will you sign?"

The girl fought a silent battle for control. Her eyes were moist, her fingers trembled. Then a flickering uncertain smile crossed her lips.

"It won't do, Inspector," she said and there was a crying hope in her voice. "It's a frame, Inspector. I won't sign."

Not only was it a frame, I decided, but it was the most amateurish frame, I'd ever heard. Allhoff was desperate, as I figured it, to get his confession signed. Well, he was licked now. He had carried the thing as far as he could. Then to my bewilderment, he carried it a step further.

"It's no frame," he said. "I don't lie about life and death. He killed himself, He's in there now. If you doubt me, look." He gestured toward the bedroom door.

The girl stood up and her gaze followed his indicating hand. I sat there silently, waiting for Allhoff to come tumbling off the throne his ego had built for him. He turned about and caught my eye.

"Simmonds," he said, "open that door. Then call the medical examiner."

I didn't move. I figured that this was just a final touch of atmosphere to make good his crazy bluff. The girl stood frozen to the spot. Her body swayed slightly.

"Damn you," yelled Allhoff. "I told you to open that door."

"All right," I said. "If you want it that way. But the only suicide in this joint is the hari-kiri you're committing yourself, right now."

I crossed the room, turned the key and flung open the bedroom door. Then my stomach turned over.

 Phillips was dead. He sat sprawled in the single chair of the room. His wrists, still handcuffed, hung limp and distorted at the right side of his body. On the floor was an automatic, lying on the little loose pile of cord that had once been secured about his ankles. Battersly's handkerchief, which had been used as a gag, lay on the bed. From an ugly hole in Phillips' brain, blood oozed down his face and dropped silently on the rich fabric of his suit.

I turned away. There was sickness at the pit of my stomach and a black horrible suspicion at the base of my brain. Ruth Murray's cheeks were cold marble. Her mouth moved convulsively, but no sound came. Allhoff reached for his coffee cup. As he picked it up his hand was steady. There was a maniacal gleam of triumph in his eyes.

It was Battersly, white-faced and craning over my shoulder, who spoke first. "My God," he said, "it's impossible. It's—"

He broke off and ran a hand across his forehead. The girl put a hand on the desk to steady herself. Then she sat down slowly. Her eyes were dry and devoid of all expression. She uttered no scream of hysteria. All the spirit, all the defiance seemed to have seeped out of her. It was as if she had died as surely as Phillips, in that moment.

Allhoff picked up his fountain pen. "Now," he said quietly, "will you sign?"

She stared at him with vacuous, unseeing eyes. She took a cigarette from her bag with quivering hands. Allhoff struck a match and held it out to her.

"Miss Murray," he said, with strange gentleness, "no matter how he lived, he died like a man. He did the only decent thing. He died himself rather than condemn an innocent man, rather than make a sacrifice of you. He has done his part. He would expect you to do yours. Now, will you sign?"

Her shaking fingers took the pen from his hand. She scrawled her name across the bottom of the paper. Allhoff breathed deeply and looked up.

"Here," he said briskly, "you two witness this thing. Then, you, Battersly, take Miss Murray downstairs. Put her in a taxi."

There was something cold and terrible in my mind now. I was slowly translating the things I felt into logical thought, gradually but inevitably arriving at a hideous conclusion.

I signed the paper and kept quiet until the door had closed behind Battersly and the Murray girl.

Allhoff sipped some coffee and looked like a gloating Caliban. He sighed a feline sigh.

"Well," he said, "I did it. I dug that one out of the clouds all right. I knew Callahan couldn't figure out a case that had licked me. Simmonds, I've just saved an innocent man from the chair."

"Allhoff," I said. He turned and faced me, startled by the vehemence of my tone. 'Allhoff," I said again,

"you murdered Phillips."

He raised his eyebrows and grinned horribly. "Simmonds," he said, "you're a damn fool."

"Allhoff"— my voice trembled with emotion—"when you say Phillips killed himself, I say you're a foul-mouthed liar. You murdered him!"

But even that accusation didn't touch him. He refilled his coffee cup, said quietly: "Simmonds, why the hell don't you shut up?"

But I went on. This time he wasn't going to shut me up. This time I was going to say what I had to say and to hell with the consequences.

"You killed Phillips!" I yelled. "Battersly served a hitch at sea before he became a copper. If there's one man in all the world I'd trust to tie a rope, it's Battersly. Moreover, I saw him tie it with my own eyes. Houdini couldn't have got out of those knots."

Allhoff sighted and put down his coffee cup.

"I tell you—"

"You'll tell me nothing. For once I'm telling you. You went in there after you couldn't break the girl down. You were in one tough spot. Phillips could have and would have broken you when he got out of your bedroom. And you knew it. Of course, if you pinned a murder on him you were in the clear. A killer has no rights, no influence. But you couldn't pin him. So you took the out. You went in there and blew his brains out. Then you untied him and left him there."

Allhoff's smile was fiendish.

"You're crazy," he said mockingly. "Why don't you go in and look the body over. You're supposed to be a detective, Sergeant. Well, go in there and start deducing."

"Sure," I said, "and I know what I'll find. I'm not accusing you of being dumb. I'm merely accusing you of murder. Oh, I know every conceivable clue in that room will point to suicide. I know further that you'll probably get away with it. But I know and you know what actually happened. You killed him because you hated him—even more than you hate young Battersly.

"What's more, you meant to do it all along, in the event that the girl wouldn't talk. That's why you had him tied up. You knew he'd been down here screaming about his stolen papers. You were waiting for him.

"You murdered him!" I roared in fury, pounding the desk with my fist. "Murdered him! Murdered him! You stinking cold-blooded madman."

I straightened up again, out of breath. Allhoff looked at me with a furious contempt in his eyes. Then, before he could speak, footsteps raced up the stairs. Battersly rushed into the room. Behind him, grave-faced and serious were the commissioner and his first-deputy.

I saluted bewilderedly. Allhoff still smiled as he

touched his fingers to his brow informally. Battersly, white-faced and tense, met Allhoff's sardonic gaze defiantly.

"Inspector," said the commissioner, "Officer Battersly has just told me an incredible story."

Allhoff nodded without taking his eyes off Battersly. Battersly shifted uneasily, then he burst out suddenly: "I don't care. I don't care," he yelled, "what I may have done in the past. My obligation to you stops short of murder. Phillips was no suicide. I tied him up and I should know. No man in the world could have broken those bonds. He never killed himself. Never!"

Allhoff's face was a terrible thing to behold at that moment. All the hate in the world was stamped on his features as he stared at Battersly. All the evil in his warped little soul was mirrored in his murky eyes.

"Well," said the commissioner, "what about it, Inspector?"

"Battersly's right," said Allhoff slowly. "Phillips never killed himself."

I gasped at that. That was the last admission I ever expected to hear him make. Allhoff leaned over his desk. He spoke to the commissioner but his yellow eyes never moved from Battersly.

"He never killed himself," he screamed almost hysterically, "because you stupid damned fools, he's not dead!"

I turned my head toward the open door of the bedroom. The first-deputy was already walking across the threshold.

He bent over and picked up Phillips' pulse. Then he turned and met the commissioner's inquiring eye.

"He's alive, sir," he reported. "Got a nasty hole in his temple. But that's about all."

There was a moment's silence in the room. Then it was broken by Allhoff's crazed, high-pitched laughter.

"Kill him? You fools, why should I kill him? Let the rat suffer. Let him go through hell at a trial, let him die a thousand deaths in Sing Sing before he burns his life away. Why should I kill him? My bullet would only kill him once. This way he'll die a dozen times over."

The commissioner looked at him sharply then shook his head. "All right, Inspector," he said. "Now take it easy. Simmonds, call for an officer and an ambulance, Get Phillips over to the hospital. We'll have him indicted the first thing in the morning.

He swung around to Battersly. "The next time you demand my personal appearance in a case," he said, "make sure of your facts first."

He left the room, his first-deputy trailing behind him. I stood still staring at the panel of the door, cursing myself for a fool.

"Allhoff," I said, "why didn't you tip us off? If you were going to smash his head in, untie him and plant a suicide to force the Murray girl's confession, why didn't you let us know? After all, we might have ruined your plant. We might have walked in, examined the body and announced Phillips was still alive, That would have shut the girl up like an oyster."

Allhoff's unhealthy grin persisted. "The trouble with me is I'm too damned smart," he said. "You don't think the fact of my always being right is sheer coincidence, do you? I know what you guys think of me. I knew you'd immediately jump to the conclusion that I'd killed Phillips. You knew I hated him, hence you figured I'd not hesitate to murder him. You were ready to believe that and you did."

I considered that and didn't answer. It was true enough.

"Furthermore," went on Allhoff, "you weren't subtle enough to realize that because I hated him, I'd prefer to have him wait in the death cell for a while instead of merely blowing out his crooked brains."

He poured himself another cup of coffee.

"You better call that ambulance," he added.

Battersly walked across the room and stood nervously before Allhoff's desk. "Inspector," he said haltingly, "I—I want to apologize for the things I said. I guess I' —er—made a fool of myself. I'm sorry I brought the commissioner over here, sorry that I made such a damn-fool mistake."

Allhoff stared at him with hard unrelenting eyes. Battersly shuffled his feet. "I guess maybe I'm a lousy copper," he added dejectedly.

Allhoff pushed his chair back and put down his cup.

"Now, now," he said and his voice was treacle, "there's no need to worry about that, What if you're not such a first-rate policeman? It doesn't matter. No one's tops at everything. Jack of all trades, master of none. So you're a lousy copper? Well, you've got other accomplishments."

He inhaled sibilantly, hunched himself over the desk, and then let fly with both barrels.

"Sure," he yelled, "other accomplishments! You're the best rhumba dancer in the entire department. It says so in the *Tribune*. You got a cup on your mantelpiece to prove it. Fred Astaire Battersly, the virgin's dream. Now get to hell downstairs and pick up a cop to accompany the ambulance to the hospital."

Battersly, white and trembling turned to the door. Allhoff lifted his head and yelled savagely after him.

"Dance, don't run down the stairs, you got plenty of time."

Then we were left in the room together. Alone with the crackling, spine chilling sound of Allhoff's hideous laughter.

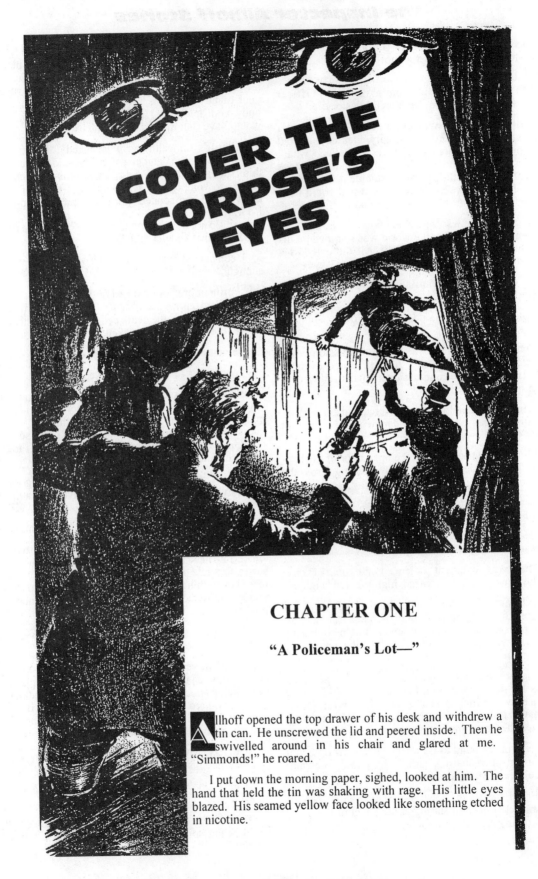

CHAPTER ONE

"A Policeman's Lot—"

Allhoff opened the top drawer of his desk and withdrew a tin can. He unscrewed the lid and peered inside. Then he swivelled around in his chair and glared at me. "Simmonds!" he roared.

I put down the morning paper, sighed, looked at him. The hand that held the tin was shaking with rage. His little eyes blazed. His seamed yellow face looked like something etched in nicotine.

Originally Published - July 1939

"Look," he said with the outraged air of a man who has discovered a knife in his back. "No coffee!"

I met his fiery eyes for a moment, shrugged, then looked around the unkempt tenement apartment. A soiled shirt and a pair of old socks lay on the chair nearest Allhoff's desk. Crumpled wrapping paper and an empty soup-can were on the floor. To the left, the door of his bedroom was open. The bed was unmade and the linen had been used at least a week.

On the desk stood a stained coffee pot attached to an electric base. A chipped cup adorned the blotter in front of the swivel chair. Allhoff sat with his back to it, holding the empty can out toward me. I took a deep breath and decided, tactlessly, to take him for a ride.

I assumed an elaborate expression of concern, clucked disapprovingly and shook my head. "No coffee?" I said, raising an eyebrow. "What can that housekeeper be thinking of? The dust is terrible, too. And I'll swear the linen hasn't been changed since—"

He called me a slimy name in a loud voice. I could hear his teeth grind. There was baleful hatred in his eyes and his voice was biting ice as he spoke. "You're fined two weeks' pay."

I dropped my air of phoney sympathy and got a little sore myself. "For what?" I said sharply.

"Insubordination."

"I wasn't insubordinate," I told him.

"Tell that to the commissioner. I'll tell him my story."

I pushed back my chair, stood up and lost my temper. "Allhoff," I said, "I'm a police sergeant, not a scullery maid—nor a quartermaster's corporal. What the hell have I got to do with your coffee?"

He glared at me. Now that I was sore, he seemed calmer himself, but there was bitterness, malevolence in his gaze. He slapped the can down on his desk, fumbled in his pocket and produced a worn leather coin-purse. He opened it and took out a dime and a nickel, put the coins on top of the can.

"Get half a pound," he said. "The loose blend. Have 'em grind it."

He swung his chair around and occupied himself with some papers on his desk.

I stood over him, staring at the back of his neck, inarticulate with rage. True, he held the rank of inspector-ex-officio, while I remained a sergeant. But his manner, his tone, implied he was an Imperator speaking to his lowliest slave. I was seized with an overpowering impulse to twist him around in his chair, hammer teeth out of his ugly head with my fist. Then, without turning, he spoke with damnable omniscience.

"Don't do it, Simmonds," he said. "It's just plain dumb to jeopardize a pension you've spent thirty years building up." He paused for a moment, then his voice took on a strident mocking quality. "Besides, there are two kids and a wife to think of. We must be fair to them."

He picked a paper up from his desk and pretended to read it. I glared at the nape of his neck for thirty seconds, then snatched up the can and the money and went down to the A. & P.

As I turned into Centre Street on the way back I ran into Battersly. He was neat and trim in his blue uniform and looked well pleased with himself.

"Hi, Sergeant," he said. "I just made a pinch." He beamed like a visiting bishop.

I was in no mood for issuing congratulations. "That's what you're paid for," I told him shortly.

"But this was big stuff, Sarge. Murder. I—"

I held the coffee tin out where he could see it.

"You're an hour late," I told him, "and you let Allhoff's coffee supply run out."

His face fell like a depth-bomb. "My God," he said. "The coffee. I forgot. But he can't squawk if I was delayed by departmental business, Sarge. I—"

"Can't he?" I said. "He'd squawk if you were delayed by your own funeral."

By now we had gained the crooked staircase that led up to Allhoff's miserable quarters. I put a hand on Battersly's arm.

"For the love of Heaven," I said, "be careful what you say. He's in one of his moods this morning."

Battersly nodded. He was tight-lipped now and that haunted expression I knew so well lurked in his eyes. He walked up the stairs like a man going to the firing-squad.

Allhoff snatched the coffee from me like a hophead reaching for a needle. He ignored Battersly as he dumped the coffee into the percolator. He turned on the electric plate and sat there in utter silence until the pot began to gurgle.

I returned to my newspaper. Battersly sat at his desk, relieved that Allhoff had not spoken to him. Allhoff filled his with black viscous brew from the coffee pot. He sipped it audibly. Suddenly he turned his head and fixed his obsidian eyes on Battersly.

"I give half my life to the Department," he said between mouthfuls. He swung his swivel chair around, revealing the two leather-covered stumps where his legs should have begun. When he spoke again his tone was a full octave higher. "Half my body, too!"

Battersly's air of well-being was completely gone now. He bit his lip and stared out the window into Centre Street. I sighed wearily. I knew every single word of the dialogue for the next ten minutes.

"So," continued Allhoff with savage mockery," as a reward they make me an inspector. Then I find out that all my work—all the work of my office—has to wait upon the convenience of a lousy incompetent patrolman."

Battersly turned a pale face from the window. "If you mean my lateness, sir," he said in a low voice, "I can explain it."

"No doubt," said Allhoff. He paused and took a deep breath. So did I. I knew what was coming.

"You can explain anything," said Allhoff. His words tumbled over each other and his voice ascended the scale. "You can even explain these!"

He wriggled the stumps of his legs like a hideous marionette. "You can explain why I sit here and lesser men walk around on my legs. You can explain—"

"Allhoff!" I said sharply.

He paid no attention to me, but for once Battersly remained steady under his blast.

"I was late, sir," he said quietly, "because I made an arrest."

"So," said Allhoff, "I've got to sit here, holding up my work while you hand out a traffic ticket."

"It wasn't traffic, sir," said Battersly. "It was homicide."

Allhoff opened his eyes at that. It burned him up when any copper in the entire department, other than himself, made an important arrest. For Battersly to presume to do so was arrant *lèse majesté*.

"You made an arrest in a murder case?"

"Yes, sir," said Battersly, and there was a little crow in his voice. "I brought in Ronnie Regan for the murder of Alfred Sontag."

For the first time in my life I saw Allhoff reduced to complete speechlessness. His mouth hung foolishly open. His little eyes were wide. His stumps twitched in a slow contorting dance.

I grinned broadly. This was big stuff. Regan was an all-around racketeer that the department had been trying to get in a cell for many years. Sontag was a retired German banker who owned several unique gem collections. And Allhoff, I knew, had not the slightest idea he was even dead.

He turned to me and spoke in a thick strangled tone. "Is Sontag dead?" he snapped.

"Very," I told him.

"Damn you!" he shrieked. "Why wasn't I told? You're supposed to clip the papers for me. You're supposed to give me the departmental reports each morning. Why didn't you tell me?"

I picked up the morning *Tribune* and a sheaf of onion-skin reports. I took them over to his desk and laid them beside his cup.

"I'm not sucker enough to tell you anything before you've had your coffee," I told him. "The Sontag murder's on top. It's the only thing there of any real importance."

"*Thank* you, Sergeant Simmonds," he said with elaborate sarcasm.

He snatched up the paper and began to read. I went back to my desk and sat down. I looked out the window and hummed that piece of Gilbert and Sullivan's about a policeman's lot being not a happy one.

If we had hung a shingle out downstairs it would have read: *Allhoff, Simmonds and Battersly. Independent Branch Office of the Metropolitan Police Department.* What our precise status was I had long since ceased to ponder. Three years ago Allhoff had been a deputy inspector—officially. Three years ago he had a pair of legs that reached all the way down to the soles of his shoes.

In those days, Battersly had been pretty much what he was now. A run-of-the-mill patrolman with most of his experience acquired at the Delehanty Institute. Then came the night of the West End Avenue raid. Battersly, in the trenches for the first time, had undergone an acute and understandable attack of buck fever. His failure to carry out an assignment to plug the desperate operator of a Tommy gun had resulted in a pound of steel plowing its way through Allhoff's legs. Gangrene was the next development, then amputation.

But the loss of his legs in no way impaired the workings of Allhoff's brain. It was a brain that the commissioner could ill afford to dispense with. However, a deputy inspector without legs would break every rule in the Civil Service book.

The commissioner solved the problem with simple directness. Allhoff was removed from the departmental rolls. Circuitous bookkeeping in the comptroller's office arranged that he receive his old salary. He had demanded and been granted Battersly's services as assistant. I, an old hand, who had come up with Allhoff, was detailed ostensibly to help with the paper work, actually to see that Allhoff's bitterness did not drive Battersly to suicide or murder.

For Allhoff, like the proverbial elephant, never forgot. He seized every opportunity to make Battersly's life miserable. When his legs had gone some part of his mind had gone, too. He retained all his old brilliant analytical qualities, all his former magnificent intuition. But there was no kindness, no humanity within him.

So here we were, the three of us, bottled up in this filthy tenement apartment that Allhoff lived and worked in because it was so close to headquarters. And I state categorically that if I'd saved a little money, if I hadn't so desperately needed that pension, I would have filled in a resignation blank months before.

llhoff replaced the Sontag death report on his desk. He picked up the gurgling coffee pot and refilled his cup. He sipped the black liquid slowly, looked at Battersly over the chipped rim of the cup.

"Nice work," he said with suspicious approbation. "Sontag was-shot through the head at midnight last night. And at eight o'clock this morning you solve the case."

"Yes, sir," said Battersly. "I—"

"Suppose you tell us just how you did it?" said Allhoff. His tone was benign enough, but somehow he reminded me of a cat preparing to pounce.

"Well," said Battersly, "on the way down here I dropped into headquarters. They were talking about the case. They happened to mention the threatening letter found in a drawer of Sontag's desk."

"What letter?" said Allhoff.

"It was written on the letterhead of the Private Property Protective Association," said Battersly. "It warned Sontag that if he did not subscribe to their service they could not be responsible for what happened to either him or his gem collection."

"So?" said Allhoff.

"So," said Battersly, "I happened to remember that Ronnie Regan ran an outfit of that name a couple of years ago. I went to his hotel and brought him in."

"And of course," said Allhoff heavily, "Regan broke down and confessed?"

Battersly licked his lips nervously. For the first time he was beginning to suspect that Allhoff's pose of affable approval was just that—a pose and no more.

"Why no, sir. He denied it. But the case seems simple enough."

"To you, undoubtedly," said Allhoff with weighty sarcasm. "Would you explain it to a couple of lesser minds?"

"It's easy enough," I said. "Battersly means that Regan was running this phoney protective association. He tried to get Sontag to kick in. Sontag refused. Regan killed him."

"Really?" said Allhoff. "Sontag's safe was open. A collection of opals was missing.

"My God," I said irritably. "That doesn't complicate it. Regan took the jewels with him."

Allhoff sipped more coffee. His little eyes were blazing over the cup's edge. He replaced it in the saucer, touched the onion-skin report with his finger.

"It says here," he said slowly, "the safe was open, the opals gone. Sontag lay on the floor, a bullet through his head. A scatter-rug which usually lay on the floor beside his desk had been placed over his face."

"Very interesting," I told him. "But what does that indicate, other than the fact that you can read?"

He glared at me, screwed up his mouth to the epithet-firing position, then decided against it.

"Listen," he said. "How many guys has Regan killed?"

"We never proved he killed any," I told him.

"Never mind what we've proved. He's a killer, isn't he?"

"He is now." said Battersly. "He killed Sontag."

Allhoff pounded the desk like an epileptic gnome. "He didn't!" he shrieked. "He never killed Sontag. He killed a dozen other guys. We all know that. That's *why* he never killed Sontag."

his time I really thought he had cracked. That last speech may have passed for logic in a madhouse, but nowhere else. I stood up.

"Allhoff," I said quietly.

He looked up at me. With his customary facility he read my mind. That made him even more furious.

"Sit down!" he roared. "Sit down, you brainless fool. It's you that's screwy— not I. You can't even see a fact when I hand it to you on a plate. It was hard to believe Battersly had enough sense to pull in a killer when headquarters couldn't do it. Now that I've read the report, I'm certain he didn't."

"Oh, he didn't?" I said. "He's got Regan in the jug, hasn't he?"

Allhoff made a noise like a wounded bull. "You half-wit," he cried. "I'm telling you Regan didn't do it!"

"But, sir," Battersly interposed diffidently. "That letter. Regan signed it. It's his handwriting."

"I don't care if he wrote his name on the corpse," yelled Allhoff. "He didn't kill Sontag!"

He picked up the coffee pot with a hand that trembled with rage and poured inky fluid into his cup. Battersly, white-faced and tense, blinked at him. I lit my pipe and fought my temper.

To me, Allhoff's behavior was childishly obvious. As far as he was concerned, Battersly could do nothing right. Now Battersly had brought in a murder suspect and Allhoff wasn't going to stand for it. He was going to spring Regan by hook or crook just to prove Battersly wrong. It meant nothing to Allhoff that he would turn a killer loose to kill again. Nothing meant anything to Allhoff when it was a question of indulging his sadistic bitterness toward the younger man.

The telephone on my desk sounded above the rattle of Allhoff's cup and saucer. I picked up the receiver, said, "Hello," and listened in amazement. I put my hand over the mouthpiece and turned to Allhoff.

"It's the D. A.'s office," I told him. "They've got Regan over there. He's squawking to high heaven. He's demanding to see you. Says you're the only guy that can solve the Sontag killing."

Allhoff put down his cup. I could almost hear him purr. "Of course I am," he said. "Bring him over."

I transmitted the message, hung up and looked at Allhoff. There was arrogant defiance in his gaze. God knows I didn't want to tangle with him again that morning, but I had to do something about this cockeyed tangent he'd taken.

"Allhoff," I said, "no matter what you feel, please try to remember you're a copper."

"You should be half as good!"

"I'm not arguing that," I told him. "The point is that Battersly's got a cold case against Regan. It's your job to back him up. We've been after Regan for years. You can't spring him for personal reasons."

I had been afraid he'd get sore again. To my surprise he smiled.

"God," he said in a low tone, "you're dumb."

CHAPTER TWO

Eight Times a Killer

Ronnie Regan was a tall, dapper Irishman. His eyes were black as a peat bog and his hair even blacker than that. His face was thin, his nose corvine. He was tall, handsome and, at the moment, worried. He sat at the side of Allhoff's desk. A uniformed copper stood behind him.

Battersly regarded the proceedings blankly. I watched Allhoff and found myself hoping that this time he'd stuck his neck out too far.

"Inspector," said Regan, "you're the only brain in the department."

"Right," said Allhoff reaching for the coffee pot.

"I had nothing to do with the Sontag killing," said Regan. "It's a bum rap. But I figure you're the only guy that can get me out. I told that to this guy who brought me in, but he didn't think you'd be interested."

Allhoff shot a quick glance at Battersly. "Oh, he didn't, eh?"

"No, Inspector," said Regan looking at him shrewdly. "He said you was washed up. Said the commissioner only kept you on out of sympathy."

Battersly leaped from his chair. His face was pale and his eyes wide open.

"That's a lie!" he yelled. "I never said anything—"

"Shut up!" thundered Allhoff, glaring at him. Then he turned again to Regan. "So I'm all washed up, eh? Regan, I don't believe you're guilty. Answer me one question honestly and I'll be sure of it."

Relief flooded Ronnie Regan's face. "Sure, Inspector," he said. "Anything at all. Anything, Inspector."

"All right," said Allhoff. "How many men have you killed, Regan?"

Regan stared at him. For that matter, so did everyone else. For six years the entire department had been trying and failing to prove that Regan was a murderer. Now Allhoff asked him point-blank, as calmly as if he were asking for a match, how many men he'd killed. And judging from his expression he actually expected an answer.

Regan smiled nervously. "Why, Inspector," he said, "I ain't killed anybody. The boys got nothing on me. I ain't ever been indicted, Inspector."

"I'm familiar with the police records," Allhoff said icily. "I asked you how many men you've murdered."

Regan looked around the room like a hunted possum. He was beginning to think Allhoff wasn't on his side after all.

"Now listen, Inspector—" he began.

Allhoff smashed his fist on the desk and his cup and saucer danced. "You listen to me!" Allhoff barked. "You'll either answer me or burn for Sontag's murder. They got you dead to rights on it. Give me an honest answer and I'll be able to help you. Now, how many guys have you killed?"

There was a long silence. Allhoff's burning little eyes stared at the Irishman, Regan's face was white, his brow wrinkled. Then, under the spell of Allhoff's dominant gaze, he yielded.

"Eight," he muttered. "Maybe nine. But you can't prove it. You can't use this as—"

"Shut up!" bellowed Allhoff again. He nodded to the policeman behind Regan's chair. "All right, Clancy. Take him away."

Regan stood up. His facial muscles twitched. His hand trembled. "Wait a minute." he said. "You can't do this to me. I thought you said you'd help me if I told you how many—"

"Shut up!" roared Allhoff for the third time. "I'm going to find out who killed Sontag. What else do you expect me to do? Arrange a jail-break for you in the meantime? Take him away. Clancy."

Allhoff filled his cup, stared at the wall opposite. He muttered in a low harsh voice: "All washed up, eh? The commissioner keeps me here out of sympathy, eh?"

"Allhoff," I said, "you know damn well Battersly never said a thing like that. Regan was playing up to you, appealing to your prejudice. Trying to get you on his side. He used Battersly as a lever. How can you be such a fool? It's transparent as glass."

He swung around in his chair. "I'll argue with you later," he said. "At the moment we're working on a murder case. The question is—who killed Alfred Sontag?"

I sighed wearily. "Regan did," I told him. "Stop being a stubborn petty fool."

"The hell he did," said Allhoff. "And the hell I am."

"Listen," I said with dogged patience. "You're sore at Battersly. You're sore he made the pinch. You fall for the obvious line Regan hands you. If you'll use your brain for introspective purposes, examine yourself internally, you'll know why you're insisting Regan's innocent."

He put down the cup, hammered the desk again and made a noise like Donald Duck in one of his more irate moments.

"If you'd examine the case *externally*," he shrieked, "you'd know Regan didn't kill Sontag! You haven't the intelligence of a—a"—he groped for an annihilating simile—"of a police sergeant," he concluded.

"Suppose you help me out," I said.

"I always have to," said Allhoff."

I filled my pipe and said: "Well?"

"The scatter rug," said Allhoff. "Remember? It was covering Sontag's face when they found the body."

"Which, of course," I said ironically, "proves that Regan couldn't possibly have done it."

"Of course," said Allhoff.

I could tell by his voice he wasn't kidding.

"Would you mind," I said, elaborately polite, "explaining that?"

"Listen," said Allhoff, "Regan is a tough guy. He's killed at least eight men by his own admission. Undoubtedly he's seen his own gorillas kill twenty more. Regan ain't afraid of a corpse."

"So?" I said.

"So," shouted Allhoff, crescendo, "he wouldn't bother to cover a corpse's face while he rifled the safe. Only an amateur murderer would get the horrors because a dead man's eyes were on him. The scatter rug proves Regan didn't do it."

He poured himself a cup of coffee. Battersly and I sat in utter silence. I screwed up my brow and considered the scatter-rug theory from all angles. For a moment it sounded all right. Then I thought of Regan's letter, signed by his own hand. I thought of the value of Sontags missing opals, of Regan's reputation. I decided it was pretty slim.

"It won't do, Allhoff." I said. "It's just a minor item and more important things, all of which point to Regan. Maybe Sontag moved the rug during the struggle. Maybe someone in the house covered him with it after the killing. Maybe—"

"Maybe," said Allhoff, "the corpse used it to blow his nose."

He clanked the cup back in the saucer and slid down from his chair to the floor. He stood there on his stumps looking like a child of Satan.

"All right," he said petulantly. "Help me down the stairs. Let's get going."

"Going?" I said. "Where?"

"To Sontag's house. Battersly! Here. Give me a hand."

We crossed the room, took his hands and headed for the stairs.

We thumped him down into the street and Battersly hailed a taxi.

It was the first time in two years that Allhoff had been out of the house.

CHAPTER THREE

Allhoff Plays Uncle

Sontag's was a cramped private house on Charlton Street. We had been there less than fifteen minutes when I began to glow internally. There were two people in all the world who believed Allhoff could do no wrong. One was the commissioner; the other Allhoff himself. The commissioner had permitted him to get away with extra-legal murder more than once on this account, but after fifteen minutes at Sontag's I was certain Allhoff was licked for once. By aligning himself with Regan he had stuck his neck out. Already I could see the axe descending.

There were four people at Sontag's— three adults and a seven-year-old child. First, Allhoff went to work on Mamie, the colored maid. She was completely dumb and hadn't the slightest idea what an opal was. Allhoff grunted and sent her back to the kitchen to make some coffee.

Now, he was sitting hunched before the desk that had been Alfred Sontag's, sipping from a cleaner cup than usual. Battersly and I stood behind him. Before him, on a couch, sat Harry and Ruth Langer. Allhoff put his cup in the saucer and yelled for more coffee. Then, assuming his most fearsome expression, he stared at the couple before him.

"How long have you two been living here?" he said.

Harry Langer cleared his throat. "We three," he corrected. "There's Minerva—our daughter, you know."

"All right," said Allhoff. "How long?" "About four months," said Ruth Langer. "You see, Mr. Sontag is—was my uncle. He had never seen my daughter. He was a bachelor with no kin but us. He wanted to leave his estate to Minerva. He promised to do so if we would live with him during the years he had left."

Harry Langer nodded. "That's right," he said. "Sontag was a lonely old chap despite his money. He wanted to have a kid running around the house. He grew very fond of Minerva. Made her his heir.

Allhoff nodded slowly. "So," he said, "your daughter gets all Sontag's money?"

"Well," said Langer, "we understand that's so. Of course, the will hasn't been probated yet."

"No," said Allhoff. "And who are the executors of the estate?"

"Probably we are," said Langer. "But we won't know until the will is read."

"The hell you don't," said Allhoff.

Ruth Langer's eyes opened wide.

Her husband sprang to his feet. "Look here, Inspector," he said angrily, "I don't know what the devil you're implying by that, but I don't like it. The case is as plain as a pikestaff. Regan demanded that my wife's uncle pay him for protection. Mr. Sontag refused. Regan killed him. At the time of the murder my uncle had taken his opal collection from the safe. Regan, finding them, took them along with him."

"I've heard that theory four times this morning," said Allhoff. "I still don't believe it."

"What do you believe?" I asked him. "Maybe," said Allhoff, keeping his little eyes riveted on the Langers, "the beneficiaries under the will killed him. That's always a good motive."

Ruth Langer gasped.

Her husband fought his wrath for a silent moment, then said quietly: "Inspector, there's a reason why it's not a good motive this time. We knew we would get Mr. Sontag's money eventually. We were well provided for while he lived. He denied us nothing. And we were at the movies when the murder was committed."

Allhoff raised his eyebrows. "You can prove it?"

"We can prove it," said Langer.

"Who was in the house with Sontag?"

"The maid and our daughter."

Allhoff's brow screwed up into a frown. He made a low humming sound, drummed a thoughtful finger on the desk-top.

I decided to throw a needle into Allhoff. "The maid did it," I said with phoney excitement. "I've got it all figured, Allhoff. The maid's great grandmother was a slave in Virginia. Sontag's grandfather was her master. He used to beat her up. For years the grandchild waited and waited. Then one night—"

That got him. He turned on me, his face like a bursting bomb. Before he could speak I drove the needle in still deeper.

"No, wait," I said, "Maybe it was the kid. Maybe the kid's a werewolf. She got thirsty in the night. So—"

Now Allhoff found his voice. And despite the presence of Ruth Langer he found a blasphemous adjective and an obscene noun. He threw them at me.

"You'll be disciplined for this," he raged. "You're obstructing justice. You're—"

He broke off as Minerva Langer came into the room. She was a sweet child with round blue eyes and golden curls. She stood on the threshold and regarded Allhoff with naive wonder. He looked at her and calmed down.

"Come in, dear," said Ruth Langer. "This is Inspector Allhoff."

The child curtseyed gravely. Then she looked at her mother. "Is he a policeman, mummy?"

"Yes, dear."

Allhoff grinned his ugly grin at her. He assumed what he considered a benign expression and spoke with the heavy playfulness of a bachelor uncle.

"Well, well," he boomed. "And how's the little lady? Come over here and say hello to the policeman."

Minerva looked dubiously at her mother. Ruth Langer nodded. The child came across the room to Allhoff, stood by his chair. Allhoff patted her head with a heavy hand. He reminded me of a Neanderthal man with a French doll.

"Well, well," he said again. "And do you like policemen?"

She nodded. "I like Dick Tracy," she said. "And Tailspin Tommy."

"Policemen and flyers," said Allhoff. "That's fine. Do you know, Lindbergh shook hands with me once."

"Lindbergh!" said the child in her thin piping voice. "I saw him once. Mummy took me to see him."

"Really," said Allhoff. "Where?"

"In a parade. I love parades."

llhoff chuckled. He sounded like grinding tin to me, but I knew he believed he was reeking with affability. "I guess you love the movies, too," he said.

The child nodded.

"Well," said Allhoff, "you get daddy and mummy to take you to the movies right now." He raised his eyes and faced the Langers. "I'd like to be alone in the house. Battersly, go along with them. You need a day off."

"Listen," said Langer hotly. "Do I understand—"

Battersly!" roared Allhoff in his brook-no-nonsense voice. "Take them all to a movie."

I lit my pipe as the Langers donned their hats. Battersly, silent and pale, joined them at the door. The kid looked back at Allhoff from the foyer. She waved her handbag.

"Good-bye," she said. "Good-bye, policeman."

Allhoff waved back at her. He watched her as they left the house. Then he turned to me. "Always had a way with kids," he said. "Should have had some my-self."

"Allhoff," I said, "what've you got up your un-washed sleeve?"

He grinned at me. It wasn't a very pleasant grin. "Get the cop off the beat," he said. "Then the two of you search the house. Overlook nothing."

"What am I searching for?" I asked him.

"You'll know when you find it," he said. "And while you're out getting the cop bring back a lollipop and a penknife. A good sharp penknife."

"Allhoff," I said. "You don't give little girls pen-knives. You give them to boys."

"A penknife," repeated Allhoff, glaring at me. "A sharp one."

I sighed, shrugged my shoulders and left the room.

At the door I heard him say into the phone: "Get me long-distance. Quick!"

wo hours later I was in the maid's room. Damrau, the cop on the beat, and I had been through the house like a pair of fine-tooth combs. Now he was finishing up in the cellar, while I was up here. Of course we didn't know what the hell we were looking for and that made it harder. Allhoff remained downstairs at Sontag's desk playing with the candy and penknife I'd brought back with me.

I conducted a routine search, but my heart wasn't in it, I was certain that Allhoff was wrong, that he had sent Damrau and myself on a fishing expedition blindly hoping we'd turn up something.

I stood on a chair inside the closet and examined a shelf on a level with my head. There were half a dozen old hats and a few dusty cardboard boxes on the shelf. I opened the boxes, went through them unenthusiasti-cally.

A moment later I was standing at the window, a cardboard box in my hand and a thumping in my breast. The light from the street streamed through the drawn curtains upon a mountain of beads inside the box. For the most part the beads were cheap and dull. But here and there, like a scattered handful of moonbeams, shone a milky radiant light.

I ran down the back stairs, through the kitchen into Sontag's study. "Allhoff!"

I yelled. "Look! Opals mixed in this box of beads. Look, man, look!"

He didn't even lift his eyes from the coffee cup. "Good," he said quietly. "Did you find the gun?"

I put the beads on the desk beside him, gave him my dirtiest look. "What gun?" I said. "You lucky copper! You haven't got the cast-iron gall to sit there and pre-tend you knew about those opals?"

"Of course I knew about them," he said impa-tiently. "But where's the gun? That's what I want."

"Allhoff—" I began, but he cut me short.

"Where's the maid?"

"In the kitchen. But—"

"Bring her in."

I went back to the kitchen and brought in the maid. She stood bored and bovine before Allhoff. He held out the bead-box.

"This yours?" he asked her.

"Yassuh." She seemed unmoved at sight of the glit-tering opals.

"When did you open it last?"

"Ah ain't seen them beads for months, suh. Most a year, I reckon."

Allhoff nodded slowly. "All right," he said. "You can go back to the kitchen. Put on some more coffee. And for God's sake make it strong. This stuff's like wa-ter."

She shuffled out of the room. There was a mocking grin on Allhoff's face as he turned to me.

"What about Regan now?" he said.

But I was ready for him. I had already figured that angle. "Those opals don't get you anywhere," I told him. "Regan bumped off Sontag because Sontag wouldn't kick in to his protective association. He didn't bother with the jewels. Too dangerous. That dumb maid walked in, saw the body and the opals. She swiped them. Figured the loss would be blamed on the killer."

He looked at me a long moment, then rocked with laughter. "My God," he said. "You can explain anything, can't you? That's almost as good as your werewolf theory."

He was still laughing when Battersly and the Langers returned from the movies. They filed silently into the room and Langer said, with what seemed to me a touch of defiance: "Find anything, Inspector?"

Allhoff went heavily avuncular again. "Certainly did," he chirped. "Found some presents for a little lady. . . Come here, Minerva."

"Shall I sit on your knee? The child asked. Allhoff went purple — and the next instant the knife was open.

The child looked at him with grave blue eyes. She deliberately removed her hat, handed it and her pocketbook to her mother. Then she crossed the room. Allhoff held up a lollipop with the air of the late Rockefeller about to bestow a shining dime on the worthy peasantry.

"Here," he said. "Now open your mouth."

The child smiled. "Shall I sit on your knee?" she asked.

The silence was deadly. Allhoff looked at her sharply. I could hear Battersly's sibilant intake of breath. Allhoff's face was purple. His lips were compressed as if he fought for control. I was prepared for the deluge.

But for once Allhoff kept his emotions in leash. He forced a smile. "You stand right there," he said. "Now open your mouth. Wide."

The child opened her mouth. Allhoff popped the candy inside. I grinned behind his back. The picture of Allhoff playing the role of benign parent was incongruous to the point of absurdity.

"And now," said Allhoff, picking up the knife and opening it, "look what I have for you."

The kid regarded the penknife without interest,

"It's sharp," said Allhoff. "You can sharpen your own pencils with it."

Ruth Langer smiled slightly. "I hardly think she's old enough for a knife, Inspector," she said.

"Of course not, Allhoff," I put in. "She's—"

The child's scream interrupted me. I never knew precisely what had happened. In one instant Allhoff was passing over the open knife. In the next it clattered to the floor, blood streamed from a jagged cut in the kid's arm, and the room was filled with howling.

Ruth Langer rushed to her daughter's side. Her husband blazed with inarticulate wrath.

Allhoff was a sudden picture of contrition. "My God," he said. "What have I done? I never thought—I— Here, Simmonds. Get Doc Bagley. Quick!"

Harry Langer glared at Allhoff. "I'll attend to it," he said bitterly. "Of all the damned fool things I ever saw—"

Allhoff looked abject and miserable. "My fault," he mumbled. "I insist on getting Bagley. Of course, I'll pay the bill. Simmonds, get on that phone. Get Bagley!"

The Langers were shepherding the shrieking child toward the bathroom as I picked up the phone. Battersly, at Allhoff's order, went along to help. I got Bagley's office and spoke to his assistant.

"This is Simmonds," I announced. "Send the doc—"

"He's on his way," a breezy voice assured me. "Ought to be there any minute."

"On his way where?"

"Sontag's—on Charlton Street. Isn't that where you want him?"

The last remark dazed me. "How the devil did you know?" I demanded. "It only just happened. How could Bagley know anything—"

"Listen!" The voice became impatient now. "All I know is that the doc's gone to Charlton Street. Answering a call for Inspector Allhoff."

I replaced the receiver slowly, looked across the desk at Allhoff. He met my gaze with bland innocence. Then, at that moment, Bagley burst in the front door.

Allhoff waved him toward the staircase. "Up there," he said. "Where all the noise is."

Bagley nodded and dashed up the stairs. I kept my eyes on Allhoff.

"What sort of a frame are you working on?" I said. "What in the—" I broke off when I noted the sudden change in his expression.

Allhoff's eyes were suddenly alert and narrowed. He was looking beyond me, over my shoulder toward the window. I swung around myself to see what he was looking at. Then the first shot cracked past my ear.

It smashed into the wall at a point some three inches above Allhoff's left shoulder. His leather-tipped thighs made a soft thudding sound as he slid from his chair to the floor. The dark figure whose eye peered around the edge of the window frame sighted his revolver again.

Now my own gun was in my hand. So was Allhoff's. When the man outside fired again, our guns roared in unison. Neither of us hit anything. Allhoff and I converged on the window. The eye disappeared. When we gained the sill, I saw a figure in a green suit desperately essaying to scale the wooden fence at the rear of the yard.

Allhoff fired at it as I vaulted the sill and raced out toward the fence. I reached it in time to clutch at a disappearing coattail, to get a single glimpse at a face as the figure disappeared into the next yard.

I ran back to the house where Allhoff stood staring blankly at the fence where the intruder had disappeared. There was a peculiar expression upon his face. It was not fear. Neither was it nervousness. It was rather stunned amazement.

"My God," he muttered. "Someone took a pot shot at *me!*"

His tone indicated his reaction. That anyone should take a pot shot at him was utterly incredible. He regarded the crime as blasphemy rather than attempted murder.

I pushed past him and headed for the front door.

"Hey!" he said. "Where're you going?"

"After that guy."

"You're crazy," said Allhoff. "He got out into King Street. He's back in his car and halfway to Brooklyn by now."

That was true enough. I came back into the room. Allhoff's brow was screwed up in thought. Well, the situation was certainly no crystal ball to me, either. "Well, Einstein," I said. "Riddle me that one. All your local suspects are upstairs under the eyes of Battersly and the doc. Regan's in the can. So who the hell is shooting at you?"

Allhoff thrust his gun back into his hip pocket. He waddled across the room and climbed back into the chair behind the desk. He stared thoughtfully at the blotting paper. I knew from his facial expression that he didn't have the answer this time.

"You saw that guy," he said suddenly. "What did he look like?"

The reply to that question had been puzzling me for the past few minutes.

"I didn't get a good look at him," I said. "But if it wasn't so utterly impossible, I'd say it looked like Benny Bagel."

"Benny Bagel," he repeated slowly. "And just why do you say that it's impossible?"

"You know as well as I do that Benny's one of Regan's gorillas. Since you seem to be the only man in the world who believes that Regan didn't kill Sontag—since you're supposed to be trying to prove he didn't—it's hardly likely that Regan would be engaged in having you knocked off."

"We sat in silence for two full minutes. I was doggedly grappling with this new problem when my futile concentration was disturbed by the hammering of Allhoff's fist upon the desk. I looked up to see an exultant grin upon his lips.

"Simmonds," he said, "we're going home now. "

"In defeat?" I said. "Or triumph?"

He slid from the chair. "What do *you* think?" he said jeeringly as he thumped his way slowly across the room toward the foyer.

I followed him. We had reached the front door when Doc Bagley came down the stairs, with Battersly at his heels. Allhoff cocked an inquiring eyebrow at the doc.

"Everything O. K., Doc?"

"Everything," said Bagley. "A scratch, that's all."

He winked slowly and deliberately at Allhoff. Allhoff nodded and yelled up the stairway to Battersly.

"We're going back to the office," he said. "When they're through bandaging that kid, bring 'em all along. The maid, too."

I opened the front door, went down the brownstone steps and whistled for a cab. Allhoff was grinning like a Buddha as we got inside.

"Say," he said as we turned into Seventh Avenue, "do ever listen to the March of Time?"

"Sometimes." I eyed him suspiciously. "What are you doing? Just making conversation?"

"You're a very bright copper," said Allhoff in a tone which implied that I wasn't at all.

CHAPTER FOUR

Allhoff Knew It All the Time

Allhoff's tiny room was crowded. Harry and Ruth Langer sat facing him on the left side of the desk. The child, Minerva, stood between them tightly holding her mother's hand. The colored maid, still utterly bored by it all, was on Harry Langer's right. Regan was handcuffed to Officer Clancy, sitting, perforce, beside him.

Battersly's back was to the window. He stood watching Allhoff like a man waiting for a bomb to explode. I sat on my desk, a little anxious. Mentally I was laying fifty to one Allhoff didn't have anything. Nevertheless, I was worried that he had.

Allhoff poured a cupful of tar from the coffee pot and sipped it. He looked around the room over the rim of the cup. Then he said in a quiet chastened voice: "I guess I owe some of you people an apology."

I nearly fell off the desk-top. Allhoff apologizing? Hitler kissing Stalin? Hoover turning Communist? Conceivably. But Allhoff apologizing? My God!

"Specifically," he went on in a meek tone, "to you, Mr. and Mrs. Langer. My conduct may have been rather brusque, but when I'm on a hard case I sometimes forget myself."

That was the sentence which should have aroused my suspicions. Allhoff never forgot himself in his life. Everything he did, even his raving at Battersly, was done for a calculated reason. But at the moment my thought processes were frozen.

"Forget it, Inspector," said Harry Langer. "After all, it's your job."

"Gracious of you," said Allhoff. He swung his head around and looked over his shoulder. "And you, Battersly," he went on. "I was wrong. You're the man who brought in Sontag's killer. I was a fool to think otherwise."

If ever a bum walks up to me in the street and hands me a thousand-dollar bill, I shall be less amazed than I was at that moment.

Battersly flushed. I thought I saw a dim affection in his gaze as he replied huskily: "Damned decent of you to say so, sir."

"It's only right," said Allhoff, reaching for the coffee pot. "I've already spoken to the commissioner about it. He's coming over in about half an hour to shake the hand of the man who solved the Sontag killing with such speed. Maybe you'd better get polished up. I'll excuse you if you want to get a shave, a shine or anything. You know, spruce up for the big guy."

"Thank you, sir," said Battersly, overwhelmed, "I'll be right back, sir."

He saluted, his face flushed with excitement. Then he left the room.

I scratched my head in wonder and looked at Regan to see how he had taken this about-face of Allhoff's. He was perceptibly shaken. His white face was whiter than usual. There was an awful anxiety in his eyes. He began to rise from his chair, but since Clancy didn't move, the chain of the handcuff pulled him back again.

"Inspector," he cried and his voice shook, "I didn't do it. I didn't kill him! It's a frame! I wrote that letter three years ago. I ain't run that protective association for two years. Sontag used to kick in to me. Why should kill him?"

"The D. A.'s office says that letter bore this month's date," I told him.

"Right," said Allhoff. "You're guilty as hell, Regan."

"No," said Ronnie Regan hysterically "No! No! I didn't kill him! I—"

"Shut up," said Allhoff. He put down his cup and leaned over his desk. He fixed Regan with his little burning eyes. When he spoke, all the softness had gone from his voice.

"You not only killed Sontag," he said "but you hired Benny Bagel to take pot shot at me."

"No," said Regan, but he didn't sound quite so vehement this time, "I swear—"

"I can prove you murdered Sontag," said Allhoff. "I can't prove you hired Benny."

"What does it matter?" I said. "He'll burn for Sontag. You can't give him any more than that."

Allhoff swivelled around and looked at me. I expected to be profanely told to mind my own business. But he only said in a dulcet tone, "Please, Sergeant."

He turned back to Regan. "What want from you," he said, "is an admission that you hired Benny to kill me."

"My God," said Regan reasonably "You say you're going to burn me for Sontag. What else do you want?"

"A confession about Benny," went on Allhoff inexorably. "You're in a tough spot, Regan."

Regan's fingers were trembling. The Langers stared at Allhoff, fascinated. The maid remained bored.

"What are you trying to do, Inspector?" said Regan. "I didn't do nothing. Why would I want to kill *you*?

You was on my side wasn't you? You was the only brain in the whole department smart enough to help me. Why would I have Benny take a shot at you, Inspector?"

That was precisely the question that was worrying me. There was savage mockery in Allhoff's face as he stared at Regan.

"You're pretty damned certain I don't know the answer to that, aren't you, Regan? Well, I do."

"Answer it," I told him, "and you're good."

"I will," he said. "And I am. Now, Regan, you did a lot of talking about the superior qualities of the Allhoff brain, but you didn't really believe what you were saying. You know you were cooked on the Sontag case. You knew that neither I nor anyone else could get you out. Right?"

Judging from the panic in Regan's countenance, it was right. Though I was damned if I saw it yet.

"So," went on Allhoff, "you sent your mouthpiece over to Benny with a message telling him to get me. It was your only chance. It wasn't a sure thing but it was a chance. Something that might swing a jury. You were in a desperate enough spot to grab at anything. Right, again, Regan?"

Regan didn't answer. He slumped in his chair, looked at Allhoff through beaten eyes.

It was still beyond me and I said so. "I often wonder how the hell you got your stripes," said Allhoff. "Look. They got Regan dead to rights for killing Sontag. But, it's a known fact that Inspector Allhoff, the brightest guy in the police department didn't believe him guilty. So what happens? Allhoff's working on the case and he's killed. All right. And what does that imply to a jury? That Regan's innocent. That Allhoff was on the verge of proving it when the real killer shot him down. Certainly Regan didn't do it. First, he was in the can. Second Allhoff was his pal. Working for him. Now does it begin to seep through your sandstone mind?"

It seeped through this time. Once again I was forced to admire, reluctantly, Allhoff's shrewd Machiavellian intelligence. Allhoff transferred his attention back to Regan.

"I'll make a deal with you, Regan," he said.

Regan stared at him, dully, without hope. "What is it?"

Allhoff held the empty coffee pot out to me.

"Water," he said. I took it into the bedroom and filled it up. After he'd got the water started boiling again, he went on. "I've got a lot of pull in this town. You know that, Regan."

Regan nodded.

"You make an oral confession," said Allhoff. "You state before these witnesses that you hired Benny to plug me. I'll guarantee you won't burn."

There was a long silence in the room. The Langer's never having seen Allhoff at work before, stared at him as if they were watching some new moving-picture star. The little girl shuffled uneasily. Even the bovine maid seemed to have lost some of her constant ennui. Undoubtedly, Allhoff had figured Benny's part in the affair dead right, but there remained one item I still didn't understand.

"Allhoff," I said, "you're crazy. You can burn him for Sontag. What the hell are you worrying about Benny for? Maybe he'd get twenty years for that, be paroled in eight."

"I don't like gorillas taking pot shots at me," said Allhoff.

So that was it! You can't take a pot shot at Inspector Allhoff, fellows. If you murder or loot anyone else, you'll get your day in court, have a fifty-fifty break with the average jury. But a pot shot at the inspector, boys, means that you're going to do time—and for that specific rap, too.

It was damned silly. Childish. And I said so.

Allhoff paid no attention to me this time. His yellow eyes were fastened on Regan.

"Admit it," he said relentlessly, "and you have your life. I'll go to bat for you in the D. A.'s office and even higher up. Keep your mouth shut and you'll fry."

Regan was licked and he knew it. He moistened his dry lips nervously. "All right," he said. "I hired Benny to plug you. I promised him five grand for the job. I did it for the reasons you already figured out."

Allhoff beamed, looked around the room and bowed. It occurred to me then for the first time that his colossal vanity was the sole reason for him dragging the Langers and the maid down here. Now that he had come to the conclusion that Regan actually had murdered Sontag, what the hell did he need them for?

"Now you got to keep your word, Inspector," said Regan. "You got me out of the chair. It's a lousy deal all around. I never killed Sontag. I never—"

Then Allhoff threw his bomb,

"This is going to kill you. Regan," he said sardonically. "I know you didn't kill Sontag. I knew it all the time!"

Regan jerked forward in his chair and the handcuffs rattled. Allhoff, tense, hateful, and throughly assured, glared about the room. The Langers watched him in amazement. Ruth held her daughter's hand tightly. Even the maid registered interest at this point. I gave up even attempting to keep abreast of Allhoff now. The gurgle of the coffee pot sounded loudly in the quiet.

"For God's sake!" said Regan excitedly. "You mean you're going to spring me?"

"After twenty years," said Allhoff. "Accessory before, during, and after the fact of attempted murder."

"Allhoff," I said impatiently. "What've you got?"

He drew a deep breath. "An indictment," he said. "Now let's reconstruct the whole case from the beginning."

"All right," I said. "Let's."

"We've got Sontag," he said slowly. "Sontag, lousy with money. No heirs. Maybe he didn't think so much of Harry Langer. Maybe he didn't have a very high opinion of his own niece either."

Langer flushed scarlet. He got out of his chair. "I resent those remarks, Inspector," he said crisply. "This has no bearing on the case. You're merely guessing."

"Sure, I'm guessing," said Allhoff, "Up to a certain point. From there on, we'll use evidence."

His little eyes met Langer's and Langer sat down. I could hear him breathing hard. Little Minerva clung to her mother.

"However," went on Allhoff blankly, "it occurs to Sontag that perhaps there is issue."

Regan blinked at that. "*What's* issue?" he said.

"A child, you fool," growled Allhoff, "It occurs to him that if there is a child, perhaps his money can go there. He writes his niece, inquiring."

"So," I said wearily, "they have a child, they tell Sontag so. He invites them to stay with him. Get on with it, Allhoff."

"You're consistent," said Allhoff. "Consistently wrong. You see they *don't* have a child."

Ruth Langer drew her breath in with a little hissing sound, Minerva stared wide-eyed at Allhoff. Harry Langer was pale. His eyes burned like smoldering cobalt. He stood up again.

"You're mad," he said in a thick voice. "We won't stay here. We—"

"Sit down," snarled Allhoff with savage enjoyment.

I ran my fingers through my hair and performed a little cerebrating myself. "You mean they borrowed a child?" I asked,

"No," said Allhoff, "They didn't borrow a child, And for the love of God stop interrupting me."

He ladled sugar into his cup and went on.

"At first things go very well with Sontag and little Minerva. He fixes up his will in her favor. Then one day he gets the idea that maybe something's screwy in the setup."

"*How?*" I said. "Granting your theory's right. How does he get the idea suddenly that something's screwy?"

"The same way that I got it," said Allhoff. "Anyway he decides to write a letter of inquiry to Quebec. The Langers realize that the reply to that letter will ruin their chances of getting the old guy's money. So they kill him."

"Holy Smoke," said Regan. "That's it, Inspector. I told you I didn't do it. I told—"

He stopped as Allhoff glared at him. Ruth Langer and the child were huddled close together. Langer leaned forward in his chair. He spoke in a high excited pitch.

"You're crazy! We didn't kill him. How could we? We weren't even in the house. We—"

"That's absolutely right," I said. "They weren't."

Allhoff lifted his eyes and hands to heaven as if he were calling on the Deity to witness what fools surrounded him. "They found the opals," he said. "They decided to hide them. They opened the back window so that it would look like an ordinary robbery. They found Regan's old letter. They changed the date on it. Maybe they'd seen it before. They put it where the coppers would be certain to find it. That would make it look like an outside job. It was all so beautifully simple that they would have got away with it save for one completely stupid move."

He paused and drank coffee while I played straight man again. "Which was?" I asked.

"The scatter rug," said Allhoff. "The killer being a rank amateur couldn't stand the sight of a corpse while all this other business was going on."

"You're still guessing," said Ruth Langer, but now her tone was low and frightened.

"I'm still guessing," said Allhoff quietly. Then his lips contorted to a horrible grimace. His voice rose and he spat words at her.

"But now I'll deal in facts. Such facts as fingerprints on those opals. Such facts as a telephone call to Quebec. Such facts as thirty-year-old arteries and wisdom teeth. Such facts as—"

Ruth Langer screamed. Her husband sat frozen and trembling on the edge of his chair. The maid glanced from Allhoff to the Langers with round startled eyes. The child alone seemed composed. She moved a little distance away from her mother and opened her handbag.

I had never seen Allhoff move so swiftly. He snatched the coffee pot from its base and flung it across the room toward Minerva. It landed full in her face, knocking her down, spilling scalding liquid over her arms and legs. She uttered a sharp cry of pain and fell to the floor.

"Allhoff!" I cried as I sprang across the room.

I picked the child up, wiped her burned face with my handkerchief. I turned my head and glared at Allhoff.

"You're crazy," I said. "Nuts. You—"

"Unless you're hankering for an inspector's funeral," said Allhoff, "take that revolver out of her bag."

I snatched up the bag from the floor where it had fallen and opened it to see a thirty-eight inside. I looked at Minerva. She glared at Allhoff like a tiger. Suddenly her blue eyes seemed ancient and filled with evil knowledge. In that instant I wondered how the hell I had ever fallen for it.

"My God," said Ronnie Regan. "Not that kid!"

"Kid?" said Allhoff. "She's thirty if she's a day. When I gave her that lollipop I saw her wisdom teeth. Before that I saw her arteries. Look at them. Blue and thick, No child ever had arteries like that. Doc Bagley bore me out."

"Bagley!" I said as light fell on my brain. "You mean you cut her arm deliberately?"

"Of course," said Allhoff, "I don't wait for the breaks. There was no way I could force her to submit to a medical examination. So I cut her arm."

The midget and Ruth Langer huddled together in each other's arms, staring at Allhoff as if he were some inhuman apparition. Langer's jaws worked spasmodically. I was aware of a queasy sensation in the pit of my stomach, caused by the fact that I was mortally certain Allhoff had done it again.

"Listen," I said. "You stated a moment ago that Sontag's suspicions of Minerva were aroused for the same reasons that yours were. Do you mean that Sontag was going around studying arteries and wisdom teeth?"

"Oh," said Allhoff, "I didn't notice them right away. I meant she must have made some dumb crack to Sontag. Like the one she made to me about Lindbergh. That, of course, made me remember the March of Time."

All that was utter jargon to me. Allhoff noted the blankness of my expression, He shook his head in well-feigned pity.

"The department's going to hell," he said. "Not a brain cell functioning. She told me that she'd seen Lindbergh in a parade. She's supposed to be seven years old. Lindbergh hasn't lived in this country for six years. On the few visits he's made, he hasn't been in any parades."

"True enough," I said, "But why should she lie to you about seeing Lindbergh?"

"She didn't lie," said Allhoff with the air of a man whose patience is sorely tried. "She did see him in a parade. But the parade was maybe ten, twelve years ago."

There was silence for a moment. Then a string of the foulest oaths I had ever heard crackled in my ear. The midget was staring at Allhoff with her suddenly aged eyes. In an expressionless tone she called him every vile name in the book. It was a horrifying spectacle. Something almost as ghastly as watching a child take dope.

Allhoff sat unmoved until she was done, then he turned to Clancy. "Can you take 'em all downstairs along with Regan?" he asked, "Book all three of 'em for murder."

"I got a gun, ain't I?" said Clancy as he stood up.

"Holy smoke, Inspector," said Regan. "I said you was the only guy in the department with a brain. I said all along that—"

"If you'd actually believed it," said Allhoff, "you'd be a free man now. You can meditate on it for the next twenty years or so."

CHAPTER FIVE

The Commissioner Congratulates

Clancy shepherded Regan, the Langers and the midget from the room. The maid followed in a daze. Allhoff took a deep breath and poured himself another cup of coffee. I didn't want to give him another chance to take a bow, but there were some things I had to know.

"I may be as dumb as you say I am," I told him, "but I'm still grappling with that March of Time crack."

"Oh, that," said Allhoff, "On the face of things it mightn't seem credible, even to me, that a midget can pass for a seven-year-old child. However, in September 1934, the March of Time people dramatized a true case that happened in London. A midget there, working with an adult, posed as a juvenile relative of the Royal Family. They worked a big swindling racket. Got away with it, too. Until a doctor noticed the arteries in a magistrate's court."

"1934?" I said. "You never forget, do you?"

"Never," said Allhoff. And he wasn't boasting. "When I'd reached that point it was simple enough. Inasmuch as a cop had been posted outside the house since Sontag was killed, it had been impossible for them to dispose of the gun or the opals outside the house. That's why I ordered that search. Well, you found the opals."

"And the gun?"

"Little Goldilocks had it in their bag. I thought of that possibility. That's why I sent Battersly with 'em to the movies. So they'd have no chance of disposing of anything. That gun killed Sontag. That's our clinching evidence.

"When I called Quebec, found out there was no birth certificate for a Langer child, I knew I had the answer. They hired this midget. They went to the movies for a perfect alibi. They left the midget in the house to do the actual killing. Who the hell would suspect a seven-year-old child? I wouldn't've myself if it hadn't been for that scatter rug."

Battersly came in. I had forgotten all about him. Now, as I looked at him, I choked. His badge, his brass buttons were polished like chromium plate. His shoes were slimed and he had changed his uniform, He was grinning from ear to ear. Allhoff watched him with glittering eyes.

It suddenly dawned on me what he was up to. I felt sick.

"Allhoff," I said. "You can't—"

I stopped as I heard footsteps on the rickety staircase outside.

The door swung open and the commissioner, flanked by his first deputy, walked into the room. Battersly swung to attention like the Prussian guards. I could almost hear his bones click as he saluted.

"Well," said the commissioner, "this is a pleasant mission. A murder cleaned up in less than eight hours. I certainly do want to congratulate the man who did it."

He thrust out his hand. Battersly, proud and happy, moved forward. Then Allhoff stuck his own hand out and grabbed that of the commissioner.

Battersly halted his forward march, bewildered.

The commissioner looked blank but shook Allhoff's hand, "Always glad to shake hands with you, Inspector," he said. "But this time I came for the specific purpose of greeting the man who solved the Sontag case."

"You're doing it," said Allhoff. "Thanks."

I turned and studied the cracked plaster on the wall. I couldn't bring myself to look at Battersly.

"But," I heard the commissioner say, "I thought Battersly—Regan——"

"Oh, that," said Allhoff. "No, sir. Regan didn't kill Sontag. I just sent the real killers over to headquarters. Battersly's a little impulsive, sir. No evidence against Regan. As a matter of fact we might've been stuck with a juicy false-arrest suit if I hadn't managed to pin another rap on Regan."

"Well, that's fine," said the commissioner in pleased surprise. "Great stuff, Inspector. Great."

His gaze grew stern as he directed it at Battersly.

"You've got to be more careful, young man," he said sharply. "Citizens, even crooks, have rights. You can't just drag them in because you don't like their faces. You can thank Inspector Allhoff for getting you out of a bad spot."

He swung around and left the room, the deputy obediently dogging his footsteps. Allhoff grinned like a fiend. His little eyes were flashing.

Battersly was pale, shaken and utterly bewildered. He appealed to me. "But how?" he said. "What happened, Sergeant? Even the inspector here admitted Regan was guilty. Who—"

"The Langers, son," I said. "Regan didn't do it. Allhoff's got a cold case against the Langers."

"No," said Battersly desperately. "He can't prove it."

"The hell I can't," said Allhoff,

"He can prove it right up to the hilt," I said.

Battersly ran his hand over his brow. "But why did he admit Regan did it? Why did he say he was wrong?"

"To force a confession from Regan" roared Allhoff. "A confession that he hired Benny. My God, you don't think I'm going to let them take a pot shot at me and get away with it!"

Battersly stood there, utterly miserable. For the only time in his life he had believed that Allhoff was capable of some decency, some humanity. Now that beautiful thought had been shattered. His Adam's apple moved and his eyes were moist as he jammed his cap down on his head and walked with bowed head from the room.

Allhoff watched him go, savage elation in his eyes.

"Allhoff," I said hotly, "if there's anything lower than a louse, you're it. You didn't have to do that to Battersly. God, man! Have you no decent instincts? Have you no feelings?"

He filled his coffee cup and picked it up, looked at me over its edge. His eyes were insane blobs of lightning.

"Have I no feelings?" he repeated slowly. He paused, and now his voice held all the bitterness of the world since the day of Creation. "Feelings, Sergeant? Well, I haven't any below the knees. Does that answer your question?"

Psychologically, I suppose it did.

DEAD AND DUMB

Allhoff banged the gun down on Battersly's knuckles till they dripped

When the taxi-drive carted that mortally wounded deaf-mute up to die in the middle of Allhoff's office floor, Battersly and Simmonds, the legless inspector's two clay-pigeons-in-uniform might have guessed hell was going to pop. What they couldn't know was that with all their cordially hated superior's other talents he also could run Eddie Bergen a close second and make a dummy sing.

CHAPTER ONE

Sweetness and Light—And Sudden Death

Of course, it couldn't last. For the past *five* days we had lived in an atmosphere of peace and tranquillity. And, save for minor routine, no work had come up at all. The bright October sunshine lit up the drabness of Centre Street and during the morning hours actually penetrated the dusty windows of Allhoff's tenement apartment.

Even Allhoff's glands were functioning normally. For forty-eight hours he had achieved a degree of benignity. Of course, he hadn't completely succumbed to the Dale Carnegie influence, but neither had he cast any profane reflection upon the ancestry of Battersly or myself. Upon one amazing occasion he had actually discussed the pennant chances of the Yankees.

And when Inspector Allhoff deigned to engage in light conversation with the help, it was an event comparable to the Archbishop of Canterbury dropping in at the corner poolroom for a fast round of Chicago with the boys.

However, on the sixth day all the sweetness and light which had been scattered around with such munificence blew up like the Munich Pact.

It was about ten o'clock in the morning. I sat at my desk thumbing through the onion-skin police reports that had accumulated during the night. Battersly stood leaning against the wall, holding the morning paper and following the adventures of Dick Tracy with incredible concentration for a policeman. Allhoff, chest pressed against his desk, brewed his second pot of coffee and a peculiar grating sound issued from his larynx.

The unpainted two-room flat was in its customary state of disorder. Allhoff's soiled linen lay piled up in a corner awaiting the arrival of the laundry boy. A half-dozen dirty plates were stacked on a table near the bedroom door. On Allhoff's desk the electric percolator began to gurgle. Allhoff rattled his chipped cup against its saucer and prepared to pour himself a draft of the vitriolic substance which he fondly believed was coffee.

The odd harsh sound that came from his throat persisted. I looked up from my papers. As I listened more intently, the noise took on a strange and vaguely familiar rhythm. I tapped out an accompanying beat upon my desk. A fragment of a half-forgotten air sounded in my memory.

Way down in Missouri,

Where I learned this mel-o-dy-

The Missouri Waltz! My God, he was singing!

This was too much. In another moment someone'd break out a Maypole for us to dance around.

"Allhoff," I said. "Allhoff, do you feel all right?" He filled his cup turned his head around to face me. "I feel fine," he said. "Here. Have a cup of coffee."

I blinked at him. Then I looked down at the black noxious brew in his cup, shuddered, and shook my head.

"Battersly," said Allhoff. "Here. *You* have a cup of coffee."

Battersly put down his paper and stared at Allhoff. His astonishment paralyzed whatever epicurean discretion he had. He got himself a cup and filled it.

"Allhoff," I said. "Do you realize that you were singing?"

"Singing?" he said. "Well, why not? The weather's great, isn't it? I see by the papers that unemployment's decreased by ten percent. I wouldn't be surprised if real recovery's begun."

I nearly fainted dead away at that. Old Pollyanna Allhoff! Looking for the silver lining with his big brown eyes! I wondered aloud precisely how the hell long this was going to last when I heard shuffling footfalls on the rickety staircase outside.

I didn't know it then, but those footsteps presaged the end of Allhoff's short excursion into the sunny-side-of-life school of philosophy.

There was a rumbling knock at the door and Battersly said: "Come in."

The door was flung suddenly open. Two men staggered into the room. One was a gaunt unshaven Italian wearing an Army overcoat with a hack-badge pinned to its lapel. With his right arm he supported a pale young man with an expressionless face and blank panic in his brown eyes.

Then as I saw the pair of them more closely, I stood up and said: "My God!" For the shirt-front of the man whom the cab driver supported was wet and red. Blood dropped and congealed on the dry dusty floor of the room. The wounded man swayed, staring at Allhoff with wild eyes.

Allhoff put down his coffee cup. He leaned over his desk, his penetrating gaze embracing the pair.

"Well!" he said sharply. "What's wrong here?"

The wounded man held up a piece of yellow paper in his hand. He waved it frantically over his head. Then his mouth opened and he uttered the most ghastly sound I had ever heard from human lips. It was something between hoarse breathing and an animal yelp.

The cab-driver reached for a chair with his free hand and dropped his bloody burden onto it. Sitting, the other still brandished his slip of paper. His lips moved convulsively and a series of bloodcurdling squeaks issued from his mouth.

The hack-driver tried ineffectually to brush some of the blood from his coat with a dirty handkerchief. Then he turned to Allhoff.

"A dummy," he said. "That's what he is, Inspector. I tried to take him to the hospital when they plugged him. But he wouldn't let me. He insisted on coming here. He—"

"Shut up," said Allhoff, his eyes upon the gesticulating mute. "Simmonds, give him a pencil. A piece of paper. He wants to tell us something."

I whipped a pencil from my pocket, snatched a scratch-pad from my desk and took it over to the swaying figure in the chair. Weak, trembling fingers took the pencil from me, balanced the pad upon a shaking knee.

The lead touched the paper, moved horizontally for a moment, then traced a jagged vertical line as the pencil shot over the edge of the pad, and fell from the inert fingers. With an uncanny and horrible gasp the red-shirted figure slid from the chair to the floor. It lay there very still.

I knelt at the side of the fallen man, my fingers groping for his pulse.

Behind me Allhoff spoke to the hack-man. "Your cab downstairs?"

"Yeah."

"All right," said Allhoff. "Battersly, lend a hand.

Take him down to the hack. Get him to the Beckman Street Hospital right away. Get him—"

I took my fingers from the pulse and stood up.

"To the morgue," I said. "If anywhere."

I glanced at the slip of paper I had taken from the mute's hand. Allhoff's name and address were scrawled upon it. I put it on Allhoff's desk, shrugged my shoulders and said: "Well?"

Allhoff grunted. He fixed his eyes on the hackie. "All right," he said. "What's the story?"

The hackman looked down at the corpse and shuddered. There was fear in his face as he looked back at Allhoff. Undoubtedly he knew Allhoff's reputation. And there has never yet been a cab-driver who got the benefit of any doubt from the police department.

"Holy smokes, Inspector," he said. "I ain't got nothing to do with it. See? I was minding my own business. I tried to get him to the hospital, but—"

"Save that speech till you're indicted," said Allhoff. "I'm asking you what happened."

The hackman gulped. 'Well," he said, "I'm cruising Penn Station. See? This guy gets into my cab and starts wigwagging his fingers at me. I figure he's a dummy all right but I don't know what he's trying to tell me. Then he holds out that hunk of paper you got on your desk.

It had your name and address on it, Inspector. So I bring him here. See?"

"I see," said Allhoff. "And you shot him in the heart on the way down. Is that it?"

The hackie looked horrified. "No, no," he said. "I tell you I didn't have nothing to do with it, Inspector. He was all right when he got in the hack. I'll swear to that. I was waiting for a light at Fourteenth Street when I seen it first."

"Saw what?"

"I looked in the mirror. I seen him slumped in the seat, I seen blood dripping all over the upholstery. So I swing the cab round and head for Saint Vincent's—the hospital. But when the dummy sees where I'm going he begins to make them funny noises. He holds up that paper with your name on it and points at it. So I figure he wants to come here more than he wants to go to the hospital. So I bring him. See?"

"You heard no shot?" said Allhoff.

The hackman shook his head.

Allhoff grunted again and looked down at the body. He said to Battersly: "Search him."

he cab-driver, convinced now that he was well in the clear, drew a sigh of relief and took a cigarette from his pocket. As Battersly proceeded to go through the pockets of the corpse the hackman began a friendly conversation.

"Well," he said, "it's a tough break all right. But what the hell. Them dummies is just as good off dead. I know I'd feel that way if anything like that ever happened to me. If I was a dummy or blind or a cripple or anything, I'd just as soon get knocked off as not. I'd just as soon—"

Battersly knelt on the floor frozen to horrified immobility. There was empty apprehension at the pit of my stomach as I cursed the cab-driver for a senseless fool. Allhoff sat hunched up against his desk. His yellow eyes were balls of amber hatred. His face was screwed up like twisted wax.

The hackman watched him with shrinking fear on his face. From his expression I realized he had not even the excuse of ignorance. He had known of Allhoff's affliction, yet he had tactlessly blundered. Now Allhoff's smile was a terrible thing to behold.

"Well," he said and his voice was poisoned honey, "you'd just as soon what?"

"Listen, Inspector," said the cab-driver, tremulo. "I didn't mean nothing. See? I was—"

I had been watching Allhoff as a man watches a time bomb, apprehensively awaiting the explosion. It came now. A feral growl sounded in his throat. He put his hands on the edge of his desk and pushed the swivel chair away so that it rolled out into the center of the room.

The hackie stared, like a chicken fascinated by a snake, at the pair of leather stumps where Allhoff's knees should have been. Allhoff wriggled his thighs like some macabre marionette.

"So you think I'd he better off dead!" he screamed. He pointed a shaking finger at Battersly. "First one rat takes my legs. Then another tells me I should be killed. By God, I'll—"

"Allhoff," I said sharply. "Allhoff. He didn't say you should be killed. He simply said—"

"Shut up!" he shrieked, beside himself now. "He has the cast-iron gall to come into my office and tell me I'm not fit to live. I'll show him. Battersly, arrest that man. Take him over and book him."

Battersly looked uncertainly at me. The hackman cowered against the wall, thoroughly subdued, aghast at the eruption he had precipitated.

"Allhoff," I said again, "you can't arrest him. You can't book a man for stupidity or tactlessness. You've got nothing on him."

"The hell I haven't!" roared Allhoff. "He brought a corpse in here, didn't he? Book him for suspicion of murder. Book him as a material witness. Anyway, you don't have to have a reason for throwing a hackie in the can. Battersly, get him out of here!"

Battersly shrugged his shoulders. He put a hand on the trembling hackman's arm and led him, protesting with quavering vociferousness, from the room.

Allhoff stared at the door as it closed behind them. His face was a study in saffron fury. He muttered blurred and frightful oaths to himself. Then he snatched up the coffee pot and filled his cup with the air of Caesare Borgia pouring a potion for a pal who had crossed him.

I sighed, returned to my desk and picked up the phone.

I got the morgue and told them to come over and remove a corpse from Inspector Allhoff's floor.

While not agreeing with the cabdriver that all cripples should be indiscriminately slaughtered, there were occasions when I held firmly to the view that both the world and Allhoff himself would be better off if his twisted body, his distorted mind were interred forever in the grave.

Today's exhibition was just another encore of a scene which was wearing me down, driving young Battersly in the general direction of a nervous breakdown, and doing Allhoff himself no good either.

It had its genesis many years ago, on the eve of an important raid. Battersly, a raw rookie at the time, had developed a sudden and understandable case of buck fever. At a critical moment he had failed to carry out his assignment with the result that a dozen machine-gun bullets had plowed their way through Allhoff's legs.

Gangrene had been the first consequence, amputation, the second. I had always believed that when Allhoff lost those legs, he lost something of his mind along with them. Still, even with that handicap he still possessed the best brain in the department. Although Civil Service rules forbade a legless inspector, he was too valuable a man for the commissioner to lose.

Devious bookkeeping in the comptroller's office contrived that Allhoff continue to receive his old pay. At the commissioner's request he had moved into this tenement flat in order to be near headquarters, and he had demanded that Battersly be assigned as his assistant.

Thus Allhoff achieved a savage and sadistic revenge. He spared no effort to humiliate the younger man. He lost no opportunity to remind Battersly of his responsibility for his condition. I, who had come out of Delehanty's with Allhoff, had been assigned to this detail, ostensibly to take care of the paper work. In reality I was supposed to pour oil on the troubled waters when Allhoff ran amok. It was a task I had sickened of long since, both figuratively and literally.

The boys from the morgue arrived and removed the body of the mute. A few moments later, Battersly returned. He was pale and obviously upset. Now that Allhoff had definitely broken with the

sweetness-and-light school of thought there was no telling exactly how far he would swing in the opposite direction.

Battersly went unobtrusively to his desk and sat down. Allhoff sat huddled in his chair. I could hear him muttering to himself. Of course, I knew that while he was in his present condition it was my cue to keep my mouth hermetically sealed. But I was suddenly possessed with an overpowering compulsion to needle him. I looked at the back of his thick neck and began to hum the opening bars of *The Missouri Waltz*.

He swung around in his chair and unleashed the roar of a wounded bull. "What the hell are you doing?" he shouted. "Trying to kid me?"

"I'm singing," I told him. "The weather's great, isn't it? Unemployment has decreased ten percent. Probably recovery's actually started."

He banged the arms of his chair with clenched fists. "You fool!" he shrieked. "You stupid fool! There's been a murder committed. Probably two. Maybe more. And you sit there clowning. Get to work. Right away!"

I raised my eyebrows at that. "What am I supposed to do? Prove that dummy didn't have cab fare? That the hackie killed him?"

"Damned fool," he said again, and there was more contempt than rage in his tone now. "Why do you think that mute came here? Why do you think someone shot him on the way?"

I didn't have the slightest idea and I said so.

"There was a crime committed," said Allhoff more calmly. "That dummy wanted to tell me something about it. Someone else didn't want him to."

Well, that was logical enough. "But how can we know what crime it might be?" I asked him. "There are a hundred crimes a day in this town."

"You've got the police reports," said Allhoff. "What's there in the way of homicides?"

I picked up the sheaf of onion-skin on my desk, thumbed through it. 'Harlem," I said. "Dead bartender, Hold-up."

"No," said Allhoff.

"South Street. Brawl. Unidentified Irishman."

"No."

"Long Island. Rickerts Institute. No, that's no good. It's a suicide."

"The hell it is," said Allhoff.

I looked up at him. He had swung his chair around again and was staring at me with hot gleaming eyes. I knew that expression well. It indicated that Allhoff's brain cells were functioning with damnable ingenuity. It meant, in short, that Allhoff had something.

"Well," I said, "it's suicide on the report. And it's

not even doubtful."

Allhoff grinned unpleasantly. "Do you know what Rickerts Institute is?"

"Never heard of it."

"It's an asylum for deaf mutes," said Allhoff. "Furthermore a railroad runs there. To be exact, the Long Island Railroad which has its terminus at Penn Station."

Battersly spoke up excitedly. "So maybe this suicide is a murder, huh? Maybe this dummy knows something about it and he's coming to let you in on it. He gets off the train at Penn Station and takes that hack. Then someone who didn't want him to spill what he knew plugged him. I bet that's it."

Allhoff stared at him until he flushed. Then he said with bitter irony: "There's no keeping a secret from you."

He emptied his coffee cup and slid down from his chair, hit the floor with two dull thumps.

"Get your drawers on," he said to me. "We're going out to Long Island to aid Battersly in finishing his solution of this case."

I put on my hat and coat and the three of us went down the rickety stairs, By now Allhoff's leaping spirits of the early morning were as dead as that deaf mute who lay on a cold slab in the morgue.

CHAPTER TWO

Dead and Dumb

Rickert's Institute for the Deaf and Dumb was situated some three miles from Forest Hills. It was a rambling granite structure set in the midst of a vast expanse of yellowing lawn. Battersly halted the police car before a pair of huge oaken doors while I proceeded to aid Allhoff out of the car. I attached a set of roller-skate wheels to his leather stumps and rolled him into a high-ceilinged corridor. A middle-aged woman seated at an information desk stared at us with surprised eyes.

"Rickerts," snapped Allhoff. "I want to see Rickerts."

His manner, as usual, was brusque and discourteous. Information lifted her brows and said distantly: "Mr. Rickerts is in conference."

"I don't care if he's in the men's room," snarled Allhoff. "I want to see him now. I'm the police department."

While information regarded him dubiously, he looked around the hall. His gaze came to rest on a door which bore Rickerts' name painted on it. Allhoff put his hands on the floor and gave a mighty push. He rolled down the hall toward Rickerts' office. Battersly and I followed him. Information rose from her chair and said: "Hey, wait a minute. You can't—"

But by that time Allhoff had reached up and turned the knob. He rolled noisily into the room, Battersly and I bringing up the rear.

We were in a large square office. Directly before us stood a big oblong table and seated around it were four men. As we entered they all stood up, stared down at Allhoff frankly astounded. Then they lifted their eyes to see Battersly and myself in uniform. A short thick man with bushy eyebrows spoke first.

"My God," he said, "more coppers. Now see here, police or no police, you'll have to wait outside until we conclude our meeting. The entire routine has been upset because of that suicide."

"Suicide?" said Allhoff. "What suicide?"

The bushy eyebrows rose and fell, "Aren't you here about the suicide?"

"Why no," said Allhoff with misleading sweetness. "I'm here about the murder."

The four men about the table exchanged nervous glances.

A tall bald individual at the head wriggled his fingers nervously. "Murder?" he said in a high alarmed voice. "Why, that's ridiculous. That's—"

Allhoff hoisted himself into a chair and interrupted. "I'm taking over," he announced. "First, who are you guys?"

The four men glared at him angrily. The man with the bushy eyebrows turned purple.

"Damn it," he said furiously. "Who the hell are you?"

I saw Allhoff hunch up his shoulders I saw the mordant gleam in his eye. I decided to come in myself before the brawl began.

"Gentlemen," I said, "This is Inspector Allhoff. He has a lot of influence and a lot of talent. He's a tough man when aroused. I'd suggest you answer his questions."

Allhoff beamed like the speaker of the evening during the introductory speech. Bushy-eyebrows calmed down somewhat. The bald man at the head of the table who proved to be Rickerts himself, cleared his throat nervously and performed the introductions.

Bushy-eyebrows, it developed, was Doctor Abbott, in charge of the medical department of the institute. The tall, rather handsome lad of about twenty-six was Latham Layne, son of Daniel Layne whose oil-and-steel millions had endowed Rickerts' Institute since its inception. The sandy-haired, loose-muscled individual who sat next to Layne wasn't anyone in particular. His name was Lucas and he was a personal friend of Layne's who had come out for the ride.

Rickerts concluded his nervous speech, then paused and added: "And now, Inspector, what makes you think we have a murder on our hands?"

"What makes you think you haven't?"

Doctor Abbott snorted. "Plain as the nose on your face," he said. "Murdoch killed himself. Acute melancholia. Brought about by brooding over his unfortunate condition. Lot's of 'em get like that. I give a series of mental tests regularly each month. I knew Murdoch was brooding. Knew it for some time."

Young Layne nodded emphatically. "That's right." he said. "Doctor Abbott had spoken to me about Murdoch's gloominess. Some of the others get that way."

Allhoff twisted his neck around and fixed the young man with his beady eyes.

"Where do you fit in here?" he asked. "Oh," said Latham Layne. "My father's money runs this place. I'm on the payroll as business manager."

Allhoff grunted and scratched his head, Old man Rickerts wrung his hands nervously. Layne and the doctor were frankly hostile, They watched Allhoff with definite antagonism. Lucas, the outsider, remained unconcerned.

Allhoff licked his lips and appeared uncomfortable, I knew he was missing his coffee. He was approaching what for him was close to a record. He'd gone without caffeine for almost fifty minutes.

"Well," he said finally, "who last saw this Murdoch alive?"

"Three of his companions were with him until he went to bed last night," said Rickerts, "Lewis, Carden and Reynolds. I'll send for them if you like."

I exchanged a quick glance with Battersly. One of those names had appeared on identification cards in the murdered mute's pockets.

"I like," said Allhoff, "But don't send for Reynolds unless you're psychic."

Rickerts pressed a buzzer at the head of the table and picked up a house phone. "Why not Reynolds? He was Murdoch's best friend."

"Because," said Allhoff. "He won't come. He's lying on a slab in the morgue."

They gasped at that. "But—" began young Layne.

Allhoff cut him short. "Shut up," he said, "Get me those two other guys."

Rickerts spoke into the transmitter, Then he looked up and asked: "What's this about Reynolds, Inspec-

tor?"

Allhoff told him, and as he spoke his little eyes carefully searched the face of each of the four men around the table. When he had finished his recital, he asked: "Is there any reason why Reynolds should have come to me specifically?"

Rickerts opened his mouth as if to speak, but Abbott cut in ahead of him. "None whatever," he said brusquely. "That is, no sound reason. Reynolds was slightly paranoiac. Delusions of persecution, you know. His friend's suicide might've scared him. He went running to the police for protection."

"Reynolds was a great reader," said Rickerts thoughtfully. "Detective stories particularly. True detective stories. He probably had read your name, your address in one of his magazines."

The door opened and two men came into the room. They wore the same strange blankness upon their faces as had Reynolds. They looked inquiringly at Rickert. Then one of them lifted his hand and proceeded to move his fingers with incredible rapidity. Rickert wigwagged back to the mute, "These are Carden and Lewis," he said to Allhoff, "Anything you care to ask them—"

Allhoff swung around and faced them. Lewis was a slight pale youth with sharp cleanly chiseled features. Carden was bulkier, fleshy faced and inclined to stoutness.

Allhoff nodded to them and turned back to Rickerts, "Ask 'em if they noticed anything wrong about Murdoch last night. If he was upset, seemed abnormal or anything."

Rickerts transmitted the question with his fingers. Carden shook his head, made a swift gesture with his thumb and forefinger. Lewis remained still for a thoughtful moment. Suddenly he thrust his hand up and signaled furiously.

Rickerts watched him for a moment, then smiled. He shook his head as he moved his own fingers in response.

"I'm afraid not," he said aloud, "That's hardly an important enough reason for a suicide."

Allhoff looked up like a hawk. "What's not?" he asked.

"Really nothing at all," said Rickerts. "Just that last night before he went to bed, Murdoch was suffering from a touch of stomach trouble. Went to the dispensary for a mild cathartic. Hardly a reason for suicide, eh, Inspector?"

Allhoff's fist crashed down on the tabletop. "No," he said. "But a damned good reason for murder, That clinches it."

Even the deaf mutes stared at ilium, "What clinches

what?" I asked.

"Listen," said Allhoff. "Can you conceive of a constipated angel? If Murdoch intended to kill himself, why in the name of God would he take a cathartic first?"

Much to my regret I had no answer to that, And judging from the shocked expressions of the others, neither did they. I was becoming very much afraid that Allhoff was going to be right again.

"Now listen," said Allhoff. "Before I go any further. I've got to have some coffee. What kind do you have in the kitchen?"

Rickerts named a brand and Allhoff shook his head.

"Lousy," he said. "I must have my special brand. The A & P carries it. Have they a store around here?"

No one seemed to know the answer to that either, then Lucas spoke for the first time.

"You could look it up in the Yellow Book," he said in a casual slow drawl. Allhoff looked at him, puzzled.

"He means the Red Book," I explained. "The classified directory."

Young Latham Layne ran his fingers through his hair. "What kind of an investigation is this?" he asked, annoyed. "Special coffee for the coppers!"

Rickerts glanced at him nervously. Obviously he was anxious to keep things on a tranquil plane.

"I'll be glad to get some for you, Inspector," he said. He scrawled something on a piece of paper and handed it to the mute, Carden. He spoke rapidly with his fingers. Carden accompanied by the second mute left the room. Rickerts turned to Allhoff.

"He'll give that order to the telephone operator," he explained. "She'll order the coffee for you."

Allhoff thanked him ungraciously and went into a brown study. We were all watching him, but he gave no indication that he was aware of our existence. Abbott wiggled his bushy eyebrows and cleared his throat rumblingly.

"Inspector," he said. "you're being very high-handed. I'm by no means sure that you have the authority to take over like this. Besides. I know that Murdoch was a suicide. You can't hang a murder case on the mere fact of his taking a cathartic last night."

Allhoff ignored him. Without looking up he said: "Battersly, what are the three possible motives for murder?"

It took Battersly a moment to recover from his surprise at Allhoff's asking him anything at all.

"Well," he said thoughtfully, "there's revenge, love and, I suppose money."

Allhoff nodded to the blank wall before him, "Right," he said. "This is hardly love. Revenge is very doubtful. Money? Well, that's—"

He didn't finish the sentence. There was a sound of running feet in the corridor outside. The door suddenly burst open. A half dozen inmates of Rickerts Institute burst into the room. Their blank faces were white. The dullness of their eyes was glazed over with fear. Their mouths were open and they desperately essayed speech.

The result was ghastly. The room was filled with high-pitched breathing sounds. It reminded me for a horrible moment of the trilling squeaks of a nest of frightened mice. Rickerts slapped his hands together to get their attention. He lifted his fingers and asked a question.

The mutes were somewhat calmer now. A number of them lifted their hands and answered Rickerts in the only language they knew, Rickerts eyes opened wide as he watched them. His lips quivered nervously.

The suspense was grating across my nerves like a hacksaw, "For the love of heaven," I said, "what's wrong?"

It was Allhoff who answered. It was Allhoff who knew without being told.

"It's another murder," he said tensely. "Another one of these guys is dead," He looked at the gesticulating mutes and slid down from his chair. "All right!" he yelled at them as if sheer volume would make his words intelligible. "Where is he? Show me where he is?"

The mutes couldn't hear him, but there was no mistaking what he meant. They led the way from the room with Allhoff rolling after them. Battersly and I followed after with Rickerts. Layne, Abbott and Lucas bringing up the rear.

The corpse, whose name was Block, lay on his bed in a small barely furnished room. His blank eyes, even blanker in death, stared upward at the ceiling. On a taboret at the side of his bed was a half-empty pop bottle. A strong smell of almonds filled the room.

Allhoff sniffed once and knew the answer to that. "Cyanide," he said. "Cyanide in orange pop."

He stared thoughtfully at the corpse. Rickerts wrung his hands helplessly. Doctor Abbott's eyebrows wigwagged and he cleared his throat again.

"Bad," he said. "Very bad. Odd thing about these institutions. One suicide starts an epidemic. Melancholia's more contagious than measles."

Allhoff looked up at him. There was an ugly sneer on his lips and an uglier expression in his eyes. "You're either a fool or a murderer," he said. "You know damned well this is no more a suicide than the others. If he wanted to take poison why the devil did he mix it with orange pop?"

Abbott's eyebrows moved faster than ever. "Well—" he began.

Allhoff cut him short. "Don't explain it to me," he snapped. "Give me twenty-four hours and I'll explain it to you. Now get out of here. All of you. I want to talk this over with my assistants."

No one moved. "Now wait a minute," said Latham Layne. "I think—"

"Get out!" roared Allhoff.

I realized that he was rapidly reaching boiling point. "Gentlemen," I said, "this is murder. The inspector is well within his rights. I'd suggest you leave."

"All right," growled Abbott. "Come on."

They filed from the room. Battersly closed the door behind them.

"Well," I said. "That's three murders. Two of them under your coffee-stained nose. And all you've got to show for it, is a hack-driver in the can."

Allhoff hoisted himself up and sat down on the bed at the side of the corpse. He drew a deep breath and shook his head, said wearily: "Why in the name of God would a guy want to knock off these dummies?"

I raised my eyebrows. For once Allhoff was asking questions instead of answering them. Somehow it made me very happy. "Money," he went on. "It's got to be money. There's no other possible motive. But I must have more facts."

I looked over at Battersly and winked, Allhoff was on the ropes this time.

"Get me facts," said Allhoff suddenly. "You, Simmonds. Take the car. Go back to town. See Daniel Latham's lawyer. Go to his bank. Go to the institute's bank, Young Layne's bank. Pick up all the information you can get. Battersly, you question those four guys in Rickerts office. Bring me back every shred of information, whether you consider it important or not. Now get going. We'll have this thing cleaned up by breakfast time."

"That," I remarked, "is an all-time high in either conceit or optimism."

But he didn't answer me, He was staring thoughtfully at the corpse. He didn't even look up as Battersly and I left the room.

CHAPTER THREE

Coffee, Vinegar and Honey

It was well after eight o'clock when I got back from town. I found Allhoff ensconced in a private office. A cup of black viscous coffee stood before him on the desk at which he sat. Carden, the deaf mute, was seated at a small table on the far side of the room. He was tending an electric percolator. I gathered he had been assigned to Allhoff as a sort of orderly.

As I entered, Battersly was standing at Allhoff's side. He held a notebook in his hand as he delivered his report to Allhoff.

Every year," he was saying, "old man Layne goes on this hunting trip in California. He picks up a guide in Los Angeles and they go off together. He leaves no address behind him. No one can get in touch with him. He wants to be completely out of the way of business worries."

Allhoff grunted. "How long's he been gone this time?"

"Three weeks."

Allhoff lifted his coffee cup, emptied it. "Hey, he said. "Carden."

The mute didn't move. "He can't hear you," I said. "Here. Give it to me."

I took the cup over to the small table. Carden filled it from the pot. As I returned the cup Allhoff said to Battersly: "This guide. What's his name?"

Battersly consulted his notes. "Claus. Stanley Claus."

"Address?"

Battersly gave him the address.

Allhoff sipped coffee for a moment and looked up at me. "All right," he said. "What've you got?"

"Nothing," I said. "Absolutely nothing."

"How would you know?" he sneered.

"All right," I said, "What I'm going to tell you will put you further away from an answer than you are now."

"I want facts," he snapped. "Not opinions."

"I saw the lawyer. It's Rex Shane who, as you may know, is blue-blood, conservative and the most honest man in town. Layne's will leaves a mess of dough to the brightest mutes in this institution. Layne figures the poor guys never had a chance. So he's splitting the major part of his fortune among a number of the best brains here."

Allhoff's eyes lit up. "Who are they?" I grinned at him. I knew what he was thinking. I'd thought the same thing myself—at first. "I don't know," I told him. "That's the rub. No one knows. No one except Shane and old man Layne."

He looked at me for a long time.

"Someone must know," he said at last.

"Someone who doesn't want those guys to get the dough. That's why they're being knocked off."

"That was my first thought." I told him. "But it won't do, Allhoff. Despite these murders Shane won't tell me even now. Not without Layne's permission. Layne has never told anyone. Not even his own son. He doesn't want the information to leak out, He doesn't want the beneficiaries to know about it. It might ruin the morale of the institution. Shane's positive about this. And with his reputation, I believe him."

There was a deep furrow on Allhoff's brow. He picked up the coffee cup and said: "How about the bank?"

"One item worth mentioning," I told him. "Latham Layne's salary is five hundred a month. That is the customary amount of the checks he deposits in his own account. Two weeks ago he deposited a check for five thousand. That's the sole item out of the ordinary."

Allhoff put his cup down. "Maybe," he muttered softly, "that's it."

I lifted my eyebrows at that. "That's what?" I asked. "It seems normal enough to me. The old man's on his hunting trip. He may be gone for some time. So he leaves the kid some extra dough in case anything turns up."

Carden rose from his post at the coffee pot, crossed the room and unobtrusively laid a slip of paper on Allhoff's desk, I glanced at it over Allhoff's shoulder, It read—

There is no more coffee in the perkolator. Shall I get some more from the kitchen?

Allhoff looked up at the mute and nodded emphatically. Carden went out of the room, I mooched a cigarette from Battersly, sighed and lit it. This place gave me the horrors. I wondered aloud how long we were going to stay here.

"Until tomorrow morning," said Allhoff. There was something vibrant about his tone which caused me to turn around and look at him. He was staring straight ahead, a gleam in his eyes. "Yes," he said again, "tomorrow morning. Then I'll—" He broke off as Carden came back into the room with a cup full of ground coffee.

Allhoff nodded his head toward the mute. "Battersly," he said, "tell him he can go to bed now. We don't need him anymore."

It took all Battersly's skill at pantomime to get the idea across to Carden. Then the mute nodded good-night to us and went out the door.

"Listen," I said to Allhoff, "do you mean to tell me you've got this thing figured?"

"I'm convinced Layne and Rickerts know something about this," he said.

"That's fine," I told him. "Shall we promise them a big chocolate soda if they'll talk?"

"Sometimes," said Allhoff, "vinegar will catch more flies than honey."

"Does a footnote go with that remark?"

"Well," said Allhoff, "there are ways of making people talk."

I stared at him in astonishment. "You're not talking about a rubber hose, are you?"

"Why not? Now listen. Everyone is sleeping over here tonight, including us. We'll wait until midnight. Then I want you to go to Layne's room, bring him here. We'll work on him. After we get through with him, we'll drag Rickerts out of bed and knock him around a little. If we smack 'em around hard enough, they'll crack."

My head was reeling now. A rubber hose was all right for a dumb Irish member of the strong-arm squad who couldn't break a petty-larceny case any other way. But for Allhoff! For the great brain of the department to descend to the extralegal tactics of third degree reminded me somehow of a chess champion beating his opponent over the head with a baseball bat.

"Allhoff," I said, "you can't do that."

"I'm not going to do it," said Allhoff.

"You and Battersly are going to do it." I looked at Battersly. He was as astounded as myself.

"Allhoff," I said, "you're crazy."

He bristled at that. "You're under my orders," he snapped. "It's my responsibility. If you refuse you're gambling your pension."

Battersly shrugged his shoulders and I gave up. "All right," I said. "And I hope they give you fifty years for assault and battery."

He looked up at me with humorless little eyes. "You can't get fifty years for simple assault," he said contemptuously.

It was a quarter to one when Battersly came back from his foray in his stockinged feet. "Say," he said, "young Layne ain't in his room. The bed's been slept in but he's not there now."

Allhoff nodded slowly. "You know," he said, "I hardly expected he would be. Now Simmonds, see if Rickerts is in *his* room."

He is," said Battersly. "I heard him snoring. Shall we bring him here?"

"On second thought," said Allhoff, "no. I think I'll go to bed, You boys are to sleep in the room off the corridor there."

I stood in the doorway and watched him. There was something very screwy going on but I was dammed if I knew what.

"Allhoff," I said, "what have you got up your sleeve?"

He grinned at me. "I'm solving a murder case," he said. "Isn't that what we came for?"

"If you're so damned clever," I said, "who's guilty?"

"Why don't you ask me who isn't?"

"All right," I said nettled. "Who isn't?"

"Rickerts," said Allhoff "Now get to hell out of here. Both of you. I've got some figuring to do. Report back here at eight tomorrow morning. Good-night." I slammed the door and walked slowly down the corridor with Battersly. If Allhoff had cracked this case I was prepared to admit that he was fifty percent the genius he thought he was.

CHAPTER FOUR

A Matter of Red and Yellow

It was five minutes before eight when Battersly and I, breakfastless, returned to Allhoff's office. Allhoff sat in exactly the same position as when we left him. He was hunched up over his desk, his little brooding eyes fixed steadily upon the opposite wall. His face was more lined than usual. A gray weariness painted his cheeks.

On the taboret near the window the percolator was gurgling. There was an empty cup on Allhoff's desk. I gathered that Carden had already been on the job. I watched Allhoff shrewdly. True, on many other occasions he had pulled a solution out of the clouds when I had been prepared to bet my life savings he was thoroughly and completely licked. But this time I couldn't see even the vestige of a clue. Three men had been murdered, two of them beneath Allhoff's prominent nose. And we had a hack-driver in the Tombs who most certainly had nothing to do with it.

Allhoff sighed heavily. He lifted his eyes from their contemplation of the plaster wall, glanced about the room. His gaze came to rest on the door of a smaller office which opened off this room. At the top of the door was a glass transom. Allhoff looked at it, grunted and spoke.

"Battersly. Open that transom."

Battersly picked up a chair, stood on it and did as he'd been ordered.

"Now," said Allhoff, "there's a key on the inside of that door. Take it out of the lock and put it in your pocket. When I slap my palm on the desk-top, I want you to lock that door as quietly as possible. Get it?"

Again Battersly did as he was told, I watched Allhoff dubiously.

"Go and gather up our hosts," said Allhoff. "All four of them. Bring them in here right away."

Battersly went out into the hall. I studied Allhoff carefully. His words were confident enough, but somehow the mocking gleam in his eyes, the arrogant cocksure manner he assumed when he had a case sewed up was missing.

"Allhoff," I said, "you're not kidding me. You can't crack this case, can you?"

He sighed wearily. "I can crack it," he said. "The whole thing's as simple as the average copper." He stopped and sighed again. "But—"

"But?" I said, puzzled.

"I'm going to have one hell of a lot of trouble getting a conviction unless I get a confession to go along with it."

I laughed aloud at that, "You've got a great trusting soul," I told him, "No guy who'd knock off three helpless mutes is going to break down and confess in the interests of simple justice."

He shook his head broodingly. I became even more perplexed. I'd never seen him in this condition before. Now Carden came into the room, carrying a bowl of sugar in his hand. He took Allhoff's cup from the desk, filled it, returned it and sat down at the little table, staring out the window with his blank expressionless eyes.

Footfalls sounded in the hall. Battersly entered, followed by our four hosts. Allhoff nodded at them.

"Good-morning, gentlemen." he said. "Will you sit down?"

Rickerts, nervous and fidgety as usual, sat down. Lucas ran his hand through his sandy hair and stared at Allhoff with an odd expression. Doctor Abbott and young Layne appeared frankly hostile.

Abbott manipulated his bushy eyebrows angrily. A frown creased his brow, "Now look here, Inspector," he said officiously. "You've completely disrupted the routine of this institution. I've given you enough leeway. From now on I must use my professional position to forbid further investigation.

It's ruining the morale of the inmates. It's definitely very bad for them."

"So is murder," murmured Allhoff.

"So is murder what!"

"Definitely bad for them."

Young Layne slapped his hand on the desk. "Damn it all!" he exploded. "I don't see you doing anything about it. One man died in your office. Another while you were in charge here."

"Sit down!" snapped Allhoff. His tone wasn't very loud but it held unmistakable command and they sat down.

For a moment there was utter silence in the room, broken only by the gurgling of the percolator. Carden stood up, crossed the room and glanced at Allhoff's cup. Seeing it half full he returned to his post, turned his back to us and resumed his bored scrutiny of the sere lawn outside the window.

Allhoff sipped some coffee, then replaced the cup in its saucer with a clatter. He lifted his head and looked around the room. "All right, gentlemen," he said. "Are you ready?"

"Ready for what?" said Layne.

Allhoff met his eye steadily. "Ready to hear who killed those helpless deaf mutes," he said evenly. "How they were killed and why. Ready to hear who killed your father, Layne. Also how and why."

Latham Layne's face was suddenly drained of blood. I heard the sharp intake of Lucas' breath. Old Rickerts moved his hands in a Zasu Pitts frenzy. Doctor Abbott alone seemed calm. Even his eyebrows were still.

"Daniel Layne dead?" exclaimed Rickerts, horrified. "No, no. It can't be!"

"You're crazy," said Latham Layne. "Utterly crazy!" It occurred to me that I had never heard as little conviction in a man's voice.

Abbott cleared his throat loudly. "Suppose you elaborate on that, Inspector Allhoff."

Allhoff lifted his cup and emptied it, "Carden," he said. "Here. Fill this up."

The mute did not move. "He can't hear you," I said, irritated, "Here. I'll get it,"

I took the cup to Carden, got it filled and brought it back. Allhoff buried his corvine nose in it for a moment, then raised his head again.

"Daniel Layne has been dead for two weeks," he announced. He leaned over his desk like a hawk about to pounce and fixed his agate eyes on Lucas, "Hasn't he, Lucas?"

I looked around the room and frowned. Allhoff's manner indicated that he definitely had something. But as usual he was approaching a given point by the most circuitous route his warped mind could devise.

Lucas said in a flat even tone: "What the hell should I know about it?"

"Listen," said Layne half rising from his chair, "what the devil are you talking about? My father's alive, He's on a—"

"I know," said Allhoff. "He's on a hunting trip in California. Well, he's in California, all right. In an undertaking establishment in Sacramento. A game warden found him yesterday." He leaned toward Layne and his eyes were blazing. "Furthermore you knew it, Layne. You knew it when you raised his five-hundred-dollar check to five thousand!"

There was apprehension in the room at that moment. I could feel it.

Abbott's eyebrows lifted and lowered. "Suppose you speak right out, Inspector," he said. "If you have a case, present it."

"All right," said Allhoff, "We'll begin at the beginning. First, this plot's been smoldering for some time. Like a bomb, prepared and waiting for a detonator. Daniel Layne's departure on his annual hunting trip set it off. Layne went to California. He stopped off in Los Angeles, as usual, to pick up his trusty guide. Off they went up the Sacramento River. Then we had our first murder according to schedule. Said trusty guide killed Daniel Layne. Didn't you, Lucas?"

There were only two people in that room who did not gaze wide-eyed at Allhoff. One was the mute, Carden, staring out the window oblivious to everything that went on, The other was myself. I'd been around long enough to sense panic and menace. I sensed them now. My right hand hung loose by my holster, My eyes watched closely every man in the room.

It was Layne who spoke first. "Again I say you're crazy!" he shouted. "Stark staring mad! What's Lucas got to do with it? How could he kill my father? I doubt if he's ever even been in California. He's lived in New York State all his life."

"If he had," said Allhoff, "he'd never call the Red Book the Yellow Book."

Something clicked in my mind at that. Lucas' blue eyes had narrowed. Allhoff gestured at him with a pencil and continued.

"In New York the classified directory has a red cover. In certain other states, one of which is California, the cover is yellow. I've been doing some telephoning myself. The Los Angeles police have informed me that a man answering Lucas' description lived, until a few weeks ago, in the Wilshire district. That man was a hunter's guide by profession. His name was Stanley Claus."

He stopped speaking and picked up his cup with the air of a man who has made everything perfectly clear.

"Well," I said, annoyed. "So what?"

"Claus," said Allhoff. "Simple transposition of the five letters in Lucas." Lucas hit a cigarette with hands that shook slightly. He stood up. I did not like the expression on his face. I touched the butt of my gun with my hand.

"Sit down," I said.

Lucas transferred his gaze from Allhoff to myself. Our eyes clashed for a moment. Then he sat down. Young Layne bit his lower lip nervously.

"Now listen," he said in a jerky voice. "I want to say that—"

"Shut up," snapped Abbott sharply. He wigwagged his eyebrows, "Thus far, Inspector, you've proved nothing. Nor have you explained the deaths in this institution."

"I'll explain them," said Allhoff grimly. "It was necessary that Daniel Layne be killed before the slaughter started here. With Layne dead, his will is ready for probate. I guess we all know what that will contained."

Rickerts' hands fluttered. "I don't see how that can have anything to do with it," he said. "That will, of course, left a great deal of money to some of the inmates here. But no one knows their names."

"I can name three of them," said Allhoff. "Murdoch, Reynolds, and Block."

Rickerts registered bewilderment. "But how—" he began.

"Yes," said Abbott and his voice was hard. "How?"

"That will," said Allhoff, "did not go beyond the bequests to the mutes. If those mutes were already dead the money would naturally revert to Daniel Layne's next of kin—his son, Latham. So he hatched, with help, of course, an intricate and ingenious scheme."

Young Layne was standing up now. There was a tremor in his tone as he spoke. "Are you accusing me of—"

"For the love of God," said Allhoff wearily, "will you stop interrupting me? In case any of you have forgotten how you did this thing I'll refresh your memory."

There was utter silence as Allhoff lifted his coffee cup, sipped audibly and set it down again. "This is the situation," he said. "Daniel Layne undoubtedly believed that young men who are not handicapped should make their own way. Hence, he made no provision for Latham in his will. Instead he left his money to the more intelligent mutes of this institution. Latham realized that if those mutes were not alive to receive the bequest, he would inherit, So he and his confederates planned to kill the mutes."

"Ridiculous," snapped Abbott, "Because no one knew who those legatees were. Daniel Layne told no one. I'm certain Shane, who drew up the will, told no one either."

"He didn't," said Allhoff.

"Then," said Rickerts, looking more harried than ever, "how can there be a plot to kill the legatees if no one knew who they were?"

Allhoff took a deep breath. "Doctor Abbott knew," he said quietly.

"That's a lie!" roared Abbott, "Layne told no one whom he had selected."

"He didn't have to," said Allhoff "You told him."

My head was reeling now. "Allhoff," I said, "will you stop talking in circles. You're not making sense, you know. What do you mean by that last cryptogram?"

"How the devil do you suppose Layne knew who the brightest mutes were?" snarled Allhoff. "How did he pick them out? I'll tell you. From Abbott's monthly intelligence tests. Abbott mightn't actually know what names are written in the will, but he can make a damned good guess—from the figures he gave Layne on the I. Q.'s he had on the inmates here. Now do I make sense?"

I nodded slowly. Reluctantly I was forced to admit that he was being very, very right again.

"So," went on Allhoff, "Layne takes Lucas into the plot. Lucas is to kill the old man during the hunting trip, to heave the body out in the wilds where it won't be found for a little while. Before Daniel Layne's death is discovered there will be an epidemic of suicides in the institution. So the money will eventually go to Layne and his confederates."

There was a chilled silence in the room. I could hear the faint ticking of my wristwatch. Carden sat over the coffee pot completely oblivious to the tenseness. Battersly stood alert behind the four seated men.

"Now," went on Allhoff, "Layne received a check for five hundred a month from his father. When he got his last check he needed money badly. Possibly one of his confederates wanted an advance. So he raised that check to five thousand dollars. He knew it would clear before his father's death was discovered. There was no danger that his father would ever learn of it. He was damned impatient to get the old man's money."

I looked around the room. I was beginning to understand what Allhoff had meant when he had told me to ask him who was innocent. Every face was white and drawn.

"Listen," said Abbott, "if I understand this theory of yours, you're accusing all of us here of being murderers. It may interest you to know that I, for one, have a perfect alibi. Quite probably the others do, too." I screwed my brow up at that, I didn't know about the other deaths but in the case of Block they were all in the clear, I had seen them all in Rickerts office at the time of the killing.

"There was one other in the plot," said Allhoff, "The actual trigger, man. Probably one of the mutes, You bought him to do the actual killing. Probably he was the guy that the check was raised for."

"All right," said Abbott. "Who was it?"

Allhoff shook his head. "I don't know."

Well, that was just dandy! Here he had built up a case on pure conjecture. He didn't have a scintilla of evidence that would hold up in the grand-jury room, and now he sat there calmly and conceded he didn't know the identity of the trigger man in the plot.

bbott laughed aloud and I didn't blame him. "Inspector," he said, "you've a lovely imagination. Unfortunately the district attorney will want something more than that. You haven't enough actual evidence to get a conviction in a traffic case."

"Well," said Allhoff mildly, "I've enough circumstantial evidence if I have a confession to go along with it, I'll give my word that the man who does confess won't burn."

That rocked me back on my heels. Allhoff, the relentless ask-no-favor-of-any-man cop, coolly admitting he didn't have a case, and equally coolly asking the killers to please break down and tell all.

"Allhoff," I said, "you're completely nuts."

The fact that he didn't get sore at that should have warned me that he had something up his sleeve. Latham Layne stood up, unmistakable relief upon his pale face.

"I take it this farce is over," he said. "I'm going back to town."

"Just a moment," said Allhoff. "You're sure that none of you cares to take advantage of my offer? Again I promise the man who confesses his life."

There was no rush to snap up the offer. "All right," said Allhoff. "I have one more request to make. Will you gentlemen give me five minutes alone with my assistants?"

"I'll give you the rest of your life alone with them," said Lucas.

Allhoff ignored that. He pointed toward the door of the smaller office.

"Will the four of you wait inside there for five minutes?"

His manner had me puzzled. The politeness with which he treated everyone was utterly unprecedented. Young Layne looked as if he were about to tell Allhoff to go to hell, when Abbott laughed shortly and said: "Well, Inspector. If you think, it'll do any good."

He turned and led the way into the smaller office, Lucas shrugged and followed him, Layne tagged along reluctantly. Rickerts appeared on the ragged edge of a nervous breakdown. His hands fluttered like frightened birds and he seemed utterly bewildered.

As the office door closed behind them, Allhoff looked at Battersly and slapped the palm of his hand sharply on the top of the desk.

It took Battersly a good ten seconds to remember his cue. Then he hastily crossed the room, quietly inserted the key in the lock and turned it. I stood there wondering what on earth the next move was, when I happened to notice Carden still sitting at his post by the percolator, still staring, oblivious to everything, out at the yellow lawn.

"What about the dummy?" said Battersly. "You want him out, too?"

"What's the difference?" I said. "He doesn't know what's going on."

CHAPTER FIVE

Allhoff Plays the Dummy

llhoff emptied his coffee cup. "There are times," he said, and it seemed to me that his voice was raised higher than usual— "There are times when an illegal act can best serve the ends of justice."

"Sure," I said, "I suppose that's why we've got a hack-driver in the can."

"There's a killer in this building," went on Allhoff. "He has poisoned two mutes in this institution. He has shot a third with a silenced revolver, It's simple justice that this man should now die himself."

"It's O. K. by me," I said, "All you have to do is to find out who he is, then build up a stack of evidence against him."

"I know who he is," said Allhoff. "And my evidence is no good without a confession."

I looked at him sharply. There was a familiar ring in his tone. It was that gloating bitterness he used when he was about to yield to the compelling streak of viciousness inside him. Battersly's face was drawn and anxious. He knew that tone, too. Perhaps even better than I did.

"So," said Allhoff and his voice rose in an almost hysterical crescendo, "I'm not only going to be the policeman on this case. I'm going to be the prosecutor, the judge. the jury—and the executioner!"

He jerked open the drawer of the desk, plunged both hands in and withdrew only his right. Now his fingers were wrapped around the butt of an automatic. He lifted it slowly, his little eyes agleam with bright savagery. He aimed its muzzle at the broad back of Carden across the room,

"Allhoff!" I cried, "You're crazy! You can't do that. You can't shoot a man down in cold blood. You can't even prove he's guilty. You—"

"I know he's guilty," said Allhoff. "Even if I can't prove it. He's murdered three of his fellows. And by God, he'll die for it!"

There was a taut silence in the room, Carden sat leaning over the taboret, looking out the window. Allhoff held the automatic centered dead at his back. I was aware of a tight, empty sensation at the pit of the stomach. Murder, God knows, is a ghastly business. And the fact of that helpless mute staring out at the lawn, utterly unconscious of the gun at his back, made it worse.

"Allhoff!" I said again. Good God, man—"

Battersly took things into his own hands. He crossed the room, reached over Allhoff's desk for the gun. Now Allhoff's left hand shot from the drawer with the speed of an eel. There was a second automatic in it. He cracked the barrel down hard upon Battersly's knuckles. Then he aimed it at us.

"Get back," he snarled. "Get back or—"

Battersly stood staring at him, blood dripping from his smashed fingers. I watched the muzzle of the second automatic trained in the general direction of my stomach. Under normal circumstances I have no relish for a gun pointed at me, and, held by a man as mentally unstable as Allhoff, I liked it even less.

"Now," said Allhoff. "You two stand where you are while I cut a huge hunk of red tape out of legal process. I'm going to blast that killer. If you try to stop me I'll blast you, too!"

I suddenly lost my temper. "Damn you," I said, "Go ahead and blast! You'll not only kill Carden with that shot, Allhoff. You'll burn yourself for it, and I'll have the time of my life testifying against you. Blast, you sadistic madman! Go ahead!"

I could see claw-like fingers tense on the butt of each gun. He jerked his head away from me and looked at Carden's back, He raised the weapon in his right hand again.

"Carden!" he shrieked as if for once he would break through the mute's deafness. "Carden, in one second you'll be as dead as those men you destroyed. Carden, here it comes!"

Then before my startled eyes the miracle happened. Into my startled ears roared pandemonium.

Carden sprang to his feet and turned around. His face was no longer expressionless. It was screwed up in frank terror. The blankness had been swept from his eyes, replaced by horror and dread. His mouth opened.

"No," he shrieked. "Don't! I—"

Then as words, articulate words tumbled from his quivering lips, there was a sudden banging at the door of the smaller office.

Abbott's voice roared through the panels of the door, "Carden! Shut up, you fool! He's bluffing you. Keep your mouth shut!"

But Carden stared at the unwavering muzzle of Allhoff's gun and kept talking. Then Latham Layne's voice came, high-pitched and fearful, over the open transom.

"Carden!" he shrieked, "Carden, you'll burn us all! You'll—"

By now Carden had crossed the room to stand over Allhoff's desk. The physical change in his features was amazing. No longer did he wear the dull, apathetic expression of the deaf mutes. His facial muscles eloquently registered his emotions now.

"For God's sake, don't shoot, Inspector!" he said. "I'll talk. I killed them, I shot Reynolds when I found he was going to your office, I—"

Allhoff dropped one of his guns. He pulled a type-written sheet of paper from the open desk drawer. "Here," he said. "Sign this. It's all down here. I know exactly how you did it," He thrust a pen into Carden's nerveless fingers.

Carden bent over the paper. "You promised, Inspector," he said. "You promised the man who confessed wouldn't burn and—"

"When you've rotted in jail for fifty years," said Allhoff, "you'll be sorry I kept my promise. Go ahead and sign."

Carden's pen scratched across the paper. Latham Layne's voice sounded almost hysterical above the pounding at the panel of the locked door.

"Carden! Carden! You're sending us to the chair. You're—"

A bullet blasted the lock of the door. It burst open. Abbott and Lucas came into the room first. There was a heavy forty-five in Lucas' hand. I sprang across the floor, seized the gun with my left hand and hammered my right into Lucas' jaw with all my strength. I heard Allhoff's voice behind me.

"All right, Simmonds. I've got 'em covered now."

I stepped back. Lucas, Layne and Abbott raised their hands silently. I looked through the door to see Rickerts, drooped in a chair in a dead faint, Camden still stood before Allhoff, talking desperately.

"You promised, Inspector," he said. "They offered me fifty thousand dollars to do it. I never made much dough. I was one of those dummy figures they use for advertising. You know, those fellows that're supposed to make the public guess if they're human or mechanical, I—"

"Shut up," said Allhoff. "Battersly, telephone for a wagon."

I stood over our three prisoners as Battersly put through the call. Allhoff regarded me with an expression I didn't like. I recalled that during the excitement of a few moments ago I had hurled some choice epithets at him. I decided it was best to apply a little oil before he remembered,

"Allhoff," I said. "It was neat. Very neat. But I'm damned if I know how you pinned it on Carden."

He registered contemptuous disdain, but I knew he was mentally taking a bow.

"That note he wrote," he said. "You remember the note he scrawled about the coffee supply being low? Well, he misspelled the word 'percolator.' He spelled it with a 'k'—phonetically. Now how the hell can a guy who's been a deaf mute since birth make a mistake like that? He can't spell phonetically for the simple reason that he's never heard the word pronounced. He's only seen it written. He's learned with the eye, not the ear, That aroused my first suspicion. Then, I clinched it."

A light began to dawn.

"You mean that speech of yours about the rubber hose?"

"Exactly. If Carden was no dummy, if he was in on the killings, he would undoubtedly eavesdrop in the hall when he heard me mention the third degree. Then he'd warn Layne to keep out of his room, to hide somewhere. You'll note he didn't warn Rickerts, That indicated that Rickerts wasn't in on it. Of the four of them he was the only innocent man."

He lapsed into silence, didn't speak again until the wagon had removed the prisoners and we were halfway back to town in our own car.

"Incidentally." he said then, "you, Simmonds, are fined one week's pay for insolence and insubordination. Battersly draws a month for attempted assault upon a superior."

I knew it was useless to protest. He had been right again and it was costing us money for having been wrong. However there was one thing I wanted to know.

"Allhoff," I said. "Suppose Carden hadn't cracked. What would you have done?"

He hooked at me with his yellow agate eyes. A bitter mirthless smile broke over his lips. "What do you think?" he said. "I'll bet Battersly knows."

Battersly looked at him and shuddered, "Yes," he said in a thin far-away voice. "I think I know, Inspector."

A CORPSE
FOR
CHRISTMAS

Originally Published - December 1939

CHAPTER ONE

Lady Bountiful and the Beast

The snow, ghostly confetti, swirled down Centre Street toward the Battery, hammered silently against the window, then turned to gray water as it trickled, discouraged, down the dirty pane. Across the street a scarlet Salvation Army Santa Claus stood huddled against the cold, ringing his bell dispiritedly. Ten feet above his head a billboard announced categorically that only two shopping days remained until Christmas.

I turned from the window, lit my pipe and looked around the unkempt room. A pair of Allhoff's pajamas hung, like an unwashed specter, from the hook over the sink where the frying pan should have been. The door of his bedroom was open and the bed was in its customary condition—unmade. A stack of dirty dishes stood like a greasy Tower of Pisa upon the stove, and I reflected that if the waste baskets weren't emptied soon we'd probably revert to that Central American custom of heaving the rubbish out the window into the street below.

Allhoff sat close up against his desk, staring at the coffee percolator upon its electric base as if the heat of his angry eyes would expedite the boiling of the water. A chipped cup and saucer, colored cafeteria gray, stood before him. A cracked tumbler half filled with sugar was on his left. He rattled a battered tin spoon impatiently as he watched the coffee pot, much in the manner a hophead watches opium cook.

I smoked my pipe quietly and thought troubled thoughts. Yesterday afternoon, in a weak moment, I had promised Battersly a favor which entailed appealing to Allhoff's better nature. Now that the time for action had arrived, I was beginning to regret it. However, I wasn't sucker enough to broach the matter until Allhoff had consumed at least two cups of the viscous fluid which he firmly believed was coffee.

The gurgle of the percolator broke the silence and Allhoff's little agate eyes lit up. He waited for a long interval while the pot performed its perverse alchemy of transmuting perfectly good coffee and water to unpotable tar. Then he snatched the pot up with a trembling hand and filled his cup. He drank gratefully and audibly.

I waited until he was well through the third pouring before I spoke. Then I cleared my throat and said: "Allhoff, do you know that in two days it'll be Christmas."

He replaced the cup in the saucer with a clatter that somehow sounded ominous. Before he answered he snatched up a pencil and scribbled furiously on a scratch pad. Then he screwed his bullet head around and stared at me with bitter narrowed eyes.

"If the conversation is taking an actuarial turn," he said unpleasantly, "I'll hold up my end by remarking that it's precisely one hundred and fifty-eight days till Decoration Day, and a hundred and ninety-three till the Fourth of July. I'll remark further—so what?"

He swung his head around again and buried his face in the coffee cup. I sighed and refilled my pipe. This was going to be every bit as difficult as I had expected. I waited while he loaded up the percolator and tried again.

"Listen," I said amiably, "I don't know if anyone ever called your attention to it, but Christmas is a period of good will and congeniality. Whole families gather for reunions. Enemies forget their hates and buy presents for each other. The world dedicates itself to joyfulness and cheer. It's a period of happiness, of gladness and unselfishness."

Allhoff swung around in his swivel chair. He stared at me over the rim of his coffee cup. There was an unholy expression in his yellow pupils.

"You've left out something," he said. "It's also a period when the storekeepers make a fortune by shilling the yokels into buying presents they can't afford. When a million morons get drunk and go home to beat their wives. Christmas is a merry period during which the Nazis will undoubtedly blow thousands of British into little pieces, and give the concentration-camp boys an extra ration of arsenic for breakfast. When a couple of million people are on relief and fifteen percent of the kids in Georgia have rickets.

"Christmas!" he concluded with a grating laugh. "I'm glad you told me about it."

After that speech it didn't take much intelligence to make me realize I wasn't making any headway. I was annoyed enough to forget discretion.

"Listen," I said. "Did you ever read Dickens?"

Allhoff regarded me suspiciously. "Why?"

"Once," I told him, "there was a guy called Scrooge. He was a louse—like you. But he met up with a ghost on Christmas Eve and it scared the hell out of him. He was a pretty good guy after that."

Allhoff refilled his cup and laughed. "I don't believe in ghosts," he said shortly.

I puffed at my pipe, sighed, and searched for a fresh approach to the matter in hand. Before I found one, Allhoff, regarding me shrewdly, said: "Simmonds, I hardly believe you're handing out all this Christmas sweetness and light for the good of my soul. Suppose you tell me in simple one-syllable words what the devil you're driving at?"

I took a deep breath and realized that was exactly what I should have done in the first place. "All right," I said. "It's about Battersly."

He scowled and his eyes blazed at the name.

"He wants to go home for Christmas," I went on hurriedly. "He hasn't seen his mother back in Indiana for a couple of years. He'd like to stay there for a week. Until after New Year's. With your permission, of course."

Allhoff's face was saffron fire. His lips twisted as he uttered a single obscene word. He was glaring at me but I knew the epithet applied to Battersly.

"So," he said bitterly, "in addition to his other charming characteristics, Battersly possesses the moral courage of a jackrabbit. Why didn't he ask me himself?"

"You know the answer to that."

"I also know the answer to the original question," snapped Allhoff. "It's no. The department grants Christmas leave to anyone not on actual duty. Battersly's entitled to it. He can have it. But he doesn't get another single hour. If he wants to go to Indiana let him do it in one day. He can fly. Better yet he can run there and back. He's got the legs for it, hasn't he? While I—"

I had been afraid of this. He was rushing up to his boiling point like hot mercury.

"Allhoff!" I said sharply.

His little eyes glazed insanely. He banged a fist on the desk like a rubber mallet. I sighed resignedly as he opened his mouth to curse me. Then, to my intense relief, the door opened.

B attersly, handsome and erect in his patrolman's uniform, stood holding the doorknob. He indicated Allhoff with a wave of his hand and said: "This is the occupant of the apartment, ma'am."

I gasped at the breathtaking beauty of the girl who entered the room. She was tall, dark, and she walked with regal bearing. Her gaze was arrogant and her eyes were blue and distant as an Arctic sea. She wore a suit which even my untutored eye recognized as an exclusive model.

On her left arm she carried a magnificent diamond bracelet and a huge covered basket. She put the basket down on Allhoff's desk, offered him a dazzling smile which, nevertheless, held a marked degree of condescension, and said: "Will someone please tell me the time? I'm sure I'll never get through my rounds before luncheon."

I didn't quite understand what she meant by that, but I glanced down at my wrist watch and said: "It's exactly seven minutes past nine."

She thanked me distantly and politely. Then she looked around the room and wrinkled her patrician nose. She shook her head in obvious disapproval.

"I should think you'd keep the place clean," she observed, "no matter how reduced your circumstances."

A llhoff blinked, looked from the girl to the basket. Like myself, he waited perplexedly for her to explain what the hell it was all about. The girl smiled down at him again, and there was something in her manner that reminded me of the local gentry bestowing a Christmas call on the worthy peasantry.

"I am here," she announced to Allhoff, "on behalf of the Society League's Holiday Aid Organization. We are giving you this basket. Each year we supply everything needed for a real old-fashioned Christmas dinner to the worthy poor."

She whipped the cover off the basket. Fruit, vegetables and canned goods were piled neatly about a huge turkey that thrust its naked torso into Allhoff's face.

"So this," said the girl as if she were talking to an imbecile, "is for you, my good man."

My good man! That killed me. Battersly looked at her apprehensively. Allhoff's face grew slowly purple. For the moment he was absolutely speechless. I took the pipe from my mouth and grinned broadly. This, I decided, was one of the high spots of my routine life.

Because Allhoff chose to live in this sordid tenement slum, he had been listed as one of the worthy indigent entitled to draw a charity Christmas meal. I saw furious baffled rage well up in his eyes and I felt uplifted.

With a mighty effort he controlled his temper, assumed a degree of distant dignity as he spoke.

"Madam—" he began, but the girl waved a jeweled, deprecating hand and cut him short.

"Don't thank me," she said. "And there's no need to be embarrassed. It is the duty of the better classes to provide for the unfortunate. We—"

"Madam!" Allhoff was a roaring lion now. His cheeks were the color of crimson orchids in bloom. There was wild fury in his eyes. "I am neither indigent nor unfortunate. My salary is ample. My bank account is healthy. Therefor, I must ask you to remove this charity basket. Give it to someone who needs it."

The girl with the regal bearing was one of the few people I had ever seen who stood in no awe of Allhoff's roaring. She watched him with her cool eyes and when she spoke it was in the tone of an adult admonishing a recalcitrant child.

"Come now," she said. "Don't let foolish pride stand in the way of your enjoying a good meal. Perhaps your circumstances are not entirely your fault. But it really is silly to pretend you don't need this food."

She paused for a moment and smiled a class-conscious smile. For the first time in my life I saw Allhoff utterly speechless. The indignity put upon him was too much for his larynx. He made an odd gurgling noise in his throat and stared at the poised beautiful creature before him with the dazed expression of a man watching water run uphill.

The girl reached over and patted the fat drumstick of the turkey. She retained her patronizing air. "Look," she said, "you'll be glad I didn't take you at your word as you munch this drumstick on Christmas day. There's really nothing as good as a turkey leg. Fat and rich. You wouldn't want your foolish pride to deprive you of two fat legs, would you?"

My stomach turned over at that. I heard Battersly's swift intake of breath. Allhoff's face was as twisted as a Communist editorial. He slammed his hands down on the desk-top, pushed the swivel chair backwards halfway across the floor. He pointed down toward his thighs, to the pair of leather pads where his knees should have been and wriggled his stumps in a little macabre dance.

"Damn you!" he shrieked, and his voice soared close to hysteria. "I've already been deprived of two legs!" He jerked his gaze away from the girl who remained calm and elegant under this outburst and glared at Battersly. "You!" he yelled. "You brought this strumpet in here. You brought her in here to mock me. You—"

Pale and nervous, Battersly interrupted him. "I never saw her before, sir. I met her in the hall. She asked me who lived in this apartment. I—"

"You lie!" screamed Allhoff, still dancing a frenzied rigadoon with his stumps. "You brought her here to jeer at me. You didn't dare do it yourself. First, you rob me of my legs. Now, you bring this slut here to sneer, to insult me with her damnable charity. A Christmas basket' My God—"

I decided to cut in before he achieved an apoplectic coma.

"Allhoff!" I said sharply.

He switched his gaze to me long enough to curse me obscenely. I looked over at the girl. She remained completely aloof. There was faint contempt upon her face and her smile was icy, totally without humor.

Allhoff looked at her, too. There was murder, unholy and dear in his eyes. She met his gaze unflinchingly. I had never before seen anyone stand like a rock before the tidal wave of Allhoff's fury. She cleared her throat and said with contemptuous indifference: "What a horrible little man."

Then she swung around on a high French heel and strode with imperious dignity from the room. Furthermore she left the Christmas basket on the desk behind her. The door slammed and Allhoff stared after her, speechless. For that matter, so did I.

I had seen Allhoff indulge in a thousand hysterical outbursts. I had seen the victims of his wrath register fear, rage, sullen resentment. But heretofore no one had ever remained remote and indifferent. The girl with the basket had subtly conveyed the impression that Allhoff was some gray crawling form of life beneath her notice.

Battersly, with rare discretion for him, went quietly into the tiny bathroom and locked the door. Allhoff turned his head slowly until his gaze rested on the turkey. Then he found his tongue.

He cursed wildly, snatched up the fowl and hurled it to the floor. He scattered the vegetables with a frenzied hand. He called the girl a string of ugly names. He swore at Battersly with all the venom of his poisoned tongue. He kicked his stumps violently and spoke for a solid ten minutes. The words poured from his twisted mouth like oil from a gusher.

I refilled my pipe and made no effort to stop him. This was one of those occasions when nothing short of a blackjack applied forcefully to the base of his skull could have accomplished that.

The genesis of Allhoff's psychosis went back to a bloody night several years ago, when he had been leading a raid on a gangster stronghold on upper West End Avenue. Battersly, a raw recruit in those days, had been assigned to affect an entrance through the rear in order to disable the Tommy-gun operator who, it was expected, would be guarding the front door.

Battersly carried out the first half of his job well enough, then developed an understandable case of buck fever and didn't shoot in time. At the zero hour Allhoff came battering through the front door to be greeted by a hail of machine-gun bullets. A score of them almost cut off his legs. The Bellevue surgeons completed the job after gangrene had set in.

But Allhoff lost more than his legs in that foray. Something of his mind went, too. He became a bitter misanthrope. Hate and venom bubbled within him, a ceaseless hot spring.

Departmental rules forbid a legless inspector and he had resigned forthwith from the force. But the commissioner did not intend to lose his best man that easily. Devious bookkeeping in the comptroller's office arranged it so that he was paid his former salary. He had set himself up in this tenement flat in order to be near headquarters. And while he had no official standing, woe betide the rookie who didn't believe that Allhoff's orders took precedence over those of anyone else. The commissioner would back him to the hilt in anything he cared to do.

Allhoff's first act in the new regime was to demand that Battersly be assigned as his assistant. When that request had been granted he proceeded to exact his bitter and terrible revenge. I, who had come up with Allhoff had been given this thankless detail, too. Ostensibly, I was to take care of the paper work. Actually, I was supposed to pour oil on the troubled waters when Allhoff gave way to his flaming temper.

It was the most unpleasant assignment I'd ever had. But all my efforts at transfer were denied by the commissioner. He knew that while Allhoff was by no means fond of me, he probably disliked me a little less than anyone else. So here we were, the three of us—me, waiting patiently until I was eligible for my pension, Battersly and Allhoff, waiting for the latter's death to release each of them from the bitter thrall in which they were held.

CHAPTER TWO

Murder—Vice Versa

It was a little after one o'clock when the Gerson case came up. For two hours Allhoff had been drinking coffee steadily and silently. Battersly busied himself with a sheaf of onion-skin reports. I sat by the window staring out into the snowy street.

A copper from headquarters came in, saluted Allhoff stiffly, laid a package and a large manila envelope on his desk.

"The commissioner wants you to look these over. Inspector," he said. "It's pretty cut and dried, but he'd like your corroborative opinion because of the prominence of the principals."

Allhoff still in a savage mood, gave him the silent treatment. He sipped coffee and didn't look up. The copper stood there, red-faced and angry, for a moment. Then he swung round abruptly and strode from the room. Allhoff continued to devote his attention to his coffee so I got up, took the package and envelope from his desk and carried them back to my own.

For the next fifteen minutes I studied the reports and exhibits in the Gerson case. A casual examination convinced me that the homicide squad already had the correct answer. But when anything out of the ordinary occurred the commissioner always liked to have Allhoff's opinion on the record, too.

Eventually Allhoff, as crammed with coffee as an A & P warehouse deigned to torn his head and grunt in my direction: "What've we got?"

"Emile Gerson," I told him. "The gold-mine guy. Been sort of wacky ever since he made his fortune, according to the papers and the report here. Lived with his nephew in that gloomy dungeon overlooking the Sound at Whitestone. The nephew's a college professor—philologist. Apparently he was something of a screwball in his own right. Both drunks. They—"

"Listen," said Allhoff irritably, "I read all the papers every morning and I've got a memory like an elephant. The Gerson family's no good. Since they got money they all proceeded to drink themselves to death. Only a couple of them left. I know all about Emile

Gerson. I know all about his nephew. Tell me something new."

"I will," I said. "They're dead."

There was a moment's silence. Battersly dropped his reports and swung around in his chair. Allhoff lifted his eyebrows and the coffee pot at the same time. He filled his cup with liquid ebony.

"All right," he said. "What happened?"

"Gerson and Harry Welch—that's the nephew—had one hell of a row yesterday. Welch threatened to kill Gerson, then kill himself. Witnesses testify that Welch claimed they'd both be better off dead. It was a real drunken brawl. Welch claimed money and booze had ruined them. This morning Welch carried out his threat."

Allhoff sipped coffee noisily. Then he put down the cup and grunted. "What's in that package?"

"Exhibits A to Z. Articles homicide took from the corpses' pockets. Random stuff they picked up."

Allhoff held out his hand. "Let me see it."

I handed him the cardboard container. He opened it and peered at the contents. "All right," he said. "Let's hear the report. Don't skip anything."

I looked at him in disgust. The report was long, detailed and deadly dull.

"Listen," I said. "This is sheer routine. The commissioner merely wants a corroborative opinion. Welch killed his uncle, then shot himself. Homicide's got the whole thing cleared up."

Allhoff took a wrist watch out of the cardboard box and examined it. "Homicide's been wrong before," he announced. "Now what's in that report?"

I sighed, picked up the single-spaced typewritten sheet and proceeded to itemize the details in a bored tone.

"At nine ten this morning, one William Leroy, the gardener, was in the greenhouse. He heard two shots, raced into the study. He found Gerson and Welch dead. Each had been shot through the head. The gun was in Welch's hand. There was a note—a suicide note written by Welch—in the roller of his portable typewriter."

Allhoff looked up from the wrist watch he still held. "Who else lives in that house?" he asked. "And where were they when the shots were fired?"

I consulted the second page of the report.

"One—" I said, "Jonas Kline, secretary to Gerson. He was at a barber shop over on Northern Boulevard. He was getting a shave, if you're going to insist on all the details. Two—Alicia Dale, second cousin to Welch, was here in Manhattan. The cook and the maid were in the laundry, some distance removed from the house. They heard the shots and rushed to the study. A W.P.A. road gang outside heard the firing, too. Homicide checked everyone. They had solid alibis all around." Allhoff snorted contemptuously. "Homicide has a habit of finding out who didn't commit the crime," he said. "Why don't they ever find out who did?"

"They found out this time," I told him. "Harry Welch."

"All right," said Allhoff. "What else?"

"My God," I said impatiently, "what else do you want? Homicide's got it cleared up, I tell you. They even interviewed Gerson's lawyer and his doctor. I suppose you'd like the doctor's report?"

"Sure," said Allhoff blandly. "What is it?"

"It won't make any more sense to you than it does to me," I told him. "Gerson was anemic, dipsomaniac, given to brooding. A marked *M. Agitata* type."

Allhoff glanced up sharply. He took an official-looking piece of paper from the box on his desk.

"This came out of Gerson's pocket," he said and there was a little tremor of suppressed excitement in his tone. "It's a federal court summons returnable at nine o'clock this morning. Income-tax stuff. Did Gerson answer it?"

I thumbed through the report. "That's on page six," I told him. "I was coming to that. No. His lawyer was down there waiting for him. Gerson was supposed to be there. The federal people were about to issue a bench warrant for him. But what the hell's all that got to do with it?"

He didn't answer. There was a faraway expression in his little eyes. Battersly watched him apprehensively. He knew that expression of Allhoff's as well as I did. It boded no good for someone.

"What else've you got there?" he demanded.

"I shrugged my shoulders. "You've got it all. All except the suicide note left by Harry Welch."

Allhoff held his coffee cup an inch away from his lips and looked at me expectantly.

I detached the typewritten note from the report and began to read aloud—

"This family was rotten without money. With wealth we are even worse. We should all have been decimated years ago. I'm doing my part now."

"The signature — *H. W.* — is typed underneath."

Allhoff bent forward and snatched the paper out of my hand. He studied it for a moment and an unholy gleam came into his eyes. He put down his coffee cup and said: "Now what do you suppose that note means?"

Battersly answered before I could. "I guess," he volunteered, "he meant the Gerson family was a bunch of no-goods and after the old man made his pile they became a bunch of drunks. He meant they should be wiped out."

"Bright boy," said Allhoff in a tone which implied exactly the opposite. He turned to me. "What do you think it means?"

"Listen," I said wearily. 'It's written in simple English, isn't it? It can only mean what Battersly has already said it means. Welch thought the family should be wiped out. He proceeded to set the example by killing his uncle and blowing out his own brains."

Allhoff smiled his prime, grade-A, unpleasant smile. He wore an air of superiority which nettled me. "Do you know what I think?" he asked loudly.

"Sure," I told him. "You think you're a combination of Sherlock Holmes, Charlie Chan and God Almighty. You think—"

"Damn you!" he yelled. "Do you know what I think about this Gerson case?"

"You tell me."

"I will," said Allhoff. "I'll tell the whole damned police department. Emile Gerson killed himself. Harry Welch was murdered."

"That's what everyone else thinks," I told him. "Only you're getting it mixed up. You—" I broke off suddenly. Allhoff never got anything mixed up. "Say that again," I demanded.

He grinned unpleasantly. "I said," he repeated, "Gerson killed himself. Welch was murdered."

I stared at him. Then I looked back at the typewritten papers on my desk. Battersly screwed up his face and watched Allhoff perplexedly.

"Allhoff," I said, "this is a beautiful flight of fancy. Homicide has been on the scene, has checked everything. They claim Gerson was killed and Welch committed suicide. You, apparently using nothing but silent communication with the stars, brazenly announce that *Gerson* committed suicide, while Welch was murdered."

Allhoff poured some coffee before he spoke. Then slowly and insultingly he said: "There are times, Simmonds, when I think you are dumber than homicide. Then again there are occasions when I think homicide's dumber than you. It's a hairline decision."

I was getting sore now. But before I could speak Battersly's curiosity overcame his natural reluctance to direct conversation with Allhoff. "But, sir," he said, puzzled, "how can you tell? How can—"

"He can't tell," I cut in. "He's impressing us. He's going to impress the commissioner too—tell him how dumb homicide is. But, of course, Inspector Allhoff wasn't on the spot and by now homicide's obliterated all the hot clues. So the inspector can't prove his case."

Allhoff's howl of rage shook the fly-specked chandelier above our heads.

"Damn you!" he roared. "Shut up. You dumb copper, I've got all the evidence in the world. You and the whole damned homicide squad are muddy minded cretins. Don't tell me Harry Welch killed Gerson and then shot himself. He didn't. Gerson killed himself. Welch was murdered. And I'm going to prove it, too."

I realized he was serious enough. But if he'd dug up enough to prove his theory from the report I'd given him, I was willing to sign my pension over to the Burglar's Union. He was glaring at me now, his eyes flashing like neon signs.

"You still don't believe me, do you?"

"No," I said. "But what was all this loose talk about evidence?"

"First," said Allhoff, and his eyes glittered, his nostrils quivered like those of a bloodhound taking the trail. "First, consider old man Gerson's condition. He's anemic. He's given to brooding, and that *M. Agitata* which seems to baffle you, means *Melancholia Agitata.*"

"Which," I said, "in turn, means . . .?"

"It means he's a manic-depressive type given to deep spells of melancholy, accompanied by a jittery nervous condition which accentuates the melancholy. Gerson was just the *sort* of guy who'd commit suicide."

I scratched my head and blinked at him. Allhoff had based a theory on some pretty slim stuff before this, but now it seemed he was going in for sheer guesswork.

"Second," he continued, "take that federal court summons. An income-tax rap is important. Gerson knew it was important. He'd told his lawyer he'd meet him in court. He was due there at nine o'clock this morning. He didn't go. Why?"

"I'm the straight man," I said. "Why?"

"If you intended to commit suicide within the hour, you wouldn't give a damn about a summons either."

"Nuts!" I said and ran my fingers through my hair.

Allhoff looked at me hotly. "You think it's thin, don't you?"

"Thin?" I echoed. "It's invisible."

"All right," said Allhoff. "There's more than that. Now let's take Harry Welch. Here's his wrist watch.

It's got his initials on it. That watch was wound up this morning. As near as I can figure, some time around eight o'clock. If Welch intended to kill himself would he wind up his watch?"

"Allhoff," I said, "do you feel well? For sixty bucks a week you can go up to Bill Brown's health farm at Garrison. In a month your mind would be as good as ever. Why, I knew a guy once who—"

Allhoff called me a filthy name, then drank some more coffee and became calmer.

"The most important item of all," he said, "is that suicide note. Welch didn't write it."

I was getting very bored. "No?" I said politely.

"No," snapped Allhoff. "Welch was a college professor before he became a booze-fighter. He was a philologist of high reputation." He swung around in his chair and faced Battersly. "You," he said. "What does *decimate* mean?"

Battersly blinked, frowned for a moment, and said: "Why it means to wipe out, to annihilate."

"Ha," said Allhoff and waved a finger under my nose. "Now, you. What does *decimate* mean?"

"It means just what Battersly said it means," I answered wearily. "And now may I please go to lunch?"

"The guy that wrote that note," said Allhoff, ignoring my question, "was as dumb as you two. He also thought *decimate* means to wipe out." He hammered his fist on the desk and raised his voice. "But it doesn't! It means to reduce by a tenth. As, for example, when every tenth man in a mutinous regiment is shot by the military authorities. Nearly everyone uses the word incorrectly, believes it means to obliterate."

"So," I said, "granting you're a purist, Harry Welch was just another of us mugs who misuses a word."

"No?" yelled Allhoff. "He was a philologist, wasn't he? Words and their derivations, their meanings, were his business. He'd never make a mistake like that. Harry Welch never wrote that note. Besides—look here."

He picked up the suicide note and held it out to me. "Note that signature. Note those initials, *H. W.* The typing there is somewhat lighter than the body of the note. Someone else typed those initials."

I took the paper from him. "My God!" I said. "Someone else wrote the note. Now a third party has typed the initials."

I studied the paper and decided he might be right, and then again he might well be wrong. Perhaps there was an almost imperceptible difference in the shading of the note itself and the signature. But it was so slight as to be entirely negligible.

"Just supposing you're right," I said. "Harry Welch was murdered. A phony note was planted. Your Gerson suicide theory suffers from an acute case of the shakes. Why couldn't the person who wrote the note have killed them both?"

"It's barely possible," said Allhoff, with the air of making a munificent concession. "But my idea is that Gerson wrote that note before he killed himself. Then after Harry was murdered, someone switched it and signed those initials to make it appear that it was written by Welch."

I thought that over and decided that I still put my faith in the homicide squad.

"You've made four points," I said. "Gerson's mental condition, the summons, the wrist watch, and the definition of the word *decimate*. Each point is inconclusive."

"Each is indicative," snapped Allhoff. "Taken all together they make the whole case look screwy. Besides, there's another important point."

"Which is?"

"I feel I'm right," said Allhoff. "I sense it."

My God, he sensed it! In another week we'd be solving murder cases by fasting, prayer and astrology.

"In any event," said Allhoff, slipping from his chair and landing on his stumps with two dull thuds, "in any event, we're going out to Gerson's right now and look things over."

"Listen," I said in disgust, "can't we wait till after Christmas? The day after tomorrow's a holiday."

"Not if we're working on a case," said Allhoff virtuously. "A copper must be prepared to make personal sacrifices for the public good."

Which was a very noble speech coming from Allhoff. To him holidays and working days were exactly the same. He spent three hundred and sixty-five days a year drinking coffee in this slum, a fact which made it a hell of a sacrifice for him to give up Christmas. I said as much aloud but he took no notice of my sarcasm. Followed by Battersly, he was already clumping off in the direction of the stairway.

I sighed, stood up and went along. As I crossed the room my foot slipped on something soft and rubbery. I looked down to see the turkey which had been presented to Allhoff for Christmas. I kicked it viciously across the room and put on my coat.

As I walked down the rickety stairs I was hoping against hope that for once in his life Allhoff would take only forty-eight hours to admit he was wrong. Otherwise we'd all be eating hamburger sandwiches for Christmas dinner out at Whitestone Landing.

CHAPTER THREE

Alibi Allhoff

We went out to Long Island in a police car with Battersly driving. Allhoff sat thoughtfully next to me in the rear seat and said nothing. I was seething with disgust and annoyance at being dragged out here on a fool's errand.

Gerson's home was an ancient brownstone structure built close to the water's edge on Long Island Sound. Secluded, it stood alone in the center of a couple of hundred acres, bleak and inhospitable.

I tugged at an old-fashioned bell-pull and a maid opened the door. She stared down at surprise in Allhoff, but he gave her no opportunity for questioning. He clumped right past her into the house. Battersly and I tagged along behind him.

Allhoff led the way through a large and empty living-room into a wide hall where we could hear the sound of voices. We paraded down the corridor in single file until Allhoff stopped before a door through which the voices sounded clearer. He jerked it open without knocking and waddled inside.

The room was obviously the study, quite probably the study in which Emile Gerson and his nephew had been found dead. Bookcases lined the walls. A broad mahogany desk stood at the far end of the oblong room like a pulpit. At the other end a vast fireplace yawned vacantly.

Two men stood up quickly as we entered. One of them, bald, ancient, and possessed of a quavering voice became indignant.

"What does this mean?" he demanded. "Who are you people? I—"

The second man interposed quickly. "Wait a minute, Kline." He looked thoughtfully at Allhoff. "This is Inspector Allhoff, I presume?"

Allhoff likes to be recognized. His mouth twisted in what he fondly believed was an ingratiating smile and he admitted his identity.

The other took a fat cigar from his lips and patted his rounded stomach. "Well, well," he said. "Glad to meet you, Inspector. Heard a lot of things about you. I'm Amberson, Emile Gerson's attorney. This"—he indicated the gray oldster at his side—"is Jonas Kline. He was Gerson's secretary."

Allhoff nodded to acknowledge the introduction. But he stood upon no further ceremony. He waddled the length of the room, climbed up on the chair behind the desk, seated himself like the presiding officer at a director's meeting.

"Now," he announced, "I want to see everyone in the house."

Jonas Kline appeared annoyed. "Good gracious!" he said. "We've had policemen here all morning. I thought everything was completed. I don't see why—"

Little Amberson interrupted him for a second time. "Now, Jonas," he said. "I'm sure the inspector knows what he's doing. Perhaps he doesn't know that headquarters is quite satisfied with its conclusions."

"I'm not satisfied," said Allhoff arrogantly. "And I still want to see everyone in the house."

Amberson hesitated for a moment. Apparently he knew of Allhoff's reputation for he turned to Kline and said: "All right, Jonas. Never obstruct justice. Get everyone down here to see the inspector."

Jonas Kline shrugged his shoulders and walked from the room without enthusiasm.

mberson puffed on his cigar and regarded Allhoff curiously. Battersly and I exchanged a glance of mutual commiseration. We knew from Allhoff's manner that he was going to play the role of super-sleuth to the hilt this time. We'd be lucky if we got out of there within the week.

The maid came shuffling through the door followed by a large competent woman, quite evidently the cook. Both of them had answered several questions for homicide in the morning and by now were quite docile. Allhoff swiftly took them over the jumps.

They had been in the laundry at the time of the shooting. They'd heard the shots, run to the study to find Leroy, the gardener, standing on the threshold staring at the corpses.

Allhoff dismissed them with a wave of his hand. Then he stopped the cook in the doorway by saying darkly: "Wait a minute. There's one very important thing."

The cook looked at him inquiringly.

"Can you make good coffee?" he demanded. "Black, thick and strong?"

The cook was quite confident that she could.

"Then make it," said Allhoff. "At once!"

Jonas Kline hustled back into the room, followed by a handsome giant, with blond curly hair and unintelligent eyes.

"Leroy," announced Kline.

Allhoff nodded. "You heard two shots, didn't you? You found the bodies."

"Yes, sir."

Allhoff leaned over the desk and shook his forefinger. "So you're the one man in the house with no alibi."

That didn't disturb the blond at all. "And no motive," said Leroy.

Allhoff scowled. He was getting nowhere at a great rate. He turned to Kline. "At the time of the killing you were in a barber shop. Is that correct?"

Kline twisted his fingers together nervously. "Absolutely. Three barbers can testify to that. I—"

But Allhoff was addressing Amberson now. "I suppose you, too, can account for your movements at the time Gerson and Welch died."

Amberson regarded Allhoff with more amusement than anything else. "I hope you don't think I killed them, Inspector. Your own homicide squad has already ascertained that I was in federal court waiting for Mr. Gerson."

"Allhoff," I said, "we can still get back to town in time for lunch."

He ignored me. He scratched his head and appeared more worried than I had ever seen him before. For once a case wasn't opening wide at his magic touch. For once Allhoff's psychic prescience wasn't working.

"This Dale woman," he said to Amberson. "She was some sort of relative, wasn't she?"

Amberson nodded, "Second cousin to Harry Welch. Even more distantly related to Gerson."

Allhoff bit his lip and looked thoughtful. Amberson shook his head. "No, Inspector," he said. "I know what you're thinking. And you're wrong. She—"

My nostrils caught a subtle odor of aphrodisiac perfume. My ear caught a rustle of silk. I saw Allhoff glaring toward the door like an enraged boar before I turned my head.

A voice said: "I'm Alicia Dale, Inspector. Did you want to see me?"

I gaped at her. It was the girl of Allhoff's charity basket!

he swept across the room toward the desk where Allhoff sat. She was every bit as calm and remote as she had been two hours ago. She smiled condescendingly down at Allhoff who looked like a bomb about to burst.

"So," he said in a thick strangled voice, "It's you."

"Yes," she said, still smiling. "I would have told you my name this morning, but when working among the unfortunate, I prefer strict anonymity."

Allhoff made a rattling sound in his throat and his eyes were yellow coals. I knew he would much rather pin a murder on Alicia Dale than on public enemies number one to ten, inclusive.

"I warn you," he said wrathfully, "you're under suspicion. I'll check everything you say. I'll do my damnedest to break down any story you tell."

Alicia Dale regarded him with sardonic mockery. "In that event," she said coolly, "you'd better begin by cross-examining yourself, Inspector. You're my alibi."

I saw a bullfight once in Juarez. The bull with a dozen darts in its back had until this moment, always been the top in baffled rage to me. Now Allhoff moved into first place by several lengths.

Since he was beyond speech, Alicia Dale spoke again.

"Someone in your office was kind enough to tell me it was exactly seven minutes past nine. As I understand it, Leroy found the bodies three minutes later. That's my alibi, Inspector. Break it down."

As I saw it, and with considerable rejoicing, Allhoff was going to be thoroughly and completely wrong for the first time in his life. If he intended to pin a murder on Alicia Dale he must first impeach the evidence of his own eyes and senses. And from what I'd heard from the others it was going to be equally difficult to pin it on anyone else.

This time homicide was right and Allhoff was wrong and great would be the gloating in the precinct locker-rooms.

"Alibi or not," snarled Allhoff, "you're a relative of Gerson's. As far as I can ascertain, the only living relative. You'd be in line for Emile Gerson's money. You had motive."

In my opinion, Allhoff was so sore he was getting childish now. Considering the girl's conclusive alibi, this motive business was a pretty slim prop. Then, to my glee, Amberson swept even that prop away.

"You're wrong, Inspector," he said. "I was trying to tell you that before. Miss Dale doesn't get the Gerson estate."

Alicia Dale's derisive smile remained steady. "Of course not," she said.

Allhoff looked like something in a cage. "Who gets it?" he snapped.

"There's a son," said little Amberson. "A natural son of Gerson's. Illegitimate. Born some ten years ago of a girl whom Gerson loved very much. She died when the boy was a baby. Exacted a dying promise from Gerson that the child would never be brought up in the Gerson family. Should never know who his father was."

Allhoff drummed an angry spatulate forefinger on the desk.

"Where is this boy?"

"In Illinois. Being brought up by his uncle on his mother's side. Everything goes to that boy. Lock, stock and barrel. The uncle, Peter Lovelace, and myself are named as executors. Gerson kept the whole thing under cover. Very few people knew about it."

"That's right," said Alicia Dale. "Only Amby, here. Harry Welch and myself."

"Four alibis," I said gayly. "And not a single motive. If we go home now, Allhoff, we'll duck the traffic on the Queensborough Bridge."

"No," said Allhoff and his voice was a hoarse, enraged scream. "There's been murder here. I know it! I know it!"

I decided to give him the works. "I've got an idea," I told him. "The kid out in Illinois had a fight with his uncle. The uncle wouldn't give him money for candy. So the kid hitch-hikes to New York, knocks off his father in order to inherit the estate. Then he can buy all the candy he wants. Oh, yes, and about Harry Welch. He—"

Allhoff let out a roar like a wounded lion and began an oath-filled diatribe.

Alicia Dale's cool voice cut in on him. "I can't stand noise and vulgarity," she said sweetly to me. "I'm going up to my room. If the inspector wants me when he gets over his tantrum, I'll be there."

She turned and swept out of the room. Allhoff stared after her and if a look could kill she'd have withered in her tracks.

"Oh, by the way," said Amberson. "I've already wired Peter Lovelace. He's flying here immediately to consult with me about the estate. Arrives at Newark airport at eleven tonight. Can you pick him up in the car, Leroy?"

"Yes, sir."

"We'll put him in the south room," said Kline. "I'll probably be in bed when he arrives."

"Lovelace is blind, Leroy," said Amberson. "Take good care of him. Take him up to the room and tell him where everything is."

Allhoff looked up swiftly. "Blind?"

Amberson nodded. "Been blind all his life. That was one of the reasons that the boy's mother wanted him to live with the uncle. Figured the uncle would be better for the boy than the Gersons. And that the blind man would be greatly aided by the lad."

Allhoff grunted and closed his eyes as if in deep thought. But he wasn't kidding me.

"Allhoff," I said. "If we leave now—"

"Damn you," said Allhoff. "We're not leaving.

We're staying here overnight. Kline, can you put us up?"

Kline admitted reluctantly that he could put us up. He left the room in order to consult with the maid. Leroy followed him. Amberson stood up and put on his coat.

"Well, Inspector," he said breezily. "Got to get back to the office. I'll be out here first thing in the morning to see Peter Lovelace and also to find out what you've picked up. Bye."

He strode cockily from the room, leaving Allhoff still registering profound cerebration, He still wasn't fooling me and judging from the expression on Battersly's face he wasn't fooling him either. We exchanged winks.

"You know," said Allhoff at last, "a woman like that Dale girl is capable of murder."

"That," I told him, "is sheer rationalization. You hate her guts, hence she's a murderess. Besides, you would look like an awful fool when she'd put you on the stand to testify for the defense. Old Alibi Allhoff. That's what the whole department'd be calling you after that." He grunted. "Well," he said, "suppose she killed Welch before she left the house." I laughed aloud at that. "So everyone's crazy," I said. "Two servants and a dozen W.P.A. guys all imagine two shots at the same time while Alicia Dale is standing in your office handing out a free turkey. No, Allhoff. For once one of your psychic hunches has collided with a fact. You're wrong as hell this time. You may as well admit it."

"Damn you," he said darkly. "I've never been wrong in my life."

The superb egotism of the guy got me. Hit him in the face with a fact and it made no difference. Allhoff had called it a murder and a suicide in reverse and that's what it would be until they laid him in a protesting grave.

CHAPTER FOUR

Blindman's Buff

Jonas Kline showed us to three single rooms in the north wing. I stayed in mine, keeping away from Allhoff and everyone else, save for an appearance at a gloomy and conversationless dinner.

I went to bed early and prayed that Allhoff would come to his senses in time to let me get home for Christmas dinner. Since Battersly wasn't going to have an opportunity to go to Indiana, I decided I'd invite him along, too. Before midnight I was fast asleep.

The shot awakened me, and the scream that followed brought me back to complete consciousness. I sprang out of bed, pulled on my trousers, grabbed my gun and went racing down the corridor. As I gained the stair-head, I saw Allhoff skidding down the steps in front of me.

Behind me, I heard doors open and the sound of footsteps. There was a ten-watt light in the lower hall that apparently had been left burning. By its illumination I saw Allhoff career down to the door of the study. His hand jerked out and touched a light-switch on the wall.

I looked down to see Allhoff prodding a man's body with the stump of his leg. Then he bent down and touched the fallen man's pulse. The prostrate figure had a thin sensitive face and deep fathomless eyes. There was an ugly red hole in the side of the head. Allhoff dropped an inert wrist and turned to me.

"Dead," he said over his shoulder, then added bitterly: "Do you figure it was suicide, Sergeant?"

At the moment I didn't figure anything. Behind me up the hall padded Battersly and Jonas Kline. They came to a full stop at the side of the corpse.

"What's wrong?" asked Battersly.

Allhoff threw him a contemptuous glance. "What do you think's wrong?" he growled. "Arson?"

Jonas Kline literally wrung his hands. "Good Heavens," he murmured, "This house is cursed. Another one. Who—who is it, Inspector?"

"If you'll look through his pockets," said Allhoff to me, "you'll undoubtedly discover that it's Uncle Peter Lovelace from Illinois."

I looked in the pockets and found a bankbook that proved Allhoff was right. Allhoff was watching Kline who muttered apprehensively, and cracked his fingers.

"You," said Allhoff. "Go to bed."

"But—" said Kline.

"To bed," shouted Allhoff in his I'll-brook-no-nonsense tone.

Kline, still murmuring to himself shuffled off toward the stairway. Allhoff entered the study and switched on the light. The first thing I noticed was that one of the sections of bookcase had been pulled away from the wall, revealing a safe set in the paneling. The safe-door was open, and examination proved it empty. Allhoff ran a hand through his thinning hair and his eyes narrowed.

Battersly stood in the doorway, staring down at the corpse. "Gee," he said. "And the poor guy was blind. Now why would anyone want to kill a blind man?"

Allhoff did an about-turn like a Prussian Guard. "What's that?" he said sharply. "Say that again?"

Battersly looked at him oddly and repeated: "Why would anyone want to kill a blind man?"

"My God!" said Allhoff. "Out of the mouths of babes! You've actually put your finger on something. No one *would* want to kill a blind man."

"But they did," I pointed out reasonably.

"Shut up," said Allhoff. "I'm thinking. Things are slowly falling into place. Peter Lovelace. A concealed heir. Empty safe."

This was gibberish to me last I knew better than to interrupt. He turned suddenly to Battersly again.

"What room's next door to this one he said. "Look on both sides."

Battersly went out into the corridor and returned a moment later.

"There's a dining-room on the left." he reported. "And a lavatory on the other side. Why?"

"Stay right here, both of you," said Allhoff. "Neither of you talk."

He climbed up into a big armchair and bowed his head in his hands, Battersly and I stood there in silence, feeling like fools. Allhoff was deep in his heavy-concentration act. And when he put on one of these seances I never knew if he actually had something or whether he was merely acting as the moving pictures had taught him a big-shot sleuth ought to act.

It was a full five minutes before he came out of it. But when he lifted his head his little eyes gleamed and his voice was hoarse with excitement as he spoke.

"Battersly, you're going back to town."

Allhoff took a notebook and fountain pen from his pocket. He scribbled something on a page then tore it from the book. Next he dragged out his checkbook and scrawled in that. He handed the check, the note and a key to Battersly.

"You'll be at the Second National Bank the instant it opens," he said. "Give 'em that note and they'll let you into my safe deposit box. That's the key there. You'll find a stack of bonds. Consolidated Motors fifties. Get 'em. Then cash that check. Get fifty twenties. Have the cashier wrap 'em up neatly with a rubber band. Be back here as soon as possible."

"What am I supposed to do?" I asked.

"You'll stand guard," he said. "You'll stay up, walk around this house and see that no one leaves it. In the meantime hand me that portable typewriter."

I picked up Harry Welch's typewriter—the one the suicide note had been written on—and carried it across the room to Allhoff. He placed it across his stumps and put a sheet of paper in the roller, began to peck at the keys as I left the room with Battersly.

Battersly went outside and drove off in the car. I strolled around the house and wondered who and what I was supposed to be guarding. Long after dawn I still heard Allhoff laboriously hammering away with two fingers. He didn't come out of the study till about half past six. But instead of going up the stairs to his room, he clumped across the hall toward the front door. I regarded him with sleepy eyes.

"What now?" I said, "Aren't we ever going to bed?"

He looked over at me and grinned unpleasantly. "I'm going out to the greenhouse," he announced. "I love to smell flowers in the early morning. It starts the day off right."

He went out into the dawn as I stared after him wondering if he was being satirical or if the millennium had actually arrived.

It was early morning and we were gathered in the study awaiting a call to breakfast. Jonas Kline stood by the window staring out at the snow. Battersly was smoking a cigarette. I sat before the big open fire and chatted desultorily with Alicia Dale.

The study door pushed open suddenly and Allhoff waddled into the room. He nodded to us all, hoisted himself up into a Morris chair and yawned elaborately.

"Terrible night," he said. "Hardly closed an eye."

Alicia Dale commiserated with him. I could have sworn I detected note of mockery in her voice, but Allhoff, usually more sensitive than I to these things, apparently did not notice it. He thanked her gravely for her interest, then looked around the room and said: "I'm sorry to have to delay this case, but we'll all be here a few days yet. I can't permit anyone to leave the house."

That was jolly news to me and, judging from the expressions of the others, to everyone else as well.

"I'd expected to break this case this morning," went on Allhoff, "but in order to clinch it I'll have to have this house, these grounds, thoroughly searched. There's some concealed evidence hidden away somewhere. This is a pretty big establishment and it'll take four or five men quite a few days to do a complete job. I'm sorry but there's no alternative."

The fact that he was apologizing should have aroused my suspicions, but the realization that I wasn't going to spend Christmas at home after all, had me too annoyed to start delving into Allhoff's private motivations. But his next sentence brought me up sharply.

"However," he was saying, "there's no point in inconveniencing anyone unnecessarily. For instance, I won't need you, Battersly. Simmonds tells me you wanted this week off, wanted to go home to Indiana. Well, go ahead. A plane leaves Newark in exactly two hours. You'll just have time for breakfast, to get home and pack."

I stared at him. Allhoff exuding the Christmas spirit was either a miracle or something exceedingly suspicious. But Battersly, overwhelmed with gratitude, took the offer at its face value. He came to his feet, beaming. "Thank you, sir," he said, "Thank you very much, I—"

Allhoff waved him to silence. "There's just one little favor I'd like to ask—"

"Sure," said Battersly. "Anything at all. I—"

"I've a few presents to send out. I'll wrap them up and leave them on the hall table for you. Pick them up on your way out and take them right out to the airport. They're all west-bound. I've let them go until the last minute and it'll save time."

Battersly kept grinning like a fool and yessing him. The rest of the assemblage was bored by the whole proceeding. But personally, if Allhoff were on the level, I was prepared to believe in fairies, Eddie Guest and the love-story magazines.

Allhoff sending Christmas presents! Reason tottered at the thought.

He turned to Kline, smiling with a cordial politeness as phony as a politician's handshake.

"I suppose I may borrow some wrapping paper and string from you?"

"I'll let you have some, Inspector," said Alicia Dale, "I've a lot of stuff left over from my own presents."

Allhoff thanked her profusely and slid down from his chair.

"I'm so sleepy I'll not bother about breakfast," he announced. "If you'll just send those wrappings up to my room, I'll get my presents ready and take a little nap. Battersly, I'll leave the stuff on the hall table for you. You can pick it up after you've eaten."

He waddled out of the room as I stared after him. And a moment later the maid announced breakfast.

I went in to the table lost in profound thought. Since my association with Allhoff, I had seen him do a number of peculiar things, but never before had he neglected his morning coffee.

CHAPTER FIVE

Without a Leg to Stand On

Half an hour after Battersly had departed for town bearing Allhoff's surprising Christmas packages, Allhoff himself thumped down the stairs, locked himself in the drawing-room. Through the panels I heard the excited hum of his voice as he used the telephone.

Ten minutes later he reappeared, eyed me coldly, ordered me to assemble the household in the study.

When I had done so the room resembled an inquisition chamber, with Allhoff, seated behind the desk at the far end of the room, playing Torquemada. I stood at his right like the Palace Guard. Scattered about the vast gloomy room were the others.

Jonas Kline was obviously nervous. His fingers constantly twined about each other like living ivy. His ancient bones cracked like rattling dice. Little Amberson, who had arrived shortly after breakfast, sat by his side to provide an interesting study in contrast. He smoked an expensive cigar almost as fat as himself, and beamed expansively and impartially upon all of us. He was on the side of virtue, law and order and wasn't letting anyone forget it.

The maid and cook stood nervously beside the door. They had entered together bringing a pot of bitter coffee and a cup for Allhoff. Unaccustomed to mixing with the gentry, their manner was anything but easy. No one had remembered to ask them to sit down and they were too well aware of their places to do so.

Leroy, however, stood upon no such feudal ceremony. He lounged back in a leather chair beside Allhoff's desk, smoked a nonchalant cigarette and kept his vacuous eyes upon the svelte figure of Alicia Dale by the window.

The girl watched Allhoff with distant, derisive eyes, cold and blue as a polar sea. She remained completely self-possessed, regal, imperious. She was the only person I had ever known who was utterly indifferent to Allhoff's nasty personality.

I turned my head away from the group and glanced out the window. It was still snowing. Tomorrow would be Christmas, and I thought with anxiety of the fifteen-pound turkey in the icebox at home. If Allhoff didn't pull whatever he had out of the hat within twenty-four hours, he would claim it was a departmental emergency and cancel my leave.

My jaundiced reverie was broken by Alicia Dale's voice.

"Inspector," she said, and the contempt she got into the single word was amazing. She somehow made it sound like an oath. "I'm tired of being held in this house under police surveillance, Will you please solve this case immediately?"

Her tone was jeering, her manner impertinent. I fully expected Allhoff to blow up. But he didn't. True, his eyes flashed, his sallow face sucked up some color, but his tone was steady enough as he answered. "Of course," he said. "Before noon, Miss Dale."

Leroy took his eyes off Alicia and stared at Allhoff. It seemed to me that there was a flicker of anxiety on his handsome countenance.

"As I have announced before," said Allhoff gravely, "Emile Gerson killed himself. He wrote a suicide note and blew his own brains out. Upon hearing this shot, Harry Welch entered the study."

Little Amberson took his cigar from his lips and clucked impatiently.

"Indeed you did tell us all this before, Inspector." he said. "I—"

Alicia Dale interrupted him. "Let the inspector finish, Amby. He undoubtedly has elaborated on that theory by now. I'm beginning to see it myself. Uncle Emile, upon seeing Harry enter the room, realized that he had forgotten to kill Harry before he committed suicide. So he slid hastily back from the grave, shot Harry, put the gun in his hand and jumped back again to Gehenna. They're both there now, playing two-handed pinochle."

I looked again at Allhoff. This was a brand of comedy he definitely did not like. The back of his neck looked like molten iron. Yet he held on to his temper with a strange tenacity, went on as if he'd never been interrupted.

"When Harry Welch entered the room, the wall-safe behind that section of bookcase was open. The bookcase was pulled out of place. In that safe were bonds and cash. As Harry Welch stood, dumfounded, staring at his uncle's corpse, someone else came into the study."

Amberson, who couldn't bear remaining out of the conversation for any length of time, came rushing in again.

"I get it," he said excitedly. "That third person saw the open safe, saw some valuables inside. He recalled the quarrel between Welch and Gerson and promptly turned it to his own advantage. He killed Welch, switched Gerson's suicide note so that it would appear Welch wrote it, planted the gun in Welch's hand and made off with the stuff in the safe."

Allhoff nodded at the lawyer like a school teacher showering approbation upon a bright pupil.

"Absolutely correct." he said. "That third person saw an opportunity to kill Welch and steal the bonds and money which were in the safe."

Bonds and money? That gave off an overwhelming piscatorial odor to me. Allhoff had sent Battersly back to town for a bagful of bonds and money and now it looked as if he were about to pin a made-to-order robbery on someone. It was very, very fishy, but I held my peace.

Jonas Kline coughed nervously behind his thin hand. "Who was this person, Inspector?" he asked, "Have you any idea who it was?"

"Certainly," said Allhoff. "It was you, Leroy. Wasn't it?"

His casual manner staggered me as much the question itself staggered Leroy. After all, you don't ask for a confession in a murder case as offhandedly as a hostess inquiring if you take two lumps of sugar in your tea.

Leroy sat upright in his chair and stared at Allhoff. There was no guilt in his expression. Rather utter and complete surprise.

"You're crazy," he said at last. "I didn't do anything of the kind. You're crazy."

Alicia Dale smiled sweetly. "Check," she said.

When Allhoff failed to blow up this time, I decided we were approaching a world's record. Three times he had been insulted in the past five minutes. Three times he had ignored it. He was just a curly little lamb this morning and that made me very suspicious that an earthquake would break loose before long.

"Leroy," he said quietly, "you'll make it a lot easier on yourself if you'll sign a confession."

Leroy stood up and appealed to the lawyer. "Mr. Amberson, he's crazy. I didn't kill anyone. He can't make me sign nothing, can he?"

Amberson nodded judicially. "You certainly can't, Inspector," he said pompously. "Not unless you've got something more than you've shown us."

Now Allhoff threw off his mask of serenity and politeness. He leaned forward over the desk and glared at Leroy. When he spoke his voice came roaring up from his bowels.

"Leroy," he shouted, "you're guilty as hell and I can prove it! Here." He pulled open a drawer of the desk. groped inside for a moment, then slapped a package of blue-and-gold-engraved bonds on the desktop. He took a swift encore on the gesture and came up this time with a packet of currency. "There." he went on. "Bonds and money. Taken from the safe. Identified by the bank as having been drawn by Emile Gerson. Found in the bureau of your room. What do you say to that?"

Leroy didn't answer immediately, but had he asked me what *I* said to that I would have told him. The bonds, I observed, were Consolidated Motors fifties. The currency was twenty-dollar bills. My suspicions were verified. This was the money and the bonds that Battersly had gotten from Allhoff's bank this morning. So this was either desperate bluff or outrageous frame-up.

Allhoff continued to shout at Leroy. "I've enough evidence here to send you to the chair! A signed confession will make things easier on you."

Leroy's face was ashen. The usual emptiness of his

eyes was occupied by fright. "Listen," he said rapidly. "You got it wrong, Inspector. Why, the murder wasn't even—"

Alicia Dale's voice sounded like a frozen bell. "Don't even bother answering him, Leroy," she said, "He's got nothing. If he had a case why would he be so eager for you to sign a confession. It's a frame."

Leroy looked at her doubtfully. Then he turned to Amberson again. "You're a lawyer," he said nervously. "Has he really got anything?"

Amberson tried very hard to look like Oliver Holmes. "If the inspector is prepared to prove that the bonds and money were in that safe, that they were later found in your room, he's got a damned good case. I wouldn't want to handle it."

Allhoff grinned unpleasantly. "Frame-up or not," he said, "it's a case. Iron-clad, Leroy here hasn't a single defense witness. I've got several for the prosecution."

If Allhoff had even one witness for the prosecution, I was prepared to perform a most humiliating action in Macy's window at high noon. But, undoubtedly, Leroy was impressed with his words.

"I suppose," he said desperately, "you're charging me with killing Peter Lovelace, too."

"What's the difference," said Allhoff callously. "I can only burn you once. However, if you'll sign a confession, it'll simplify things. I'll guarantee you don't get the chair."

Leroy was close to panic now. He bent over Allhoff's desk and his face was the color of the snow on the windowsill.

"No," he said vehemently. "No! No! I didn't do it! I won't sign. You—"

"Leroy," said Alicia Dale, "sit down and tell him to go to hell. If he's got a case let him give it to the D.A. He hasn't got a leg to stand on! Have you, Inspector?"

That last crack was a bombshell to me.

I glanced quickly from Allhoff to the girl. She was smiling with diabolical ingenuousness and looking squarely at Allhoff. He glared back at her and there was a terrible threat in his eyes.

Allhoff took a deep breath and cleared his throat. Fearing the worst, I came rushing up to stem the tide.

"Allhoff," I said, "Miss Dale is a thoughtless young girl. I'm sure she meant nothing. Anyway you're solving a murder case." I figured he'd like that. "You can attend to her later."

To my surprise he nodded. Then he said a peculiar thing. "Of course," he murmured quietly. "Of course. That was my original intention."

He thrust his hand into his vest pocket and withdrew a typewritten sheet of paper. He unfolded it and handed it to Leroy.

"Here," he said. "A typed confession. All you have to do is sign it."

"No!" screamed Leroy, pounding the desk frantically, "I'll never sign it! It's a lousy frame-up. It's—"

Amberson said sententiously: "You can't use coercion, Inspector."

"Nor force," said Alicia Dale.

"Look," said Allhoff to Leroy. "I've got you dead to rights and you know it. You'll never get an acquittal with what I've got. All I ask is that you read this confession. If it's true sign it. If not, hand it back to me unsigned." He paused for a moment, then added something I didn't understand. "Remember, Leroy, you're not getting paid any more."

I was damned certain Leroy wasn't guilty. Aside from Allhoff's bond-and-money plant there was the matter of the shots. According to the evidence, those two reports had sounded within a very short time of each other. If Leroy had entered the study at the time of Gerson's suicide—always assuming it *was* a suicide—he must have thought fast and acted faster to have killed Welch and rifled the safe before the cook and maid arrived upon the scene. Of course Allhoff was framing Leroy cruelly. But Leroy was certainly convinced that he'd go through with it.

He took the paper from Allhoff like a man handling a rattlesnake. He sank back in the Morris chair and began to read. The rest of us stared at Allhoff. Personally, I thought he was a little wacky. Under any circumstances Leroy would be an utter fool to sign that confession. What optimistic idea convinced Allhoff that he might was beyond me.

Leroy reached the end of the page and laid the paper down on the desk. His face was deathly pale and he was breathing hard. He hesitated for a moment, then held out his hand.

"Inspector," he said in a voice that was scarcely audible, "give me a pen."

That staggered all of us. There was deadly silence as the nib of Allhoff's pen scratched across the paper. Allhoff picked it up and put it back in his pocket.

Leroy, speaking through livid lips said: "You promised I wouldn't burn, Inspector. You promised."

"You damn fool," said Alicia Dale evenly.

Amberson got out of his chair and sputtered excitedly. "You can't promise immunity on a first-degree murder case, Inspector. You—"

Jonas Kline cracked his knuckles in a frenzy. "Leroy," he said. "I can't believe it. I—"

I turned on Allhoff with bitterness and astonishment. "You damned lucky copper. You were guessing. You ran a wild madman's bluff. You hadn't the slightest vestige of evidence that Leroy was the killer."

Allhoff twisted his head around and grinned crookedly at me. There was a grimace on his face I couldn't quite classify. "As a matter of fact," he said distinctly, "he isn't the killer at all."

"Goodness gracious," said Kline. "You accuse Leroy of murder. You get him to sign a confession. Now you say he isn't guilty. It's most irregular, Inspector."

"Allhoff," I said wearily, "what've you got up your sleeve? Let's hear it and we'll all go home."

"All except one of us," said Allhoff. "One of us is never going home again."

CHAPTER SIX

Cold Turkey Christmas

There was utter silence in the room. I could hear Leroy's heavy breathing and that was all. Allhoff leaned over his desk and his face was a flaming lamp of triumph.

"Miss Dale," he said. "Yesterday morning you called on me. You very kindly brought me a turkey which I didn't want. I now have the opportunity of repaying you, by giving you something you don't want either."

Alicia Dale lit a cigarette. She looked bored.

"All right, Allhoff," I said. "And what doesn't Miss Dale want?"

"Death," said Allhoff melodramatically and the word rolled gloatingly off his tongue. "It is quite true, Miss Dale, that you were legitimately engaged in delivering food to the indigent. Further, it is quite true that your errands for sweet charity's sake brought you into the neighborhood in which I live. But your call on me was deliberate. Not accidental."

Alicia Dale watched him with her cold steady eyes. Not a muscle of her face moved.

"You have a perverse character," went on Allhoff grimly. "Perverse and ironic. You needed an alibi. Any one of your indigent families could have given it to you as well as I. But it amused you to have the best copper in the department to cover you up."

"What the devil are you talking about?" I asked him. "Whether you like it or not, she is covered up. If she was in our office at seven minutes past nine—and, by God, she was—she couldn't have shot Harry Welch at nine ten."

"No," said Allhoff. "She couldn't. That's why she killed him a half-hour earlier."

Alicia Dale studied her coral nails for a moment. Then she looked up and blew smoke from her patrician nostrils.

"Inspector," she said, "do you make a habit of drinking this early in the day?"

Across the room, Leroy uttered an odd choking sound and buried his head in his hands. I considered Allhoff's charge, decided he was talking through his hat and told him so.

"According to you," I said, "everyone else is nuts. You can't go behind the obvious testimony in this case."

"Can't I?" said Allhoff, "Now get this! Emile Gerson came down to the study early yesterday morning. He'd been brooding all night. He'd made up his mind to kill himself. He'd typed out a note on his nephew's typewriter, then proceeded to blow his brains out. At this time the servants, still in their living-quarters over the garage did not hear the shot. That W.P.A. gang hadn't come to work yet, so they didn't hear it either. Shortly afterwards Miss Dale came into that room. Maybe she heard the shot and came to investigate. Maybe Harry Welch found Gerson and called her, I don't know and it doesn't matter. It's enough that she and Harry Welch were in the study together. That no one else in the house knew of Gerson's suicide yet."

If Allhoff were right, the girl was magnificent. She smoked a cigarette as calmly as if she were being accused of a misdemeanor by the local constable.

"Now," went on Allhoff, "Miss Dale who thinks swiftly and logically, saw a tremendous opportunity. She killed Harry Welch and went in search of Leroy."

Leroy's face was still in his hands. The Dale girl yawned and looked out the window.

"In my book," said Allhoff, "Leroy was more to Miss Dale than a gardener. He's probably nuts about her. She can wind him around her finger. She told him of her plan and he agreed."

"What plan?" I said impatiently. "For heaven's sake, Allhoff, come to the point."

"It was simple enough," said Allhoff. "All Leroy had to do was to give Miss Dale about twenty minutes to get to town. That twenty minutes would also be time enough for the maid and the cook to begin their laundry chores. It also permitted time enough for that W.P.A.

road gang to go to work."

I watched him closely. From the hard twisted expression of his face I knew he wasn't bluffing this time.

"So in twenty minutes," he continued, "Leroy entered that study again. He fired two shots out the window. Those two shots were heard by the servants and the W.P.A. boys. They all came running along to investigate. Leroy—"

"Wait a minute." I said. "If Leroy fired two more shots there would have been four bullets fired from the gun in Harry Welch's hand. There were only two."

"You're a fool," said Allhoff quite amiably. "Leroy fired his two shots with another gun entirely. He had plenty of time to hide it, between the time of his notifying the police and their arrival."

"Of course, you've found that gun, Inspector," said Alicia Dale with heavy irony.

"Of course," said Allhoff. "I have it here in my pocket. Leroy, you know, has a rather obvious mind. It seemed logical to me that he'd hide the gun somewhere in the greenhouse. I found it early this morning, buried in a box of humus."

I recalled his sallying forth to bid a bright good-morning to the flowers and kept my mouth shut.

"Leroy," continued Allhoff, "took his own sweet time about calling the coppers with the result that the medical examiner arrived on the scene over an hour later. Of course, he couldn't ascertain the time of death within twenty minutes or so. So, Miss Dale had her alibi. Leroy needed none. He had no motive."

Alicia Dale smiled pleasantly at him. "I had no motive either, Inspector," she said. "You overlook that."

"The hell you didn't," said Allhoff. "You wanted to get your fingers on the Gerson estate."

"But listen," said Amberson. "The Gerson money goes to that illegitimate kid in Illinois."

"A little thing like that doesn't bother the inspector," said Alicia Dale. "I've already sent the kid a poisoned lollipop. The inspector's coming to that, aren't you, Inspector?"

"You never knew there was a kid in Illinois," said Allhoff. "Not until Amberson told you yesterday afternoon."

"But she said—" I began, when he interrupted me.

"I know what she said. I've already told you she thinks like a rattlesnake strikes. The fact of the money going to that kid was a body-blow to her. But she never showed it. She pretended at once that she'd known it all the time. The instant she lost the money, she pretended knowledge of the will and immediately lost the motive as well."

Alicia Dale lit a second cigarette from the butt of the first one. Her hands were as steady as the West Wall before Gamelin began pecking at it.

"Let me finish that theory for you, Inspector," she said evenly. "Realizing I'd lost the estate I became very angry, so angry that I decided to kill Peter Lovelace just for spite. Is that it?"

"Partly," said Allhoff. "You killed Lovelace. But not for spite. You killed him through ignorance."

"My theories can't keep up with yours," she said. "You'd better explain that one."

"I will," said Allhoff, "When you realized you weren't going to get the Gerson money, you began to worry. One reason was that you'd be unable to keep your bargain with Leroy, pay him whatever you promised him. So you needed cash to get away before anyone could break him down."

"So I held up Uncle Peter?" she suggested brightly.

"No," said Allhoff. "You knew that there was money, valuables of some sort in that safe behind the bookcase. You didn't bother to take it yesterday because you were sure it would revert to you legally and legitimately when the will was probated. But when you found it didn't, you decided to take it yourself last night."

"What's that got to do with Lovelace?" asked Kline.

"Lovelace opened the study door as Miss Dale was rifling the safe. She realized at once that if there were a witness to what she was doing, I might well figure out why she was doing it. So she shot Lovelace, ran from the study, up the backstairs to her room."

"Allhoff," I said, "that won't do. Lovelace was no witness to what she was doing. He—"

"Sure," said Allhoff. "I know. But Miss Dale didn't. She was out of the room when Amberson told us about it yesterday. She doesn't even know it now."

"Know what?" asked Alicia Dale as now for the first time I caught some tension in her tone.

Leroy lifted his head from his hand and told her in an agonized voice. "He was blind, Alicia! He was blind. My God he couldn't see what you were doing."

He groaned and replaced his head in his hands. I thought the girl had paled a little but her bearing was that of Queen Mary.

"It sounds very good, Inspector," she said. "But I don't quite understand what a blind man was doing wandering about a strange house in the middle of the night."

"That had me worried for a little while," said Allhoff. "Then I remembered something. Leroy brought him into the house after the rest of us had gone to bed. Undoubtedly, he asked to use the lavatory, to clean up after his trip. Leroy showed him to the one next door to the study. During the night he wanted to use the lavatory again. The one downstairs was the only one he knew the location of. He tried to find his way there."

"And got the wrong door," said Amberson eagerly. "Opened the study door by mistake."

Alicia Dale crushed out her cigarette in a hammered-silver ash-tray. She looked Allhoff squarely in the eye and said in an even, low voice: "Are you quite sure of all this, Inspector?"

Allhoff's tone was soaring and triumphant. "I can prove it," he said. "Before a jury composed of the Skeptics Society and foremanned by Robert Ingersoll, I could prove it."

"Suppose you do?"

Allhoff leveled a forefinger at her. "Last night," he said, "you took from that safe exactly four thousand three hundred and eighty-five dollars in cash. Six thousand dollar Arkansas Railroad Bonds, and a diamond necklace that had belonged to Gerson's family. Furthermore, you left fingerprints all over them."

It still didn't seem right to me. Murderess or no, Alicia Dale wasn't dumb enough to hide the stuff in a place where Allhoff could have dug it up so soon.

"This is a big house," said Allhoff. "There's a lot of acreage surrounding it. That gave you the edge. It might have taken me weeks to find what you took from the safe. I didn't want to spend the time."

"Then," I demanded impatiently, "how do you know what the loot consisted of? How do you know Miss Dale's fingerprints are on it?"

Allhoff grinned unpleasantly. "Since I didn't want to search for the missing items." he said, "I gave Miss Dale an opportunity to produce them for me. Miss Dale has a habit of thinking quickly. She thought quickly enough to take advantage of that opportunity."

"Goodness gracious!" said Jonas Kline. "What are you talking about, Inspector?"

"Those Christmas presents of mine," said Allhoff. "The telephone book, the dirty sheet and the glass tumbler I so neatly wrapped up, addressed at random, and had Battersly take out with him."

"Allhoff." I said wearily. "Will you stop talking Choctaw."

"It's not Choctaw to Miss Dale," he said. "Is it?"

I looked at the girl. Though she still held on to her magnificent poise, her face was pale and her lips compressed.

"You will remember," said Allhoff to the rest of us, "that I did not tell Battersly how many packages I would leave for him. You will note further that I announced I would be resting in my room at the time he

picked them up. Those two facts offered a golden opportunity to Miss Dale. She took it."

At last I saw it. I said, grudgingly: "So Miss Dale, knowing the house would be searched and desiring to get that incriminating stuff out, wrapped it up as a Christmas package and put it with your stuff so Battersly would mail it for her?"

"Right," said Allhoff, "She addressed it to some place where she could pick it up at her convenience. But in the meantime, I called headquarters—the I-bureau. Told them to get hold of Battersly at his apartment. Told them to check the prints on the loot with the prints on a tumbler I'd sent in one of my packages. It was a tumbler Miss. Dale had used while cleaning her teeth this morning."

"You've a lot of clues, Inspector," she said. "You've done a lot of ingenious reasoning. But it won't look any too strong on an indictment."

"Perhaps not," said Allhoff, "But I've provided for that." He leered at her. "I made Leroy believe I'd frame him for murder. I pointed out to him that since Miss Dale did not inherit the Gerson money she would be in no position to help him financially. Then, when I slapped a typewritten statement under his nose, detailing exactly how the crime had been committed, he cracked."

"Then that wasn't a confession of murder he signed?"

"No," said Allhoff, "Accessory after the fact. That's bad enough, but Leroy didn't know it, Leroy can turn state's evidence now. He can help send Miss Dale to the chair."

Up to this point, Allhoff had remained remarkably calm. Now he leaned far forward over his desk. He glared at Alicia Dale and his wicked little eyes burned.

"You came to my office." he said. "You insulted me. You mocked the loss of my legs. You jeered at me. You derided me. Well, you'll burn now. I hope you'll remember, when they strap you in the chair, that Inspector Allhoff sent you there! I hope you keep remembering while you burn in hell!"

His manner indicated that the State of New York was about to electrocute Alicia Dale for contempt of Allhoff rather than for first-degree murder.

It was then the girl cracked. The garments of Boadicea fell from her like a chrysalis from a butterfly. Her lip quivered. Her eyes were suddenly moist. She moaned and fell back in her chair.

Allhoff regarded her with a horrible grin, then he snatched up the telephone from the desk, called the precinct house, and demanded a wagon. From the savage triumph in his little eyes, I knew he was having a very merry Christmas.

Then, as he hung up the receiver a horrible suspicion occurred to me.

"Allhoff," I said. "Did you send Battersly away from here merely to—"

"I sent Battersly out on departmental business," he snapped, glaring at me.

My suspicion became a crystallized fact. "You mean you're not granting him a week's leave? You mean—"

"We're in the police department," said Allhoff, "not a kindergarten. I told him he could go home to provide a logical excuse for his carrying those packages out of the house. I told headquarters to rescind that permission when they went to his apartment."

I felt physically sick at that. "Allhoff," I said bitterly, "how can you build the kid up like that and then let him down? Haven't you a single decent instinct? After all, it's—"

"It's Christmas," said Allhoff, "You don't have to tell me again. And once it was the thirteenth of May."

There was hate and bitterness in his gaze. May 13th was the date upon which his legs had been amputated. And all the words in the world would never assuage the wound that operation had opened in his soul. I was still looking at him, feeling utterly frustrated, when we heard the howl of a police siren outside.

Allhoff took his eyes from me and stared at Alicia Dale, who cowered in her chair.

"A merry Christmas, Miss Dale," he said, as the coppers pounded at the outside door. "A very Merry Christmas."

SERGEANTS SHOULD NEVER SLEEP

Originally Published - March 1940

CHAPTER ONE

Yes-Man in Uniform

It was twenty minutes past nine. I had read the morning papers, conned the police reports and thoroughly digested two confidential memoranda sent over from headquarters across the Street. From those last two communications I had extracted information which I knew would interest Allhoff even more than it had interested me. But I wasn't telling him about it yet.

Five minutes ago we had run head-on into a crisis which forced all matters of police routine into the background. Shortly after I had reached my desk, Allhoff had dumped moodily out of his bedroom, climbed into his swivel chair and set the machinery of his electric percolator into action.

Young Battersly, neat and trim in his patrolman's uniform, had arrived just as the coffee began to bubble. He bade Allhoff an unreciprocated good-morning. Allhoff, his cup filled at last, prepared to imbibe his initial draft of the day, when he suddenly discovered nothing but space in the tin can which was supposed to contain the sugar.

At no time was Allhoff's nature anything that Eddie Guest could write a poem about. And in the morning before his second cup of coffee it was even worse than that. With a maniacal shriek he flung the empty can to the floor, hammered his fists on the desk as if it were an anvil. He hurled his whole profane vocabulary like a bolt of lightning at Battersly's hapless head.

Battersly retreated swiftly and strategically to the corner grocery on Lafayette Street, and returned a few moments later with a box of sugar. So now, at last, Allhoff was noisily drinking the black and bitter liquid much in the manner of a misanthropic camel who has come to the first oasis since it left Damascus a week ago last Wednesday.

I estimated it would take at least three cups of the brew to get him to a quiescent stage where he would listen to me. So I silently watched him pour his second cup, filled my pipe and waited.

Outside a cold winter morning. Snow, streaked with dirt, lay piled in the gutters of the city. Inside the cramped two-room tenement flat our oil stove spluttered, giving, more offense to our nostrils than warmth to our bodies.

The door of Allhoff's bedroom was open, revealing an unmade bed with sheets the color of the snow outside. Shirts, drawers and pajamas were strewn across the floor. Opposite my desk stood the metal sink. Plates, cracked with age, yellowed with egg, were piled in depressing array. A half-filled laundry bag slumped under Battersly's chair and a cockroach waddled across the floor toward the garbage can to take pot luck for breakfast.

Allhoff hunched over in his swivel chair pulled up close to his desk. He drank greedily from the chipped cup, then with a sigh replaced it in the saucer. He leaned back in his chair and fished a cigarette from his pocket.

"All right, Simmonds," he said to me. "Now what've we got for today?"

"Hamtrack," I said. "Sergeant Paul Hamtrack of the Headquarters Squad."

Allhoff turned his head around, looked at me suspiciously as if he thought I was trying to be funny.

"What the devil do you mean by that?"

"Sergeant Paul Hamtrack," I repeated, consulting the special memorandum in front of me, "is temporarily transferred from headquarters to special duty under Inspector Allhoff."

The blood was coming into his face now. His little eyes glowed.

"When I want help from headquarters, I'll let them know," he exploded. " I never fell down on any job they ever gave me. Who the hell do they think they are to assign some half-baked Civil Service sergeant to me? Alone, I'm a damn sight better man—"

I grinned at him. "Why don't you wait till you hear the rest of it?"

He subsided while I read verbatim from the paper in my hand.

"Citing the unparalled success of Inspector Allhoff in the solution of cases which have baffled the rest of the Departmental detectives, Sergeant Paul Hamtrack has, this day, requested the Commissioner to assign him temporarily to Inspector Allhoff's staff so that he may study the Inspector's methods at first hand.

"The Commissioner, quite cognizant of Inspector Allhoff's competence and services to the Department has approved this request as of February twenty-ninth."

I looked up from the memorandum. Allhoff's color was normal now. His eyes had lost their fire. He was beaming like a second-rate actor taking his third curtain call. I was sorely tempted to get up, kiss him on both cheeks and pin my prize pistol-shot medal on his breast. However. I restrained myself.

"Well," he said, completely mollified, why didn't you say so in the first place?" I knew the answer to that but I didn't give it to him. Battersly, I noticed, was staring miserably into space, wondering, undoubtedly, how the addition of another member to our triumvirate would affect the situation. For that matter, so was I.

Allhoff picked up the coffee pot, dumped the used grounds into the wastepaper basket and refilled it. Battersly, recognizing his cue, got him fresh water from the sink.

"Well," said Allhoff as he turned on the electric plate, "this Hamtrack guy can't be any dumber than the assistants I have now.

I let that go and told him: "We also have a case."

"Worthy of my talent?"

I looked over at him sharply and decided he wasn't kidding.

"Hardly," I said. "Homicide reports a killing done by a sneak thief. From the data I agree with them."

Allhoff grunted and there was malice in his eyes. Did you used to read Heywood Broun?"

"Sometimes," I said. "Why?"

"Broun once observed," said Allhoff, "that whenever he was doubtful of his stand in any controversy, he waited until Bishop Manning declared himself. Then Broun felt he was fairly safe in taking the opposite view. If he wanted to be doubly certain, he'd wait until Bishop Manning and Nicholas Murray Butler agreed. That would clinch it."

"So?"

"So," said Allhoff. "That's how I feel when you and Homicide see eye to eye."

By this time I realized we were in for a very jolly morning. I went back to the onionskin report on my desk.

"The dead guy," I told him, "was a retired importer. Name of Kling. Milton Kling. Shot in his own study night before last. The killer quite obviously entered through the window, which was open. Ground-floor apartment. Robbery at the point of a gun seems to fit the case. Kling must have put up a fight. He was shot in the head. His wallet and a wrist watch were missing. A ring had been wrenched off his finger. And if that case isn't clear enough, I'll drink a cup of that black hemlock you call coffee."

"If it's as easy as you say," said Allhoff, "why are they sending it over here?"

"Officially, I don't know," I told him. "Unofficially, I got it from Barrow over at the office, that Kling's widow got in to see the commissioner through influential friends. She believes she has some important evidence Homicide didn't get. She's coming over to see you this morning."

"Well," said Allhoff. "I guess we can handle it, eh?"

The caffeine had seeped through his stomach lining and been picked up by the blood stream. For a moment he smiled almost affably. Then his gaze fell upon the sugar tin and he remembered suddenly that he was a persecuted man. With unnecessary clatter he dumped the sugar from its box into the tin, glaring at Battersly as he did so. Battersly sedulously avoided his gaze.

ootfalls sounded on the stairs outside. Knuckles rapped against the panel. Battersly got up, opened the door. A tall stout individual brushed past him into the room. The newcomer wore the uniform of a police sergeant. His metal buttons had been polished like the brass-work on a battleship. His shoes gleamed like moonlit ink, and his golden badge of office was a blinding thing to behold.

He marched up to Allhoff's desk like a West Point flag-bearer, saluted in two precise movements and said: "Sergeant Hamtrack reporting to Inspector Allhoff for duty."

Allhoff blinked up at him. He wasn't used to such military formality but, from the sudden light in his eyes, I knew he liked it.

"Ah, good-morning, Sergeant," he said with unusual cordiality. "I'll have a desk brought over for you later. We're a little crowded here, you know."

Hamtrack remained at attention and said: "Yes, sir."

"We've a case coming over this morning," went on Allhoff. "I understand from the commissioner's memorandum that you admire my methods, that you want to observe them more closely."

Hamtrack smiled like an ingratiating footman. "Yes, *sir,*" he said enthusiastically. "The whole department admires your methods, Inspector. We can all learn from you. I consider it a great privilege to be associated with you."

Battersly and I exchanged a disgusted glance. We already had enough trouble without being saddled with this career yes-man who would further inflate Allhoff's already bursting ego.

I hoped, for a moment, that Allhoff would see through Hamtrack's nauseous flattery and proceed to blast him. But he was grinning from ear to ear as he and Hamtrack agreed on the fine quality of the Allhoff brain.

"Yes, sir," said Hamtrack again. "We're all quite envious of Battersly and Simmonds working here with you, Inspector. Only the other day the whole gang of us over at headquarters quite agreed with Battersly when he said you were the greatest detective that ever walked on two feet."

Something turned over at the pit of my stomach. Battersly winced as if suffering an invisible blow. Allhoff's face flamed like an angry rose. His eyes widened, hot and angry. "He said *what*?" he roared. Battersly, white-faced and biting his lip, stood up. "I never said that, Inspector," he said quietly. "I only said—"

By now Hamtrack saw his error. He made an eleventh-hour move to retrieve it. "He—he mightn't have used those exact words— sir," he said stumblingly. "He simply meant that you were—"

"Shut up!" yelled Allhoff.

He pushed his chair away from the desk with such force that it rolled halfway across the room. At the end of his thighs where his knees should have begun were a pair of leather pads. These he wriggled furiously as he fixed Battersly with a murderous glare.

"You!" he shrieked. "You have the damnable gall to tell headquarters jokes about my legs. You, who cut them off!"

Battersly stood, pale and unmoving under the explosion of Allhoff's tongue. Obscenity piled on obscenity. Bitter epithet hurled itself on savage insult until, at last, I could stand it no more.

"Battersly," I said. "Go downstairs and get me some tobacco. Take your time. I'm in no hurry for it."

That served to divert Allhoff's attack to me while Battersly hastily made his way out of the room.

"So," yelled Allhoff. "You're on his side, too! Persecuting a legless man! You—"

I sat down at my desk again and closed my ears. It was a trick at which I was unusually proficient. All the bitterness that the years had stored up in Allhoff's soul was being distilled into savage sentences. I knew there was nothing short of a bullet in the head that would stop him. And there were several times when my trigger finger itched to fire that shot.

It had all begun several years back during a surprise raid on a gangster hideout on upper West End Avenue. Allhoff was in charge of the squad. Battersly, a raw recruit on his first real assignment. Battersly's orders had been to affect an entrance through the rear at zero hour, to disable the machine-gunner whom we believed was covering the front door from the stairway. Battersly got in all right. Then he underwent an understandable attack of buck fever. Instead of carrying out his assignment, he remained frozen on the back stairway as Allhoff, at the head of his men, came charging in the front.

The chief result had been a spray of machine-gun bullets that buried themselves in Allhoff's legs. Gangrene and amputation had followed in that order.

But if Allhoff had lost his legs he had gained a terrible compensatory bitterness. Never a congenial companion, he had developed into a savage misanthrope, a complete psychopath, and the finest detective inspector in all the metropolis. His two passions were coffee, of which he drank three quarts a day, and an awful compulsion to make Battersly suffer for the loss of his legs.

Of course, a legless inspector was something that would have tossed all the civil-service requirements out the window. But the commissioner was not going to be deprived of his best brain because of any physical disability. He had arranged, through devious politics in the comptroller's office that Allhoff receive his old pay. Allhoff, himself, had taken this dilapidated tenement apartment because of its proximity to headquarters. He had demanded as his pound of flesh that Battersly be assigned as his assistant.

I had been transferred from a good job uptown to do his paper work. That was a sinecure. The other part of my job was to keep Allhoff from Battersly's throat, to pour oil on the troubled waters whenever the storm broke. Which it did—far too often for comfort.

Now, with a glib yes-artist like Hamtrack blundering about the place, my task was going to be even harder than before.

It struck me as odd that Allhoff had not seen through Hamtrack's transparent flattery. Even odder that he had not raised several kinds of particular hell when Hamtrack made his tactless crack about his feet. But he hadn't. As a matter of fact he was far more cordial to the new arrival than he had ever been to me.

CHAPTER TWO

"Someone's Going to Burn"

It was almost noon when a burly copper brought in Mrs. Kling, the widow of the murdered importer. She was a short dark woman of obviously Semitic heritage. Her eyes were black and tragic and it seemed as all the suffering of her race was reflected in her face.

Battersly had taken advice and still had not returned with my tobacco. Hamtrack sat at Battersly's desk, stiff and upright. The burly copper saluted Allhoff and helped the widow into a chair facing his desk. Allhoff waved him out of the room with one hand and poured a cup of coffee with the other.

The widow leaned forward in her chair. There was sorrow in her face. Sorrow and, I thought, a trace of bitter anger. "Listen," she said with a strong accent. "It was no cheap crook that killed Papa. The police are dumb. *Fericht!*" Well, that was a point on which Allhoff wouldn't argue. He spooned sugar into his coffee, stirred it thoughtfully and said: "Tell me about it. Tell me exactly what happened."

The widow opened her mouth to speak. Her face became suddenly red. She gasped as she breathed. She opened her bag, took out a glass bottle of pills and quickly swallowed one, then leaned back in the chair for a moment.

"I am not well," she said apologetically "Pills I must take. Sed—sedatives, the doctor calls them."

Allhoff sipped his coffee and waited. That was not the kind of information that interested him.

Mrs. Kling bent forward in her chair again. She looked at Allhoff with a desperate sort of hope in her eyes.

"No," she said. "I do not believe an ordinary crook killed my Milton."

"But, madam," said Hamtrack in his oily voice.

"Consider the evidence. Consider the fact that your husband's wallet was missing, that his watch and ring were taken."

I glanced over at Allhoff, fully expecting him to blow up like the Royal Oak. When he was working on a case, he expected neither aid nor comment from his assistants. But he seemed so much under Hamtrack's slimy spell that he said nothing.

"It was the money, Inspector," she said.

"If it had been a crook, he would have stolen the money, wouldn't he?" Allhoff put down his coffee cup and evinced a little interest. "Money?" he said. "What money?"

"The money on the desk," she said excitedly. "There was eight hundred dollars on the desk. A blind crook couldn't miss it. But it was still there after my husband was—was dead."

"She took a handkerchief from her bag and held it to her eyes. Allhoff leaned over his desk and came to point like a setter.

"You mean," he said incredulously, "that there was eight hundred dollars in full sight on your husband's desk? That it was still there after the murder?"

The widow nodded her head without removing her handkerchief. I saw her shoulders move slightly, heard the sound of a faint sob.

Allhoff frowned. First at Mrs. Kling, second at Hamtrack, finally—most darkly—at myself.

I knew what he was going to say so I answered him before he said it.

"There's nothing about eight hundred dollars in the police report," I told him. "Apparently Homicide knew nothing about it."

Allhoff grunted, turned back to Mrs. Kling. "Where is this money now?"

She sat up straight again and looked at him through moist eyes. "In my bag. I have it here."

Allhoff slapped his palm on the desk. "Why didn't you tell the police about it?"

"I forgot. I was upset. When I found my husband dying there, I phoned for the ambulance. Then I picked up the money and put it in my bag. I forgot until yesterday when I heard the policeman had said a crook killed Milton. Then I remembered. I knew no crook would leave that money behind."

Allhoff was frowning again. But this time it was perplexity, not rage. "But," he said, "there was a wallet and watch and ring missing?"

"That's right," said Hamtrack. "The police established that beyond all doubt."

Allhoff ignored him. "Can you explain that, Mrs. Kling?"

Mrs. Kling wiped her eyes again. It was obvious she couldn't explain it.

There was a long silence in the room. Allhoff stared at his coffee cup, his brow screwed up in thought. Hamtrack scratched his blond head, pretending he, too, was thinking. I grappled with the problem for a moment, then quickly gave it up.

Hamtrack spoke first. "If the inspector doesn't mind," he said deferentially, "I believe I have a theory which will fit the facts."

Allhoff looked at him over the edge of his coffee cup. There was a danger signal in his eyes but Sergeant Hamtrack didn't see it.

"Yes," he went on, "I've got something. The killer enters through the window. Motive—robbery. He sees the money on the desk and intends to take it. He puts his gun up against Kling, demands his watch, wallet and ring, intending to take the money last. Kling hands over the first three articles and by that time has got over his first shock. When the crook reaches for the cash, Kling fights, gives the alarm. The crook kills him, gets panicky and flees, leaving the money behind him."

He stopped and looked around the room like a bright pupil who has just answered all the questions. Much as I hated to admit it, it sounded logical.

Allhoff shook his head. "No," he said. "I don't like it."

"Why not?" I asked him.

"It's too damned easy," said Allhoff.

Hamtrack, unaccustomed to the Allhoff thought processes, blinked at that. It was a typical Allhoff remark.

Mrs. Kling nodded her head emphatically. "You're right, Inspector," she said. "I know it wasn't no crook who did it. I know it. I know it."

Her insistence on the point was remarkable. But I had observed enough recent widows to realize they are mentally and emotionally overwrought.

I could tell from Hamtrack's expression that he had accepted his own solution of the problem and had ceased thinking about it. For that matter, so had I. But Allhoff still frowned into his coffee cup as if the answer lay in the depths of the dark liquid within.

The outer door opened suddenly and Battersly came back. He had with him my tobacco, a man and a woman. He put the tobacco tin on my desk and conducted the couple over to Allhoff.

"Inspector Allhoff," he announced.

"This is Mr. and Mrs. Arnold Pearl. They, have some important information in the Kling murder. Headquarters told me to bring them over."

We all looked at Mr. and Mrs. Pearl. Pearl was slim-waisted, and light-complexioned. He was well dressed and there was cold intelligence in his blue eyes. His wife was plump, handsome and very well dressed. It seemed to me that we were acquiring one hell of a lot of witnesses for a petty hold-up case.

Battersly dragged two chairs out of the bedroom and Mr. and Mrs. Pearl sat down. Allhoff introduced them to the Kling widow, then got right down to business.

"All right, Pearl," he said. "What is it?"

Pearl sighed, exchanged a swift glance with his wife and said: "It's a hard thing to tell you, Inspector but it's my duty."

"The eradication of crime is every citizen's duty," said Hamtrack glibly, quoting without credit from the editorial in yesterday's *World-Telegram.*

Pearl rubbed a hand over a lean jaw. "Many years ago," he said, "I had a very good friend. He has been dead for some time. A week ago, his son came to our apartment. He was broke, ragged. and hungry. We took him in."

Well, we certainly were going far afield from the Kling murder and I expected Allhoff to comment on it. But he didn't. He poured more coffee and remained strangely silent.

"Yes," said Pearl's wife. "We took him in, Inspector. Treated him like one of the family. I never would have thought it of him. He seemed like such a quiet sort. He—"

Allhoff held up a hand. That sort of feminine chatter drove him mad. He said, pointedly, "Go on, Mr. Pearl."

"Well," said Pearl. "As my wife says, he seemed a nice boy. But a few nights ago, he found a bottle of wine on the sideboard and got pretty drunk. That seemed to change him. I was away from home at the time or perhaps I could have done something about it."

Allhoff slapped his coffee cup down in the saucer with a bang. "Done something about what?" he demanded. "For the love of heaven will you come to the point?"

"He had a gun," said Pearl. "He showed it to my wife. He boasted drunkenly that although he was broke he always knew how to get money. He announced he was going out and hold someone up."

"So," said Allhoff slowly. "He went out and held up Milton Kling."

But Pearl wasn't going to be hurried. "My wife tried to stop him," he went on, "but she couldn't. The boy went out of the house with his gun. Now, since I didn't come back home until the whole thing was over, I think my wife better tell you what happened."

Reluctantly Allhoff turned to Mrs. Pearl. Eagerly she took up the story.

"He came back to the house about an hour later. He had sobered up and he seemed scared to death. I asked him what the matter was. He told me he had climbed through a ground-floor window of a house on Eighty-eighth Street. He had seen some money on the desk through the window. There was an elderly man there who seemed frightened at the sight of the gun. The man gave up his watch, ring and wallet. Then he got over his fright and began to fight."

"That's right," said Pearl. "So the boy shot him. Then he got panicky and ran away leaving the money on the desk."

I looked around the room. Hamtrack smiled with a superior air. He had explained all this theoretically before we had the facts. He had thought faster than the great Allhoff. And Allhoff wasn't going to like that at all.

Mrs. Kling was staring at Pearl. Her deep tragic eyes had a darker shadow in them. Her face was set oddly and her whole body seemed tense.

Allhoff growled, "So?" over the edge of his coffee cup and Mrs. Pearl continued.

"He came back to the house, took a suitcase and ran away. After he had told me what he had done I begged him to give himself up to the police, or at least to wait for my husband's advice. But he wouldn't do it. He ran away that night."

"It is a very silly thing," said Hamtrack primly, "to bother the inspector with a trivial case like this."

I thought so, too. But I knew Allhoff wouldn't give up without a struggle. He never lost an opportunity to demonstrate Homicide wrong. Besides, if he accepted the obvious explanation of the Kling killing it would make Hamtrack the mister mind instead of himself.

Allhoff put down his cup and addressed Pearl. "What was this boy's name?"

"Levy. Samuel Levy."

Allhoff grunted. "How old?"

"Twenty or thereabouts."

"His father," said Allhoff. "Your old friend. What was his name?"

"The same as the son's," said Pearl. "Samuel Levy."

Allhoff grunted again. "How long's he been dead?"

"About fifteen years."

This cross examination was so futile, it annoyed me. "Allhoff," I said wearily, "the case is cold as a relief investigator's heart. What are you fishing for? A cheap hold-up punk killed Milton Kling and that's an end of it."

Allhoff swung around in his chair and I prepared

myself for the blast—but it never came.

Mrs. Kling stood up. Her face was twisted and her eyes were wild. Her voice touched a hysterical pitch as she spoke.

"No," she cried. "No, It's a lie. No crook killed him. It's a lie! There was no money on the desk. It's all a lie. There wasn't any money on the desk, I tell you!"

She staggered suddenly and her eyes closed. She fumbled at her bag. Battersly sprang to his feet and saved her from falling. Allhoff watched her through narrowed little eyes.

"Take her in the bedroom," he said. "Give her one of those pills."

Battersly carried the woman across the floor to the other room. He laid her on the bed, took the bottle of pills from her bag and went to the sink for a glass of water. Allhoff said: "Mrs. Pearl. you'd better go in there. Loosen her clothing."

Pearl's wife nodded and went into the bedroom. Battersly poured a pill down the stricken woman's throat and came out closing the door behind him.

Hamtrack cleared his throat and said: "Hysterical. Naturally upset about her husband. Doesn't know what she's talking about."

"I'm inclined to think she does," said Allhoff grimly.

"Look here," I said. "Either you accept Pearl's story which explains the money being left on the desk and proves Kling was killed by a petty hold-up artist. Or you believe Mrs. Kling's second statement that there wasn't any money on the desk, but a ring, a watch and a wallet missing. Which also proves Kling was killed by a petty hold-up artist."

"This case," observed Allhoff profoundly, "is getting less and less petty every moment."

Mrs. Pearl came out of the bedroom. "She seems all right now," she announced. "She's conscious and says she feels all right."

Allhoff spoke to me over his shoulder. "Take a look at her, Simmonds. See if she wants a doctor."

I took a look at her. She lay, pale and exhausted on Allhoff's gray pillow. She smiled weakly up me.

"I'll be all right," she said, "if I can just rest here for a little while."

I assured her that she could, closed the door and reported back to Allhoff.

Pearl got up, laid a card on Allhoff's desk, and said: "If you want me, Inspector, there's my address. Anything that I can do—"

Allhoff took the card and waved the Pearls discourteously from the room.

A silence descended. Hamtrack looked expectantly at Allhoff for a while, then, being completely ignored, gave it up. He pulled a Civil Service booklet from his pocket and proceeded to bone up on the lieutenant's examination. Battersly delved into the comic section of the evening paper, while I attended to some routine work. Allhoff gulped down coffee and glared at the wall opposite.

After two hours of this congeniality, he spoke. "Battersly. Get Mrs. Kling out here. There are a few questions I want to ask."

So he hadn't given up. If Hamtrack and Homicide and myself were going to be right, Allhoff wanted more evidence than he'd had yet. Battersly went into the bedroom. He came out again ten seconds later.

"Inspector," he said nervously. "I think—I think she's dead."

I sprang up, raced across the room. At the bed, my fingers felt an unresponsive pulse, touched a breast that had no heartbeat. I came into the other room again to face Allhoff's dark inquiring face.

"Is she?" he asked.

"As Dizzy Dean's arm," I told him.

He smashed his fist on the desk and fury was in his eyes: "Dead!" he yelled. "In my own apartment. Right under my nose. By God, they can't do that to me! The colossal gall. I—"

"Who can't do what?" I asked. "It's simple enough. She probably took an overdose of that sedative. That's all."

"You're a bright little boy," said Allhoff in a savage tone that indicated I wasn't at all. "Bring me her bag."

I brought the bag from the bedroom and laid it on Allhoff's desk. He opened it and withdrew the pill bottle which was empty and a change purse which wasn't. It held precisely eight hundred dollars in bills.

"Ah!" said Hamtrack. "So she wasn't lying about that money on the desk after all."

"Of course not," I said. "Why should the Pearl's invent such a story?"

Allhoff didn't comment. He was staring down at the money and the empty bottle. His lips moved slowly and he said in a scarcely audible voice, "Someone's going to burn for this."

"Who?" I asked him.

He swung around and fixed me with his little slit-eyes. "Ask me in forty-eight hours," he said. "I'll tell you then."

"Are you a gambling man?" I asked.

"A month's pay," he said. "Mine against yours." Then he rubbed it in a little, and added: "That's odds enough."

CHAPTER THREE

The Dead Diamond Merchant

I arrived downtown the following morning to see Battersly already at his desk and Allhoff thumbing the onionskin police reports that had come from across the street. The mess in his saucer indicated he had already had his first quart of coffee. Hamtrack wasn't in evidence.

"Listen," said Allhoff as I took off my hat and coat. "There was a guy killed last night. Jacob Weinberg. A diamond merchant."

"The hell there was," I told him. "It was a suicide. I just read the morning paper."

"I'm going to prove differently," said Allhoff.

"Listen to me," I said wearily. "Won't you ever let Homicide be right? Doesn't the law of averages work for them, too? You're sore as hell because both Hamtrack and Homicide out-theoried you yesterday. Now, you're out to show them that what they call a suicide is a murder. Well, you can't do it. That guy—what's his name? Weinberg? He even left a death note behind him. Written in Hebrew, too."

"Exactly," said Allhoff. "Did you read the note?"

"No. It wasn't in the paper."

"All right," he said, handing me a typewritten piece of paper. "Here it is. Fresh from the interpreter."

I took the sheet from him and read aloud: *"Friends, good-bye. Welcome is death. Sad and old am I."*

"Well," said Allhoff, "and what do you make of that?"

I shrugged my shoulders. "It isn't the clearest literary construction in the world. But the meaning is plain enough. He's a tired old man and he kills himself."

"Maybe," put in Battersly, "it's written in Hebrew idiom."

Allhoff laughed — unpleasantly and without mirth. "You've each got an assignment," he said. "You, Simmonds, get up to Kling's apartment. Question everyone you find there. Bring back any and all of Kling's personal effects you find. Battersly, you do exactly the same thing at Jacob Weinberg's residence."

"Listen," I said, "what are you expecting from us? A miracle for you to use to put Homicide in its place? You have absolutely nothing to connect the Kling and Weinberg killings. Furthermore, you have absolutely nothing to indicate that the first wasn't a stick-up, the

second a suicide. Besides, if you want someone to go out on a wild-goose chase, send your pal, Hamtrack. I've got work to do."

Allhoff picked up his copy of the day's *Police Departmental Orders.* He ran his finger halfway down the sheet, then looked up at me and read aloud.

"Patrolman Roberts, Harold. Badge number 58346. 11th Precinct. Refusal to obey a superior's Orders. Fined two months pay. Sixty day's suspension. Loss of twenty places on the promotion list."

He put down the paper, stared at me with his hateful little eyes. "Are you going uptown, Sergeant Simmonds?"

I was licked and I knew it. "I'm going uptown," I told him. "And I hope to God I don't find anything."

I went downstairs with Battersly, wondering how much longer it would be before I cracked completely and smashed my fist into Allhoff's ugly, arrogant face.

I took my time and it was almost half past two when I returned to the tenement. Hamtrack had arrived and was busily engaged in looking over the scrapbook which recorded the magnificent feats of Inspector Allhoff. Every minute or so he would look up and congratulate Allhoff, who sat beaming at him over a cup of coffee. From the appearance of things, Allhoff had at last discovered a blood brother.

I tossed a package of papers on his desk. "Nothing," I announced triumphantly. "Absolutely nothing except a ream of innocuous personal correspondence and a batch of international postal-money-order receipts."

"Receipts?" said Allhoff. "Money orders? Sent where?"

"Holland mostly," I told him. "A few to Belgium."

"Ah," he said, unwrapping the package. "I rather expected that."

"You are an unqualified liar," I told him. "You expected nothing and you got it. Weinberg was a diamond merchant, wasn't he? Diamonds are bought in Europe. Holland, principally, aren't they? So what?"

I walked over to my desk and sat down. Before Allhoff could answer me, Battersly came in. He, too, was armed with a mass of documents.

"Well," said Allhoff. "And what've you got? Money-order receipts, too?"

Battersly's normally wide eyes opened wider. "Why, yes," he said. "How did you know?"

"To what countries were the orders sent?"

"Denmark and Switzerland. Why?"

"Allhoff," I said. "You're not kidding me. Kling

was an importer, wasn't he? Why shouldn't he send money abroad?"

"Why should superannuated sergeants ask damnfool questions?" said Allhoff. Then, to Battersly, "What else?"

"A screwy housekeeper," said Battersly. "But I think you can discount her testimony."

"You think?" howled Allhoff. He drew a deep breath to continue but teacher's pet, Hamtrack, got his word in first.

"I should think the inspector's the best judge of whether testimony is important or not," he said with the air of an impecunious clergyman endorsing the bishop.

Allhoff smiled upon him, then turned back to Battersly, who continued.

"This housekeeper told me Weinberg had a visitor earlier in the evening—before she went out to the movies. Weinberg let him in so she didn't see him. But she heard them arguing in the study. She heard Weinberg say—" Battersly paused and consulted his notebook—"something about how no one who knew the names would give them out. Then Weinberg said that the visitor had just taken another four hundred million dollars from him. Then the housekeeper went out to the theater and didn't hear anything else."

Allhoff digested this information in silence. Then he asked suddenly: "And why do you say the housekeeper is crazy?"

"Because," said Battersly, "how could any crook get four hundred million dollars from anyone. No one has that much money."

Allhoff poured himself another cup of coffee. He was registering deep thought. But I still believed it was an act to impress Hamtrack and myself.

"Allhoff," I said, "what's your intense interest in these two murders? They're petty enough no matter who did them. Why don't you leave it to Homicide?"

"Homicide," snorted Allhoff. "Leave it to Homicide and the whole town'll be wiped out. Besides, I don't like to see Jewish people killed. A lot of my best friends are Jews and," he added cryptically, "some of the most influential."

He spent the next half-hour examining the papers Battersly and I had dug up for him. Then at four o'clock he looked at his watch, pushed his cup and saucer away from him and made an announcement.

"Tomorrow," he said, "Simmonds and Battersly will round up Weinberg's housekeeper. Mr. and Mrs. Pearl must be brought here, too. I want them not later than three o'clock in the afternoon."

Hamtrack smiled over at Allhoff and said: "Is there anything I can do, Inspector?"

"Indeed there is," said Allhoff. "I've been saving the most important assignment for you, Sergeant."

Hamtrack's smile grew broader and more servile, if possible. "Yes, *sir,*" he said. "Anything at all, Inspector."

"You will proceed immediately," said Allhoff, "to Seventeen East Thirty-sixth Street. You will take up your position outside that building. You will remain there until eight o'clock tomorrow morning. Then you will report here to me at nine."

Hamtrack blinked at him. "And what am I looking for, Inspector?"

"Suspicious happenings," said Allhoff. "Particularly watch out for a man in a camel-hair coat. If any such person loiters around the building, call the beat copper and have him booked for disorderly conduct. Record such arrests in your notebook and when you report to me in the morning, I'll take care of them."

Hamtrack, I knew, was as bewildered as Battersly and myself. But he pulled himself together, saluted stiffly, said, "Yes, sir," and walked out of the room.

There was a hard ironic smile on Allhoff's face as he listened to the diminuendo footsteps on the stairs.

"Allhoff," I said. "Have you gone crazy?"

"Sure," he said without turning around. "Like Einstein."

"Seventeen East Thirty-sixth Street," I told him, "is the Second Federated Bank. Will you please tell me what in the name of God that has to do with the deaths of Weinberg and Kling?"

Allhoff gave me a twisted, bitter grin. "Nothing," he said. "Absolutely nothing."

CHAPTER FOUR

The $400,000,000

Battersly and I were at our desks and Allhoff was working on his first cup of coffee the next day when Hamtrack came in. Obviously he had been to a barber's but despite his shave and massage, his face looked tired. His eyes were red and sleepy.

"I got him, sir, he announced as he entered the door. "Picked him up about four this morning. He's in the Tombs right now."

Allhoff looked up from his coffee. "Got who?" he said. "Who's in the Tombs?"

"The man in the camel-hair coat," said Hamtrack triumphantly.

"Oh," said Allhoff. "Him." Hamtrack, a little miffed that Allhoff hadn't congratulated him, lapsed into silence. Allhoff remained engrossed in his coffee and his thoughts for an hour or more, and a beautiful serenity reigned over the sordid tenement apartment.

Then Allhoff came suddenly out of his reverie. "Sergeant Hamtrack," he snapped.

Hamtrack sprang out of his chair like the mechanical man, saluted and said "Sir?"

"You did very well last night," said Allhoff. "I'm very happy about your work. Now, since you've had no sleep, and a I'll need you this afternoon, I want you to get some rest. Go in my bedroom there, and lie down."

Battersly and I stared at his back. Allhoff considering someone else's comfort was utterly unheard of.

"There's a closet by the head of the bed," said Allhoff. "You can hang you clothes up there. I'll give you a call about two o'clock."

Hamtrack rubbed his sleepy eyes and thanked him profusely. I watched Allhoff suspiciously. Whenever he got benign, I felt nervous. It usually presaged something particularly terrible.

"Simmonds," he said to me. "Take Battersly with you and get out of here. Have your lunch. Then get those people down. Take your time. Get yourselves a drink in Noonan's on me. Here."

He handed me a dollar bill. Shocked to the very core of my nervous system I took it.

"Allhoff," I said. "This is unprecedented."

He made a peculiar strangling sound, looked at him for a moment and decide he was laughing.

"Well," I said, "what's so riotously funny?"

"There's a man with a camel-hair coat in the Tombs," said Allhoff, and his roaring laughter filled the room.

It echoed after us as we went out.

It was late afternoon when the company assembled. Hamtrack, Battersly and myself were at the rear of the room, facing Allhoff's back and the people beyond him. The Pearls sat side by side on a pair of battered Windsor chairs. On their right Weinberg's housekeeper, Mrs. Everard, wrinkled her Irish nose in manifest disapproval of the domestic disorder room. At Allhoff's right was a tall, distinguished man with a vandyke beard, Judge Irving Rose of the State Supreme Court.

Heaven only knew what hat Allhoff had pulled the judge out of, and why. He had arrived with the air of a man who has an appointment and Allhoff had apparently been expecting him. The others had trickled in shortly afterwards.

Now Allhoff sat like a Roman magistrate prepared to deal out justice. The lifted coffee cup in his hand, the *fasces* of his office. We watched him expectantly and he thoroughly enjoyed it. He was very cocky and it irritated me.

"Now," he said as he put the empty cup back in the sloppy saucer, "we are here to solve three murders. Those of Milton Kling, his widow and Jacob Weinberg."

Pearl smiled uncertainly. "I was under the impression I'd already explained one of them," he said.

"And I can explain the other two," I put in. "Weinberg was a suicide as indicated in his own note and Mrs. Kling died from an overdose of sedative. The medical examiner, incidentally, corroborated that this afternoon, Allhoff."

Allhoff swung around in his swivel chair and fixed me with eyes that were hard and relentless. "Your explanation, Simmonds," he said, "is as inaccurate as that of Mr. Pearl. The prime difference is, while you are merely stupid, Pearl is a downright liar." He swung around in the chair again and said very politely: "Aren't you, Mr. Pearl?"

Pearl flushed. "I resent this, inspector," he said hotly. "I reported what I knew to the police because it was my duty as a citizen. It wasn't too easy to turn in the son of an old friend."

"There never was an old friend," said Allhoff. "There never was a son."

If ever there was a fact that couldn't be checked on, this was it.

"You're prepared to prove that?" I asked him.

"I'm prepared to prove it," said Allhoff.

"That's utterly ridiculous," said Pearl, "How can you prove that I never had a friend named Sam Levy? How can you prove he didn't have a son?"

"If there ever was a Samuel Levy," said Allhoff, "if he ever had a son, that son's name was not Samuel Levy."

"What've you been doing?" I asked him. "Peeping into your crystal ball?"

Judge Rose cleared his throat. "The inspector is right," he said. "Jewish families never name their children after living relatives."

No one spoke as Allhoff reached for the percolator and filled his cup. Pearl and his wife were staring at him, The judge had an odd bitter expression on his face. Mrs. Everard gazed at the pile of dishes in the sink with mounting horror.

"Perhaps," suggested Hamtrack, "the Levys weren't at all orthodox. Perhaps they paid no attention to the customs and religion of their race. After all, Inspector, why should Mr. and Mrs. Pearl invent such a story?"

"That's easy," said Allhoff. "In order to cope with the story about the eight hundred dollars that Mrs. Kling invented."

"Invented?" I said. "The money was in her bag, wasn't it?"

"There was money in her bag," said Allhoff. "Money she drew out of the bank the day *after* her husband was killed. I've checked the withdrawal."

"Well," I said, not having the slightest idea what he was driving at, "if Pearl invented a story to counteract a lie of Mrs. Kling's, why the hell did she invent *her* story?"

"That," said Allhoff smugly, "took me almost twenty-four hours to figure out."

"The way you're talking," I told him, "it's going to take you twenty-four hours to tell us about it."

"All right," said Allhoff, "consider this. Milton Kling is murdered. The killing is made to look as if it had been done by a petty hold-up man. Mrs. Kling knows that isn't true. She has a very good idea who killed her husband. She has an excellent idea why. So she cooks up that story about eight hundred dollars lying on the desk. From that fact the police *may* conclude that it wasn't a stick-up artist that killed her husband at all."

"That's positively profound?" I told him. "So if she knows who killed her husband why doesn't she just tell us the guy's name?"

"First," said Allhoff, "she doesn't know it. Second, she's sworn an oath of secrecy and third, she's frightened to death."

"Listen, Inspector," said Pearl. "Do you mind telling us what the hell you're talking about?"

Allhoff sighed and fixed Pearl with his little eyes.

"Kling is killed," he said in the weary tone of a man explaining something to an idiot. "The police decide a thief killed him. His wife knows better. Afraid to tell the police what she does know, she tells that tale about the overlooked cash. That, she reasons, will force the police to discard their original theory and perhaps get to the truth of the matter."

"So?" I said.

"So," said Allhoff, "Pearl, here, and his principals are as strongly in favor of the hold-up theory as Mrs. Kling is against it. Hence, Pearl invents his own story about Samuel Levy to counteract Mrs. Kling's story about the money."

"I see," I said slowly. "That Sam Levy story still makes it look like a hold-up even though money *had* been left on the desk."

"Now," said Allhoff, "let's get on to Weinberg."

The Pearls were staring at Allhoff as he filled his coffee cup. There seemed to be a quiet confidence on Pearl's face and I thought I knew the reason. No matter how correct Allhoff's theory might be, there was absolutely nothing that put the finger on Pearl, and he knew it.

"Weinberg," said Allhoff, "is supposed to leave a suicide note behind him before he blows his brains out. Very pretty. Weinberg who was something of a Hebrew scholar turns out an exceedingly screwy note. It reads, in case you have forgotten: *Friends, good-bye. Welcome is death. Sad and old am I.* Your knowledge of Jewish culture, Pearl, is appalling."

Pearl's wife held on to his arm. She stared at Allhoff with wide and frightened eyes.

"If you're making an accusation," said Pearl coldly, "please do so in understandable English."

"All right," said Allhoff, "I will. You wrote that suicide note, Pearl. You wrote it in Hebrew, copying it word for word out of an English-Hebrew dictionary. The construction is screwy because you wrote it backwards. You wrote it from left to right just as English is written. Neither Hebrew nor Arabic are written that way. They are written from right to left."

I lit my pipe and observed that Allhoff was beginning to make some sense.

"So," I said, "the interpreter naturally translated it from right to left since he was reading Hebrew. Reversed, it would read—*I am old and sad. Death is welcome. Good-bye, friends.*"

"That's how Pearl meant it to read," said Allhoff. "He's a very illiterate murderer."

The judge was looking at Pearl and there was a terrible expression on his face. Pearl shifted uncomfortably beneath his scrutiny. He said: "You're a fool, Inspector. What possible motive could I have for killing either Kling or Weinberg. I never even knew the men."

"That's quite true," said Allhoff. "You didn't."

Battersly, Hamtrack and myself exchanged glances. After all, you can't have a murderer without a motive and you can't have a motive, save robbery, if the accused doesn't know the victim. But Allhoff seemed very sure of himself.

"Judge Rose and Mrs. Everard are here to establish the motive for me," he said. "First, Mrs. Everard."

The housekeeper who had been looking at the disorder of the apartment much in the manner of a society matron examining a stable, gave Allhoff her attention for the first time.

"You said, Mrs. Everard, that Mr. Weinberg had a caller early on the evening that he died."

Mrs. Everard shook her head emphatically and her earrings jingled. "He did that."

"You said, further," continued Allhoff, "that you overheard two fragments of conversation from the Weinberg study. Once you heard Mr. Weinberg say, 'No one who knows the names will talk.' Is that correct?"

Mrs. Everard conceded that it was correct.

"Now," said Allhoff consulting a sheet of paper before him. "You also heard Weinberg say, 'And you've just taken another four hundred million from me.' Is that right?"

Mrs. Everard attested that was right.

"Now think," said Allhoff. "Think hard, Mrs. Everard. Is it possible that you've made a slight mistake? Is it possible that Weinberg could have said, 'You've taken another four hundred million from us?' Us instead of me?"

Mrs. Everard screwed up her brow and thought. "It's quite possible," she said at last. "As a matter of fact, I think he did say 'Us.'"

Allhoff looked triumphantly around the room. "There," he said. "Add those facts to the money-order receipts. Money orders sent to Denmark, Switzerland Belgium and Holland. There's your motive."

With the exception of the judge who still stared with terrible intentness at Pearl, everyone seemed as baffled as myself.

"Allhoff," I said. "What's whose motive."

He sighed as if the stupidity of the rest us was more than he could bear. "Four hundred million dollars," he said. "It's a lot of money. What does it mean to you?" I rolled that over in my mind. It didn't mean anything at all to me and I was about to say so when Battersly spoke excitedly.

"It was the last levy," he said. "Hitler's levy on the Jews of Germany. Last October."

"Click," said Allhoff. "So Weinberg said to his visitor, 'You've just taken another four hundred million from us.' So whom do you think he was talking to?"

"You mean an agent?" I said. "A German agent?"

"Put everything together," said Allhoff.

"See what you get. Four hundred million dollars. One murder that is made to look like a hold-up. Another made to look like a suicide. The fact that Weinberg said that no one who knew the names would tell. Names—get it? It suggests an organization. A secret organization. The fact that Mrs. Kling was afraid to tell what she knew corroborates it."

"Why should she be afraid?" I asked him.

"Why not?" he snapped. "First, perhaps, for her life. Second, the exposure of the organization. Had she told the police what she knew, what she suspected, it is quite probable that Homicide, in its customary blundering way, would have tried to get those names from her for investigation. She didn't want to reveal them. The moment those names were made public every life was in danger."

"Allhoff," I said, puzzled, "what names? What organization?"

"God, you're a fool!" he snarled. He was working himself up to a nice pitch now. "Money orders to border countries in Europe. A list of names Weinberg's killer tried to get from him. What does it add up to? The fact that there is a secret organization of well-to-do Jewish businessmen who finance the exodus of Jewish goods, Jewish people from Germany. How they do it, or why, I don't care."

"Wait a minute, Allhoff," I said. "This is all conjecture, isn't it?"

"Of course not. As soon as I figured out what must be the answer, I went to work on the telephone. I told you that some of my best and most influential friends were Jews. I phoned a number of them. I asked them all the same question—the question that I have already asked Judge Rose."

"And that question?" asked Pearl in a low tone.

"I asked them," Allhoff said, "whether or not there was such an organization as I suspected. I asked them if Kling and Weinberg were members. I promised that if they answered me truthfully I would ask no more questions. I would not ask the names of other members nor the duties of the organization. Judge Rose had already answered me. .. . Judge."

Judge Rose answered him without taking his eyes from Pearl. "The inspector is right. There is a secret organization of my people. Milton Kling and Jacob Weinberg belonged to it. I am forbidden to speak of the purposes or the living membership of the organization. For it has certain political enemies who have sworn to kill each member."

I noted that Pearl's wife held his arm more tightly. Mrs. Everard stared at the couple. At last something had happened which interested her more than Allhoff's housekeeping.

"To recapitulate," said Allhoff. "Pearl assigned by his principals to wreck this organization somehow found out that Kling and Weinberg belonged to it. He killed Kling, planted the evidence to make it look like a hold-up. When Mrs. Kling invented the story of the money on the desk, Pearl invented another story to explain how his mythical hold-up man overlooked it. Fearing Mrs. Kling might talk after her collapse here, this woman who calls herself Mrs. Pearl, killed her."

Pearl's wife was pale. Her blue eyes stared at Allhoff reflecting the fear in her heart. "No," she said. "No. You can't prove that."

"He can't prove anything," said Pearl.

As I saw it, he had something there.

"Mrs. Kling died from an overdose of sedative," went on Allhoff. "Probably morphine. The M.E. will tell us that later. But when she went into my bedroom her own pill bottle was half full. After she died it was empty. It is incredible she took all those pills herself. It is not incredible that Mrs. Pearl emptied the bottle of Mrs. Kling's own pills and put in one single morphine tablet that she had in her own bag for just such emergences. Mrs. Kling, awakening, would probably take one of her own pills. In her condition she would hardly note the difference in size, or the fact that her supply had been suddenly reduced to a single pill. She took it and died."

"You're guessing now," Pearl said. "You're further away than you were before."

"It is quite customary," said Allhoff, "for persons in Mrs. Pearl's profession to carry a single heavily charged dose of morphine or other poison with them in case of emergencies. Either suicide or murder. Mrs. Kling was the emergency."

Allhoff grinned at him. It was a twisted horrible grin that I had seen before. And it boded no good to its recipient.

"Then," he said, "we come to Weinberg. Pearl called on him, demanded to know the names of his associates, Weinberg wouldn't talk. Pearl killed him and wrote his phony backwards suicide note. There's the whole case."

CHAPTER FIVE

Sergeants Shouldn't Sleep

Allhoff made a gesture with eye brows, hands and shoulders that indicated there was nothing more to it save the making out of the State executioner's check. But as I saw it. Even if he were right, we had a long, long way to go.

The judge had his eyes on Allhoff now and from the expression on his face it was evident that his thoughts were the same as mine.

"Inspector," said Pearl. "it's been quite, an ingenious and amusing story. But if you don't know quite well that you haven't enough evidence to hold me overnight, I'm sure the judge here does."

"Oh," said Allhoff, suspending his cup in mid-air. "The confession will be evidence enough."

"The *what*?" I said.

For the first time in the last hour Pearl seemed highly amused. "And do you really expect me to confess, Inspector?"

Allhoff emptied his cup, replaced it in the saucer and leaned over the desk.

"I expect you to confess," he said. "There are two things of which you are very much afraid, Pearl."

'Namely?" said Pearl.

"The first one," said Allhoff, "is the *Associated Press.*"

"What do you mean?"

"Your government," said Allhoff slowly, "has little regard for human life, Pearl. At the moment they are fighting for their lives. It is of great importance to them that the United States does not become antagonized. All their propaganda strives to make a good impression over here. A newspaper story exposing you and your government as murderers, Pearl, would not make them very happy on the Wilhelmstrasse."

"That's ridiculous," said Pearl, but there wasn't too much assurance in his tone.

"Is it?" said Allhoff. "You were given a job to do. Undoubtedly you were instructed that that job must be done in the utmost secrecy. You bungled it, Pearl. Your government will not like that. You can either confess and stand trial here or you can be deported and handed over to the German headsman. Your blond head will roll off the scaffold, Pearl. You'll have no lawyer. You'll have no trial. Your government will make you the scapegoat in order to appear guiltless itself. Now do you care to fight for your life in an American courtroom or lose it on a German scaffold?"

"It's absurd," said Pearl but his eyes were harried. His voice scarcely audible.

"Maybe we can't convict you in court without a confession," said Allhoff, his little eyes boring like hot diamonds. "But we can convict you in the newspapers. That story will be a blow to your propaganda department, a blow they will never recover from. And they'll make you pay for your failure, Pearl. Your relatives in Germany will find themselves in concentration camps. You'll find yourself on the scaffold, after, of course, the customary torture."

"I—" began Pearl, but Allhoff interrupted him.

"I said there were two things you feared. I am going to use them against you now. In a moment I shall telephone the *Associated Press.* First, I shall make another call."

He picked up the telephone. He said into the mouthpiece: "Bowling Green 9-5285."

Pearl sprang to his feet. There was black terror in his eyes now. "No!" he cried. "No. Don't tell them. I'll confess. I'll—"

Then a voice at his shoulder sounded harsh and commanding. "Hang up that telephone," said Hamtrack. "Sit down. Pearl."

We all stared at Hamtrack. He stood with his back against the sink. His Police Special was in his hand covering us all. I was stupefied with astonishment. Allhoff played with his spoon and seemed cool enough as he spoke.

"Ah, Hamtrack," he said "So a phone call to the Nazi Consul General brought you out of cover, eh?"

"Shut up," said Hamtrack. "You stinking little cripple. You damned near ruined us."

Allhoff's eyes flamed. His cheeks were purple and he looked very much like a gas bag filled to double its safe capacity. He opened his mouth as if to speak, then closed it again.

"Good work." said Pearl to Hamtrack. He was completely self-possessed again now.

Hamtrack was frowning over the barrel of his gun. "We still are not in the clear," he said. "We can escape but we'll always be hunted."

Pearl laughed. "Not necessarily," he said. "There are five people in this room, Hamtrack. It's their lives or ours."

That, I saw, was unpleasant, but logical. If Hamtrack and Pearl were working together they could only get away with it by making certain that none of us who had heard Allhoff's words lived.

Judge Rose stood up. "Do you mean to kill five innocent people?" he asked. "Is it—"

"Shut up," said Allhoff "He's not going to kill anyone."

He seemed so damned positive that I wondered for a moment if Hamtrack's play was part of some act Allhoff had plotted himself. Then he turned calmly around in his swivel chair and said an amazing thing.

"Battersly, take that gun away from him."

I stared at him. His tone was as casual as if he'd asked Battersly to get him some coffee. He sat back in his chair calmly watching Battersly and his eyes were glowing.

"The first man who moves toward me," said Hamtrack, "will have the dubious privilege of dying first."

"Battersly," said Allhoff, "take that gun away from him. That's an order."

"Allhoff," I said, "you're crazy. You can't issue an order like that."

He didn't answer me. His gaze remained on Battersly. Battersly's face was white. His lips were set tightly. He got up from his chair and faced Hamtrack.

I knew what he was doing. In some crazy way he believed the bullet from Hamtrack's gun would expiate his sin. Obeying Allhoff's order would even matters between them forever. That would be small consolation in the grave.

"Battersly," I said. "Don't do it. I accept full responsibility for your refusal to obey. There's nothing in regulations that makes you subject to an order like that."

"Battersly," said Allhoff relentlessly. *"Take his gun away."*

Battersly moved a step forward. I could see Hamtrack's finger tighten almost imperceptibly on the trigger of his gun.

"No!" I shouted. "You don't—"

But Battersly paid no attention to me. He walked slowly like an automaton toward Hamtrack. Marching deliberately to his death.

"All right," said Hamtrack. "Here it is, Rover boy."

His right hand contracted slowly. The trigger went back. Battersly neither increased nor slackened his pace. He reached his hand out to touch the gun when I heard a hollow click, Hamtrack stared down at the weapon in his hand. Hastily he pumped the trigger again. Two, three times. Three answering clicks sounded through the room, then Battersly was upon him.

He wrenched the gun with his left hand and swung with his right. I dived into my shoulder holster for my own gun and became suddenly aware that the room was filled with Allhoff's horrible ringing laughter.

Hamtrack lay very still on the floor. There was a little streak of blood on his chin where Battersly's knuckles had torn the skin. Allhoff rocked from side to side in his chair and peals of maniacal laughter came from his twisted lips. Pearl's wife clung to his arm, shaken and trembling. Battersly stood staring at Allhoff with glazed, stunned eyes.

"Now." said Allhoff controlling his ghastly mirth, "the situation remains the same as before, Pearl. Will you confess and take your chance with a lawyer and a jury in an American courtroom? Or do I tell my story to the German Consul and the newspapers and send you to the tender mercies of Berlin?"

There was a long silence. Pearl's face was drawn and his eyes were tired. Then he suddenly capitulated. "We'll stand trial here." he said. "The three of us."

The judge put his hand on Allhoff's shoulder. "But I don't understand, Inspector," he said. "This man, this police sergeant—you mean he's also a foreign agent?"

"He's a Bund member," said Allhoff. "I checked on that with a long-distance call to the Dies Committee yesterday. I figured that in order to tell that weird story about the legendary Samuel Levy, Pearl must have had information that Mrs. Kling was going to testify that money had been left in the desk. How could he find that out? Only through a headquarters leak."

"I'm beginning to see it," I told him. "Mrs. Kling

saw the commissioner the day before she saw us. Hamtrack knew of it. He tipped Pearl off."

"Right," said Allhoff. "Then, fully aware of my talents he applied for a transfer under me when he knew I was going to work on the case. He figured he could keep an eye on me if I got too close to the truth."

"You were lucky," I told him. "Those were very slim reasons for figuring he was a phony."

"Do you think I'm a fool, Hamtrack" he shrieked me. "I had two stronger reasons."

"Which were?"

"Do you think I fell for his slimy flattery?" demanded Allhoff, "When anyone in the department pays me a compliment it's for, an obvious reason. Besides, didn't he figure out that hold-up theory even before we heard Pearl's story? How could he think of that when I hadn't thought of it? He had to have advance information. He couldn't out-think me. That was why I sent him to watch the bank last night."

Battersly still stared at him like a corpse looking at its murderer.

"What was why you sent him to watch the bank?" I asked.

"I don't like armed enemies," said Allhoff. "I had Hamtrack stay up all night that I'd have an excuse to get him asleep this morning. While he slept I unloaded his gun."

Understanding and anger came to me simultaneously. "You knew Hamtrack's gun was unloaded," I said hotly. "Why didn't you tell us? Why didn't you pull your own gun on him? Why did you make Battersly think he was risking his life?"

I glared down at him, furiously angry. But he was paying no attention to me. His eyes were fixed on the unconscious figure of Hamtrack. And I think, for the moment, his hatred of Battersly was a secondary thing.

Under his breath he muttered: "Stinking little cripple." He picked up the coffee percolator, hurled it viciously to the floor. It smashed full in Hamtrack's face and a muddy mixture of blood and coffee trickled across the floor.

"Are you mad?" I said. "Have you no sense of decency, of justice—"

"Justice," said Allhoff sharply. "I knew I'd forgotten something. While Battersly books these people you'd better get over to the Tombs."

I looked at him, puzzled. "For what?" "You've got to spring a guy in a camelhair coat," said Allhoff. "He's got a suit for false arrest against Hamtrack."

TURN IN YOUR BADGE!

"They pulled his body out of the river this morning. His feet were stuck in a block of concrete . . ."

Originally Published - June 1940

CHAPTER ONE

Allhoff Gets the Sack

I sat down at my desk with an odd feeling that something was wrong. For the past six years the morning routine and the physical appearance of Allhoff's apartment had never varied. Today, it seemed to my subconscious, something was amiss.

I looked about the room. It was in its normal disarray, Allhoff's pajama coat lay crumpled on the window sill. A pile of unwashed dishes leaned precariously against the side of the sink. The bedroom door was open and the unmade sheets looked like a drift of slovenly snow. Certainly nothing was changed.

Battersly sat at his desk conning the adventures of Superman with grim interest. His face was pale as usual and his eyes held a dark beaten shadow. Allhoff bent forward in his swivel chair and sipped coffee with a loud unpleasant sound.

I sighed and came to the conclusion that my sub-conscious was wrong. Our little menage was as it always had been. As I was very much afraid, it was always going to be. I buried myself in the *Tribune* and read with interest of the death of Lieutenant Arnold of the Racketeering Squad.

I reached the final paragraph without interruption when I heard the clatter of Allhoff's cup and saucer as he pushed them away. His chair creaked as he half turned his body. He said to me over his shoulder: "All right, Simmonds, let's have the reports."

I put down the paper, reached in the wire basket on the back of the desk and realized my instinct had been more accurate than my eyes. For the first morning in six years the basket was empty.

"There are no reports," I told him. "They haven't come over yet."

Allhoff glared at me over his shoulder as if I, personally, were responsible. His little eyes narrowed.

"My God," he said in the tone of a man who has too much to bear, "I don't ask those coppers across the street to bring in the super-big-shots. Eddie Hoover handles that for them. I don't ask them to clean up the local murders. I attend to it myself. All they have to do is handout traffic tickets and send me over the police reports once a day. Even that taxes their mentality."

"The commissioner's in Miami," I told him. "Six weeks vacation. Our reports come direct from his office. Without him they may be a little pressed."

"Pressed!" he shouted. "Pressed! They've time enough to sell tickets to the Police Games. They can chase the kids playing ball in the streets. If a guy passes a red light the hand of justice is laid swiftly and relentlessly upon him. But they can't find time to send three sheets of onionskin paper across the street before ten o'clock in the morning. Damn them! I—" He was pounding the desk now and his face was red as a Russian diplomat at a Finnish tea party. I stepped in hastily before things got worse.

"Battersly," I said, "go across the street to headquarters. Get the inspector's reports. Hurry."

Battersly stood up and walked toward the door. Allhoff glared at him. His little eyes shone like balls of neon. "The sergeant said, 'Hurry'!" he roared. "You're not ambling through an art gallery. Run, don't walk. What did God give you legs for? What did—"

Battersly disappeared rapidly through the doorway. In order to cut off what I knew was coming, I said: "Allhoff, Arnold's dead."

That stopped him effectively enough. He screwed up his brow and reached for the coffee pot.

"Arnold?" he said. "Mike Arnold? Lieutenant, Racketeering Squad?"

"Mike Arnold," I told him. "The story's here in the *Tribune.*"

A thick viscous liquid gurgled from the percolator into Allhoff's chipped gray cup. He shoveled in sugar with a lavish hand.

"What'd he die of?"

"Everything," I said, "except natural causes. They pulled his body out of the river this morning. His feet were stuck in a block of concrete. His tongue was cut out. His forehead had been slashed with a knife, and there were nine bullet holes in his body."

Allhoff froze, his coffee cup suspended in mid-air. "Ah," he said, "they'll be coming to me with that one."

"They will not," I told him with malicious satisfaction. "It's already solved, tied up and in the bag. The grand jury will indict tomorrow and the state executioner will draw a check for a hundred and fifty bucks within three months."

His cup clattered down upon its saucer. Coffee slopped over the edge. Allhoff turned his face to me. Three things he hated with all his shriveled heart and twisted soul. The world in general, Battersly in particular, and the idea of anyone other than himself solving a murder case.

"Who broke it?" he snapped. "He's either wrong or lucky."

"The crime was solved," I told him happily, "by Acting Commissioner Blakely. He—"

"That damned bookkeeper," snarled Allhoff. "He couldn't solve a crossword puzzle. That lousy, bespatted—"

He delivered himself of some choice epithets. And for once he was etching the ideas of the rest of the department. Blakely, the first deputy-commissioner, was an insurance executive, who had achieved his high appointment for political reasons.

While the commissioner was in Florida, Blakely was in full charge of the department. A fact which caused many an old-timer to use similar, though more discreet, language than Allhoff.

I waited until he paused for breath, then added more detail.

"The guy in the can," I told him, "is Raphaelson. Legs Raphaelson. I think you sent him up once yourself. It seems he was mixed up in some sort of hot-fur racket. Arnold was collecting evidence against him. So Legs got him. Luckily, Arnold had turned in his report to Graham at headquarters the day before he was killed. That established motive. Besides, Raphaelson rolled Arnold after he killed him, took his ring and wallet. They were found on him when he was arrested this morning."

Allhoff snorted into his coffee cup. "Phony," he said. "That Raphaelson guy is really tough. The hardest thug in town. He'd never pull a killing like that."

"That," I told him, "is about as logical as the current European unpleasantness. Tongue cut out. Knife slashes. Bullets and a concrete sinker. If that isn't a tough-guy killing, I'm Dick Tracy. Or maybe you think the whole thing a childish prank?"

"If your nose was five inches longer, you couldn't see it in front of your face. That job was done by an amateur who's been to too many movies. It's overdone. That's why Legs Raphaelson didn't do it."

"Well," I said, "that's wonderful. Following the same reasoning we can argue that Arnold appears so damned dead that it's overdone. He's not dead at all. He's only pretending so he can have a nice long vacation in Woodlawn and hand us all the horse laugh when he gets up out of the grave and comes back to work."

He swung around in his chair and opened his mouth. I braced myself for the blast he was about to deliver, when Battersly came back and temporarily stilled his throbbing tongue. The familiar onionskin reports were not in Battersly's hand, a fact which Allhoff profanely remarked.

"Where are they?" he yelled. "Twenty-five thousand men in the police department and they can't send a lousy piece of paper across the street. Where the hell are my reports?"

Battersly's face was paler than usual. He looked acutely uncomfortable.

"There aren't any reports," he replied with the air of a man announcing the demise of a relative. "They're not going to send any over."

Puzzled, Allhoff and I stared at him. He shuffled uneasily but didn't speak. Then I heard the sound of footsteps on the rickety stairs outside.

Two men strode into the room. One was Captain Graham of the headquarters Squad. The other was Blakely, the acting commissioner, himself. I dragged myself up out of my chair and saluted. Allhoff, who possessed an anarchist's respect for authority, nodded briefly and said, "I'm glad you're here, Commissioner. I want to call your attention to the negligence of your own office. The police reports should be here at nine every morning. They haven't arrived yet."

Blakely cleared his throat. "Not negligence, Mr. Allhoff," he said in his dry clerical voice. "They were withheld by my orders."

It was the first time in my life I had heard Allhoff called 'mister.' He blinked at Blakely in bewilderment. For that matter, so did I.

I noted that Battersly and Graham sedulously avoided Allhoff's eye.

"It is my considered opinion," said Blakely briskly, "that the police department is quite capable of functioning without civilian help. Civilian authority over the rank and file weakens morale. There are other reasons for my decision we need not discuss at this time."

Allhoff's mouth was open. He sat stunned, as if Blakely had swung an invisible bat and cracked him on the skull. His little eyes were blank and glazed. His cheeks, gray and hollow. I sat with a high-beating heart and utter incredulity in my brain as the significance of Blakely's speech seeped into my mind.

Allhoff was being fired! Chucked out of the department on his large, unhandsome ear. This was a day for which I had waited hopelessly for five weary years.

Allhoff, for once reduced to complete silence, reached forth a trembling hand and, picked up his coffee cup. He sipped loudly. Then he said hoarsely: "You mean I'm through? You mean I'm no longer on the force?"

"Officially," said Blakely coldly, "you've been through for several years. I'm merely severing your unofficial connection, Mr. Allhoff. Let's see. Today is Tuesday. I'll give you the rest of the week to clean up your affairs. Next Monday, Sergeant Simmonds and Patrolman Battersly will report to me for other duty. You will return all departmental documents and files in your possession."

I watched Allhoff like a man waiting for an air raid. I expected a detonation like the Black Tom explosion. But nothing happened. Dazed incredulity was stamped on Allhoff's face. His eyes were wide open and filled with disbelief. He resembled a mathematician looking at a ghost. When he spoke his voice was high and off key.

"Commissioner, you can't do this to me. I'm indispensable. Every tough case in the department comes to me. I've never fallen down yet. I'm the only brain on the force, I—"

"You may be a brain." said Blakely, 'but I'll thank you to remember you're not on the force. I'm running things now. Certain laxities will be repaired. As for your solving the tough cases, well"—he laughed deprecatingly—"I'm not doing so badly myself. I cleaned up the Arnold murder this morning. My first day on the job. Of course, I had Captain Graham's help."

Graham smiled obsequiously like a moving-picture producer's secretary. Allhoff's eyes suddenly narrowed. His voice was tight and closer to normal when he spoke.

"You mean Legs Raphaelson? You mean you've broken the Arnold case by putting Raphaelson in the can?"

Blakely smiled smugly. "Exactly."

Allhoff drew a deep breath. His fist banged on the desk-top and his saucer danced clatteringly. He raised his voice in an intolerant shout.

"You damned actuary's clerk! Raphaelson didn't kill Arnold. The very method of killing absolves him. Would a ball player kill a guy with a baseball hat, then leave it there for the cops to find? Would a piccolo player beat a guy's brains our with his instrument and leave it behind him as a clue?"

Blakely lost his tongue at this outburst. Graham said: "All of which has what to do with what?"

Allhoff didn't answer him. He centered his attack on Blakely.

"You grubbing bookkeeper," he yelled. "How the hell could you solve a murder? What right have you in the department anyway? What've you ever done for the force? I've given it my brains, my life. And that's not all."

As Blakely stood speechless before this tirade, Allhoff pushed his swivel-chair away front the desk. It rolled halfway across the room. His thighs were capped with a pair of leather pads where his knees should have begun. The pads wriggled furiously, danced a frenzied rigadoon in the air.

I gave my legs to the law," he screamed, his voice breaking just this side of hysteria. "Didn't I, Battersly? Gave it half my body. And for what? For the sake of a yellow rat over there." He pointed at Battersly who turned his face to the wall. But for once Allhoff was more enraged at someone else. He turned back to Blakely. "For the sake of getting fired by a lousy insurance peddler. A stupid stuffed shirt who puts the first gangster he finds in the can and says he's solved a murder!"

He picked up the half-filled coffee pot and glared with insane rage at Blakely. "You damned idiot! Get out of here. Get out!"

He raised the percolator over his shoulder and hurled it with all his strength at Blakely. The acting commissioner ducked without dignity. The pot crashed against the wall. Coffee flew about the room like black rain.

Cold fury glittered in Blakely's eyes. You'll answer for this," he said brittlely. "I'll prefer charges. Assault, insubordination. You'll—''

"I'll thank you to remember." said Allhoff savagely, "I'm not a member of the police force."

Their eyes met, clashed. Then Blakely turned abruptly on his heel and strode from the room. Graham glanced at Allhoff shook his head, and followed.

I stood up, picked up the percolator, filled it with water and set it back on the electric plate on Allhoff's desk. He was staring silently and sullenly at the door through which Blakely had disappeared.

I went back to my desk, not daring to reveal the ela-

tion in my heart. Monday might be the end of Allhoff, but it was a golden dawn for me. Battersly was staring out the window, a faraway expression in his eyes.

As I picked up the *Tribune* cross-word puzzle, I heard a low, rhythmic, rumbling sound. It took me some minutes to realize that for time first time since I had known him, Battersly was humming a tune.

CHAPTER TWO

The Late Lieutenant and the Ladies

It was some six years ago since Battersly and I had begun to serve our sentence under Allhoff. It had its genesis in a raid on upper West End Avenue in the days when Battersly was a raw rookie. Allhoff, leading his squad had broken in the front door at the zero minute. Battersly's assignment had been to affect a rear entrance, disable the Tommy gun which was guarding the staircase. At the last moment, Battersly, developing a quite understandable case of buck fever had flunked on the job.

The immediate result of his failure was a blast of machine-gun bullets in Allhoff's legs. Gangrene and amputation followed in short order and during that operation Allhoff lost far more than a pair of legs.

Of course it was impossible for the departmental roster to carry an inspector who was a cripple. On the other hand the commissioner had no idea of losing the best man he had. Wires had been pulled and it was arranged that Allhoff still be paid his old salary. He took up residence in this slum principally because it was just across the street from headquarters.

Allhoff had demanded that Battersly be assigned to him as his assistant. The commissioner with ironic justice granted the request I, who had come up front the ranks with Allhoff, had been sent over, too. Ostensibly to look after the paper work. Actually to see that he didn't ride Battersly too far.

For six years I had labored in an atmosphere of bitterness and hate. Allhoff never missed an opportunity to remind Battersly that his cowardice had cost two legs. And Allhoff's mind had become as crippled as his body. Had it not been for a pension which my family was going to need sorely I would have walked out of this gloomy tenement years ago.

So today my heart was light, as was Battersly's. Allhoff was through, relieved of duty by the officious Blakely. I knew it was a pretty raw deal from Allhoff's point of view, but I didn't see any point in conducting a dental examination on a gift horse. Within six days I'd be back at a precinct desk doing a normal day's work among normal people.

Allhoff lifted his bead from its meditative position on his chest. He said to me: "What do you know about this guy, Arnold?"

I put down my paper. "Allhoff," I told him, "you'd better quit gracefully. They've got Raphaelson cold. You couldn't spring him with the aid of Charlie Chan, Sherlock Holmes and a crowbar,"

He swung around in his chair and glared at me, "What do you know about Arnold?" he yelled. "I demand an answer."

I shrugged. After six odd years of Allhoff I certainly could hold on until Monday.

"A competent copper." I told him. "Something of a playboy off duty. Quite a hand with women. Worked under Graham and they were close friends. Most of this is hearsay, of course."

Allhoff grunted into his coffee cup. "Any relatives? Who gets his dough, his insurance if any?"

I consulted the news story in the *Tribune*, "A brother." I said. "Matt Arnold. Sole living relative. He gets the insurance, It doesn't say how much."

Allhoff stared long and thoughtfully at the panels of the door. Somehow he reminded me of the walls of Jericho just before the trumpet blew. I felt so elated I couldn't refrain from using the needle.

"Allhoff." I said excitedly, "maybe Blakely killed him. Why don't you check the insurance records? Maybe he sneaked in a policy on Arnold, making himself the beneficiary. Then he kills Arnold and—"

Allhoff turned around. "A wise guy," he said in a tight voice. "A very wise guy who believes I'll be through on Monday." He paused for a moment and lifted his tone to a shout. "Well, I won't! I'll be here when you're dead! I'll be here after Blakely resigns in disgrace. I'll always be here. Always!"

His hand shook as he lifted his cup. Over its edge he mumbled to Battersly: "Ask Graham to come over here a minute. Then bring me in Matt Arnold."

He drained the cup as Battersly left the room.

"Allhoff," I said, "I don't like to see a guy beat his head against a wall. Why don't you quit gracefully. Legs Raphaelson's guilty as hell."

"You are as dumb," said Allhoff, "as a giraffe with laryngitis. Would an iceman kill a guy with ice tongs and leave the tongs behind him? Would—"

"We've already been over that," I reminded him, "using a second baseman and a piccolo player. So what?"

"Then would a known gangster, a notorious tough guy, use every known thug-method of killing Arnold? He might use one but not all. It aims the murder right at a gangster. Raphaelson is a gangster, and since Arnold was investigating him, a damned obvious suspect. Why should he call attention to himself? Besides, why should Raphaelson who makes God knows how many grand a week, bother to swipe Arnold's lousy paycheck from his wallet? Well, have you got any answers?"

I had, but since Graham came into the room just then, I didn't give them.

Graham sat down with an uncomfortable air. He took off his cap and mopped his brow with a huge handkerchief. "Inspector," he said, "I didn't have anything to do with what the commissioner said. I—"

"Forget it," said Allhoff. "There are a few things I want to ask you about Arnold."

Graham shook his head slowly. "You're all wrong there, Inspector. This Raphaelson, now—"

"Will you answer my questions or not?" snapped Allhoff using his grade-A, nasty tone.

Graham gulped. Whether Allhoff was through on Monday or not, Graham still had a wholesome fear of him.

"Sure, Inspector," he said. "Anything at all. Go right ahead."

Allhoff fished a cigarette from his pocket and lighted it. "All right," he said. "You were a pretty good friend of Arnold's, weren't you?"

"Sure. He practically lived at my house."

Allhoff inhaled deeply, blew the smoke out from twisted lips. "You had different tours of duty, didn't you?"

"Sure we did. But Arnold'd hang out at the house even if I wasn't there. Practically one of the family."

Allhoff grunted skeptically. "Arnold was a drinker and a chippy-chaser. Why should he suddenly become so enamored of the Graham domesticity."

Graham didn't answer immediately. After a while he said, "Well, I'll tell you, Inspector. This is confidential though. Arnold was engaged to Donna, my daughter. I wanted to keep her name out of the trial if possible."

I watched Allhoff closely and remarked happily that he seemed completely baffled.

"Has the M. E. estimated the time of death?"

Graham nodded, "They figure he was killed sometime late Saturday night. While he was on duty."

"Where were you that night?"

"Me? Home. Why?"

"What were you doing?"

"My God," said Graham, "do you think I killed him?"

"What were you doing?" yelled Allhoff.

"Reading."

"Reading what?"

"The paper. The evening paper."

"What paper?"

This cross-examination was becoming so pointless that I butted in, "What color drawers were you wearing, Captain? Name three."

Allhoff swung his head in my direction and his eyes glittered dangerously. But this time he managed to keep his profanity to himself.

"What paper were you reading?" he asked Graham again.

"*The Herald.* I read it every night."

Allhoff grunted. "That all you did." he said. "Read the paper all night."

"Well," said Graham. "I did the crossword puzzle. It was, a tough one, too. Didn't get it finished till almost bedtime."

Allhoff grinned at him unpleasantly.

"*You* finished a crossword puzzle?" he jeered, incredulity in his tone. "You, an illiterate flatfoot of the old school."

Graham flushed angrily. "I did every word of it," he said. "You ain't the only smart guy in the department, Inspector."

Allhoff played with the handle of his coffee cup. "So," he said more to himself than to anyone else, "You read the paper and you finished the crossword puzzle, eh?"

"I beg your pardon," I said with mock politeness. "Is this a murder investigation or a cultural discussion?"

"It'll be an inquest." said Allhoff savagely. "if you don't shut up. That's all Graham."

Graham stood up and replaced his cap. "I still think you're wrong, Inspector," he said, "This Raphaelson. now—"

"I don't take advice from the police force," snapped Allhoff, "I give it."

Graham smiled weakly, saluted and walked out the door, Allhoff looked at his watch and said: "Where the hell's that Matt Arnold? I've got no time to throw away."

"You've got the next hundred years." I told him, "From here on in you've nothing to do and a lifetime to do it in."

He didn't answer me, There was a very smug expression on his face as he filled his cup.

"So," I said, "you're going to pretend that you actually found out something from Graham."

"I did," he said. "I found out that he indulges in such erudite pastimes as crossword puzzles."

"So what? It makes you jealous to have any other copper even solve a puzzle in a newspaper. Is that?"

He snarled something at me which I didn't catch because I was hearing too many other sounds at the moment. Two cracking reports resounded from the hall below. There was a sudden shriek of pain, a shout and two more shots.

I was halfway across the room in nothing flat. Allhoff slid out of his chair and clumped across the floor behind me. A slim dark figure pushed past me on the stairs. He held his left wrist in his right hand and left a trail of blood behind him. He was howling like a banshee with a toothache.

At the first landing I looked over the banister and saw Battersly enter the doorway below. He was panting and his revolver was in his hand. He raced up the stairway, saw me, and announced breathlessly: "He got away. I lost the car in traffic on Lafayette Street. Where's Arnold?"

"Is that the guy with the blood?"

"Yeah. They nailed him in the wrist. Where is he?"

I led him back to Allhoff's apartment. Matt Arnold stood whimpering over the sink, running warm water on his wrist. Allhoff regarded him unsympathetically.

"Better take him over to the doctor," I said to Battersly. "He—"

"Doctor, hell," said Allhoff. "He's got a nick on the wrist, that's all. The way he's howling you'd think he'd lost his legs. You'd think—"

"Let me look at it," I said hastily more to shut off Allhoff than because I was interested.

Matt Arnold extended his hand. The bullet, I saw, had smacked across the top of it, nicking the skin, leaving the bone intact. I rinsed the wound with warm water, poured iodine on it, despite Arnold's protest, and bound it up with a clean handkerchief, Then I ushered him to the chair by Allhoff's desk and sat him down.

"O.K., Lombroso," I said. "Here's your witness."

"All right," said Allhoff, "Now what happened downstairs? Who plugged you?"

Matt Arnold was pale and shaken, Battersly came forward with an explanation. "A car, Inspector," he said, "A sedan drove by just as we were coming in here, Fired two shots. The second one got him. I fired twice at the tires. Must have missed, though. I ran after it but lost it in traffic."

Allhoff fixed his eyes on Matt Arnold. "Who's shooting at you and why?" he snapped.

Arnold licked his lips nervously. "I ain't got any idea, Inspector. I got no enemies, I ain't even got a job.

I got nothing."

Something flickered over Allhoff's face. "You've got your brother's insurance, haven't you? You've got what dough he left?"

"Yeah." said Arnold uncertainly. "Yeah. Sure. But you don't think—"

"Never mind what I think. When did you last see your brother?"

"Saturday. Saturday around noontime. We had lunch together, then I went to the movies. My brother went on duty at four o'clock.''

Allhoff grunted. ''Saturday was the fifteenth. Your brother got paid that day, didn't he?"

"I suppose so. He usually picked up his check when he went on duty."

"He had a bank account, didn't he?"

"Sure. Right around the corner from where we lived."

"But nowhere near headquarters."

"Why no," said Matt Arnold, as puzzled by this question as I was. "The bank's a good three miles from here."

Allhoff sighted, reached for the percolator and filled his cup. He drank very slowly and his brow was wrinkled in thought. I caught Battersly's eye and winked. Never in his entire career had I seen Allhoff flounder around like this. Apparently, after all, he wasn't a money player. With his whole future at stake he had evidently joined the question-at-random-and-pray-for-a-break school of cross- examination.

He emptied the cup at last and turned again to Matt Arnold.

"Your brother, I understand, was quite a hand with the ladies?"

Arnold twisted his hat nervously in his hands, "Well," he said, "he wasn't no saint."

"If he ran true to type," said Allhoff, "it's my guess he did a lot of talking about his women. Sort of bragging about his conquests, eh?"

Matt Arnold nodded. "Mike wasn't no quiet-mouthed guy," he conceded.

Allhoff's eyes narrowed and his finger drummed nervously on the desk top.

"Did he ever mention a girl named Graham to you?"

Matt nodded emphatically. "For the past few weeks he never mentioned nothing else, Inspector. He was nuts about her, All day long it was the Graham dame this, the Graham dame that, I never seen him go overboard like that before."

"Damn," said the Allhoff in utter disgust.

I looked at him curiously. "What do you care?" I asked him. "What's it to you whether he was nuts about Graham's daughter?"

"Shut up," he snarled, "I'm solving a murder case."

"Oh," I said, "Pardon me all to hell."

He was staring into the inky depths of his coffee cup, too dejected to flare out at me. He waved Matt Arnold away. "All right." he said, "That's all for now, If I want you I'll send for you."

Arnold stood up and wet his lips with a nervous tongue. "What it that guy takes another shot at me, Inspector?" he asked. "I think I ought to have a bodyguard."

"Don't be silly," said Allhoff. "If he takes another shot at you he might leave a clue behind. It'll give me another angle to work on."

All of which was going to be very consoling to Matt Arnold in the morgue, as I mentioned when I ushered him from the room.

CHAPTER THREE

The Commissioner's Quandary

Three idle days passed. Once, on Thursday, Allhoff sent Battersly uptown to buy a back copy of the *Evening Herald*. He buried his corvine nose in it for a long time, leaving me strictly alone and Battersly to his uninterrupted perusal of the comic strips. The rest of the time Allhoff drank coffee and scowled at the wall until, I swear, the dirty paint grew darker.

The atmosphere was gloomy and no inspiration to one of those keep-smiling-your-troubles-will-fly-away lyric-writers. But I figured I could stand it very easily. A kid doesn't care if it rains three days before Christmas and that's just how Battersly and I felt.

On Monday, we'd go back to duty and that beautiful thought had the effect of a deep draft of fifteen-year-old Bourbon.

Just before quitting time Thursday, Allhoff slammed his coffee cup down suddenly, snatched up a pencil and scribbled rapidly on a piece of paper. He called Battersly to his side and handed him the note.

"Here," he said. "Take that over to Captain Graham. Stay there while he reads it. Bring me his answer back right away."

Since Allhoff hadn't bothered even to fold the paper and I was standing right at his shoulder, I couldn't help reading the message.

It said—

Graham, Since I was your mystagogue when you were a rookie, I'm asking you a favor now, I have enough white paper to get through the week but none at all which is xanthic. Further will you ascertain when my ultimate guerdon for police services will be sent me.

Sincerely,

Allhoff.

I blinked, first at the note, then at him. "What is it?" I said. "Code?"

He smiled without answering and waved Battersly out the door. His complete ignoring of me as he filled his cup was irritating.

"Allhoff," I said, "are you crazy?"

"Sure," he said almost pleasantly. "They locked Galileo up for being nuts, too."

I shrugged my shoulders and went back to my desk.

A few moments later Battersly returned. He didn't look very happy.

"Well," snapped Allhoff. "What'd Graham say?"

"Well," began Battersly, acutely uncomfortable, "he said—er—he said—"

"He said I was nuts, didn't he?"

Battersly swallowed hard. "Yes, sir. He did. He said if you'll tell him what you want in plain English he'll see what he can do."

I turned my head quickly. This called for a loud and profane explosion. To my surprise I saw Allhoff smiling dreamily into the viscous depths of his coffee cup.

That was such a violation of everything in the book, I didn't even try to figure it out.

On Friday morning when I came in, Allhoff was already up. Obviously he had consumed his first quart of coffee and, very much to my surprise, Gregory Garfield was sitting in the chair at the side of his desk.

Garfield was an assistant D. A. and there was no more hatred in the Wilhelmstrasse than existed between him and Allhoff, Garfield was aggressive and officious.

He had climbed to his present position by bullying cross-examination and pitiless pounding of witnesses. He was far too much like Allhoff for them to get along.

But now the pair of them reminded me of a couple of Siamese cats plotting against the canary. They were grinning at each other with a nice mixture of suspicion and smugness on their faces.

"All right," said Garfield as I came in. "As long as I get the credit. But if you're wrong, Inspector—"

"I'm never wrong," said Allhoff and no religious fanatic ever stated his beliefs with more conviction, "Never."

Garfield got up, shook hands, picked up his lawyer's inevitable brief case and departed. I looked questioningly at Allhoff. He smiled most unpleasantly and said: "You'll be sorry to lose me on Monday, eh, Simmonds?"

"No," I said shortly. "I won't."

"I'd suggest neither you nor Battersly spend any money celebrating my departmental demise just yet," he said.

I looked at him suspiciously but he vouchsafed no further information.

Battersly arrived a little later and the morning ticked past.

At noon Allhoff took his nose out of his coffee cup long enough to say: "Battersly, tomorrow morning at ten I want you to bring in Donna Graham. That's Graham's daughter. I also want Matt Arnold. Ten o'clock, sharp."

I scratched my head. I wondered if he actually had anything up his greasy sleeve that might grant him a reprieve beyond Monday. His next order took my breath away.

"You, Simmonds, will have Blakely and Graham here at the same time. Ten o'clock sharp."

"That's one sweet assignment," I told him. "I probably can talk Graham into coming over, but how am I going to get Blakely? Throw a net around him?"

"Yes him to death if necessary," said Allhoff. "Spread the salve, the slime all over him. You've been doing it to me for years. Drag my years of faithful service into it. The last request of an old departmental war horse. But get him here."

He put his nose back in the coffee cup.

I said aloud to Battersly: "Do you think his mind has cracked at last?"

Surprisingly enough Allhoff chuckled. "Sure," he said. "Me and Archimedes— both crazy as hell."

I dug the encyclopedia out from beneath the pile of laundry and went searching through the A's. It seemed this Archimedes was a very smart guy, indeed.

Donna Graham and Matt Arnold sat uneasily on a pair of Allhoff's more secure chairs and sedulously avoided each other's eyes. Battersly stood by the window staring out into Centre Street. There was an odd expression on his face and I knew he was calculating the chances of Allhoff's solving the Arnold murder against his failing to.

Allhoff, his swivel-chair turned parallel to the desk, beat a typewriter laboriously with one hand and hoisted a cup of coffee with the other. The clicking of the keys, the occasional rattle of the cup in the saucer were the only sounds in the room.

I watched him speculatively. True, I had seen him pull many a triumph out of the clouds when things looked very, very black indeed. But this time I was certain he had no evidence to spring Raphaelson.

I heard footsteps mounting the stairs outside and raised my eyebrows as I saw Blakely and Graham enter the room.

I had poured polite deference into Blakely's ears yesterday afternoon but he had remained noncommittal. I had never really believed he would heed Allhoff's summons.

Blakely stared at Allhoff, annoyance written plain on his countenance. Graham frowned at his daughter. He said: "What are you doing here?"

Donna looked up at him and it seemed to me there was a shadow of anxiety in her eyes.

"One of the Inspector's men brought me," she said. "I thought you'd know about it."

"I didn't," snapped Graham, He turned on Allhoff. "What authority have you to bring my daughter here? What—"

Allhoff ignored him, drowned out the rest of his sentence by rattling his cup and saucer, He took the sheet of paper from the typewriter and put it on the desk before him.

Blakely's highly polished shoe tapped in irritation on the floor.

"Allhoff," he said sharply, "because of your record in the department, because of the sacrifices you've made in the line of duty, I've been courteous enough to come over here. Now, quickly, what is it you want?"

Allhoff turned to me and bowed. "You laid it on very nicely, didn't you Simmonds?"

Blakely made a clucking sound of impatience. "Come now, What is it?"

Allhoff sucked the tar from the bottom of his cup. He picked up the sheet of paper and handed it to Blakely.

"This," he said. "I want you to sign this."

Blakely snatched the paper and began to read, Matt Arnold and Battersly looked on, puzzled. Graham and his daughter exchanged glances. I kept my eyes on Blakely's face. Color came into it, and sudden anger. He looked up from the paper to Allhoff.

"Are you crazy?" he shouted. "Have you lost your mind? This is a resignation, dated today."

"Correct," said Allhoff, "And if you'll keep on reading you'll note the reasons for that resignation are admitted incompetence which endangers the lives of innocent citizens, stupid blundering which reflects on the good name of the department, egregious inefficiency and no aptitude whatever for police work."

Blakely's face resembled an apoplectic poinsettia blossom in a tropic dawn. He crumpled the paper, threw it down on Allhoff's desk and roared hike a bull.

"You insolent maniac! How dare you ask me to sign that? You belong in the psychopathic ward. By God, I'll send you there for observation?"

The fact that Allhoff did not lose his temper should have warned me that he had something. As Blakely's tirade fell about his ears he went calmly about brewing another pot of coffee.

Graham cleared his throat nervously and said: "We'd all better get out of here. The guy's crazy. Come along, Donna."

Donna Graham stood up. Blakely, looking like a man who restrains his tongue only by superhuman effort, turned toward the door. Allhoff, hand on the percolator handle, said: "Don't go, Donna. Come back, Graham. Sit down, Commissioner."

There was a whiplash of authority in his voice that halted them. He caught Blakely's eyes, deliberately picked up the crumpled paper and smoothed it out.

"So you refuse to sign, Commissioner?"

Blakely glared at him. "I'll sign a commitment paper for you when I get back to my office," he snapped. "That's all."

The phony affability Allhoff had been registering fell front him. He leaned over the desk and his voice was grim.

"You have your choice," he said. "You can sign this now and resign of your own free will. You can wait three months and be drummed out of the department in disgrace. You will see yourself branded a bungling murderer in every paper of the country. You'll lose every friend you have. You'll lose your insurance-company sinecure. Your own family will be ashamed of you. And," he concluded with vast satisfaction, "you'll probably take to drink and finish in the gutter."

Blakely was no longer angry. He stared at Allhoff as if the legless inspector had just claimed he was Napoleon. So did I.

"What are you doing, Inspector?" I asked. "Reading futures in coffee grounds?"

He ignored me. He laid the smoothed out sheet of paper before Blakely. "Listen," he said, "You got this guy, Raphaelson in the can across the street?"

"So?"

"So he's innocent."

I sighed. He was harping on that again. Blakely scratched his head and appeared exasperated.

"You've already told me that," he said. "Several times. Moreover you've told me why you think so. In my opinion your theory is ridiculous."

"It's not a theory any more," said Allhoff. "I can prove it."

We all stared at him, I noted that Matt Arnold appeared acutely uncomfortable.

"Go ahead, then," said Blakely. "Go ahead and prove it."

"Sure," said Allhoff with a terrible grin. "As soon as you sign this paper."

For the first time it dawned on me what he was driving at. It dawned on Blakely too, for he was staring at Allhoff with horrible incredulity in his eyes.

You mean," he began. "You mean that—"

"I mean," said Allhoff, "that if you sign this paper, I'll prove Raphaelson didn't kill Mike Arnold."

"And if I refuse?"

"If you refuse. I'll prove it, too. But not now. I'll wait until you indict Raphaelson. I wait until you convict him. I'll wait patiently, until you burn him. When he's been a corpse for twenty-four hours. I'll produce my evidence."

I stood up. "Allhoff—" I said, but he cut me short.

"So you'll sign now," he said to Blakely, "or wait until you've burned Raphaelson. Then I'll present my proof. You'll go down in the newspaper files as a bungling murderer. You'll die more deaths than Raphaelson—ever will."

Blakely sat in frozen silence. Undoubtedly, he still believed Raphaelson guilty as hell. But you can't gamble a man's life with the same careless abandon that you ante a dime in a cheap poker game.

"Now look here," said Blakely. "Leave me out of it for a moment. Forget your personal dislike of me. Frankly, I don't know whether you can prove Raphaelson's innocent or not. But if you can, humanity dictates that you do so, You can't let an innocent man die. Forget me. Think of Raphaelson."

Allhoff put down his cup with a bang. "*You* think of him." he said and his voice lilted high and hysterical. "*You* think of him, Commissioner. Think of him frying in the seat up the river because of your stupidity. After you've amused yourself with that, think of yourself, twenty-four hours afterward when I prove Raphaelson didn't kill Mike Arnold."

Blakely quite evidently thought of these things. His face was pale.

"Inspector," said Matt Arnold suddenly. "You wouldn't do it!"

Looking at him then, watching his glinting little eyes, the bitter sardonic twist to his mouth, I knew damn well he would do it, if he could, Blakely squared his shoulders suddenly and took a deep breath.

"I'll make a deal with you," he said. "Produce your evidence. If it's conclusive, I'll sign that resignation."

Allhoff leaned over the side of his chair, picked up a dirty handkerchief front the laundry pile, blew his nose, and replaced the handkerchief. He looked down at the watch on his wrist. He said, without looking at Blakely: "You'll give me your word before these witnesses?"

"My word," said Blakely and his voice was scarcely audible.

CHAPTER FOUR

Till Monday Morning

Allhoff smiled gloatingly. "All right," he said, "First let us consider the circumstances of the crime. Is it likely that a well known gangster would kill a man by—"

"Allhoff," I said wearily, "we've been over that several times. We've used as examples a second baseman, a piccolo-player and an iceman. Is that all the case you've got?"

"If you don't appreciate the reasoning there," said Allhoff amiably, "I offer you something else. The day Arnold was killed he drew his pay check. He drew it after the banks were closed and it's most unlikely he cashed it. Coppers, as a general rule, don't carry much cash with them on pay day."

"Well," said Blakely, "where's all this leading?"

"Would Raphaelson steal Arnold's pay check? Why? He would never be dumb enough to cash it. What good would it do him? And what about the ring? Raphaelson, vulgar as most thugs are, wears a huge diamond on his finger and a larger one in his tie. What in the name of God would he want Mike Arnold's lousy signet ring for?"

"It was found on him," said Blakely.

"It was planted on him, you mean," said Allhoff.

"By whom?" I asked, "How can anyone plant a wallet and a ring, unobserved, in a man's pocket?"

"I'll get around to that later," said Allhoff, "Just now I want to discuss Captain Graham's mental recreations."

"Recreations?" said Blakely, puzzled.

Allhoff looked down at his wrist watch again and sighed. "Yeah," he said, "On the night of the murder Graham was at home. Reading the paper. Working the crossword puzzle. Weren't you, Graham?"

"*Why*, sure, Inspector. I already told you that."

"You did, indeed," said Allhoff cheerily. "You were curled up in your favorite chair, culling your extravagant vocabulary, eh, Graham?"

Graham nodded uncertainly.

"It was the crossword puzzle in the *Herald*, Commissioner." went on Allhoff, "Quite a literate puzzle. But Graham did it. Did every single word of it before he went to bed."

"Which," said Blakely, "has a great deal to do with the Arnold murder."

Allhoff deliberately missed the irony in his tone. "Why, of course. Commissioner," he said. "I never thought you'd see it."

"Damn it," roared Blakely. "I *don't* see it! What the devil are you talking about?"

Allhoff drank a cup of coffee with maddening deliberation before he answered.

"Well," said Allhoff, "Graham does a crossword puzzle. He fills in all the words. Hence he must know what they mean. Yet when I check back on the copy of the *Herald* containing the answer, when I select a few of those words at random and incorporate them in a note to Graham, he hasn't the slightest idea what I'm talking about."

Something clicked in my mind as I recalled that screwy message Allhoff had sent across the street yesterday.

"The words xamithic, guerdon, and mystagogue were in that puzzle. Words which, if Graham solved the puzzle, he certainly should know the meanings of. I sent him a note with those words in it. A simple note which reminded him I'd taught him the rudiments of police work when he first came up, and asking him to let me have some yellow paper. I requested further that he find out when my last pay check would be due."

"So?" said Blakely, drawing out the syllable.

"So," said Allhoff, "Graham lied. He never worked that crossword puzzle. I doubt if the flatfooted moron ever worked one in his life. He told me that on the night of the killing he was home. To make it sound better he said he was reading the paper. To make it sound even better, he said he did the crossword puzzle, added it was so tough it took him until bedtime to finish it."

"Granting all this is true," said Blakely, "what?"

"You tell me," said Allhoff, "What did Graham lie for?"

Blakely turned to Graham. Some of the ruddiness had gone from the captain's face, He shook his head emphatically.

"The inspector's got me wrong, sir." he said. "He misunderstood me. He—"

"Shut up, said Allhoff, "Do you think I'm staking my case on a confession from you?"

He underlined the last word faintly and I began to puzzle over what he meant.

"And that," said Allhoff, "wasn't the only lie he told me. He told me that Mike Arnold and his daughter were in love."

Donna Graham gasped. But this time I was dead certain that Allhoff was wrong.

"That fact was corroborated," I told him, "by Matt Arnold, here."

"Ah," said Allhoff. "Matt lied, too."

att Arnold got out of his chair and his knees were trembling. "Inspector," he said. "I didn't tell no lie. Why should I lie to you? I only told you what Mike said to me. Honest to God, I—"

Battersly put his hand on his shoulders and gently sat him down again. Graham said hoarsely: "I told you the truth. Didn't I, Donna? And if you don't believe me, what about Matt.

"Matt didn't lie intentionally," said Allhoff. "He said that his brother was constantly raving about that Graham broad or that Graham dame. That's what Matt told me."

"Well," said Blakely, hopefully, I thought, "isn't that enough. That's corroboration, isn't it?"

"No." said Allhoff, "Because when Mike Arnold was raving to his brother he wasn't talking about Graham's daughter."

"Then," I said, "who in the name of God was he talking about? His grandmother?"

"No," said Allhoff. "His wife."

There was complete silence in the room, broken only by a hissing sibilant sound as Graham inhaled air through his lips. Allhoff looked around the room over the rim of his coffee cup and there was dancing mockery in his eyes.

Graham's voice cracked through the silence, high and rasping. "That's a lie. A filthy lie. It's—"

"Shut up," said Allhoff savagely. He leaned over his desk and fixed Blakely with his hot little eyes. He spoke so swiftly that his words seemed missiles tumbling out of a machine-gun barrel.

"Graham discovered Arnold was having an affair with his wife. He killed him, using all the gangster methods he could think of, to fool the coppers into believing it wasn't a personal killing. He took Arnold's wallet and pocketbook. He talked you into believing you had solved the case yourself from the facts in hand and you sent him out to bring in Raphaelson. He did. He searched him himself and reported he had found the wallet and ring which clinched the case."

"But," I said, "his wife, his daughter. What's all this about?"

"Simple enough," said Allhoff. "After murdering Arnold he realized that the fact that the dead man had been visiting his wife in his own absence would be noticed by neighbors. It might arouse suspicion. So he invented a story to cover it. He announced that Arnold had been courting his daughter."

"It's a lie," yelled Graham. "Donna, tell him it's a lie!"

Donna Graham stood up. Her young chin was held high and defiant. "It's a lie," she said evenly.

"Sure," said Allhoff bitterly. "It's a lie. It's a lie, too, Graham, that when you heard me say I was waiting to talk to Matt Arnold you got panicky. Afraid that Mike had told his brother about your wife. Knowing Mike was a braggart, had probably talked to his brother, you figured two killings were no worse than one. You took a pot shot at him as Battersly was bringing him in here."

"That's another lie," said Graham.

Allhoff sighed and looked down at his watch again. There was an odd frown on his brow, Blakely stroked his lean chin thoughtfully. Graham stood glaring at Allhoff, an impartial admixture of rage and fear on his face. Matt Arnold's eyes were glued on Graham, slow wrath welling up in them. Donna stood erect and self-possessed, her arms folded over her small breasts. Battersly caught my eye and shrugged. I shrugged back at him. The situation was rapidly outdistancing me.

Blakely pursed his lips and narrowed his eyes. "Allhoff," he said at last, "I admit you've made out something of a case, But it's theory. Pure theory. If Donna Graham insists Arnold was going to marry her, you can't disprove it. You, yourself, concede that Matt Arnold's testimony is worthless in that respect. He only heard his brother mention the Graham girl. Have you any proof?"

"My watch says eleven thirty-one," said Allhoff. "Is it fast?"

A quick check around the room assured him his watch was right.

"Can you prove it, man?" said Blakely impatiently.

"I think so," said Allhoff slowly, his eyes still on his watch.

"You think so?" exploded Blakely. "A man's life is at stake. You've thrown suspicion on a police captain. What do you mean you think so?"

Allhoff opened his mouth to speak. His eyes lit up suddenly and he closed it again. Then I heard racing footsteps on the stairs and I knew Allhoff's keen ears had heard them before mine.

Garfield, the assistant D.A., ran into the room, his yellowish face lighted with excitement. In addition to his briefcase he carried a large sheet of foolscap in one hand and a woman's pocketbook. The last two he threw down on the desk before Allhoff.

"There it is," he shouted triumphantly.

"A full confession, signed and sealed. And here's her pocketbook. Some of his letters were in it."

Graham leaned forward, his eyes riveted to the purse. "That's my wife's bag," he said in a hoarse voice. "Where did you get it?"

Neither Garfield nor Allhoff paid the slightest attention to him.

"A complete confession," said Garfield again. "She helped him with it. Helped him dispose of the body. We can hold them both. She's an accessory before, during, and after the fact of first-degree murder. We'll burn them both!"

"No!" said Donna Graham. "For the love of God, no!"

There was awful vibrant emotion in her voice, but Allhoff seemed deaf to her too.

"Both of them," he said to Blakely. "Here's the proof you asked for Commissioner, I'll give you two killers instead of one, I'll give the executioner three hundred bucks instead of half that."

"No!" said Donna Graham again. "No, you fools! You've bullied her until she's hysterical. She didn't know what she was saying. She had nothing to do with it. She knew nothing about it till it was done. Dad! You can't let her suffer for this. You did it all yourself. Mother didn't know till it was done. Dad, tell them that's the truth."

Graham closed his eyes. He swayed back and forth on his feet for a moment and I thought he was going to fall.

"I killed him," he said heavily. "I killed him myself. Neither my wife nor daughter knew of it till it was done. I killed him."

All the tense animated excitement which had possessed Garfield suddenly drained from him like blood from a torn jugular. He slumped down in his chair. He wiped the sweat from his sallow brow with a handkerchief. He emitted a long-drawn sigh. "Thank God," he said to Allhoff. My career was at stake. Thank God!"

Allhoff regarded him quizzically. "You mean she wouldn't talk?"

Garfield shook his head, "I've been screaming at her, pounding at her for a solid hour. She wouldn't say a word. Then I realized it was half past eleven. I knew we'd have to do it your way." He sat upright in his chair again and added rather conceitedly: "I did damn well, didn't I?"

"Damn well," said Allhoff, "I believed you myself."

"Could you spare a moment." I inquired, "to tell me what the hell this is all about?"

"Sure," said Allhoff. "Garfield arrested Mrs. Graham this morning. While I was working on Graham here, he was working on his wife over in the D. A.'s office. If she cracked, he was to bring her confession over right away. If she didn't—"

"If she didn't." I put in, "he was to come over anyway and pretend that she had."

"With variations," said Allhoff. "He was to pretend not only that she had confessed but that she'd implicated herself as an accessory. We gambled that would break Donna down into convicting her father. The handbag was good atmosphere, too. It assured Graham that we actually had arrested his wife."

Matt Arnold stood up. He eyed Graham with murderous gaze. He took a step forward when Battersly seized his arm, Graham stood leaning against the wall, his face bloodless and gray. His daughter wept softly unto a handkerchief.

I went out into the hall, leaned over the balustrade and blew a loud blast on my police whistle. While I waited for the beat copper to come up the stairs, I reflected that Allhoff had not only solved a murder case but had brought my own dreams of freedom from his savage thrall crashing about my ears. It was quite evident that not only would Allhoff be at his desk on Monday but on every Monday hereafter until the day he died.

The copper pounded up the stairs. He departed a moment later with Graham in his custody. I sent Matt and Donna Graham home.

I closed the door behind them to see Blakely standing over Allhoff's desk with his hand extended.

"Very nice work, Inspector," he said. "You've done a first-rate job."

Allhoff looked up at him, but did not take the proffered hand. He pushed the typewritten resignation across the desk. He said: "I'm always glad to see a civilian take an interest in the world of the police department."

Their eyes met for a moment and held. Allhoff took a fountain pen from his pocket and handed it to Blakely. Blakely stood perfectly still for a moment. Then he sighed and stretched forth his hand. He scrawled his name at the bottom of the paper, swung around on his heel like a guardsman and marched from the room.

Allhoff filled his chipped cup with coffee. He glanced over his shoulder at Battersly and myself. There was a wicked glint in his eyes.

"You guys can go home now," he said. He drank his coffee in silence as we donned our hats and coats. He didn't speak again until we were halfway down the stairs. Then the mocking voice roared after us."

"I'll see you on Monday morning!"

His raucous laughter followed us down the staircase out into Centre Street.

THERE WAS A CROOKED MAN

 Originally Published - August 1940

CHAPTER ONE

Murder at 103° in the Shade

The brick and concrete of the tenements sucked up the heat like the sands of Sahara. Humidity rose from the bay and swept over the city like a wet and stifling blanket. Centre Street was a klieg-lighted Turkish bath in the blinding sunlight. Opposite the window, the dull red bricks of police headquarters withstood the temperature with the dispirited indifference of old age.

It was bad enough outside, but within Allhoff's cramped apartment it was hot as a clarinet solo played in hell's furnace room by Benny Goodman. The tin roof above us conducted the heat down upon our heads like anathema. Wet, reeking air pushed lazily through the open unwashed window and there were dark steaming patches on the blue of my uniform shirt.

At a hundred and three in the shade the flat was in its usual disarray. The bedroom door stood ajar revealing an unmade bed and a carpet of soiled clothes upon the floor. Dishes rattled in the sink as Battersly, from sheer boredom, began to wash the stack of china, accumulated through God knew how many weeks. His young muscular shoulders were bent over the sink as he pursued this task with the same dogged, unemotional persistence that he applied to everything else.

A cockroach moved wearily across the floor to join its family at lunch by the garbage can. I lit my pipe, sighed, and wished with all my heart and soul that I had enlisted in the Northwest Mounted Police. At the moment, the Arctic held no terrors for me.

Allhoff squatted, characteristically, in his swivel chair. Huddled over the desk like a gnome, his corvine nose was buried in a thick gray cup. It had no handle and its chipped and stained exterior gave it a leprous appearance. At his right the electric percolator gurgled in macabre glee as its heat lifted the already unbearable temperature a few more degrees.

I stood up and pulled my sticky underwear away from my flesh. I glanced over Allhoff's shoulder into the murky depths of his coffee cup. I felt so unutterably lousy that I had resolved to brave his curses and ask for the afternoon off. Then as I opened my mouth to speak, I heard footsteps on the stairs.

The outer door opened and a well-tailored body came briskly through the heat. As he stepped across the threshold, his manner, his smile reminded me of a ship's cruise director. His eyes were blue and bright. He wore a salesman's smile. His collar was crisp and unwilted. His demeanor was jaunty. He was, I wagered mentally, a very active member of at least three fraternal organizations.

Inside the room his face fell for an instant as he looked around at the dirt, the disorderliness, the apparent poverty. But he recovered in a split second, stepped forward and stood before Allhoff's desk. He thrust out his hand and spoke crisply.

"Inspector Allhoff, I presume. My name's Williams. Henry Fairchild Williams. I've got a case for you."

Over at the sink, Battersly put down an egg-stained plate and turned around with interest. If Henry Fairchild Williams expected his cordiality to arouse a similar response in Allhoff, it was quite obvious he knew very little about the inspector's habits.

Allhoff, disregarding Williams' hand fluttering over the desk, took his nose out of his cup. He reached for the coffee pot, poured a dark libation, spooned in a lavish amount of sugar and put his nose back where it had been at the time of Williams' entrance. Williams

looked down at his own outstretched hand and flushed. Allhoff sipped his coffee noisily as Williams cleared his throat.

"Perhaps you don't understand, Inspector," he said with rather less assurance than before. "I'm a nephew of Morgan Murtry. A son of—"

Allhoff took his face out of his cup and finished the sentence for him with a single insulting word. Rage flamed in Williams' blue eyes. Allhoff planked his cup back in its saucer and spoke harshly.

"I take cases only from the commissioner. I never welcome visitors. I do not care to be disturbed at my coffee."

Williams stared at him incredulously. Then slowly an expression of understanding came over his closely shaved face.

"Ah," he said breezily, "I guess I didn't make myself clear. Inspector. I dare say you're bothered a lot with cranks and nuisances who expect you to drop everything and solve their cases for nothing. I'm not one of them. No, sir. Cash on the line. That's me."

Battersly glanced nervously at me. I took a deep breath and waited for the detonation. Offering Allhoff money was rather like tendering the Russian flag to a bull. Allhoff pushed his cup away. He lifted his head and his little yellow eyes stared at Williams. His face was contorted. His parted lips revealed stained teeth.

Williams remained completely unaware of the danger signals. He chattered on gayly.

"My uncle. Morgan Murtry was killed yesterday. Although, I guess I don't have to tell you police news, eh, Inspector. Well, they've got my cousin. George— that's Murtry's son, in jail charged with the murder. Now that's ridiculous, Inspector. Utterly ridiculous. But the police won't listen to me. So I've come to you."

Allhoff didn't say anything. He sat quite still, breathing deeply. Somehow he reminded me of a gun that was loading.

"No, sir," continued Williams. "They even ignored my important evidence. Uncle Morgan had a visitor last night. No one knows it but me. Walking past his study door I heard voices. I distinctly heard my uncle say. 'Your coming in the window tells me all I want to know.' Now that certainly indicates a burglar, Inspector. But the police wouldn't listen to me,"

He broke off and reached into his inside pocket. Allhoff still looked at him like a muzzle watching a target. Williams withdrew a wallet from which he pulled out a thick stack of bills.

"And don't worry about money, Inspector. There's plenty here and plenty more where this came from." He laid the bills on the desk and looked around the wretched room, "And I guess you could use a little cash, eh, Inspector? Get yourself out of this dump. Get something decent."

took a step forward, intending to interrupt him. But before I could speak he established himself as the top-flight candidate for the tactlessness championship of the decade.

"Besides," he rushed on. "I've heard of your affliction, Inspector. I know a man does wonders with artificial legs. Never know them from the real thing. Of course it costs money. But that's what I'm offering you. Now shall I sit down and tell you my theory?"

Allhoff snatched the money up from the desk. He hurled it to the floor. He pushed his swivel chair out into the center of the room, revealing a pair of leather stumps attached to his thighs where his knees should have begun. His voice rose through the heat of the room like shrill thunder. "Get out!" he yelled. "Damn you! Get out! You grinning, blatant smug-ugly. I want neither your filthy money nor your murder case. I don't want your lousy artificial legs either. I lost my legs honorably, in the line of duty. I'll not be mocked about it. Pick up your money and get out of here. Get Out! Get Out! Or, by God, I'll arrest you."

Williams' jaw had fallen almost as far down as his chest. He goggled at Allhoff in terrified amazement.

"Arrest me?" he echoed faintly. "For what? You can't arrest me."

"The hell I can't!" roared Allhoff, You're a disorderly person. You're trespassing. I can hold you on suspicion for forty-eight hours. I can put you—"

I took a step forward, "Allhoff," I said sharply. He turned his wrath on me as Williams, dazed, bent down and scooped up his money.

"Shut up!" he yelled at me, Then his eyes met Battersly's and I braced myself for the worst. "You," he roared, "I bet you sent this pompous idiot up here. Trying to sell me a set of wooden legs to ease your own conscience. Trying—"

The slam of the door punctuating Williams' exit interrupted him. I tried to stem the tide.

"Allhoff," I said, cajolingly, "maybe the case is worth looking into after all, Murtry was a pretty big shot. His son is in jail and headquarters seems pretty sure of itself. It's just the sort of thing you like."

But at the moment he wasn't having any flattery. He moved his hot little gaze from Battersly and hurled it at me.

"You, too," he said bitterly. "You want me to buy a pair of lousy wooden legs. You want me to take his dirty dough to get back the legs I lost honorably in the line of duty."

This statement was as reasonable as a Goebbels speech and I said so. I added that I still thought the case was interesting, that perhaps he should look into it. But at the moment, it appeared. Allhoff was looking into nothing but his coffee cup. From its unclean depths I could hear the rumble of his voice.

"The case is cold. The kid killed the old man after a quarrel about his impending marriage. I read the reports. Besides I don't need his damned oaken legs. I don't need his damned money. I wouldn't touch the lousy case. I lost my legs—'"

"I know." I said hastily. "Honorably and in the line of duty."

He swung around again in his chair. Battersly turned to the sink and made a hellish clatter as he resumed his dish-washing. To my relief Allhoff ignored him. His wrath was directed solely at me.

"I want to hear nothing more about it.'' he shrieked. "Nothing more about the Murtry case. Nothing more about wooden legs. Nothing. Nothing. Nothing!"

He slammed his fist against the desk until the cumbersome cup rattled in its saucer. He snatched up the coffee pot, poured, and drank deep.

I retired to my desk, picked up the afternoon paper, thoroughly decided against requesting the rest of the day off. Battersly washed the dishes listlessly. Allhoff sipped his coffee. And the heat came down on my head as I inwardly cursed the day I had ever seen Allhoff, Battersly, this damned tenement and the uniform I wore.

he circumstances which had engendered our happy little family had occurred several years ago when Battersly was a raw recruit and Allhoff an inspector whose legs ran all the way down to the floor. The department's crack stoolpigeon had reported that two wanted and notorious public enemies were in hiding at an upper West End Avenue rooming-house. Allhoff had volunteered to lead the raiding party.

The informant had stated further that the gangsters had mounted a Tommy-gun upon the stair head, thus commanding the door from within. Battersly's assignment had been to affect a rear entrance, disable the operator of the gun at zero hour just as Allhoff came crashing through the front door. Battersly had affected his entrance all right. However, once inside the house, he had contracted a quite understandable case of buck fever. Instead of overpowering the thug behind the gun, he had run into the upper story.

A moment later the raiding party came bursting through the doorway. Allhoff at their head. The Tommy-gun operator went into action, with the immediate consequence of twenty machine-gun bullets tearing their way through the lower half of Allhoff's legs. Gangrene had set in swiftly. Amputation had saved his life.

I often doubted if it had saved his mind as well. Minus his legs Allhoff had become a bitter, misanthropic old man—older by ten years than he actually was. His physical loss had been compensated for by a psychological hatred, directed at the world in general, and young Battersly in particular.

He retained, however his keen, analytical mind, and the commissioner had no intention of losing his best man. Of course, a legless inspector violated every rule in the book. However, devious bookkeeping saw to it that Allhoff received full pay each month. He had rented this fragrant slum because it was close to headquarters, had demanded of the commissioner that Battersly be assigned as his assistant. I, as an old-timer, who had known Allhoff ever since he came up from the ranks, had been thrown in on the deal to see that he stopped just this side of apoplexy whenever he cursed young Battersly.

It was a miserable job from which the commissioner flatly refused to transfer me. Allhoff lived introspectively with his bitterness. Battersly's attitude was that of a man devoting his life to the expiation of a mortal sin. I, completely normal, was caught beautifully in the middle.

CHAPTER TWO

Cripple to Cripple

The day wore on. Battersly finished the dishes, returned to his desk and scanned the comic strips. I lolled by the window inhaling what little air came over the dusty sill. Allhoff brewed coffee constantly.

Once, I thought I heard footfalls on the rickety stairway outside. On second thought I decided I was mistaken. True, the boards seemed to creak wearily but there was no rhythm in the sound such as regular stepping would make. The sound, however, continued. A moment later a diffident knock came at the door.

Battersly stood up, went to the door and opened it. A man came slowly into the room. I half rose in my seat and stared at him with wide eyes, half in horror at what I saw, half in horror of Allhoff's reaction when he lifted his face from his coffee cup.

The stranger hobbled into the room on a pair of crutches. His face was twisted in pain and his brow was wet with agonized sweat. His left leg was contorted horribly behind him. His right foot which touched the floor was pointed inward as if he were about to embark on some grotesque variation of the Charleston. The fingers of his left hand bent down almost touching his own wrist. There was misery in his eyes and his grimacing face wore an expression which was repulsive and pitiful at once. He looked for all the world like an apparition. As if Lon Chaney had broken the tomb and come back to haunt a damned and cursed planet.

Allhoff looked up. His head jerked back in a sudden start as he beheld the apparition. His eyes narrowed. I could hear his sudden and quick breathing across the room. He swung his chair around and yelled at Battersly.

"A chair, you oaf. A chair for the gentleman. Damn you, get him a chair!"

Battersly dragged a chair across the room, placed it by the side of Allhoff's desk and aided our visitor into its uncomfortable seat. The cripple sat down, handed his crutches to Battersly and wiped his brow with a handkerchief. A sultry sigh escaped his parted lips.

"Excuse me, Inspector," he said. "The name's Leamington. I can't talk till I get my breath."

"Of course," said Allhoff, and there was a strange gentleness in his voice. "Take it easy. Here, have a cup of coffee. Battersly! A cup for the gentleman."

It was the first time in my life that I'd ever heard Allhoff refer to anyone as a gentleman. Moreover, it was the first time I'd ever seen him proffer a cup of the asphalt he called coffee to a stranger. The reason, of course, was obvious. There is a bond between the lame, the halt and the blind which transcends the ties of religion, race, or even blood.

Leamington sipped his coffee gratefully. Then he replaced the cup on the edge of the desk and spoke.

"I've been over to headquarters, Inspector," he said, "but they won't listen to me. They say I'm crazy, that what I have to tell them isn't evidence. Maybe it isn't, but I know I'm right. So I came to you for help. I thought—"

He looked down, embarrassed, at his twisted legs. "I thought maybe, seeing as how—Well, I thought, somehow, you might be able to help me."

"I'll help you," said Allhoff, with that odd softness still in his tone. "Anything I can do. What is it?"

"The Murtry case, Inspector. Young Murtry never killed his father. I know he didn't."

Allhoff blinked. I watched him closely. He had strictly forbidden all mention of the Murtry case and here it was bobbing up again. Rather to my surprise, he didn't blow up. He said in a low confidential tone: "Tell me about it, Leamington."

Allhoff picked up the percolator and refilled the cripple's cup. Leamington nodded his thanks, and spoke again.

"I've known George Murtry for several years. Used to work for him before—before my accident. He's a kind and good man. He visited me at least once a month. Gave me money, helped me in every way he could. Spent hours talking with me, trying to make me more cheerful, trying to interest me in hobbies, things that's take my mind off my troubles."

His voice became suddenly husky with emotion. He broke off and sipped some coffee.

"You see, Inspector," he went on, and there was terrible earnestness in his tone, "George Murtry has a heart of gold. He'd never kill anyone. Least of all his own father."

ell, that was a speech I'd heard many times before. Laymen never seem to realize that every man's a potential killer under certain circumstances. I waited for Allhoff to make that point clear. To my surprise, he didn't.

"I see your point," he told Leamington. "I'll look into the case."

That irritated me. Allhoff's sympathetic feeling for a fellow sufferer was swaying him away from the path of logic.

"Allhoff," I said, "you're crazy. If headquarters says the case is open and shut, it probably is. Besides, Williams had a better story than this man and you threw him out of the office."

"The hell he had a better story," snapped Allhoff. "If this George Murtry was kind to this man it argues he wasn't his father's killer. Leamington, leave your name and address with Sergeant Simmonds, there. I'll look into this case for you."

That, of course, was as reasonable as numerology. But I took Leamington's address and kept my mouth shut. If Allhoff wanted to stick his neck out for purely emotional reasons it was quite all right with me. If he botched up a perfectly good case and got hell from the commissioner while doing it, it was even better.

Battersly handed Leamington his crutches and aided him to the doorway. En route, the cripple stumbled. Allhoff's fist smashed hard on the desk-top.

"Be careful, you blundering fool," he shouted at Battersly. "Must you specialize in breaking legs?"

Battersly flushed but didn't answer. He disappeared down the stairway, holding on to Leamington's arm. Allhoff drained his coffee cup and turned to me with a businesslike air.

"Now," he said, "what've we got on this Murtry case, Sergeant?"

That 'Sergeant' was to show me that the great Inspector Allhoff had embarked on another case, that from here on in things were strictly official. However, I decided to give him one more warning before he acted on anything as flimsy as Leamington's suspicions.

"Look here," I said. "Headquarters has a good case against young Murtry. Whether he's guilty or not I don't know. But I'm damned if there's any reason to think he's innocent merely because he's been good to his mother or because he once gave a dozen bananas to a guy who uses crutches."

Allhoff waved that aside with a gesture. When he spoke he sounded like an admiral addressing the lowest dog-robber in the fleet.

"Sergeant Simmonds," hue said, "I'll hear the evidence."

I sighed and picked up the onion-skin report. "Murtry," I said, "Morgan F., banker, industrial entrepreneur and all around big shot. Found stabbed to death in his study yesterday morning. Found by the beat copper who was called in by the butler. That afternoon he'd had a terrific brawl with his son George. Headquarters figured the son killed him. Moreover they figure they can prove it."

"Without my aid," said Allhoff loftily, "headquarters couldn't prove the world is round. What was the Murtry brawl about?"

"A woman. Young Murtry was going to marry a girl named Margie Hope. On one occasion, at least, she was engaged in a profession which is somewhat older than that of radio engineer. The old man said no. Said he expose the girl for what she was in every paper in the country."

Allhoff grunted. "So the son said he'd kill him, eh? Who heard him say so?"

"The butler, your old pal Henry Fairchild Williams, and the girl. The girl says he elaborated on it. Said he'd use a knife instead of a gun so as not to arouse the household."

Allhoff lifted his coffee cup. "Estate to the son, too, I suppose?"

"No. Half to Williams, the nephew. Half to a Doctor Raynor. The son was lousy within his own dough. Got it from his dead mother's estate."

"All," said Allhoff, a note of triumph in his voice, "there's one motive out of the way."

I put down the report. "Listen," I said. "do you mean to say you're still pursuing the golden-heart theory? George Murtry apparently had enough motive without money."

"Now," he said, playing his role of super-sleuth to the hilt, "call headquarters. Ask them when I can question the prisoner."

I shrugged my shoulders, made a gesture of helplessness at Battersly, who had returned to sit slumped by the window. Then I picked up the phone and put my call through. A moment later I hung up again and faced Allhoff.

"Well," he said as I didn't speak, "when do I talk to George Murtry?"

"Never," I told him.

He glowered at me. "The hell I don't," he bellowed. "Who do they think they are over there? They can't keep a prisoner incommunicado from me. Get me the commissioner on the wire. They're scared I'll smash their case for them."

"You don't want the commissioner," I told him. "To question George Murtry you'll want a spiritualist."

His agate eyes opened wide. "What do you mean?"

"He's dead. Found poisoned in his cell less than an hour ago."

"Poisoned with what? When? Who did it?"

His little eyes were gleaming and his finger rattled excitedly upon the desk-top.

"The M. E.'s looking things over now. They figure it was probably suicide. If not, the stuff must've been in his food."

"I knew it," exclaimed Allhoff. "I knew there was more to that case than met the eye. I knew headquarters couldn't solve a murder on their own book."

I regarded him with a fishy and dubious eye. "A few moments ago," I observed, "you told Williams the case was cut and dried."

"That was before I gave myself over to it. Before I felt psychically that something was screwy."

Before he felt it psychically! I clapped my hand to my head at that one.

"All right." said Allhoff briskly. "We're going to work. We're going to clear this thing up." He turned his head and shot a venomous glance at Battersly. "We'll show Leamington that half a body doesn't mean half a brain."

Ever since I'd heard of the death of George Murtry, I'd been thinking. Now I thought I had a very simple answer.

"Allhoff," I said. "let's look at the most obvious theory. Granted George Murtry was a very nice guy, granted he was in the habit of sending flowers to invalids. Nevertheless, he's in love with a girl. His old man threatens to publish some very unsavory facts about her. He goes berserk. He kills the old guy. Because he was a decent kid while normal, his cousin and Leamington intercede for him. But alone in his cell he gets the horrors and poisons himself. That's simple obvious, and quite probably true. Now suppose we all go home, have a cold shower and go to bed."

"That," said Allhoff, "clinches it."

"What clinches what?"

"The fact that there's something screwy about this case. You've never been right in your life, Simmonds. Now here's what you guys are going to do tonight."

Whatever vision I'd had of a cold shower and a night of relaxation vanished. Allhoff was playing Sherlock Holmes and when he was in this mood, Battersly and I were reduced to a pair of docile Doctor Watsons.

"First," said Allhoff, "see that doctor. What's his name? Raynor. Pump him. See why he gets half the estate. Then get out to Murtry's house. Go over the whole place carefully. See what you can find. Pay particular attention to Williams. After all he's a beneficiary un-

der the will. And if you can pin the killing on that louse. I'll see you get a week's leave, both of you. I don't like him."

"Good old prodigal Allhoff," I murmured. "How the hell could Williams have killed the old guy when he came here offering you more dough than I've seen this year to turn up the real killer."

Allhoff shrugged his shoulders. "That's what I'm offering you a week's leave to find out."

Battersly had put on his cap and was standing in the doorway. I mopped my wet brow, buckled on my holster and followed him.

"Wait a minute," said Allhoff thoughtfully. "We may as well cover all angles. Go to this Leamington guy's apartment, too,"

"With a basket of fruit?" I asked him.

"Damn you, no! See what you can find out about him. Search his rooms. See what—"

"How are search going to search his rooms while he's there?"

"My God," said Allhoff, "what sort of a detective-sergeant are you? Get him out of there. I'll tell you what. Take him out to Murtry's with you. Say I wanted him to go along to help out with suggestions, You get started with him. Battersly can stay behind and frisk his joint. I know rolling cripples is a pretty low pastime, but I'm sure Battersly'll enjoy it. Now, get going. I want to think."

I followed Battersly down the stairs watching the red flush at the back of his neck and I knew Allhoff's last words were still stinging his ears and his heart. We got into my car downstairs and I didn't speak to him as we drove through the seething streets to Doctor Raynor's Park Avenue office.

Raynor turned out to be a fat, ineffectual-looking guy addicted to expensive Klassy-Kut suits. His shirt was lavender and lovely. His tie cost a cold five bucks. He literally wrung his hands in misery over Murtry's death when we announced the purpose of our visit. Murtry was his oldest friend, a great guy, good to the poor and his mother. It sounded very much like the spiel Leamington had given us about the son.

Raynor sat at a desk in his office with a huge checkbook in front of him. Apparently he had been going over his accounts when we arrived. Casually, I noted that his bank was the Second Federated. Beyond that I observed that he bore a single tuft of hair in the very center of his bald head. And that was all.

As we left, I decided the visit had been fruitless. Allhoff had nothing, knew nothing, suspected nothing. Battersly and I had been assigned to a fishing expedition to turn up whatever fell into our lap. These reflections caused me to think of the dinner and shower I was missing and my temper mounted. Battersly, still mulling over Allhoff's parting crack, was wallowing in just about the same mood as myself.

We left Raynor's and drove crosstown to Leamington's place, having a very low opinion of the world in general and Allhoff in particular.

After a long wait in the hallway. Leamington opened the door. He was twisted around on his crutches and greeted us with a wan smile, through the tortured pain on his face. I grew even more annoyed with Allhoff. There was as much point in searching this guy's apartment as there was in rolling Bishop Manning's vestry room. I became throughly convinced Allhoff's had ordered it merely to get his nasty crack in at Battersly.

I told him what we wanted and felt like a heel when he beamed at me and said: "Why, that's damned white of the inspector. I'd be delighted to come along. I always wanted to watch a detective at work. And I really may he able to help. I know a lot about George Murtry."

"O. K.," I said. "You come along with me. Battersly here has a little chore to do downtown before he joins us."

The cripple kept beaming at us as we helped him on with his jacket and hat. A moment later he was sitting beside me in the coupe. We drove off with Battersly standing on the sidewalk staring miserably after us. I knew he felt like a poor-box robber on his present detail.

Murtry's estate was just beyond Forest Hills out on Long Island. Leamington chatted desultorily during the drive and it was evident from his enthusiastic manner that he was having the time of his wretched life playing copper for real.

As I turned into the gates of the estate a cool breeze came in from the bay and I felt somewhat better. There was a caretaker's lodge near the gates and about a quarter of a mile up a gravel driveway, a huge colonial mansion stood whitely in the dusk.

A butler ran out on the porch to open the car door and helped Leamington into the house. Greeting us in the foyer was Williams who seemed very happy when he discovered Allhoff was investigating after all, and a girl. The girl, tall, worldly and damned good-looking turned out to be Margie Hope, George Murtry's fiancé who had precipitated the brawl between the old man and the son. Despite a touch of hardness in her eyes, they were moist with tears.

Williams and I maneuvered Leamington into a chair. The butler got us drinks while Williams paced up and down the drawing-room and talked.

"A terrible thing," he said, "Young George's suicide. A terrible thing. I can't understand it at all."

The Hope girl stood up and glared at him, "Suicide hell!" she said. "George never killed his father and he never killed himself. But there were those who'd profit by his death."

Williams turned to her, horrified. "Do you mean—"

"You know damned well what I mean," she said bitterly. "Who gets the old guy's dough?"

"Take it easy," I interposed. "Allhoff's on this case now. If there's any dirty work he'll uncover it."

I didn't believe that myself, but a copper can have a bedside manner, too.

"That's right," said Williams. "Very decent of the inspector to take the case for me after refusing a fee."

I didn't enlighten him by announcing that Allhoff hadn't taken the case for him at all. Williams and the girl seemed puzzled enough at Leamington's presence without my complicating matters. I had introduced him as a friend of mine interested in police work.

Some twenty minutes later Battersly arrived. I told Williams the pair of us had orders to roam around the house with our eyes open, left Leamington in his care and walked out of the room with Battersly.

Without difficulty we discovered "the room that had been Murtry's study—the room in which he had been killed. It was a huge oblong chamber with an enormous desk in its center. Books lined the walls and deep dark heather chairs were scattered about the room. The big double windows opened on to a garden distinguished by a magnificent oak tree that towered above the house. A polished mahogany half-sized cupboard stood opposite the desk against the east wall.

"Well," I said to Battersly, "did you find anything at Leamington's?"

He shook his head and flushed. "Nothing important. There was a suitcase full of papers. I didn't have time to look 'em all over. I brought 'em along. Let him look at 'em."

I saw his point. If anyone was going to invade Leamington's unhappy privacy, let Allhoff do the dirty work himself.

"Good enough," I said. "I'll look over the study, here, son. You get upstairs. I don't know what the hell we're looking for, so anything you decide's worth reporting is all right with me."

Battersly left the study. I sat down at the desk, lit my pipe, opened the drawers and proceeded to rummage. I found a lot of dull business letters, financial statements which were utterly beyond my four-thousand-dollar- a-year understanding and then, after a while, I came across a museum piece. It was a driver's license, made out to Morgan Murtry and dated 1919.

At this point I put everything back in the drawer, decided Allhoff was screwy, got up and scanned the bookshelves for something to read until Battersly finished his futile search of the upper stories. I pulled out Herbert Lewis' *Gentleman Overboard*, and settled down in one of the easy chairs.

Fifteen minutes later Battersly bust in the door like the vice squad. "Sergeant," he said breathlessly. "For God's sake! Look what I've got!"

He held up a knife in one hand and a sheet of typewriter paper in the other. There was a brown stain on the knife blade and I'd seen enough lethal weapons in my day to know it was neither rust nor nicotine.

"It's the murder weapon, Sarge," said Battersly, talking like a tabloid in his excitement. "I bet it is. And look what it says here." He handed me the piece of paper. A message was typewritten upon it.

Henry: It is easier to write you about this than to speak to you. Various matters, none of which are your fault, have caused me to change my mind about the disposition of the estate. Next week I am changing the will. Hoping you will take this in good part. MM.

"See," cried Battersly, "it's a cinch. Williams didn't want the old guy to cut him out of the will. He knocked him off before he could change it. My God, Sarge, I solved a case. All by myself. The inspector ain't got nothing to do with this. Has he, Sarge?"

I examined the knife and the note. Everything seemed cold enough save for one item.

"Why," I asked, "would Williams come and ask Allhoff to take the case if he were guilty? Why would he be so calm about our looking over the house with this evidence against him?"

Battersly thought a moment. "Maybe," he said shrewdly, "he asked the inspector to take the case just to make things look good. Maybe he's smarter than he looks. Maybe he figured out how to get the inspector sore, talked to him like he did deliberately, so he'd get thrown out. Then everyone would say he tried his best."

"Where'd you find this stuff?"

"In the basement, Sarge. At the bottom of a big pile of old paper. Williams probably never figured anyone'd look there. He figured the stuff would go to the incinerator in a day or two."

I stood up and thought it over. "Well," I told him, "I hope you're right and I hope you're wrong. There's nothing I'd like better than to see you break a case under Allhoff's nose. On the other hand, I'd hate like hell to be around when he found it out. Let's pick up our cripple and get back to town. We've done better than I thought we would tonight."

On the drive home Leamington bombarded us with questions that we didn't answer. It was so late when we arrived in town that I told Battersly to go home. The stuff we had for Allhoff could wait until morning. We dropped Leamington at his place and went to our respective apartments. It was almost midnight when I finally got my shower.

CHAPTER THREE

Allhoff and Freud

The percolator was brewing its second batch of ebon poison when I arrived at Allhoff's apartment the following morning. Battersly came in a few minutes after Allhoff had ignored my "good-morning."

After a half -hour of silence Allhoff deigned to take notice of, our existence. He pushed his cup away, lit an evil-smelling stogy, and said: "Well, what did you find last night, if anything?"

"There's a very good chance that Battersly solved your case for you," I told him.

He laughed unpleasantly. "That's good. Solve a case for me! Well, what did you find? Tell me about the doc first."

"Nothing there," I told him, "An innocuous sort of a guy. Old pal of Murtry's. I gather Murtry went in for a lot of medical clarity. That would explain the bequest."

"I'd like the facts," said Allhoff arrogantly. "Not opinions."

By this time Battersly was bubbling over. He could keep silent no longer. "I've got facts, Inspector," he said eagerly. "Look here."

He pulled a parcel out of his pocket and unwrapped it on Allhoff's desk to reveal the knife and sheet of paper he had found. Allhoff frowned and examined the articles.

"What's this?"

Battersly told him. He kept his eyes anxiously on Allhoff like a dog waiting to be patted or kicked.

"Well," I said, "has he solved your murder for you?"

"My God." said Allhoff in a voice several degrees lower than his normal bellow. "Out of the mouths of babes. Maybe he has solved it, Simmonds. But certainly not the way you think, I'm beginning to see a faint light."

That, frankly, I didn't believe, Allhoff wasn't seeing a damned thing beyond the fact he was going to let neither Battersly nor myself get an iota of credit no matter which way things broke.

"Anything else?" he said after a long silence.

"Sure," I told him. "A butler with a stiff collar an' everything. A rather good Scotch and soda. A good-looking girl, George's fiancé who's pretty sore about everything. Oh, and a driving license, dated 1919. Anything else you'd like to know?

"Driving license? 1919? Made out to whom?"

"The deceased, Morgan Murtry. What's odd about that?"

"Go way," said Allhoff. "I'm thinking."

Within the aid of another pot of coffee he thought, or pretended to, for a long while. Then, he came suddenly out of his reverie and snapped at Battersly: "What about Leamington? Did you roll his joint?"

"Oh," said Battersly, "I forgot. Here are the papers I took. I didn't have time to look them over in his place so I brought them along."

Allhoff took the papers from his hand and glared at him.

"You're dumb enough to become commissioner some day," he said scornfully. "Leamington's going to miss this stuff. If it's at all important, he'll be warned."

He left us alone for a while as he pored over the papers. After some five minutes reading he banged his fist upon tile desk.

"Listen," he said excitedly. "Listen to this."

He began to read from a piece of heliotrope paper in his hand. From the salutation it seemed to be a love letter. After he got through the second paragraph there was no doubt about it.

It was not only a love letter but it was what the boys on the corner would call a hot love letter. It was frank to the point of lewdness. What it lacked in spiritual qualities it more than made up for in its carnal trend. It had obviously been written by a nubile and passionate woman who was very much in love with Leamington.

Battersly's neck was red as Allhoff read the lascivious details, I became annoyed. It wasn't the sort of thing I liked to hear anyway and Allhoff's obvious relish made it worse.

"Damn it, man," I said at last. "Will you lay off? That letter's got nothing to do with the case. It's a personal matter and I think it's damned indecent of you to read it."

He put the letter down and swivelled-slowly around in his chair. "You are very brilliant copper," he said and his voice dripped irony. "Suppose I told you that there were several letters in this vein among these papers. Would that mean anything to you?"

"Nothing. Except I'd ask you not to read them."

Rather to my surprise he said nothing. He swept the pile of papers into a drawers, screwed up his brow in thought and said: "I suppose neither of you sleuths thought to get the name of Raynor's bank?"

"It's the Second Federated. Why?"

"I want to call them up," said Allhoff. "That is, right after I call the license bureau."

By now I figured he was simply being cryptic for effect, for during the whole rest of the morning he made no phone calls at all.

When Battersly and I came back from lunch he was beaming. "Say," he said, "do you know that thousands of dollars went into Raynor's account from Murtry?"

"So what?" I said. "I told you Murtry was his pal. It went in for medical charity."

"Ah," said Allhoff with suspicious sweetness. "so you did. And what would you say if I told you the license bureau reports that 1919 was the last year Murtry took out a driving license, was the last year he ever registered a car?"

"I wouldn't even say it was mildly interesting."

"I didn't think you would. However, now I'll tell you both something you'll find personally interesting. You're working tonight. The two of you."

"For Heaven's sake, Allhoff," I protested. "What are you master-minding now? If you're going to charge Williams with murder can't you do it on what we've given you? Must we rush all around town in this heat digging up futile information for you?"

"Yes," said Allhoff with devastating finality. "But first tell me about Murtry's study. What's it like?"

I made a gesture of resignation. What in hell did he want to know that for?

"It's big," I told him. "Books all over the walls. Easy chairs. A desk. A phone."

"Any closets?"

"No closets."

"Hmm. How high is the window from the ground?"

"Maybe eight feet."

He grunted again. "Any cabinets in the room? Cupboards?"

"No," I yelled at him. "And there are no grand pianos, cello cases, or rifle racks either. Anything else you want to know?"

He opened his mouth to scream at me but fortunately Battersly spoke first. "There's that what-not, Sergeant?"

"A what?"

"A what-not. That little low cabinet against the wall. Opposite the desk."

"Oh, that," I said. "That's not a whatnot. It's a—"

"Well," snapped Allhoff impatiently. "What is it?"

"It's a little cabinet. About three feet high."

"All right. All right. You guys get out to Murtry's place at exactly nine thirty. Under no circumstances leave before eleven thirty. Oh, and by the way, take Leamington with you. He'll probably get a kick out of it. Poor devil can't get much out of life. Got those instructions?"

"We've got them," I told him. "But what do we do when we get to the house. Sit around and wait for a confession?"

"Ah," said Allhoff. "I almost overlooked that, didn't I? Let me see. Oh, yes. I want you to gather everyone in the study. Then I want Battersly to ask that Hope girl if anything has been going on between her and Williams. Ask that question in front of Williams. You, Simmonds, study their faces carefully as they answer."

That was the insanest instruction a police sergeant ever had and I said so. Allhoff merely chuckled.

"Oh," he added, "there's one other thing. A friend of mine's passing through town tonight. Big-shot medical guy. Specializes in cases like Leamington. I've arranged for him to see Leamington at his hotel at eleven thirty. His name's Wheeler. Tell Leamington about it."

"All right," I said. "We understand. But do you mind telling me why Battersly has to ask that embarrassing question of the Hope girl?"

Allhoff laughed unpleasantly. "There are only two people in the whole world who might figure the answer to that question," he said. "The other one is Freud."

"You mean the Austrian psychologist?" I asked. "But I thought he died a few months ago." "Ah, so he did. I'd forgotten. Then that leaves only me, doesn't it?"

The big grandfather's clock at the south end of Morgan Murtry's study indicated it was a few minutes past ten. Uncomfortably the five of us stood gathered around the big open window drinking the cooling breeze. Leamington sat in a huge leather chair we had pulled up for him. The rest of us, Williams, the Hope girl, Battersly and myself, stood chatting idly.

I stared morosely out into the night. I noted, sitting beneath the splendid oak tree of the garden, a fat elderly woman taking the air. I assumed she was the cook. I glanced at my watch, then at Battersly.

He met my eyes sheepishly. He had been stalling ever since we arrived and I couldn't blame him for that. The question he had been ordered to ask was tough enough for a hard-boiled veteran, much less a kid like Battersly. Still, we couldn't stand around and talk about the weather all night. Then just as I was about to nudge him into action, I recalled Allhoff's message to Leamington, about Doctor Wheeler.

No sooner had I delivered it, than Battersly, red of face and none too facile of tongue, touched Margie Hope lightly on the elbow and having gained her attention, blurted out: "I beg your pardon, Miss Hope, but have you-er-I mean there's nothing been going on between you and Mr. Williams, was there?"

Had he hit her on the head with his blackjack he would have surprised her less. Williams gasped. The Hope girl stared at Battersly with her hard eyes. Her mouth twisted into a nasty sneer. Williams spoke first.

"Good Heavens." he said. "Do you mean to imply—"

"He's a copper, ain't he," said Hope harshly. "What the hell can you expect from that breed?"

Battersly hung his head like a schoolboy who has been caught concealing pornography in his history book. To cover up, I said hastily: "Suppose we all have a drink?"

"Certainly," said Williams. "Let's go down to the bar."

"What about Leamington? He's comfortable here. No sense in moving him."

"Right," said Williams. "Well send his back up here. We'll be back in a few moments, old man."

Leamington smiled his thanks and we left the room.

From the bar the butler took Leamington's drink back up to the study, then returned and served us. By now it was only twenty minutes past ten, our embarrassing question had been asked and Allhoff had specifically instructed us to wait until eleven thirty. I certainly didn't know why. The conversation was languishing and I was sure Williams was wondering why the hell we didn't go back to town.

After a little time at the bar we flocked aimlessly back to the study and rejoined Leamington. From then on the conversation became deader and deader.

Just before eleven o'clock. I heard the doorbell ring. Then we heard footsteps in the hallway and a moment later Doctor Raynor entered the room. He shook hands effusively with Williams and the Hope girl. "Sorry, I haven't been out sooner," he said. "A terrible thing these two deaths. Terrible. God knows—" He broke off suddenly as he caught sight of Leamington. "My God!" he said, "What are you doing here?"

I became mildly interested. "You know Leamington. Doc?"

"Know him? He's my patient. And a damn bad one. He should be in bed. The man's crazy wandering about at night in his condition. He's ill. By God, I'm taking him right home!"

Leamington protested but Raynor stood on his professional dignity. He bade us all a hasty good-bye, promised to see Williams tomorrow and aided

Leamington out of the room, still muttering about the foolhardiness of patients who disobeyed doctors' orders.

When they had gone Williams yawned. The evening had become deadly boresome. "If you gentlemen don't mind," he said, "I think I'll go up to bed. Very tired. Hard day. If you want anything while you're investigating, the butler will get it for you."

Hope said, "You ain't leaving me alone with any coppers," and followed him out of the room.

As the door closed behind them, I turned angrily to Battersly. "What's that damned fool making us stay here till half—past eleven for?" I demanded. "Curse him. I'm going to call him up and get permission to leave."

I snatched the phone from the cabinet and started to dial. I became suddenly aware that the familiar buzz wasn't sounding in my ear. I jiggled the receiver. The phone was quite dead. I handed it to Battersly.

"How do you figure that?"

He listened, frowning for a moment. Dead," he said. "Sounds like the wire's been cut."

He put the phone down slowly and we exchanged puzzled glances. I shrugged. "Well, to hell with it. Probably the wire got broken somewhere. We'll just have to hang on for another half-hour. That's all."

We sat and smoked for a long while in silence. Then I gave utterance to a thought that had long been on my mind. "Son," I said, "why don't you get out?"

"Get out?"

"Of the department There's no reason why you should stick around letting Allhoff drive you crazy. With me, it's different. A few more years, a pension and my life's over. But you're young."

Battersly sighed and shook his head. "No," he said. "I made him like he is today. It's up to me to stick around."

"All right," I said, realizing it was useless to argue. "But don't let him get you down. Treat him like the harmless lunatic he is. Remember he's completely pathological and don't take him too seriously."

I know. He's like a savage who must be humored. But sometimes the going is tough."

"Well, take it easy," I said inadequately. "Some day he'll finish in the grave where he'll really be better off with the worms eating the hatred out of him so he can rest in peace."

Down at the end of the study the big clock clanged out the half-hour. I stood up.

"Come on," I said, "That officially ends our vigil. Though if there's any sense in what we've done tonight, I'll eat my pension."

We went out into the night, climbed into the car and headed back to town.

Home, I found a message left by Allhoff with my wife. It ordered me to round up Raynor, Leamington, Williams and the Hope girl, to have them all present at Allhoff's apartment at eleven o'clock the following day.

I had a shower, went to bed, and had a very odd dream in which Allhoff was perfectly sane.

CHAPTER FOUR

Allhoff Plays God

Allhoff's coffee pot gurgled sullenly, showing no respect for the gathered company. Fanwise before the desk sat the group of people. Immediately on Allhoff's left, facing the begrimed coffee pot was Leamington. His crutches leaned against the wall behind him and his twisted legs lay coiled beneath the chair like a pair of tweed covered snakes. His face was wet with perspiration that he made no effort to wipe off.

On the cripple's left was Margie Hope. Her silken legs were crossed revealingly and defiantly. She regarded Allhoff, Battersly and myself warily. Her early life had taught her that a copper was a copper and not to he trusted under any circumstances. She was dressed in white and remained crisp and damned good-looking even in the awful heat.

Facing Allhoff, his back to the door, Henry Fairchild Williams sat upright in his kitchen chair. A faint shadow in his eyes revealed a slight apprehension, but his salesman's smile persisted and his social-director demeanor remained unimpaired. From time to time he chatted briskly with Doctor Raynor who was seated next to him.

With the temperature of the room an even hundred and five, Raynor resembled a drooping five-day-old gardenia. His elegant lavender shirt was wet, his once stiff collar had long since wearily collapsed. His tie was awry and the little tuft of hair in the middle of his head shone wetly in the single sunbeam that reached him from the open window.

Battersly's chair having been commandeered for the company, he stood leaning against the sink watching the assembly with a detached air. I sat on the top of my desk, looking at Allhoff, wondering if he was going to pull a rabbit out of a hat once again and hoping very much that he wasn't.

Then, after keeping everyone waiting for a dramatic ten minutes, he took the rim of his cup away from his lips, set it down with a clatter on the saucer and looked around the room.

"It may interest you all to know," he said, smug as the Book of Proverbs, "that the Murtry case is solved. *I* solved it."

Which was quite a broad statement considering Battersly had dug up the evidence and I had done most of the leg work.

His audience, with the exception of the Hope girl took the pronouncement calmly. Hope uncrossed her legs, rather to my disappointment, and leaned forward in her chair.

"You mean you can prove George didn't do it?" she asked. "You mean George is clean?"

"Naturally," said Allhoff magnificently. "I don't dabble in the obvious."

He poured himself a cup of coffee as if he had all the time in the world. Then he looked up suddenly and fixed Raynor with his metallic eyes. "Doctor," he said sharply, "was Morgan Murtry a sickly man?"

Williams answered before Raynor could find his voice. "Not at all, Inspector" he said boomingly. "Never had a sick day in his life. Picture of health. I always used to say—"

"Your voice," snapped Allhoff, "has a cathartic effect upon me. Now, Doctor Raynor?"

"He was a healthy man," said Raynor in his tired voice. "Usual colds and so forth. Nothing serious."

"Then," said Allhoff, "why do your bank statements show such a hell of a lot of money paid into your accounts by Murtry? If he wasn't paying your bills what the hell was he paying?"

The lethargy went out of Raynor's eyes. A startled expression came in. "Uh," he said. "Money? From Murtry? Oh, that. He was a very generous man, Inspector. Very generous. Constantly paying the bills of those unfortunates who couldn't afford to pay themselves. Ordered the best for them, too."

Allhoff grunted. "Can you produce any of these unfortunate people?"

Raynor appeared very uncomfortable. "Well, if you gave me time. Yes, of course I can."

"You couldn't." said Allhoff flatly. "But we'll let that go for a moment."

Battersly and I exchanged glances. In my wildest theory I didn't see how the hell Raynor fitted into this.

"Now," said Allhoff, "I have a reputation in this town for infallibility. It is undeserved. People forget my talented assistants." He gestured toward Battersly and myself like Toscanini permitting the first violins to take a bow.

We stood uncomfortably as the assembly looked at us. My immediate astonishment at Allhoff's compliment rapidly gave way to suspicion. I was certain he had something up his sleeve that boded no good to anyone save Allhoff.

"At times," said Allhoff, "I concede I lose my temper to the point of becoming completely pathological. However, I hope I'm fair enough to give credit where credit is due."

Completely pathological. The phrase struck some responsive chord in my brain. But, for the moment, I couldn't quite place it.

His sweet smile terrified me. I was convinced something awful was going to happen any minute.

"Yes," went on Allhoff, "it was Patrolman Battersly who really solved this case, who found the missing link which I needed to complete the chain of my reasoning."

He opened the desk drawer. From its muddled depths he withdrew the knife and the typewritten sheet of paper which Battersly had found in Williams' bedroom. His audience leaned forward in their chairs, craning their necks.

"Yes, sir," said Allhoff, "here we have the weapon that killed Morgan Murtry. Here we have a typewritten slip of paper which apparently furnished the motive for the murder."

"What is it?" said Henry Williams, tensely. "Where did it come from?"

"From your bottom bureau drawer," said Allhoff affably. "In your raincoat pocket was the slip of paper. Initialed by Murtry and informing you that he intended changing his will."

For the first time since I had known him, Williams dropped his Kiwanis Club air. His face was suddenly pale and his eyes seemed to sink deeper into their sockets.

"My God," he said hoarsely, "what is this? A frame up?"

"Precisely," said Allhoff.

"Allhoff," I said, "get on with it. You're accusing Williams. Can't you do it without all this cryptic hocus-pocus."

"My invaluable assistant," said Allhoff, and his voice was thick with sarcasm, "I am not accusing Williams. Despite the fact that I merely appear a harmless lunatic, I know exactly what I'm doing."

For the second time it seemed to me that there was a familiar ring to his words. But at the moment I was too concerned with other things to examine my memory.

"Someone killed old man Murtry," said Allhoff. "Someone who overlooked the fact that the police department is composed of some very heavy muscles and some very light minds. The killer did his job with despatch. He planted the evidence on Williams, here. Then went home to bed waiting for the police to do the rest. The coppers, as usual, fell down badly."

Raynor and Williams exchanged glances. Behind the gurgling coffee pot, Leamington, the cripple, stared blankly at Allhoff. The sweat was running down his face, leaving little gray streaks in its wake. Margie Hope looked over Allhoff's shoulder at me. Her face was screwed up in puzzlement.

"Sarge," she said, "what in hell's he talking about?"

"He'll tell you," I said. "It'll probably take him several hours, but he'll tell you."

Allhoff ignored this conversation. "As I was saying," he continued, "the police made their customary mistake of accepting the easiest and obvious thing. Hearing of the quarrel between George Murtry and his father, they looked no further. They dragged George off to the can and never even looked for the murderer's planted evidence. Which was most annoying to the killer."

I decided it was time someone played interpreter. "Are you saying," I asked, "that someone planted that knife and that note, purporting to be signed by Murtry, in Williams' room?"

"That's what I'm saying," said Allhoff. "Much as I regret it."

"Regret it? Why should you regret it?"

"Because," said Allhoff, smiling his terrible grimacing smile at Williams, "I'd like to see Williams in the chair. His death would remain among my happiest memories."

Williams' face grew paler. He swallowed something in his throat, tore his eyes away from Allhoff and intently studied the cracked plaster of the wall.

"Why in the world should anyone want to plant evidence against Williams?" I asked.

"Well, if Williams *did* burn for the murder—and that's still a beautiful thought to me—Doc Raynor would get all the old guy's dough, wouldn't he?"

Raynor shook his head like a waking dog. He opened his eyes wide. "Me?" he said. "My God. Me?"

The effort of those four words was too much for him. He sat back in his chair again, breathing hard. Leamington took his gaze from Allhoff and stared hard at the doctor.

"Listen, Allhoff," I said. "Who're you charging with murder? If it's Williams— if it's Raynor—say so. And if it's neither of them, please tell me why George Murtry died. If he killed himself, why? If he was murdered, again why? There's no point in his death that'll fit any theory, if he wasn't guilty."

"Ah, a very keen mind, Simmonds. Very keen," he said in a tone which indicated that it wasn't at all. "George Murtry was killed. Killed because the murderer feared George would expose him."

"All of which makes no sense," I said. "If George knew who the murderer was he would have talked before he went to jail. Why should he cover up for his old man's murderer?"

"Ah," said Allhoff, "he didn't know who his father's killer was."

By this time I was as dizzy as anyone else in the room. Allhoff invariably approached an explanation by a route as devious as a schoolboy going to the dentist. But today he was setting new records.

"All right," I said, "I'll be straight man for you. What do you mean by saying George was killed for fear he'd expose the killer when he didn't even know who the killer was?"

Allhoff sighed. He poured fresh coffee with the air of a man who is greatly put upon by the stupidity of the world. "Perhaps I'd better explain it as simply as possible. I concede I'm something of a savage but I think I should be humored." That last sentence was not only vaguely familiar to me but it struck me as damned odd. It didn't make much sense. However, I let it pass. If Allhoff was going to talk lucidly at last, I didn't want to do anything to hinder him.

"You see," said Allhoff, "when Murtry died his estate would be split between Williams and Raynor. Note, Raynor would get half. With Williams in his grave for murdering the old guy, Raynor would get it all."

Raynor looked like a mass of putty clad in a Kollege-Kut suit.

"Are you saying Raynor killed Murtry?" I asked,

"He didn't wield the knife," said Allhoff, not taking his eyes off the little doctor. "But he'll burn for it just the same."

Raynor spoke and his voice seemed projected from a great distance. "You've nothing on me, Inspector. I'm a respectable professional man. Never a breath of scandal. Never—"

"Shut up," said Allhoff, "you remind me of Williams. Now why did Raynor collect all this dough from Murtry while he was alive? Why did he go down in the will for such a huge hunk of cash? Why?"

"All right," I said, "Why?"

"Because," said Allhoff, "Murtry never took out a driving license since the spring of 1919."

Then he shut up and reached for the coffee pot. That was no unexpected gesture to me. After as cryptic a remark as he had just made, he was going to give us all time to be completely baffled before he cleared it up. There was nothing to do but wait.

CHAPTER FIVE

"There Was a Crooked Man—"

While I waited, I looked at the faces around the room, trying to read the answer to Allhoff's crack in them. The doctor and Williams looked as if the F. B. I. was hiding in the closet, prepared to leap out and pin the Charlie Ross kidnaping on them. Leamington stared unblinkingly at the percolator, his face wet and pained. Hope had recrossed her legs, I noted, which Battersly had already observed. Allhoff sucked up some coffee with what for him was a cultured noise, put down his cup, and having enjoyed his moment of suspense, continued.

"Here's Murtry— a guy who's owned a car ever since the day Henry Ford scrapped the family team and put a four horse-power motor in the buggy. Every year since then Murtry bought a new car. Right up to 1919. Then he quit. He never owned another automobile. He never took out another driver's license. And from what we can ascertain, he never drove anyone else's car either. Now what, my mentally alert assistants, does that argue?"

Battersly screwed up his brow in deep thought. I didn't even bother with it.

"It argues," I said, "that he got tired of driving. Maybe that he didn't like cars anymore."

Allhoff's sneer made an awful heel out of Humphrey Bogart. "It argues," he yelled, pounding the desk with his fist, "that he'd had an accident. It argues he was scared to death to drive. That his conscience was bothering him. That was so apparent I checked on it. On April Seventh, 1919. Morgan Murtry had an automobile accident. He hit a guy."

"As an elementary lesson in detection, that's not bad," I told him. "However, I'm still patiently waiting to see what the hell it has to do with the matter in hand."

"I am a bitter old man," said Allhoff, strangely. "Don't try me too far." He leaned over the desk and shook a threatening and dirty forefinger under Raynor's quivering nose. "Now, Doctor, you received a telephone call at about thirteen minutes past ten last night, didn't you?"

"Yes," said Raynor, startled. Then quickly, "That is, I—er——I don't know. I receive lots of phone calls professionally, Inspector. I don't remember."

"You remember this one," said Allhoff grimly. He spun around in his chair and fixed Battersly with his gaze. "You. There was a phone call made from the Murtry estate last night at approximately thirteen minutes past ten. Who made it?"

Battersly looked bewildered as he always did when Allhoff fired a direct question at him. "I don't know, Inspector. I didn't. Oh, the phone was out of order. The wires were cut. Weren't they, Sergeant?"

"They were," I said. "Though exactly when I don't know. It was about half-past ten when I found it out."

"The wires were cut at a quarter to nine," said Allhoff decisively. "But I'm not discussing that. I'm trying to find out who telephoned from the estate at ten thirteen. Or if I can't discover that, let me know who didn't."

"My God," I said not unreasonably, "if the wires were cut at a quarter to nine, although I don't see how you can figure that so damned accurately, how the hell could anyone use the phone at ten thirteen?"

"Did *you* phone?" snapped Allhoff.

"No."

"Battersly said he didn't. Anyone else who can prove he didn't?"

Sure," I told him. "Williams didn't. Because he was with me at that time. So was Miss Hope. The butler didn't because he was serving us drinks."

Ah," said Allhoff, "and where was Leamington?"

I don't know," I said, "And I don't know where the cook was either. Do you?"

"Yes," said Allhoff. "The cook was sitting in the garden outside the study window taking the air. Leamington was down at the caretaker's lodge."

That staggered me. I recalled now that I had seen the cook sitting under the big oak tree. For a moment I was prepared to believe Allhoff as psychic as he claimed he was.

Now," went on Allhoff, "what time was it when Williams asked you all to have a drink?"

"Oh, that," said Williams, "It must have been about ten minutes past ten. I remember because I—"

"Shut up " roared Allhoff, "I can't stand your greasy voice. Simmonds!"

"He's right. About ten minutes past ten."

"So you left the study then. What time did you next see Leamington?"

"My God," I said again. "I don't know. We left Leamington in the study. His drink was served to him there because it was difficult for him to walk down to the bar. When we came back again, certainly not more than ten or twelve minutes later, he was still there."

"Damn you, why didn't you say so before?" He whipped open the drawer of his desk, jerked out a Police Special and the taut silence of the room was broken by the click as he took off the safety catch.

He swung his chair around sideways and leveled the gun at Leamington over the top of the coffee pot. "Leamington," he said, and there was a hideous note of triumph in his voice, "you can't move without your crutches, can you?"

The expression on the cripple's face was one of utter and complete bewilderment. His face grew white beneath the running perspiration. He shook his head wonderingly.

"No," he said. "No."

"Of course, he can't," snapped Raynor. "If you want a professional opinion."

"What profession?" said Allhoff. "I'll give you a copper's professional opinion right now. Battersly, take those crutches away."

Battersly obeyed the command as gingerly as a general taking orders from Hitler. He picked up the crutches, took them back to his desk and leaned them against the sink.

"Now," said Allhoff squinting down the barrel of the revolver, "I'm going to count three, Leamington. Then I'm going to fire dead at the middle of the chair you're sitting on. I'd suggest you'd better not be there when the bullet comes."

By this time Raynor had stopped his wilting. He stared, horrified, at Allhoff. Williams adjusted his colorful tie with trembling fingers. Margie Hope drew a deep breath and recrossed her legs. Battersly looked helplessly at me.

"One," said Allhoff. Then, "Two."

I took a step forward. "Allhoff," I said. "For the love of God, man, are you—"

"Three!" said Allhoff.

The gun thundered in his hand. The sound smashed against the wall and banged back into our ears. The bullet hammered into the pine wood of the chair boring a neat little hole. Leamington had taken Allhoff's advice. He wasn't there when the bullet arrived.

He had moved faster than any cripple I had ever seen and quite as fast as Joe Louis in the ring. He had straightened up like a released bow string, jumped to one side like a pendulum, and was now standing with his back against the wall, both in a literal and figurative sense, breathing hard and staring at Allhoff with red hatred in his eyes.

It was Williams who recovered first. "Inspector, what does this mean? Did he—did he—"

"Yes," yelled Allhoff banging his hand up and down on the desk-top like a pile-driver. "He did! He did! If he was a cripple how the hell could he get out of the study, run down to the caretaker's lodge a good quarter of a mile away, put in a call to Doc Raynor and get back all in ten minutes?"

llhoff was screaming now in a wild frenzy of excitement. His eyes glittered like angry coals. His lips were wet with saliva which splattered over the papers on his desk as he bit off his words.

"I sent him that phony message about Doctor Wheeler to see what he'd do. If he'd been on the level he'd have jumped at the chance. If he was a phony it'd terrify him to death, That's just what it did. The instant you guys left him alone he sprang to the phone to get advice from his pal, Raynor. He found the wire dead. That got him more panicky than before."

He paused for a moment and lifted the percolator with a hand that trembled. Leamington glared at him like a wolf at bay. Oddly enough the sweat dried on his face now, leaving it whitish and scabrous looking.

"He remembered the caretaker's lodge. Figured that phone would be O. K. It was the nearest one anyway, so he took a chance. He leaped out the window, got there, called Raynor and got back again. All inside of ten minutes. Once I knew that, I knew he was a fake. After a while Raynor arrives, orders Leamington to bed so he won't have to see Wheeler."

To myself I conceded Leamington looked very much like a guilty man. Still I was damned if I saw all the angles and I said so.

"Look," said Allhoff. "It's 1919. Murtry's car hits Leamington. Leamington goes to the hospital. Murtry has a large attack of conscience. He pays all the bills, sends his own doctor, Raynor, to take the case. He pours money and gifts upon Leamington. So why, then, should Leamington get cured?"

"You mean he faked it all these years merely to take Murtry for dough?"

"Use your head, man," shouted Allhoff. "All that dough checked from Murtry's account into Raynor's. For what? Why new cures of course. New specialists to cure the helpless cripple that Murtry's careless driving had created. Thousands of dollars to the high-priced medicoes. All for Leamington. But, of course, the specialists never even heard of the case, much less got the dough. But Leamington got his half. It was fifty-fifty, wasn't it, Doctor? Even George, the son, contracted some of the old guy's horrors. He visited Leamington sympathized with him, gave him dough."

"But the will?" I asked. "What about the will?"

"It's as obvious as your own stupidity. Murtry was going to die some day. Maybe after he was dead some super-specialist would be able to cure Leamington. Murtry made sure they'd have the dough for it. For anything as long as it would expiate his sin. Battersly knows how he felt, don't you, Battersly?"

That was a cruel remark. Battersly's face was suddenly ashen.

"As soon as I knew of that old driving license, of all that dough going from Murtry to Raynor, I suspected the answer. So I set my trap last night. That proved I was right," Allhoff finished.

"But George," said Williams, whose curiosity momentarily overcame his fear of Allhoff. "Who killed George and why?"

"You did," said Allhoff.

"Me?" Williams' voice was a crescendo howl of horror.

"Indirectly," said Allhoff, "The first day you were in this office you spoke of a visitor in Murtry's study. You quoted Murtry as saying, 'Your coming in the window' tells me all I want to know. Remember that?"

I remembered it and said: "So what?"

"So," said Allhoff, "it was an easy window to get into. You told me that, Simmonds. And if my theory was correct, and it usually is, Murtry's remark had to be directed at our phony cripple. Get it? *Your coming in the window* (thus avoiding being observed by anyone) *told Murtry all he wanted to know.* In short it told him that if Leamington could climb in that window he was a fake, had been a fake all these years."

"All right," I said. "But what's that got to do with George?"

"Everything. Williams liked his cousin and his visit was bona fide. When Williams was in this room offering me his munificent fee, Leamington came along to ask me to handle the case. He and Raynor, bitterly disappointed that the dumb headquarters coppers had overlooked their planting evidence against Williams, figured I'd be smart enough to find it. They figured, too, that one cripple would be likely to help another.

"Anyway, Leamington was outside the door, ready to knock when he heard Williams' loud and oily voice. He heard what he said about that crack of old man Murtry's and he knew immediately that when George heard of it, and he was bound to sooner or later, George would figure it out just as I figured it out. Far more easily, in fact, because George was well aware of the whole situation. Once that remark was repeated to George he'd know that Leamington had visited the old man that night. He'd also figure he was a phony since he climbed through the window. And that would explain a number of things to George."

ight and grudging admiration for Allhoff were slowly dawning upon me. "But, Allhoff," I said, "there's one more thing. If they were draining the old man so successfully why knock him off?"

"Ask them. Greedy, I guess. Couldn't wait, Didn't want to divide the estate with Williams anyway. Knock off the old man, frame Williams, and Doc gets it all. Of course he splits with Leamington. Or had you planned to get rid of him, Raynor?"

I had never seen a man in such a pitiable condition as Raynor. His lavender shirt was dripping wet. His face was gray putty. His eyes were rolling marbles and when he spoke his voice was poisoned with terror, "God." he said, pointing a finger at Allhoff. "He's in league with the devil. How could he know? How *could* he?" He looked from Allhoff to Leamington, standing, a wolf's snarl on his lips, against the wall. "But I didn't actually do it. I didn't knife Murtry. I was against sending that poisoned food in to George. Leamington'll tell you I was against it. Tell him Leamington. Tell him!"

For the first time that afternoon, Leamington spoke. "You've told him enough." he said savagely. "At least I'll know you're burning with me when I go."

"You will indeed," said Allhoff cheerfully. "Battersly, get a copper to take them out of here."

here was complete silence in the room as Battersly went downstairs. It held until he returned with two policemen who dragged Leamington, minus his crutches, and Raynor down into the street.

Williams stood up and extended his hand over Allhoff's desk. "Congratulations. Inspector." he said. "I think—"

"My God." said Allhoff wearily. "Are *you* still here."

Williams flushed, turned on his heel and walked out. Hope got up, pulled her dress down over her legs, walked to the door and handed Allhoff her accolade.

"I never thought I'd live to see a cop who wasn't dumb," she said. Her footsteps sounded diminuendo on the rickety stairs.

"Allhoff," I said, "I admit you were good. But what made you think Leamington was a phony? You must have had something to go on before you began to theorize."

He turned his face to me and there was a wry, twisted smile on his lips. "Those letters," he said harshly. "Those damned love letters. How the hell could a cripple get them?"

That took my breath away. His own complete misanthropy had led him to the trail. Yet I was sure he had been wrong.

"Why not," I said, "Do you argue no one would ever love a cripple? There are a million cases. What about Browning? What about—"

"You fool." he said. "Can't you see that was different. Maybe a cripple could be loved by someone. Though I assure you as far as I'm concerned it's purely an academic question. But they couldn't love him like *that*. A girl might have loved Leamington, assuming he was on the level, in a spiritual sort of a way. The sort of love a wife of eighty feels for her husband. But not passionately, physically, obscenely, as those letters indicated. It was a dead give-away. I knew Leamington was a fake ten seconds after I read those letters."

I digested that for a long time. Sometimes he was so damned right it drove me crazy. I was still mulling it over when Battersly spoke.

"I'm puzzled about one thing, sir. Those cut wires. Without that you wouldn't have trapped Leamington. Was it just luck?"

"Luck!" snorted Allhoff. "Luck! I leave nothing to luck. I never have and I never will. Not even when I'm in the grave and the worms are eating the hatred out of me so that I can rest in peace."

He shot a venomous glance at me and I suddenly recalled where I had heard all the strange abnegating phrases he had been uttering all day. They were taken almost verbatim from the conversation I had had with Battersly out at Murtry's place.

"Allhoff," I cried, "You were there! You were out at the house. You made Battersly ask that question about an affair merely to fool us. You were there! You cut the wires yourself!"

"I don't trust either of you completely. Simmonds, I wanted to watch the effect of my own trap. I did cut the wires myself. I sneaked in the study window an hour before you arrived."

"But you couldn't have been hiding. Not in the study. There's nowhere to hide."

"The hell there isn't," said Allhoff. "That thing that Battersly said was a what—not."

You're crazy. It's too small. A man couldn't hide in there."

He focused his eyes upon me. And I swear all the bitterness that has flourished in the world since time began was concentrated in his gaze.

"Half a man could." said Inspector Allhoff with savage finality.

CHAPTER ONE

Allhoff and the "Hysterical Type"

The Commissioner said thoughtfully: "Perhaps you're right about this thing, Simmonds. I'll speak to Allhoff about it later this morning. I have to see him on another matter anyway. That's all Simmons."

 Originally Published - October 1940

SUICIDE IN BLUE

I stood stiffly at attention before his desk. Before I made my parting salute. I figured I'd better get myself in the clear.

"I'd be obliged, sir, if you—if you—"

He looked up, grinned and anticipated me. "If I didn't tell Allhoff you had anything to do with it, eh, Sergeant? Don't worry. I won't."

I thanked him, saluted, and swung around on my heel. I strode down the corridor, out of the red brick building which housed police headquarters, into Centre Street. I had the warm satisfied feeling of a man who is

acutely conscious that he has put something over. More than that, I felt like a Boy Scout who is three good deeds ahead of himself and can rest on his oars for the remainder of the week.

I crossed the street. entered the dank hallway of a dreary tenement house which was a crime against the Federal Housing Act, and climbed a flight of creaking stairs. I opened the door of Allhoff's apartment, walked in, and noted with some surprise that he had not yet rolled out of his sagging mattress.

The bedroom door was ajar. The sun shone through the unwashed window with reluctance. It landed, a diluted spotlight on Allhoff's face. Even in slumber, I observed, his ugly features were not relaxed. Beneath the skin the muscles seemed taut and the heavy vertical lines on his brow attested that he frowned even in sleep. A snore, harsh and restive, floated through the doorway, came to rest in my ear. I sat down at my desk and sighed.

I looked around the room, shook my head, and wondered how any man could live in it. The sink, with more enamel chipped off it than remained, was half filled with greasy water. An egg-stained plate floated like a discouraged garbage scow on its top. Thick cafeteria cups, spattered with coffee stains stood in a precarious tower beside the water. Silverware, which was that only nominally, lay strewn and blackening over the drain board. Beneath the sink an uncovered garbage pail furnished a self-service breakfast for a score of buzzing flies.

Opposite this delicate scene, by the side of the bedroom door a pile of soiled clothing and linen lay on the floor. In itself this was no unusual sight. But it seemed to be getting out of hand. In five years I had never seen it so mountainous. It stretched a gray, dank peak half-way to the cracked ceiling. Allhoff, the chatelaine of all this luxury, snored on. I lit my pipe and went to work.

I pored over the departmental reports that had been sent over early this morning. I conned the crime news in all the papers. I had all the answers ready at my tongue's tip, in case Allhoff, upon rising, had any questions.

Finished, I glanced at my watch and noted that the sounds of snoring had ceased. In their place mumbled oaths emanated from the bedroom. It was now a few minutes after ten o'clock. It was unusual for Allhoff to sleep so late. More unusual was the fact that Battersly had not yet put in an appearance.

The bedroom door creaked open wider. Allhoff emerged like something zooming out of Pandora's box. He was unwashed and his hair looked as if someone had starched it during a moment when he was very frightened. I offered him no greeting. Allhoff observed no social amenities, uttered no word, save his guttural oaths while dressing, until he had consumed at least two pints of coffee.

He clumped across the floor, squatted in his swivel chair and proceeded to dump coffee with a prodigal hand into the percolator. Silently, I got up and filled the pot with water. Allhoff put it on the electric plate, switched on the current and awaited its boiling with all the patience of an insomniac alcoholic hanging on until eight o'clock for the saloons to open.

The minutes ticked by. Allhoff glared at the glass top of the percolator awaiting for the first bubble to appear. Outside, I heard a footfall on the stairs. A moment later the door opened and Battersly neat and trim in his patrolman's uniform, came in. Allhoff, of course, didn't look up. I nodded a greeting, which Battersly ignored. He stood in the doorway staring apprehensively at Allhoff's percolator. He swallowed something in his throat then came nervously into the room and took off his cap. At the moment he looked more like a dip who has just seen a member of the pickpocket squad, than a policeman.

He reached his hand out and touched the switch that controlled the overhanging light. It clicked as he pressed it.

The light did not go on. Battersly looked at me with wide fearful eyes until I felt like a hammer murderer who'd just come into his bedroom.

"My God," he muttered. "Oh, my God!"

He turned around and approached Allhoff's desk as if it were the gallows. He cleared his throat nervously and said: "Inspector—"

Intellectually, I had always known that Battersly was not even a distant cousin of Einstein. But until now, neither had I considered him a complete idiot. For anyone to venture a remark to Allhoff prior to his morning coffee was dangerous. For Battersly to do so was suicide.

Allhoff kept his eyes fixed on the percolator and didn't answer. Frantically, I tried to get Battersly's eye, to flag him away. Miserably, he shook off my signal and said again: "Excuse me, Inspector, but I—"

Allhoff's head spun around on his shoulders so savagely that the swivel chair creaked. His little eyes were hot slag. His lips were contorted grotesquely. His voice vibrated like an angry dynamo.

"Damn you!" he yelled. "Get to your desk. Don't bother me in the mornings. I've told you that a million times. Get to hell away from me. Can't you see I'm making coffee?"

"I beg your pardon, sir," faltered Battersly. "But—but that's what I wanted to tell you, sir. You're—you're not."

"I'm not what?"

"You're not making coffee, sir. You see yesterday I forgot to—"

He never finished that sentence. Allhoff had reached out his hand and touched the electric plate. It was, as I had figured by now, stone cold. Allhoff's face was reminiscent of a desert dawn. His eyes were dark and burning charcoal. Battersly looked like a man awaiting the drop of Doctor Guillotine's blade. Despite myself, I grinned. The idea of Allhoff thirstily awaiting the coffee's boiling while the electricity was turned off did not appeal to my better nature.

"You see, sir," said Battersly hurriedly, "that electric bill I was supposed to pay for you yesterday afternoon—well, I forgot. I didn't think of it until this morning. When I got there they told me they'd already turned it off. It'll take an hour or so before it comes on again."

"Idiot!" howled Allhoff and his enraged voice rose and scraped the ceiling. "You blundering dull-witted fool! Or are you? Damn you! You did this deliberately. You've made a fool of me."

"No, no," said Battersly unhappily. "I'm sorry, Inspector, I forgot, that's all. I—"

That was another sentence he never finished. Allhoff reached down deep into the sewers of his mind for the rest of his vocabulary. He smeared the unfortunate Battersly with language which would have impelled a corpse to rise from its bier and smack him. I knew full well where this conversation was leading us. I got up and essayed to head it off.

I pressed a quarter into Battersly's cold palm. "Here," I said. "Go downstairs to the Greeks. Get a container of the strongest coffee he's got. Hurry."

attersly hurried. He needed no urging to flee the room. Allhoff flung a biological remark after him, then turned the vials of his wrath upon my head. "I won't drink that damned slop from downstairs. Hell, that's not coffee. You want know what it is?"

I didn't want to know what it was, but he told me in roaring obscene chemical detail. He was still protesting profanely, vehemently, that he wouldn't drink it when Battersly returned. Allhoff snatched the container and ingested a full pint before he took it away from his twisted, dripping lips.

I went back to my desk and ran through the reports seeking a diversion to keep him away from the thing I knew he was going to hurl at Battersly when he had finished the coffee. Battersly crossed the room, stood by the window, staring down into Centre Street with shadowed eyes.

"Allhoff," I said casually, "did you know that Wheeling killed himself last night? You remember Wheeling. He came up when we did. Sergeant. Safe-and-loft Squad."

Allhoff grunted into the coffee container. "That's over twenty police suicides since the first of the year," I went on. "There's a committee of three psychiatrists looking into it."

Allhoff put down the container. "Psychiatrists!" he said, and his voice curled with so much scorn I knew I had diverted him temporarily, from Battersly. "What the hell do they need psychiatrists for? I could've told 'em ten years ago Wheeling would probably kill himself. I could've told 'em that about most of those other coppers who've blown their brains out."

I raised my eyebrows at that. I had always known that Allhoff's opinion of himself reached Himalayan heights, but heretofore he had never boasted he was occult, that he could detect a crime before it had been committed.

"Well," I said, permitting my incredulity to seep into my tone, "that's a very good trick if you can do it."

He spun around in his chair and glared at me. "It's no trick, you muddy-brained copper. It's simple observation and reason."

"All right. Let's take Wheeler's case. Go ahead. Observe and reason."

"An hysterical type," said Allhoff. "Never should've been allowed in the department. Remember the time they brought him up on charges? He was innocent. He was cleared. But he had a breakdown immediately afterwards. Then there was the time he saw his kid brother's corpse after those dope runners shot him down. He wept over the body. A copper, mark you," he said indignantly, "crying."

I blinked at him. "Do you actually mean to tell me that you could have predicted Wheeler's suicide on those two items?"

"Not definitely. But those two episodes are indicative, I've observed a hundred other things since I knew Wheeler. There's a lot of people like that. With most guys it doesn't matter. They get hysterical, so they get drunk and sleep it off. And that's an end of things. With a copper, it's different."

"Why," I asked, "is it different with a copper?"

"Because, you stupid flatfoot, he's always got a gun handy. When a copper broods and considers suicide he's only got to unlimber his Police Special and it's all over. A layman has to devise some means of killing himself, then go out and buy the weapon. That gives him time to think it over. Wheeler was a natural to kill himself. Always worrying, always brooding about the least thing."

I lit my pipe, digested this theory, then decided I didn't believe it.

"So you really think that only coppers of the hysterical type, as you call them, kill themselves. And then only because there's a gun handy."

"Of course. Every rookie should be put on six months probation under my supervision, I could tell in that time if he was the hysterical type or not. If he was, we could get rid—of him. Stop the department getting a bad name with all these suicides."

I puffed at my pipe and asked: "Am I the hysterical type?"

Allhoff snorted. "Hell no. You're too damned bovine. It takes a degree of sensitivity to be the hysterical type. Like Wheeler, or—" He looked around the room and his bitter little eyes settled on Battersly. "Or Battersly over there. He's a real hysterical type. Wouldn't be a bit surprised if he blew his brains out some day."

If he does, I reflected. I'll know damned well who drove him to it.

"So there you are," said Allhoff with the air of a man who has settled the problem of creation. "Hysterical types make bad coppers. Wheeler kills himself just because he belongs to that type. So three psychiatrists delve into their books to discover why instead of asking me. Hell, I've known why for ten years."

In front of him the discolored coffee pot gurgled morbidly as the electricity came on. Allhoff stopped talking and grabbed his cup eagerly.

He was pouring a tarlike concoction from the spout when I heard someone coming up the stairs. A moment later the commissioner entered.

attersly and I saluted. Allhoff bowed with the respect he offered no one else. The commissioner put his hat on Allhoff's desk and sat down.

"Inspector," he said, "I have something for you. It has to do with the death of Sergeant Wheeler."

Allhoff buried his nose in his coffee cup. Then he took it out again and said: "I'm not surprised at that suicide, Commissioner. Not surprised at all. Now there's—"

The commissioner interrupted Allhoff's pursuit of the "hysterical type" theory. "It wasn't suicide, Inspector. It was murder."

Allhoff appeared very annoyed that Wheeler had not killed himself. He would far rather be tubercular than wrong. And here was his "hysterical type" theory blowing up in his face before he'd fairly got it under way. I grinned at Battersly as Allhoff said: "Of course, you have proof of this, Commissioner?"

"Here. Inspector. Read this."

Allhoff took the sheet of typewritten paper from his hand. He read it, aloud.

"Wheeler

"You will withdraw from your bank ten thousand dollars in small bills. At four o'clock Tuesday afternoon you will be instructed how to get them in my possession. Failing this you will die at precisely three o'clock the following afternoon."

Allhoff put down the paper and picked up his cup. "So." he said very slowly. "And when did Wheeler die?"

"As closely as the medical examiner can figure," the commissioner told him, "somewhere between two and three on Wednesday afternoon."

Something clicked in my brain at that. "Say," I said, "there've been three or four notes like that in the last

month. They were found in the houses of men who'd just died. It's here in the reports."

"Precisely," said the commissioner. "That's what I want you to look into, Inspector. The sergeant's reports will tell you as much as I can. Well, I must get along now."

He stood up, walked to the door then turned around again and winked broadly at me. "Oh, and by the way, Inspector, I've been thinking of giving a transfer to Battersly here. Can you spare him?"

I held my breath as I waited to see how Allhoff would take that. Battersly swung around from the window, surprised and anxious. The commissioner, himself, was aware of the tension in the room.

"Transfer him?" repeated Allhoff in a taut voice. "To which bureau, sir?"

"Detective. He's due for a promotion. And he certainly should have picked up something from you, Inspector. Can you think of any reason why not?"

Allhoff was silent for a long time. He could think of several reasons why not, but not which he was willing to admit. Finally, he said: "Yes, sir. Battersly'd be no good in the Detective Bureau, sir. No good at all."

The commissioner lifted his eyebrows. "Why not?"

"The hysterical type, sir. Definitely the hysterical type. They make very bad policemen, sir. And worse detectives. Better leave him here, sir, where I can keep an eye on him."

Well, if the "hysterical type" theory hadn't served one purpose for him, he was certainly trying to make it serve another.

"Oh, come now, Inspector. I have great regard for your gifts but you're not a psychologist, you know."

"I'm right," said Allhoff stubbornly. "I'll prove I'm right, if you'll give me time."

The commissioner shrugged. Allhoff was the white-haired boy in his book. "All right." he said, "I'll give you time. Say a month. But you must have definite evidence by then that Battersly is what you call the hysterical type. No opinions, no theories. Facts."

We saluted again as he turned around and left the room.

s the door slammed behind the commissioner Allhoff blew up like a bomb. His face was twisted wrath. His eyes flashed with hell's own light. He jerked his head around on his spinal column until he was facing Battersly. Then he opened his mouth, his voice was a cascade of rage.

"You slimy anaconda," he roared. "Not only are you a yellow coward, but a backbiting snake as well. Behind my back you sneak to the commissioner asking for a transfer. Trying to run away as you did on the night you cost me my legs!"

He pushed his chair away from the desk with such force that it rolled halfway across the room. At the edge of his chair where his knees should have begun, his two stumps wriggled furiously. Battersly stared at him, scared and startled.

I breathed a heavy sigh and took my rap. "Allhoff," I said, "it's not Battersly's fault. He knows nothing about it. I asked the commissioner for that transfer. I figured the kid was entitled to a promotion by now. It was all my fault."

But there was no diverting him this time. True, he didn't like me a great deal, but he hated Battersly with all the venom that had collected in his warped brain for the, last five years. He paid no attention to my confession. He raved on, obscenely and blasphemously at Battersly.

I gritted my teeth, turned to my reports and kept my mouth shut. Long ago I had learned that words merely poured oil on the fire of his wrath. Battersly stood, pale and miserable, before the outburst as we both waited for him to subside through sheer exhaustion.

The affair had had its genesis some five years ago in the days when Battersly had been a raw rookie. A raid had been scheduled on a West End Avenue apartment where a notorious gangster and his aid were hiding out. The department had learned through a stool-pigeon that the front door was guarded by a machine gun planted on the stairway. Battersly's assignment had been to affect a rear entrance and close with the machine-gun operator at the precise moment that Allhoff, at the head of the raiding squad, charged through the front door.

Battersly had got in the house all right. Then at the last moment had suddenly developed a quite understandable case of buck fever. Instead of disarming the man at the tommy gun, he had fled upstairs as soon as the battle began. That resulted in Allhoff's crashing though the door just in time to receive a hail of machine-gun bullets in his legs. Gangrene and amputation had followed in the order named.

However, despite the loss of his legs, the commissioner had arranged for Allhoff to continue to work and draw his former salary, although he was no longer an official member of the department. Allhoff, with some grim idea of poetic justice in his head had demanded and received Battersly as his assistant. I had been sent over from headquarters to handle his paper work and act as peacemaker between the pair of them. I relished neither job.

CHAPTER TWO

Five Who Died on Time

Noon came and went. When Battersly and I returned from lunch Allhoff had apparently numbed his fury with caffeine. At least he appeared to have forgotten Battersly temporarily. He was ready to go to work.

"Simmonds," he snapped. The commissioner has sent over all the data on those extortion notes. The Wheeler case and the others. It's on your desk. Look it over. Tell me how many guys got those notes before Wheeler."

I picked up the stack of documents from the desk. Battersly retired to the other side of the room to brood. After a moment's research, I said: "There were four of them before Wheeler was killed."

"Damn you," he snarled, "I didn't ask you for an opinion."

"Opinion? I didn't give you one."

"The hell you didn't. You said Wheeler was murdered. I'm going to prove he was a suicide."

I raised my eyebrows. So that was it! Allhoff had said Wheeler was a suicide, and Allhoff was going to be right no matter what the evidence.

"Now," he said. "Those notes. They're all there including Wheeler's. I glanced at them. They all read exactly the same, don't they?"

I checked them. The phrasing was identical and I said so. Allhoff grunted.

"What about the death certificates? What causes of death do they give?"

"Edwards, cancer" I said. "Robertson, pernicious anemia. Wheeler, suicide. Gelberstson, heart failure. Graham, Bright's disease."

Allhoff pursed his lips thoughtfully and poured himself another cup of coffee. "That all looks very kosher," he said. "Yet all those notes predicted the death within one or two hours."

"Has it occurred to you," I asked excitedly, "that the murderer might be a doctor? A doctor could deliberately fake the death certificates and get away with it."

"Brilliant," said Allhoff in a tone which implied I was ripe for the loony bin. "Coruscating. Especially considering that each of those guys had different doctors."

I sat there, the papers in my hand watching him. He was registering heavy thought and I knew better than to interrupt him. Then his face lit up. He nodded his head slowly and said: "Now assuming Wheeler was a suicide—"

"Which I don't," I told him.

His eyes blazed and he slammed his fist on the desk. "Damn you, Wheeler was a suicide! He was the type, the hysterical type. He—"

I was saved further expatiation of the theory by the entrance of a dignified elderly man. He strode with military mien toward Allhoff's desk. He stood there stiffly for a moment, his gray mustaches bristling and his blue eyes fixed upon Allhoff.

"Inspector Allhoff?"

Allhoff sullenly admitted his identity. "I'm Colonel Whittaker. The commissioner's a friend of mine. He sent me over to see you. To show you this."

He handed Allhoff a folded piece of white paper. Allhoff took it, opened it and read aloud.

"Whittaker

"You are herewith given notice of an assessment of twenty thousand dollars ($20,000). This money to be paid in cash as per instructions you shall telephonically receive. Failure to accede to this demand will result in your demise. Said demise to take place at precisely 4:15 post meridian on the 29th Inst."

"Damn," said Allhoff as he finished. "This interferes with my theory."

"Ah," I said happily, "you mean Wheeler wasn't a suicide?"

He didn't answer me. He looked up at Whittaker. "When did you get this, Colonel?"

"In this morning's mail. I took it to the commissioner at once."

Allhoff gulped some coffee. "You don't intend to pay this money?"

The colonel bristled. "Most emphatically not! I shall pay no money to extortioners."

"Well," said Allhoff, glancing at his desk calendar, "this is the 23rd. That leaves six days before your extortioner gets serious. I don't think you need worry, Colonel. I rarely take that long to clean up a case."

Despite the arrogance in his voice I was compelled to admit that as a general rule, he didn't. The colonel shook his hand and left.

As soon as the door closed, I blurted out the discovery I had made several minutes ago. "Hey," I said, "did you notice that the colonel's note is different from the others? The wording is changed.

Maybe it's from another guy, a different extortionist."

"My God," said Allhoff, "how many times must I tell you that if you think of it, I've *thought* of it.

"All right," I said, nettled, "But if you insist Wheeler killed himself, how do you explain the colonel's letter?"

Allhoff shrugged his shrunken shoulders, "I don't know yet. We'll have to wait."

"For what?"

"Goodman, Regan and Langley."

"Who are they? Vice-presidents? I never heard of them."

"One," said Allhoff, "was Wheeler's lawyer. Regan is Wheeler's cousin, probably next of kin. Langley's an employee of the Acme Paper Company."

A little light penetrated my skull. "You mean you can trace the paper the notes were written on?"

Allhoff nodded none too enthusiastically. "Maybe. Most of them were written on unmarked cheap paper. One of them, however, the letter that went to Edwards, was written on bond paper. Paper put out by the Acme people. They're sending up one of their men for me to question. I can't do anything until I've tried that."

I went back to the sport pages of the evening paper I'd brought in from lunch. Battersly conned the funnies with moronic intentness. Allhoff sucked up coffee, registering profound thought over the chipped cup.

Some twenty minutes later Goodman, a wiry, restive little lawyer, arrived with Regan. Regan was young and well built. I particularly remarked the size of his shoulders. Then, before they had been properly introduced, the door opened again and Langley came in.

Langley was a typical clerk. His shoulders were bent and he wore a worried air. Allhoff greeted him and sat the trio down in chairs arranged fan wise about his desk.

"I may as well tell you at once," he announced, "that no matter what may have happened in the other cases, I am of the firm conviction that Sergeant Wheeler committed suicide."

I watched both Goodman and Regan. It was difficult to say which of them registered shocked surprise most heavily.

"Good heavens, no," said Regan. "I'm sure my cousin'd do nothing like that. It's impossible."

"Ridiculous," said Goodman. "No reason for it at all."

"You don't convince me," said Allhoff. And I knew

no one ever would since he'd already gone on record with a contrary opinion. "You, Goodman, what do you know about this?"

"Nothing much. As soon as I heard of the—the tragedy, I went up to Wheeler's place, to look over his papers. I took the beat copper in with me. I always like to have a witness under such circumstances. While there we met Regan, who'd heard of the death of his cousin and come down from Utica."

"Ah," said Allhoff, "and as next of kin, Regan, I suppose, gets what money Wheeler left."

"He's probably entitled to it," said Goodman, "but he's waived any claim, in favor of distant relatives in Ireland. Regan believes they'll need the money more than he does."

Allhoff uttered an annoyed grunt. "And that's all either of you can tell me?"

"That's about all."

Allhoff sighed and turned to Langley, who'd been sitting in deferential silence.

"You," he said, "what do you know about this?"

Langley flushed nervously as if Allhoff were pinning the rap directly on his stooped shoulders. He took the Edwards letter from Allhoff's hand and examined it closely. He read the writing with moving lips. Then he said with the air of a man coming upon a remarkable discovery. "It's our paper, Inspector. Made by the Acme Company."

"Magnificent," purred Allhoff. Then he roared: "You idiot, I know damned well it is. Why do you think I sent for you?"

Langley became white, then flushed again.

"To whom was it sold?" demanded Allhoff. "Can you check that?"

Langley shook his head unhappily. "No, Inspector. There'd be no way of telling. We've given reams of this stuff to the jobbers recently. There's no way of telling at all."

Allhoff filled his coffee cup and looked annoyed. He waved his three visitors away with an angry hand. "All right," he said, "that's all. You can all go now. If any of you thinks of anything, remembers anything pertinent to this case let me know."

As Goodman led the trio out the door, I watched Allhoff closely. I began to think that the thing I had long hoped for had come to pass. Allhoff, apparently, had run up against a brick wall. For the first time in his career he had no clue, no inkling about anything. Beyond a rather shakey theory about the hysterical type to account for Wheeler's death, he had drawn a complete blank. I stood up, lit my pipe, and told him so with vast satisfaction.

Then, observing it was five o'clock, I put on my cap and got out of the room in a hurry.

Battersly followed right at my heels, before he could answer me.

The following day was Saturday. Since I was going fishing early Sunday morning, I prepared my tackle and outfit before I went to work, with the net result that I was a good hour late. I steeled myself for profane admonition when I entered Allhoff's slum. However, I found him alone, grinning into his coffee cup, almost happily.

"Well," I said, "and what are you beaming about?"

"Langley," he said. "The paper guy. He's dead."

"What are you so happy about? He was no enemy of yours."

"If what I think happened," said Allhoff. "He will always be my friend." Which would be a warning thought for Langley in his tomb.

"There was one of those extortion notes in his apartment," said Allhoff. "Battersly's across the street picking it up for me now."

As he spoke Battersly returned. He handed the letter to Allhoff. I read it over his shoulder. It was an epistle demanding payment of five thousand dollars, threatening Langley with death on Friday night if he failed to pay it.

"Listen," said Allhoff to Battersly, "what have you got on this? Has Homicide decided that this is a suicide or a naturally caused death?"

Battersly shook his head. "No, sir. Murder. Window broken. Langley shot through the head in his chair. No weapon found. Murder all the way, sir."

"Good," said Allhoff.

"Good?" I repeated. "Why?"

"I wouldn't expect you to know. Look here, do you notice anything about this letter?"

"One thing. Its wording is exactly the same as that received by Whittaker. It's different from the first ones we got."

"And what do you figure from that?"

"Precisely nothing."

"You're not only more than ordinarily stupid," said Allhoff reaching for the coffee pot, "you're a completely useless adjunct to this office. Since you've made plans to go fishing tomorrow why the hell don't you go today? Your absence may permit me to get some work done."

I put my hat on before he could change his mind.

"Thank you, inspector," I said, striding from the office as Battersly stared after me with wide and envious eyes.

CHAPTER THREE

Half a Ghost

It was a little after ten o'clock on Sunday night when I drove back to town after a day's fishing in Connecticut. A healthy weariness was in my muscles. The country air, after a week of the constricting atmosphere of Allhoff's tenement, had loosened my nerves, cleared my brain, and deluded me into believing that I was yet young enough to pound a beat.

Nothing was more remote from my mind as I unlocked the door of my apartment. Nothing was closer to it a moment later.

My wife came bustling out of the kitchen. She took my arm, kissed me and said without preamble: "Tom, the inspector's dead."

I dropped my fishing tackle on the floor and, stared at her in wide-eyed amazement. "Not Allhoff? You don't mean Allhoff's dead?"

She nodded her head. "Killed. Torn. Blown up by a bomb in his own apartment. It's here in the Sunday papers, And that poor lad, Battersly's been trying to get you on the phone all day."

I raced into the living-room, snatched up the Sunday *Times*. Apparently the news had reached them just in time for the last edition. They'd run barely a stick of type which stated prosaically that Inspector Allhoff had been killed late Saturday evening when an explosion had occurred in his apartment. Headquarters had announced that the inspector had been experimenting with amonol explosives.

For a moment, I stood stunned. Then I ran down the stairs, jumped in the car and headed for Centre Street as if I were on radio patrol. I drove recklessly with at least two conflicting emotions in my breast. If Allhoff were dead, I most certainly could not feel sorry. In my book he was much better off. Battersly and I most assuredly were.

However, a doubt remained in my mind. I had heard nothing about Allhoff's bomb experiments. And I knew him well enough to suspect anything connected with him until it had been well checked.

I parked the car before the tenement house across the street from headquarters. A uniformed copper was on duty outside the door. I identified myself.

"Happened about midnight last night," the patrolman told me. "Lieutenant Hayes was coming out of headquarters when he heard the explosion. He came right over. Found the inspector's apartment wrecked,

the inspector dead. The M. E. said the percussion killed him. The commissioner himself took charge of the body. They're trying to locate relatives."

I took off my hat and mopped my brow. This certainly looked on the level.

"All right." I said. "Thanks. I'll go upstairs and look around."

The copper saluted, then said: "Say, Sergeant, this guy Batterslys' been hanging around all day. Been trying to get hold of you. He seems pretty hard hit."

"Battersly? Where is he?"

"Down there at Noonan's. He's been soaking up whiskey all day. Better take a look at him Sergeant."

I spun around and headed down the street to Noonan's. At a table against the rear wall sat Battersly staring at me through red-rimmed sleepless eyes.

"Sergeant." he said. "For God's sake, where you been? You hear about it. Sergeant? He's dead. I killed him. First, I chopped his legs off, then I killed him."

I yelled for Noonan and ordered black coffee and spirits of ammonia.

"Battersly." I said, "don't be a damned drunken fool. He blew himself up, didn't he? What did you have to do with it?"

Battersly shook his head with drunken earnestness. You don't know the facts," he said leaving out the t's and slurring the s's. "It was me who done it. Oh, my God, I killed him. I killed him!"

There was small profit in arguing the point at that moment. I kept my mouth shut as I poured the coffee and ammonia into him. Then I dragged him to his feet.

"Let's get out of here. We'll go upstairs. You can sleep it off in Allhoff's bed."

He looked at me as if I'd suggested he violate the corpse. "Good God, no!" he said, horrified. "Sleep in the bed of the man I've murdered! I—"

He broke off into wild drunken laughter. I grabbed his arm and led him from the saloon. I practically carried him up the creaking stairs to Allhoff's apartment. I switched on the light and deposited him in his own chair.

Half the room—the bedroom side— was normal enough. The other half was a wreck. Allhoff's desk was a splintered ruin. The back of his swivel chair lay on the floor over by the sink. Plaster from the wall was scattered everywhere. Papers from the desk were strewn all over the room. A handful of dark reddish stains dotted the desk and plaster.

I surveyed the scene for a long silent moment. Then I shook my head and said:

"My God, it's true!"

Battersly lifted his brooding gaze to me. "True?" he said, and his voice broke just this side of hysteria. "Of course, it's true! And I did it." He sprang suddenly to his feet. "I can't stay in this room. Sergeant. I can feel his presence. Everything here is his. His clothes, his coffee pot. They all remind me of him."

As he spoke I automatically looked at the pile of laundry which leaned grayly against the wall at a height of some three feet. I looked on the desk for the coffee pot, didn't see it. I walked around the room and found the electric plate and percolator placed neatly under the sink. I screwed up my brow at that. In seven years I'd never seen that pot anywhere save on Allhoff's desk. Then the unnerving sound of Battersly's sobbing brought me back to other things.

I went across the room and shook his shoulder roughly. Battersly," I said harshly, "you're being a hysterical fool. You've as little to do with Allhoff's death as I have. You've—"

"No," he said. "No, no. You don't understand, Sergeant. I mixed that explosive for him. I must've mixed it wrong. And that's what killed him."

I stared at him blankly. "What explosive? I've never seen an explosive around here in seven years. What are you talking about?"

"After you left yesterday he told me he was conducting some experiments. He gave me some chemicals to mix for him. Told me to be very careful. Gave me exact measurements. Told me it was dangerous if I made a mistake. He gave me so many instructions all at once that I forgot some of them."

"Well, why the devil didn't you ask him again?"

"I did. Once. He repeated them and called me all kinds of a damned fool, I was scared to ask again. I trusted my memory, hoping I was right. But now I know it was my fault. I killed him!"

"Have you told anyone else this?"

"No. I wanted to tell you first. But what the hell's the difference? It's my fault. I killed him and the only thing I can do now is kill myself."

He was sobbing aloud now. I went to the doorway and whistled up the copper from downstairs.

"Look," I told him, "this kid's drunk and almost out of his head. Get a taxi and take him up to my house. Tell my wife to put him in my room and watch him."

The policeman saluted. He took hold of Battersly and propelled him, still sobbing, from the room.

I sighed, went into Allhoff's bedroom and sat down on the edge of the sagging mattress. My wife had had more experience with weeping infants than I.

I switched out the light in the living room, returned to the bedroom and undressed. I climbed into the creaking bed in my underwear, flicked off the reading lamp and closed my eyes. I lay there in the dark hazily speculating on a number of things. . .

I awoke abruptly and alarmed. There was empty apprehension at the pit of my stomach as I oriented myself. It took a full five seconds to remember where I was. I sat up in bed and listened.

Thin sound trickled to my ears from the other room. A shuffled footfall, the rustle of paper. Silently I cursed the fact that my gun was in the second bureau drawer at house. Slightly less silently, I maneuvered myself out of the squeaking bed and tiptoed to the door.

Beyond the window was moonless night. A faint yellowish ray of light traveled up from the street-lamp below and formed an odd pattern on the ceiling, which shed almost no light at all in the room. Yet there was someone, something, there.

I stood with my body pressed against the bedroom wall so that the white of my underwear would not give my position away. My head was thrust around the door-jamb, my eyes straining into the darkness, staring at a moving dark blob that was not part of the night.

I took a deep breath to still my leaping nerves. I hadn't been in a rough-and-tumble for years. And at my age I was going to need a lot of luck. Carefully I moved one foot through the doorway. The moment of surprise was an ally I intended to keep. Then, just as I was prepared to spring upon the intruder, my aching eyes blinked once and I froze to horrified immobility.

A ghost was rising on the far side of the room. Whitely, eerily, it crawled waveringly up the side of the wall. Through no volition of mine, my voice came out of a dry throat, high-pitched.

"Who's that?" I yelled. "Who's there? Put up your hands. You're covered!" The darkness suddenly became Stygian madness. The ghost uttered a vehement and foul oath, and sprang across the room. There was a crackling noise of crumpled paper. Feet raced across the floor-boards toward the open window. I emerged from the bedroom to make a futile flying tackle at a figure suddenly silhouetted against the windowsill. A fist swung full into my face. I clutched at the figure as I reeled backward. My outstretched fingers touched a pocket, somehow closed about a pencil. Then the dark form had straddled the sill and now the ghost was upon me.

The ghost, I noted, as I fell to the floor, was only half a ghost now. At first it had been completely white. Now it appeared spotted. White on top and at the side, black and disembodied everywhere else. I heard a curse in my ear as it tripped over me, got to its feet again and raced to the window. I saw a revolver thrust itself over the windowsill, fire two crackling shots into the street below.

I scrambled to my feet, lurched across the room to the electric-light switch and clicked it on. I stood staring across the room, my eyes wide as the Grand Canyon.

For over by the window, glaring at me balefully was Allhoff! Allhoff with a pair of dirty drawers resting on his head, hanging down over his ears, a soiled pillow case dangling from his shoulder, and an old shirt flapping around the stump of his left leg.

"You drooling idiot!" he screamed at me. "You damned meddling lunatic!"

I kept on staring at him too utterly astonished for resentment. Then, when he paused for breath, I said in bewilderment: "But where did you come from? I though you'd been killed?"

"I'm a miracle," said Allhoff bitterly from the grave. Buried beneath a pile of dirty laundry, I have broken the tomb. Only to find that you are still the same damned interfering cretin that you were when I died."

I cast my gaze in the direction of the laundry pile. The mountain of linen had 'erupted, a huge crater was in its center. "You mean you were hiding under that pile of clothes? What for? And who was the other guy. The guy that came in the window?"

"That, said Allhoff disgustedly, "was the guy I was waiting for. That was the guy we've been looking for. That was the guy whose capture would've solved this case."

"But I—"

"But you, you stupid ox," he roared savagely, "screwed everything up. You butted in and he got away. Neither of us could see him in the dark."

I looked down at my right hand, noted it still clutched the pencil I had inadvertently grabbed from the intruder's pocket "Look," I said, "I've got his pencil. Maybe that's a clue."

"A pencil," sneered Allhoff. "A plain yellow pencil. There are fifty million of them in the country. Hell, *I've* got his glove."

He held up an ordinary canvas workman's glove. It was one of the sort that can be bought in any ten-cent store. I shrugged my shoulders and said: "So what? That's about as good as my pencil. There are fifty million of those gloves in the country, too."

Allhoff bobbed his head up from beneath the sink where he was reaching for his coffee-making apparatus. "And there are fifty million dumb police sergeants," he snapped. "Now get the hell out of here. I'm going to have a cup of coffee, then I'm going to bed."

I went into the bedroom and began to put on my clothes. My brain was still dizzy from the events of the evening.

I put on my coat and emerged from the bedroom.

"Allhoff," I said, "what was all this business about experimenting with bombs? This cock-and-bull story your being killed?"

Allhoff turned on his electric plate. He filled the percolator to the brim.

"It's three o'clock *in* the morning," he said. "You usually manage to botch things up earlier than this. For God's sake, go home and let me think."

I went to the door in silence. I could see one of his moods coming on him.

"Say," he said as I stood on the threshold. "Tomorrow morning, get that lawyer fellow and Wheeler's cousin down here at about ten thirty. Get Colonel Whittaker, too. You might tell the commissioner as well, that if he drops over here a little after eleven, I'll have his case all wrapped up and ready for him."

I blinked at him. "How can you break the case when you say the guy got clean away, didn't leave a clue? If you didn't know who he was when he came in the window, how in hell do you know now."

He looked up at me and came as close to smiling as he ever did. "I've got his glove, haven't I?" he said. "Now for heaven's sake get the hell out."

CHAPTER FOUR

A New Kind of Sadist

We gathered in Allhoff's slum a little after ten o'clock the following morning. Battersly sat glumly at his desk staring blankly at the wall with red sleepless eyes. Despite his horror at Allhoff's death last night, he didn't appear overjoyed to see him alive this morning. He had come to the conclusion that Allhoff's fake demise had been planted for the sole purpose of embarrassing him.

Colonel Whittaker, looking as if he had stepped from a full page Arno cartoon, sat at the side of Allhoff's new desk.

Goodman, holding a brief case on his knee, fidgeted in his chair like a man who has an engagement elsewhere. Regan smoked a cigarette and seemed bored by the whole proceeding.

On Allhoff's desk the battered coffee pot, that he had so carefully preserved from damage during the explosion, gurgled invitingly. Allhoff rubbed his hands together.

"Well, well," he said and he sounded as if someone had buttered his vocal cords with margarine. "I see we're all here on time. *I* always say there's nothing like a cup of good coffee to get the brain cells functioning in the morning. Battersly, cups!"

Battersly looked up at him wonderingly. "Cups, sir?"

"Cups," said Allhoff testily. "For everyone. We'll all have a cup of coffee to begin with. Come on, hurry it up."

Battersly got up and went over to the cupboard above the sink. I regarded Allhoff with a fishy eye. Allhoff going hospitable was rather like Hitler patting a neutral country on the back and assuring it everything was going to be all right.

Battersly laid five cups on Allhoff's desk. I counted them mentally and said hastily: "Count me out, inspector. I just had breakfast."

The colonel contemplated the chipped, unsterile china. His blue eyes looked upon the stained and battered coffee pot. He regarded the pair of amorous flies that flirted above the sugar bowl and his mouth pursed until he looked like Calvin Coolidge.

"Thank you, no, inspector." he said. "Just came out of a restaurant. I—"

Now Goodman and Regan entered their polite refusals. Allhoff, however, paid no attention to anyone. He filled the five cups with a liquid that looked as if it had come from Trinidad's pitch lake and pushed the mugs around the desk.

"Nonsense," he said. "You can always stand a good cup of coffee. I insist. Come now, drink up or I'll feel insulted."

Allhoff insulted! I nearly slid off my chair at that one.

Reluctantly everyone picked up his cup. We all sipped the pungent black liquid with the enthusiasm of a Greek patrician knocking off a hemlock and soda. The colonel downed his bravely. He replaced the cup on the desk and said: "Now, inspector, will you tell us what's on your mind?"

"In just a moment," said Allhoff. "I'll clear the cups away. I hate disorder."

Battersly and I exchanged glances. Allhoff couldn't stand disorder much as I couldn't stand a million dollars. Battersly stood up, went over to the desk and reached for the cups.

"No, no," said Allhoff affably. "Don't bother, son. I can manage it by myself." He slid down from the chair, picked up the cups and carried them across the room. "I won't bother washing them now," he said over his shoulder. "Just get them in the other room out of the way."

He disappeared into the bedroom, Battersly staring after him like a man witnessing a miracle. Personally, I was becoming very, very suspicious.

A moment later Allhoff reappeared, clambered back into his chair. "Now," he said, "let's get down to business." He cleared his throat, opened his mouth to speak when a knock came at the door. I got up and opened it. A white-coated lad entered the room.

"Came for the laundry," he said. "Someone phoned us a while ago."

"Oh, yes." said Allhoff. "Over there. That pile. You might take the sheets off the bed in the other room, too."

The laundry boy went about his task and left.

Goodman squirmed uneasily on his chair. "Listen, inspector," he said. "I've got to he in court at noon. I—"

"I've an engagement too," said Regan. "If possible, I'd like—"

Allhoff held up a silencing hand. "Don't worry, gentlemen." he said. "We'll be all through in less than half an hour. I simply thought you'd all be interested in the explanation of the extortion notes. You've all helped me so much on the case I thought it would be only courteous of me to invite you to hear the explanation first."

All this sweetness and light Allhoff was casting about was beginning to overwhelm me. Past experience warned me that something terrible was going to happen.

I observed a swift exchange of glances between Goodman and Regan. The colonel twisted his mustache impatiently and waited for Allhoff to begin.

"You see," said Allhoff, "everyone—except me, of course—had the wrong angle on this case from the beginning. Everyone was looking for a murderer, a subtle murderer who effectively concealed his method of killing."

"And," I said ironically, "what were you looking for?"

"An extortionist," said Allhoff.

"You mean he didn't kill those guys, after all?"

"He did not," said Allhoff. "I told you I knew Wheeler was a suicide. It was obvious. He was—"

"I know," I interposed hastily. "He was the hysterical type. You've already explained that."

"Wait a minute," said Goodman. "If the extortionist, as you call him, didn't kill these guys, who did?"

"Well," said Allhoff judicially, "Wheeler killed Wheeler. Cancer killed Edwards. Pernicious anemia killed another of them. You'll find it all on the death certificates."

"That's crazy," said Regan. "What about those notes? Do you mean to say it was sheer coincidence that all those guys died just when the notes predicted they would?"

"Those notes predicted nothing," said Allhoff, helping himself to more coffee, "They were based on past occurrences, not future contingencies."

The colonel leaned forward in his chair. His blue eyes were alertly gleaming. "I think I see what you're driving at."

I was damned if I did and I said so.

Allhoff put his cup down in its sloppy saucer. He drew a deep breath, leaned forward over his desk and said: "Those notes were planted *after* the recipients had died, Not *before!*"

There was silence in the room broken only by Allhoff's triumphant and stertorous breathing. Each of us considered the import of this information.

Goodman was the first to decide it wouldn't do. "That doesn't make sense, inspector," he said. "Why should anyone plant notes in the house of a man who was already dead. You can't extort from a corpse—legally or actually."

"You can't," agreed Allhoff placidly. Then his tone changed suddenly. It came loud and savagely. "But you can use a corpse to scare the drawers off the living!"

I still didn't see it. "Allhoff," I said, "are you sure you're not developing into the hysterical type?"

He swing around in his chair and glared at me. All the saccharine Shirley Temple qualities he had assumed dropped from him now, His face was weirdly contorted and I could hear the stumps of his legs rattle angrily against the under part of the desk.

"You blind, blundering fool!" he roared, "Did you bribe your way through the Civil Service examination? It's as obvious as your own damned stupidity. Look here. Men die. Our extortionist finds out quite easily when and how they died. He steals into their homes. He plants his note demanding money upon pain of death. He predicts that death to the hour, because he knows when his victim has already died. Now, do you see it?"

Whittaker nodded his head before I could speak. "I see it, inspector," he said. "By so doing, the extortioner would build himself up a terrific reputation as a killer. Once he'd established that reputation through the newspapers, the living recipients of his letters would pay what he asked."

"Right," snapped Allhoff. "First he plants his letters on corpses. Then when he's received the attendant publicity, he plants 'em on live guys. The live guys, believing he's murdered all these other mugs in a manner which has completely baffled the coppers, promptly reach a condition where they need no cathartic and pay through the nose."

"Damned ingenious," said Regan slowly. "And who is this extortioner?"

"I don't know," said Allhoff blandly. "But I will in a very short time,"

Goodman pursed his lips. "Of course, then," he said, "your killer is no killer at all. He gained all the menacing reputation of a murderer, but legally he can never be indicted for homicide."

Allhoff lifted his coffee cup. "Oh yes, he can," he said over its rim.

"How?" I demanded. "If he killed no one, how can you get him for homicide? Besides, I've been thinking this over and it sounds screwy to me. What about Langley?"

"Well, what about him?"

"There was no point in planting a note on him. Hell, he only made about forty bucks a week, It'd arouse suspicion, at once if an extortioner went to work on him. His later victims might start figuring there was something funny about the whole deal. Why should he take that chance?"

"Ah," said Allhoff, "I'm glad you mentioned Langley. What did you notice, if anything, that differentiated Langley's death from the others?"

"Well," said Regan, "what?"

"It looked like murder," said Allhoff. "All the others looked like something else. Langley's death didn't."

We all stared at him.

"And why was that?" asked the colonel.

"Two reasons," said Allhoff. "First, it *was* murder. Second, our extortionist, who, by the way, has now become a killer, *wanted* it to look like murder."

"Go on," I said, "Why?"

"Good God," said Allhoff, "do you mean to say you don't see it yet? Our man began to worry that perhaps his system was defeating itself. Heretofore none of these deaths had looked like murder. Of course, considering they weren't that's not odd. Perhaps his living victims would begin to wonder, to believe that our extortioner wasn't a killer at all. One genuine murder, with no doubt about it, would do his reputation a lot of good. So he killed Langley."

"It was a damned poor choice," said Regan. "Why didn't he kill a guy with dough?"

"I'm glad you asked that. He didn't kill Langley primarily for reasons of profit. He killed him because Langley had knowledge which would give the whole thing away. Since he had to kill him anyway he made no attempt to conceal its being murder and he planted one of his notes."

I said: "Well, since Langley told you nothing of any importance when he was here, since he was killed shortly afterwards, I gather you've been in touch with your astrologer again."

"You're a damn fool," said Allhoff contemptuously. "It struck me as damned odd, too, that an extortioner would pick on a guy who made as little dough as Langley. So then I began to think. I came to the obvious conclusion that Langley had been killed for some other reason. What?"

The colonel did straight man for him this time. "All right, Inspector," he said. "What?"

"If not money," said Allhoff, "it must have been to silence him. There was no other reason. If he knew something, it was in all probability something to do with the paper. So I called Langley's firm. I examined and cross-examined about that paper. Finally, I got the answer."

Goodman shifted uncomfortably in his chair and said: "Which was?"

Allhoff leaned over his desk and jabbed his finger at the air to emphasize his point. "The paper on which the note found at Wallace Reading's house was written was not put on the market until July 17th."

I took my pipe out of my mouth. "And Reading died on July 15th. Is that it?"

"That's it," said Allhoff. "As soon as I knew that, I knew everything. The whole scheme was obvious. Langley neglected to mention that item while he was here. But he thought of it later. He was killed before he could tell me."

"Well," said Regan, "that's all very ingenious. But who was it? Who is this guy? Do you know?"

"I will."

"How?" I asked.

"I've got his glove," said Allhoff triumphantly.

The telephone on his desk rang. Allhoff snatched it up. For once, I noted, the guy at the other end of the receiver did more talking than Allhoff.

He was still holding the receiver intently to his ear when the outer door opened and the commissioner walked in. He sat down quietly, didn't speak until Allhoff hung up.

"Good morning, Inspector," he said. "I have a message that you've cleaned up the case of these extortion notes. Who's the guilty man?"

"Number three," said Allhoff. "Number three is the murderer. I told you I had his glove!"

The commissioner nodded as if he understood what Allhoff was talking about.

"So what?" I said. "A moment ago you didn't know who the killer was. Now you know. How did you find out?"

"I blew myself up," he yelled, beating the desk with his fists. "Are you so dum you don't see it yet? Listen. This guy's building up a reputation. He's a subtle murderer. Pay me or I'll do to you what I did to those other guys, see? Well, he hears I'm dead. Me! The smartest copper in the world! Is he going to pass up a chance like that. The hell he is. He's going to plant a note on me so the whole world can see what a great guy he is."

Allhoff was laying it on rather thick, but still I saw what he meant. "So," I said, "you framed your own death, then hid in the laundry pile waiting for him to climb in the rear window and plant his note. Then you could jump him red-handed?"

"Sure. It was perfect. How could I figure on a dope like you wrecking my plans. If I hadn't snatched his glove, he'd be in the clear now, thanks to you."

The commissioner looked at me sternly. For a moment I felt like a one-man fifth column who had been sabotaging the police department. I covered my confusion quickly by asking: "How could you trace that glove? There are thousands of glove's like that? And who in the devil is number three?"

"I couldn't trace the glove." snapped Allhoff. "But if a guy had to climb down that waterspout outside the window there, with only one glove, he had to leave fingerprints, didn't he? Fingerprints that would tally on one of those coffee cups this morning. I had those cups numbered. I took 'em into the bedroom and wrapped them up in tissue paper. The laundry guy wrapped them up, in turn, in the dirty clothes and took them over to the Identification Bureau. The prints on the waterspout tally with the prints on cup number three."

"Who's number three?" asked the commissioner.

"Regan." said Allhoff, and his gun was in his hand.

Regan got out of his chair. His face was ashen and his fingers trembled. He shot a swift glance at Goodman. The lawyer leaned forward and said: "That's ridiculous. Wheeler's own cousin. It's too coincidental. How could he—"

"He's not Wheeler's cousin," said Allhoff, "and no one knows that better than you, Goodman."

"Are you accusing me—" Goodman started to bluster.

"I am," snapped Allhoff. "I'll tell you just when and where you came into this thing. You were Wheeler's lawyer. You first met Regan when you found him in Wheeler's apartment planting his note. You went into that apartment with a policeman. Regan claimed he was Wheeler's cousin. You knew damned well he wasn't, but you let the claim go until you found out what the angle was. When you did find out, you cut yourself in, instead of turning Regan over to the police."

Goodman laughed. Not a very mirthful laugh, either. "Absurd," he said.

"Sure," said Allhoff. "And I'll tell you something even more absurd. Before and including Wheeler's death, various brands of paper and different typewriters were used to write those notes. Since Wheeler's death there has been a uniformity of both paper and typewriter. As soon as I knew you were involved in it, I had all the machines in your office checked. I've just heard over the phone that a locked Royal portable in your private office has been identified as the machine that wrote all the notes since Wheeler's death."

"Including." asked the commissioner, "the one found at Langley's home?"

"Including that," said Allhoff. "Langley left here with those two on Friday. It was undoubtedly in their company he remembered that fact about the paper. He mentioned it to them, and died as a result."

Regan sat down again. He looked appealingly at the lawyer. Goodman stood up, clasping his briefcase to his breast.

"You still haven't a case," he said and there was desperation in his tone. "Not a homicide case."

"We know you wrote the notes," said Allhoff. "We know Regan tried to plant one here in this house. That's all we have to tell a jury. They'll believe you killed every one of those guys."

The commissioner nodded. "That's right. You can take your chances confessing to Langleys murder or stand an indictment for a score of killings."

Regan's white lips moved. "All right," he said, "I killed Langley." He pointed at Goodman. "But he was in it with me."

The commissioner got up and went to the door. He called one of his personal bodyguards who had been stationed outside. The copper took Goodman and Regan out of the room.

The colonel leaned over and shook Allhoff's hand. "Wonderful work," he said. "Wonderful. Now that those two are in jail, undoubtedly all those living men they extorted money from will come forward and testify. But there's one thing I still want to know. How did you realize that Goodman was mixed up in it?"

I wanted to know that, too. I leaned forward and listened. Allhoff poured himself some more coffee.

"Did you ever see a lawyer who didn't know it all? Who simply didn't have to be the general of any enterprise he got his fingers into? No? Neither did I. All those notes, up to Wheeler's death, were written simply, as you or I would write them. After Goodman got in on the deal, he, holding a college degree, had to write the notes himself. Then they were written in stilted language using the barbarous syntax that all attorney's affect. I could see a lawyer's hand in it miles away."

"And," put in the commissioner, "because before that the notes were different, you figured Goodman came in at the time of Wheeler's death. And you figured how."

Allhoff nodded. He didn't seem much interested anymore. He had solved another case, taken his bow and was now to bury his nose in his coffee cup for the rest of the day.

Whittaker got up to take his leave. The commissioner told Allhoff what a terrific copper he was and walked to the door. He paused upon the threshold.

"By the way, Inspector," he said, "Have you made up your mind on that Battersly transfer yet?"

Allhoff put the coffee cup back in the saucer with a bang. His little eyes flashed mordantly and he shot a malevolent glance at the brooding Battersly.

"I was right the first time, sir," he said. "He'll never make a detective, sir. He'll never make much of a policeman. Better leave him here where I can keep an eye on him. He's quite definitely the hysterical type, sir."

The commissioner raised his eyebrows. "You said that once before, Inspector. Can you offer me any evidence of it, other than your own opinion."

Allhoff inhaled deeply. He looked very much like a cat that has just swallowed a very bloody canary. "Yes, sir. Last night he was drunk and unnerved. Threatened to kill himself, sir. Very unstable character, sir."

The commissioner frowned. Departmental suicides preyed on his mind. He liked them even less than he liked homicides.

"Is this true, Inspector?"

"Indeed it is," said Allhoff grinning. "The sergeant heard him, too. Didn't you, Sergeant?"

I gave him a dirty look.

"Yes, sir," I said reluctantly. "But there were certain circumstances which—"

"There are no circumstances which excuse a man's taking his own life," said the commissioner angrily. "Either morally, legally or ethically. Battersly will stay here, Inspector."

Allhoff nodded, grinning, and went back to his coffee as the commissioner left the room.

Battersly stared at Allhoff through beaten eyes.

I didn't take it so calmly.

"You're a louse," I told Allhoff. "You could have managed your fake death without involving Battersly. You didn't have to get him to fix your damned bomb. You only did that to break him up, to make him think he'd killed you. You're a stinking, uncivilized little sadist. Nothing more!"

He fixed me with glittering eyes.

"And just what's your definition of a sadist?"

I was so damned sore at him I stumbled right into the trap. "A sadist," I told him heatedly and without too much accuracy, "is a guy who goes around hurting other people's feelings."

"*Ah,*" said Allhoff. "You mean the sort of guy who blows another man's legs off with machine-gun bullets? I'm glad to hear there's a name for it."

He buried his nose in his coffee cup leaving me staring at his back with insensate, outraged and thoroughly futile fury.

The 10:30 to Sing Sing

CHAPTER ONE

Joe Alibi

The blizzard had raged two days and for the first time in my departmental career I found myself grateful for the fact that I sat warmly in Allhoff's tenement apartment instead of pounding a snow-driven beat.

Outside the window, down on Centre Street, a snow plow was stalled like a disabled tank. The boys from the sanitation department, red-faced, with heads bowed

Originally Published - January 1941

against the storm, struggled to get it going again. A copper, muffled up like a Russian general with a head-cold, plodded wearily around the corner and disappeared in the haze that fell white and silent from the clouds.

I turned from the window, sighed with vast satisfaction and lighted my pipe. I stretched out my legs and toasted my feet before the electric heater on the floor, reflecting comfortably that half the uniformed force was out in the cold combing the town for Big Joe Petroni. The sense of well-being that pervaded me was so rare in Allhoff's slum that I enjoyed it to the full.

Allhoff, himself, sat across the room, crouched over his desk, his little eyes riveted upon the coffee pot before him. He awaited with all the serene patience of a lustful rabbit, the brewing of his morning cup of coffee. Following his most rigid rule no word had yet been spoken, no police business had been transacted. Allhoff needed at least three cups of coffee in the morning before either his tongue or brain cells began to function.

Around me the room was in its customary condition of disarray. Soiled linen was piled carelessly in one corner. The dishes stood stacked and unwashed in the sink. Through the open door of Allhoff's bedroom, the unmade bed was visible, the sheets colored a dispirited gray.

The coffee pot began to gurgle and Allhoff pulled his thick chipped cup toward him. Outside I heard footsteps upon the ricketty stairs. I heard voices, one of which I recognized as Battersly's. A few moments later Battersly entered the room alone.

He nodded to me behind Allhoff's back and took his seat at his desk, disturbing in no wise the episcopal silence of the apartment. Allhoff's hand shot suddenly out, snatched the coffee pot off its electric base and poured viscous fluid from its spout into his cup.

He shoveled sugar in with a prodigal hand, raised the cup to his lips and ingested the liquid with the sound of a cow delicately sipping a bowl of soup. He repeated this procedure three times in as many minutes. Then he uttered a bass melodic belch, pushed the chipped cup away, swung his head around and regarded Battersly and myself with obvious distaste.

"*Well*," he said with the air of a man making the best of his company, "what's new this morning?"

I put down the onion skin reports I had been reading. "Nothing," I told him. "Apparently the entire force is too busy looking for Big Joe Petroni to bother about anything else."

Allhoff grunted. It was a deep grunt and an eloquent one. It meant, I was well aware, that the police department in general and Battersly and myself in particular were unutterable idiots, that Inspector Allhoff was the only departmental brain in the whole city. It meant, moreover, that he calculated the chances of the force finding Big Joe were something in the neighborhood of

twenty to one, while he, Allhoff, could have done it on his left ear if the commissioner had thought to ask him.

He grunted again and looked at the coffee pot speculatively as if considering whether his membranes could absorb another beaker of the black brew.

He decided in the affirmative, poured his cup full and remarked over his shoulder: "You'd think they'd work up a case first. From the reports they've got nothing on Big Joe. What do they want to pick him up for? Big Joe Petroni won't talk even if they borrow the rubber hose from the fire department."

I raised my eyebrows at that. "No case?" I said. "What do you want? A signed confession? There were two murders, weren't there? Buggsy Davis and Wally Rugene. They were both deadly enemies and competitors of Joe Petroni's. Joe had publicly threatened Buggsy for chiseling in on his Shylock racket, promised he wouldn't live a month. Wally Rugene was Buggsy's right-hand man. It was his testimony for the state that sent up Big Joe's kid brother only last year."

Allhoff turned a belligerent profile in my direction. "So what? Is that evidence?"

"It'll do until they turn up something else," I told him. "Who else had a motive for the murders?"

"You can't burn a guy, my thick-witted friend, by going around demonstrating no one else had any reason to commit the crime so it must have been him. The whole damned department's searching for Big Joe. All right, what are they going to do with him when they get him? Always provided they *do* find him. Joe's no dope. I bet he's not even in town. I bet—"

Battersly interrupted him by leaping to his feet and snapping his fingers. "Gee," he said, "I forgot."

Allhoff glared at him balefully. He didn't care much for my company, but his emotional attitude toward young Battersly was that of an enraged bull toward a matador.

"Forgot what?" he snarled. "Your corn plaster?"

Battersly flushed at that inference and I became alarmed myself. Allhoff was directing the conversation toward a channel that was deep, treacherous and conducive to headaches.

"No," said Battersly hastily as he strode toward the door. "The guy outside. He came in with me. I met him downstairs. He wanted to see you but I wouldn't let him. I told him to wait outside."

"Why?" snapped Allhoff.

The question was unnecessary. He knew the answer quite well. No one was permitted to speak to Allhoff before he had gulped a quart of his morning coffee. No stranger was permitted to enter his August and disheveled presence until he had steeled himself with caffeine.

Battersly tactfully let the question go. He went

through the door to the hallway beyond. I heard the rumble of voices down the stair well and a moment later Battersly reentered followed by a short wide Italian whose shoulders looked as if they had been constructed by a master brick layer.

Allhoff stared at the visitor with amazed and blinking eyes. I stood up myself, surprised. Allhoff's gaze moved suddenly to Battersly. His mouth contorted savagely. He took a deep breath and his voice pitched through the room, battered itself against our ears and the walls like an angry wave.

"You fool!" he roared. Every copper on the force is combing the town for Big Joe Petroni and you—you won't let him in the house. You keep him waiting in the hall. Suppose he'd changed his mind and taken a powder. I'd've been the laughing stock of the whole damned city. You did it deliberately! You tried to make a fool out of me. My God, is there no end to the injury you do me? Wasn't it enough that—"

Apprehensive, I threw myself into the middle of his sentence in an effort to stem the tide.

"Allhoff," I said sharply. "Battersly didn't recognize Big Joe. He'd never seen him before. He—"

"Shut up," yelled Allhoff, his voice rising to a squeak. "You dumb, interfering louse. You—"

Big Joe Petroni cleared his throat. "It is a very bad thing for mor-morale," he said primly, "for flatfeet to fight among themselves, particularly in front of civilians."

This was a rather surprising maxim from Big Joe Petroni, but I was grateful for it. It took Allhoff's attention from Battersly. He turned his hot little eyes on Big Joe Petroni.

"That was a very beautiful thought, Joe," said Allhoff bitingly. "If you've any more of them you better talk fast because in ten minutes you'll be locked in a cell alone. With no audience."

"I don't want to go to the can, Inspector."

"Well, well," said Allhoff with a politician's phoney heartiness. "He doesn't want to go to the can. Neither did Mulenbroich. Neither did Capone. But they went, didn't they? And who the hell's going to keep you out of the can, Petroni?"

Big Joe Petroni took a thin cigar from his pocket and lighted it. It seemed to me that there was a flicker of nervousness in his eyes, yet his manner was assured enough as he spoke.

"I was hoping you would, Inspector. Seeing as how you got such a reputation for fair play and honest dealing, I come direct to you."

I exchanged a swift glance with Battersly. Big Joe was certainly laying it on with a trowel. If Allhoff had a reputation for fair play and honest dealing it had never

reached my ears. However, at the moment, Allhoff nodded sagely and accepted the tribute as something rather too obvious to comment upon.

"So," went on Big Joe, "I come direct to you figuring I could get a fair shake."

Allhoff's lips twisted into what he firmly believed was a benignant smile. The one hole in his armor was flattery and it was apparent that Big Joe Petroni knew that as well as I.

"You'll get a fair shake," said Allhoff. "But headquarters wants you for questioning. There's nothing I can do about that."

"Sure there is," said Big Joe. "I didn't kill them two guys, Inspector. I'm clean."

"Why not tell that to the guys who're looking for you? I'm not on the case."

"I'll be honest with you," said Big Joe slowly. "I don't want to get smacked around by those dumb flatfeet who use nightsticks instead of brains like you, Inspector. I don't want to sit in a cell while my lawyer cuts the red tape. Besides, I don't want to be stuck for a big legal fee, if I don't have to."

In all probability, I reflected, Big Joe was being honest. Though undoubtedly for reasons of expediency.

"Well," said Allhoff, "Where do I come in?"

"I didn't kill them guys," said Petroni. "And I can prove it. But if them flatfeet take me in they'll hold me for forty-eight hours. They'll smack me around a little just for the hell of it, whether I prove I'm innocent or not. So I figured if I give myself up to you, Inspector, if I prove to you that I'm clean, you'd fix things up so's I don't have to stand for the pinch."

An unholy light came in Allhoff's eyes. I knew what he was thinking. If, while the entire department was hunting for Big Joe, assuming he was implicated in two murders, Allhoff could produce him and also prove him innocent, it would once again be a great victory for Allhoff over the rest of the force.

He swung around in his swivel chair and faced me. "Simmonds, give me that first murder. Buggsy Davis, What've you got on it?"

I thumbed through the old reports.

"Davis," I read, "Robert Eugene, twenty-seven. Previous record—"

"The hell with the previous record," snapped Allhoff. "What about the actual killing."

"Found dead," I told him. "A bullet through his conniving skull, on February fourth. In his own home. The copper on the beat heard the shot at precisely two forty-three. He entered the house, found the body. The killer undoubtedly exited through the open rear window.''

Allhoff nodded curtly. He turned to Big Joe Petroni. "All right," he said. "Now what have you got to say?"

"February the fourth," said Big Joe slowly. "Two forty-three. I got an alibi."

Allhoff snorted. "Don't expect me to take the word of stoolpigeons, punks, or that assorted mob of racketeers you keep on your payroll."

"Why, of course not," said Big Joe as if such a thing would never occur to him. "You'd take the word of the Federal Life Insurance Company, wouldn't you?"

"Go on," snapped Allhoff. "Give me the details?"

"On February fourth from twelve thirty until some time after three I was in the offices of Federal Life applying for insurance. I filled out the papers, went to their doctor, waiting for a half-hour till he was ready for me, then took my physical examination. I didn't leave there until at least half past three."

"Check that," said Allhoff to me. "Right away."

The room was silent as I picked up the phone. Battersly watched Big Joe and Allhoff like a child enjoying his first play. Big Joe chewed blandly at his cigar, apparently quite calm beneath Allhoff's searching gaze. I talked over the telephone for some ten minutes and then hung up.

"Click,"— I said, "Joe has his alibi."

Allhoff grunted. "All right," he said. "Give me that other case."

"Wally Rugene," I read, "Shot through the heart, found in a Brooklyn alley. February twelfth. Time of death uncertain. The M. E. estimated he'd been dead anywhere from twelve to twenty hours when a street cleaner found him."

"Go ahead. Joe," said Allhoff. "Alibi that."

"Cruise." said Big Joe.

"Cruise?"

"Bermuda. Left on the tenth. Got back six days later. Atlas Steamship Company."

"Check that," said Allhoff to me.

I checked it telephonically. Big Joe Petroni was so serene during the call that I knew the answer before I got it.

"Right," I told Allhoff. "Joe was in Bermuda."

"See, Inspector," said Big Joe. "I'm clean, see. I come to you for a fair shake, I want you to take the heat off of me."

Allhoff expelled his breath thoughtfully and

reached for the coffee pot. I considered the situation and decided that for once Big Joe was telling the truth. If the coppers picked him up, he would probably sit in a cell all night, he would undoubtedly get stuck for a fat legal fee and it was not beyond the realm of possibility that some Irish sergeant who didn't like crooks would take a poke at him.

To avoid these things Big Joe had shrewdly played on the fact that Allhoff loved to show up the uniformed force, to demonstrate how perennially wrong they were while Allhoff, by his own admission, had never made a mistake in his life.

Allhoff emptied his coffee cup, put it down and grinned. "Well, Joe," he said, I—"

The telephone ringing on my desk interrupted him, I picked it up and listened to the voice on the other end. I hung up and announced to the room in general: "Paul Wexler was killed fifteen minutes ago. Headquarters thought we'd like to know."

I met Big Joe's eye and I thought I saw a flicker of amusement there.

"Paul Wexler," said Allhoff, "Policy guy, wasn't he? He'd been chiseling in on your district, hadn't he, Joe?"

Big Joe Petroni lied with his face. He looked blank and thoughtful as he said: "Wexler? Wexler? I don't believe I know the name, Inspector."

"Joe," I said, "you're a Sicilian liar. You know Wexler as well as you know your own name. There's been stoolpigeon talk that you were going to get him, take over his policy game."

Big Joe took his cigar from his mouth, "I'm clean, Inspector," he said. "I got an alibi."

"Sure," I said bitterly. "And we're it. Besides, headquarters said that they got the guy that killed him. Nailed him running away from Wexler's car, a gun in his hand."

Big Joe sighed gently. "Well, will you take the heat off of me, Inspector."

Allhoff lifted his coffee cup and spoke over its chipped rim.

"Joe," he said with suspicious softness, "I'll take the heat off you. But it strikes me that maybe you've overplayed the hand. It occurs to me that there's more to this case than meets the eye. I'm looking for it."

Big Joe Petroni shrugged. "Go ahead, Inspector," he said. "I'm clean. All I was asking was a fair shake. I knew you'd give it to me. I'm at the Royal Hotel if you want me." He turned around and went out the door.

Allhoff stared after him for a long time, until the sound of his footsteps died out down the stairway.

"Gee," said Battersly, who could appreciate the obvious as well as any man. "Petroni had fool proof alibis. The department would've looked pretty silly if they'd put him in jail."

Neither Allhoff nor myself paid any attention to this profundity. Battersly, who possessed the tact of a Japanese diplomat, continued: "Anyway, by letting him go, the inspector didn't put his foot in it."

I got to my feet, drew an involuntary breath of horror. Battersly looked at me and, as the significance of his ill-chosen phrase dawned upon him, his face turned white. Allhoff's coffee cup struck the desk-top like a falling bomb. He swung around in his chair pushing it away from the desk.

As his body came clear, two wriggling stumps revealed themselves at the point where his thighs should have begun. He hammered his clenched fist on the wooden arm of his chair. His eyes blazed with furious fire. His face was a twisted mask of evil. His lips contorted as if he were on the verge of a sudden epilepsy. Then his voice roared through the room like a diving plane.

"You dare say that to me!" he shouted. "Put my foot in it, eh? Damn you, my foot is buried six feet in the ground. Thanks to you and your lousy yellow belly manners! You filthy—"

He groped down in the sewers of his vocabulary and came up with a group of nouns whose vileness was equaled only by the adjectives.

Young Battersly's face was deadly pale. His lips were tightly compressed and there was a misery in his eyes that made my stomach turn over.

"Allhoff," I said shortly. "Allhoff, listen to me."

He took his eyes from Battersly and turned them on me, I could almost feel their heat.

"Keep out of this. You hate me as much as he does. Sometimes I think that if he hadn't robbed me of my legs you would have done it. You're the same yellow type. The same—"

The deeper pools of his vocabulary, I learned, were by no means plumbed yet. He hurled invective at me until he was exhausted. I took it calmly enough. I was used to it and I preferred to have the storm of his wrath gather about my head than about Battersly's.

At last, out of breath, Allhoff abruptly turned back to his desk, filled his cup with coffee and, still breathing hard, buried his corvine nose in its murky depths.

I went back to the papers on my desk. Battersly stared savagely out the window into the snow-driven depths of Centre Street below. I had dwelt in the middle of this situation for some five years now without learning to relish it.

It had its genesis some time back when Battersly was a raw recruit and Allhoff, legs and all, an Inspector on active duty. A raid on a gangster's hide-out on upper West End Avenue had been scheduled with Allhoff as leader of the raiding party. Battersly's assignment had been to affect a rear entrance, disable the Tommy-gun operator, who, our stoolie had informed us, was guarding the stairway facing the door.

Battersly obeyed the first part of his orders, all right. That is, he gained entrance to the house. Then he developed a quite understandable attack of buck fever. Instead of closing with the thug at the machine gun he fled up the stairway at the precise moment that Allhoff, at the head of his squad, axed in the front door.

The first burst from the machine gun riddled twenty holes in Allhoff's legs. A week later gangrene set in and amputation was necessary to save his life. There were many times when I found myself wishing it hadn't.

Of course, all of us in the department had figured that this was the end of Allhoff's career. But the commissioner was of no mind to lose his best man so easily. Since a police inspector minus his legs was a Civil Service impossibility, the commissioner had arranged things so that Allhoff, through devious bookkeeping, still drew his former salary and still did a full day's work for it.

Officially unattached to the force, Allhoff had rented this slum tenement because of its proximity to headquarters. There, well in the commissioner's graces because of his undoubted ability, he wielded as much influence as ever before. Which was far too much for my liking.

With a nice sense of ironic justice the commissioner had granted Allhoff's Machiavellian request that Battersly be assigned to him as assistant. I, as an old-timer who had come up with Allhoff, had also been detailed to his office, ostensibly to take care of the paper work, actually to step in when Allhoff became too hysterically angry at the younger man.

For that amputation had cost Allhoff more than his legs. It had cost him some of his reason, too. He had become a bitter, brooding old man who at times teetered over the balance line which divides sanity from madness.

Anyway, here we were, the three of us, for better or worse. Each day's routine was a hell that had to be lived through. Though, had it not been for my family and the pension which was due me in a few years I would have quit long ago. Battersly, with a martyr's sense of expiation, resolutely stuck to his job no matter what indignity Allhoff heaped on his head.

CHAPTER TWO

Protection for a Killer

I arrived at Allhoff's apartment the following morning some forty minutes late, Battersly was already there and Allhoff had consumed his matutinal gallon of coffee. He looked up as I entered and surprisingly enough, grinned.

"We've got a case," he said. "And they're sore at me."

"Who's sore at you?"

"Those uniformed morons across the street. They're sore because I sprung Big Joe."

He grinned happily as I regarded him curiously. The single thing that seemed to give him any measure at all of enjoyment was the fact that someone was sore at him.

"Yeah," he went on. "They say they might've got some information out of Big Joe if they'd got their hands on him, Those three killings have got 'em licked. Especially the last one. You know, Wexler."

"Wexler," I said, taking off my coat. "I thought they caught the killer red-handed. That's what the morning paper said. A guy named Muller."

"That's what they thought," said Allhoff. "But they can't figure it. They're sending him over here to me."

I sat down and scratched my head. "But the beat copper heard the shot, caught the guy with the gun in his hand."

"No motive," said Allhoff,

"There must be a motive. Or else the guy is nuts. What the hell do they mean no motive?"

"For once you're right," said Allhoff.

"Of course there's a motive. They're just too dumb to figure it. That's all. They claim this guy Muller is a thirty-dollar-a-week bookkeeper. They claim he never knew Wexler at all. That there was absolutely no connection between him and Wexler. This Muller, they say, is an ordinary clerk. No underworld connections at all."

"Well," I said, "Someone's wrong."

"Naturally. *They* are. That's why they're sending him over to me,"

At that moment I heard heavy footfalls on the stairs, Battersly stood up and opened the door. A heavy Irish copper named Reardon came in. Handcuffed to him was a thin insignificant-looking guy whose pinched face was pale, whose blond moustache was twisted upward with what seemed pathetic bravado.

Reardon saluted and in response to Allhoff's ges-

tured invitation sat down. Muller perforce, sat down in the chair next to him. Allhoff reached for the coffee pot, filled his cup and stared at little Muller with his evil eyes.

Muller looked more frightened than ever. Allhoff lifted his coffee cup and drained it without removing his gaze from the prisoner. He banged the cup back on the desk and said: "So this is the killer, eh. Reardon? And he won't talk?"

"He'll talk," said Reardon, "but what he says don't make no sense, He says he held a grudge against. Wexler checked and checked and there ain't no tie-up between them. None of Wexler's guys ever seen him. He was never in none of Wexler's hang-outs neither."

Allhoff eyed Muller unpleasantly as if he had one hell of a nerve coming along and confusing the police department. Muller, without waiting for Allhoff's question, said suddenly: "It's a lie. I knew Wexler. Saw a lot of him around the night clubs."

"So." said Allhoff. "You run around to night clubs."

Muller nodded. "Sure. Every dime of my salary goes on liquor and women. Money's only made to spend. I was on a lot of parties with Wexler."

I looked at Muller and got the impression of an anemic Flatbush Don Juan.

Allhoff said: "And how much is your salary?"

"A little under forty dollars a week."

"And it all goes on night clubs and women, eh? What's your wife have to say about that?"

"She's dead," said Muller. "I'm a widower."

"No family?"

"One daughter."

Allhoff refilled his coffee cup and picked it up. "Where's she? Does she live with you?"

"Yes, but—but—she's not home now."

Allhoff put down the cup and looked at Muller as if he had something. "Where is she?"

"Upstate. Visiting an aunt. Now look here. Inspector. I admit shooting Wexler. Isn't that enough? Isn't that the end of the matter?"

"I hardly think so," said Allhoff showly. "As a matter of fact, I think it's only the beginning. Reardon, take him away."

Reardon took him away and as their footsteps vanished down the stairs Allhoff turned to us. "You, two, go out to Muller's apartment. Look around. Test your powers of observation. And for once in your lives bring me back some evidence voluntarily without my having to drag it out of you."

Battersly and I donned our hats and coats and went

out, none too happily, into the blinding snow storm.

A little more than an hour later, Battersly and I returned to Allhoff's apartment with a collection of varied, and as I saw it, thoroughly futile information. He tore the coffee cup away from his lips as we came in proceeded to fire questions at us.

"Well, what did you find? Papers? Letters? Any tie-up with Wexler that the dumb coppers overlooked? There must've been something there."

He stared at us eagerly. I reflected that Allhoff's interest in justice was nothing compared to his desire to show the lads in blue across the street that he was their master.

"Take it easy," I told him, "and prepare yourself for a disappointment, we found nothing. Absolutely nothing."

He scowled at me and said insultingly:

"How would *you* know? Battersly, tell me what you saw in Muller's apartment. Never mind how trivial you think it is. Tell me everything."

"Well," said Battersly uncomfortably, "it was a pretty ordinary apartment, Inspector. Maple furniture. Neat and clean but cheap. You know."

"The sort of a place," I broke in, "where the average thirty-five-dollar-a-week clerk would have if he had a child to support."

Allhoff sipped his coffee sibilantly. He lifted his head from the cup and said suddenly: "Papers? Any papers in the place?"

"The usual papers," I told him. "Gas bills, rent receipts, a time-payment book, old circulars—"

"Payment for what?" snapped Allhoff, turning on me.

I shrugged my shoulders. "I don't know. I just happened to notice the book. You don't think he bought the gun he shot Wexler with on time, do you?"

His angry gaze hit me with almost physical impact. "Damn you!" he yelled. "I get no cooperation in this office. You two deliberately try to hinder me. Back from that day when—"

He glared balefully at Battersly who temporarily stemmed the tide of his wrath by murmuring: "Them time payments was on the radio, Inspector. I happened to notice that."

Allhoff grunted, somewhat mollified. "Radio, eh? What sort of radio? Did either of you happen to notice?"

"There were two radios in the house," I told him, "Which one would you like described?"

"Both of them."

I sighed. The conversation was fruitless and pointless. Allhoff was gathering not a single bit of evidence from our facts. But, by God, he was going to pretend he saw significance in each tiny item merely to show us what a subtle gigantic brain functioned beneath his uncombed hair.

"There was a small radio, a ten-dollar one in the room which I figured belonged to Muller's daughter. There was a big one in the living-room. Undoubtedly it was the big one that he was making the installment payments on. Now that you have that fact, I suppose you can easily tell us why Muller killed Wexler."

To my surprise he let that crack go.

"What was it worth, do you figure? The big radio?"

"Oh, I don't know. Possibly a couple of hundred dollars, Eh, Battersly?"

Battersly agreed it was worth a couple of hundred dollars.

"Ah," said Allhoff with vast satisfaction. "That's the first thing I've had to work on since they dropped this damned case in my lap."

I was too tactful to obey my immediate impulse to call him a liar. Allhoff didn't have a thing. I was certain. His pretense that he did was calculated to impress Battersly and myself.

Grateful silence filled the room. Battersly turned to his favorite intellectual pastime—a scrutiny of the comic pages in the evening paper. I lit my pipe and attended to some routine, while Allhoff sipped coffee with horrible sounds and glared at the wall thoughtfully.

The steps came up the stairway outside swiftly, noisily, and with staccato panic. The door pushed open and Frankie Hadderman burst into the room. He stood near the door for a moment, his twisting lips almost as white as his sagging cheeks. His hands moved nervously at his sides, His eyes were wide open, gray, and filled with terror.

"Inspector," he said and his voice quavered. "You got to help me, Inspector. You got to save my life, The coppers laughed at me. Wouldn't give me no help. They can't do that, Inspector. It ain't right. You got to help me, Got to give me protection."

Allhoff eyed him with distaste. Frankie Hadderman was the sort of crook that every copper regards with hatred and contempt. Frankie had dipped into every sordid crime in the book, White slavery and dope peddling were two of his more elevating avocations. Headquarters knew damned well that he had killed at least a dozen men. Time and again the D. A. had tried to convict him. Time and again he had failed. The witnesses had strange ways of dying, disappearing, or changing their testimony every time Frankie Hadderman stood in the dock.

"Protection?" said Allhoff. "Give you protection? Hell, I'd clean the gun of the guy who killed you. Get out of here!"

Hadderman shook his head like a feverish aspen leaf. His chin trembled and he clasped his hands before his chest. He rushed into the room and threw himself on his knees at the side of Allhoff's desk.

"No," he shrieked and his voice hit the ceiling, crescendo. "No. You can't do this to me. He got the other guys, didn't he? He killed the other guys. Now he's trying to get me. I gotta have police protection, Inspector. You can't turn me down."

Disgusted, I turned my head from Hadderman. Allhoff, for the first time, evinced some interest.

"Who killed three guys? Get up, you rat. Get up and tell me who killed three guys?"

Hadderman stood up on trembling knees. "Joe Petroni." he said in a rustling whisper. "He killed them other guys, didn't he? He knocked off Buggsy, Rugene and Wexler, didn't he? The finger's on me next. He's going to get me unless I got protection."

"Petroni had cast-iron alibis on those three killings," said Allhoff. "And the guy who killed Wexler's in the can right now."

Hadderman shook his head stubbornly. "I don't care who's in the can. I don't care what alibis Joe's got. Lookit. Three guys—all guys Joe was sore at—got theirs. Joe was sore at me, too. And a guy just blasted at me. No, sir. It's Joe Petroni. And he's going to get me, too. For God's sake, Inspector—"

"Shut up," said Allhoff blandly. "Shut up and tell me just what happened."

Frankie Hadderman pulled himself together with almost a physical effort. He spoke rapidly and jerkily as he strove to keep the fear out of his voice.

"I come out of the house today, see. I go down to the saloon where I hang out. I'm being extra careful, too, because I don't like the way them three other guys got theirs. Still I ain't really sure Joe done it. Not then. A guy comes up in a car just as I'm going in the saloon. He fires two shots at me and scrams. He misses twice. But I'm scared, see."

"Wait a minute," snapped Allhoff. "Who was this guy? Did you see him?"

"Sure, I seen him, But it ain't no guy I ever seen before. He don't look like a hired gunman, either. He's a little guy. A little guy in a gray suit. Looked like a clerk or something."

"So," said Allhoff, "like a good solid citizen and taxpayer you went to the police, eh?"

"Sure," said Hadderman slightly relieved as he took Allhoff's irony for commendation. "Sure, that's what I done, Inspector. I went to the precinct house. I asked the sergeant for protection. He laughs at me."

"What'd he say?"

"He told me to go to hell. Said he was in favor of someone knocking me off. Said the city'd be better off without me. Told me to see you, Inspector. Said the coppers weren't on the case any more, that you took it away from them. He was sore at you, too. He called you a name."

Allhoff beamed. He relished being called a name by the uniformed squad.

I saw the sergeant's point quite well. In the first place I understood why he wasn't at all interested in the sudden demise of a rat like Hadderman, Second, he was nettled at the fact of Allhoff's fluking Petroni's capture and springing him before the boys could ask him some pointed questions. So, since Hadderman wanted protection from Petroni, he had been sent to Allhoff.

Allhoff spilled coffee into his cup. "I'm beginning to like this case," he said to me. "I think I'll solve those three killings."

"Two," I said, "You can't get around the fact of Muller."

"Maybe I can," said Allhoff thoughtfully. "Call Big Joe at his hotel."

I picked up the phone. I tell him when I get him?"

"Oh," said Allhoff, "he probably won't be in. I just want to see if I'm right."

I looked up the number and dialed it. "If you're so damned omniscient," I said, "where is Big Joe?"

"Well," said Allhoff, considering, "he may be calling on a big-shot lawyer on business. He may be down at the license bureau getting a driver's or a hunting license. He may even be in church."

That sounded like gibberish to me until I got the call through and spoke to the hotel operator. I hung up the receiver, looking at Allhoff in bewilderment, He met my eye mockingly.

"Well?"

"Mr. Petroni," I told him, repeating verbatim what the hotel had reported, "has gone over to Saint Malachi's chapel to discuss a personal matter with Father O'Brien."

"I thought so," said Allhoff with a touch of grimness. He turned to Hadderman. "Frankie, I've decided to give you protection." He shut off Hadderman's thanks with a gesture. "Simmonds, you and Battersly accompany Hadderman to his home. Tail him down the street at a discreet distance. Keep out of the way when you get to his house. I don't want it to look too obvious that he's traveling with a bodyguard."

Frankie Hadderman shook his head again.

"That ain't no good, Inspector. They got to keep up close to me. That guy's liable to try to get me again. He's crazy as a—"

"Shut up," said Allhoff again. "I don't give a damn about you, Frankie. I want to see the guy who's shooting at you. If he thinks you've got a couple of coppers with you he might lay off, I want him to try again. When he does, Simmonds, grab him. Bring him in to me. Bring Hadderman back, too. *Now* get going, the three of you."

Battersly and I stood up and walked toward the door, Frankie looking like a guy at his own funeral, stood still, stretching his hands out in appeal.

"No, Inspector. You can't do that. Suppose he shoots me. I gotta have—"

Allhoff glared at him over the rim of his coffee cup. "Get out!" he yelled. "Get out, or by God, I'll shoot you myself."

He made a movement to open the upper desk drawer. There was scurrying movement in the room as Frankie Hadderman hastened toward the door. He beat Battersly and myself into the street by a good twenty seconds.

CHAPTER THREE

Little Man With a Gun

Frankie Hadderman lived in a three-room flat on West 54th Street. The living-room, in the rear, opened on a typical New York garden, small, square, floored with dispirited grass, a flourishing ailanthus tree in its center.

Hadderman, as calm as a hurricane, paced up and down the living-room floor. From time to time he would deliver his profane opinion of a police department that refused to protect the life of a taxpayer. Battersly smoked cigarettes glumly while I looked at my watch and wondered how long I was supposed to sit here. Allhoff had set no time limit so I was looking forward to no dinner and an all-night vigil.

A little after six o'clock Battersly got up and wandered into the bathroom. I suddenly became struck with an idea and asked Frankie if there was such a thing as a drink in the house. Without marked hospitality he directed me to the kitchen. I went in there and proceeded to pour myself a slug of dubious blended whiskey.

I stood frozen with the bottle in my hand as I heard Frankie's sudden yell of terror.

He cried out: "Don't shoot me, pal. Don't shoot, I ain't done nothing to you. I don't even know you. I—"

A voice, tense and almost as fearful as Hadderman's answered.

"Why should I care about you? Why? There are those to whom I owe protection. Others—"

There seemed to me to be a sob in his voice as the word broke off in his throat.

Battersly, gun drawn, charged past me from the bathroom, I followed on his heels, We burst into the living-room to find Frankie Hadderman cowering in a corner. His face was the color of desert sand. His jaws worked convulsively and his eyes were the eyes of a man already dead.

Facing him, an automatic in his hand, was a man of middle height and medium build, His cheeks were pale and the hand that held the automatic trembled. All in all he appeared almost as afraid as Frankie Hadderman.

He took his eyes from Hadderman as we came into the room. He stared for a moment at the Police Specials Battersly and I had drawn. His fingers slowly relaxed and his own weapon thudded to the carpeted floor.

Then just as Battersly and I were upon him he did a peculiar thing. He buried his face in his hands and wept, frightfully and horribly, his shoulders moving convulsively as the sobs wracked his body.

I took his arm as Battersly snatched the automatic from the floor. Hadderman, observing his assailant disarmed, found fresh courage. He stood up straight and walked across the floor with his fists clenched.

"You yellow rat," he said. "I'll knock all your teeth out. I'll—"

He grabbed the other by the hair and jerked his head up. I moved forward and slapped Hadderman hard in the face. He looked at me in astonishment.

"He tried to knock me off, didn't he? Leave me take a poke at him. Just one poke. I—"

"There ought to be a reward for knocking you off," I told him. "Grab him. Battersly. We're all going back to Allhoff's."

By the time we reached Allhoff's slum. Frankie Hadderman had thoroughly convinced himself that he was the outraged citizen. No sinless bank president could have been more indignant, more resentful at police conditions which allowed such things to happen.

I told Allhoff what had happened at Frankie's house while Hadderman stood before Allhoff's desk and pointed a trembling forefinger at the man who had entered his apartment with the gun.

"I never did nothing to him," he declaimed. "I never even seen him before. And the rat tried to knock me off. Sneaked in over the back fence wearing crepe soles. I never even heard him till he was in the room, And them two coppers was outside drinking."

Allhoff put down his coffee cup. He looked at Battersly and myself as if he were about to deliver a diatribe on the evils of drinking in uniform, Then he thought better of it. He told Hadderman to shut up once again and turned to the other prisoner.

"Name?" he roared. "What's your name?"

The man lifted a frightened face. He spoke in a low dull tone as if he were beyond all caring. "Weldon," he skid. "Wallace Weldon."

"Occupation?"

"Junior accountant."

Allhoff sloshed coffee in his cup and ladled in sugar as if national rationing was imminent. He lifted the cup to his lips and closed his eyes registering deep and 'profound thought. He put the cup down again and said very slowly: "Of course, you're married, Weldon."

Weldon nodded dispiritedly. "Yes, I'm married."

I scratched my head and exchanged a glance with young Battersly. It was obvious Allhoff, completely baffled, was merely asking questions for the sake of asking them. I decided to needle him a little.

"Why don't you ask him how many kids he's got? That ought to clear things up."

Allhoff lifted his lids slightly. "It probably will," he said without losing his temper. "I'm going to ask that question in a very little while. Now, Weldon, why did you try to kill Hadderman here? Did he ever do anything to you?"

"I never even seen him before," screamed Frankie. "How could I do anything to him? How could I—"

Allhoff picked a ruler up from his desk. He swung it through the air like a sword and slapped Hadderman's face with the flat side, leaving a swathe of red an inch wide across his cheek,

"Now," he said sweetly, "will you shut up?"

Weldon spoke in a dispirited monotone. "He's right," he said. "He's never done anything to me."

"Well," I said, "why did you try to kill him?"

Weldon shook his head, He reminded me very much of a Belgian peasant sitting in the middle of the German invasion. He just didn't care about anything anymore.

"All right," said Allhoff. "Now, Weldon. Let's get back to the question propounded by my brilliant colleague. Have you any children?"

"Yes," said Weldon in a low frightened voice. "Two children. A boy and a girl."

"Where are they?"

Weldon lifted his eyes to meet Allhoff's for the first time since he had been in the room.

"Home, I suppose," he said scarcely audibly.

"Really?" said Allhoff. His manner was casual but I knew him well enough to realize that his mind was working at top speed, that there was hidden significance to what he said. "Are you sure, Weldon? Stop and think, Perhaps one of them is away? Visiting some relative, perhaps?"

Weldon clutched at the suggestion like a drowning man at a straw, "Sure," he said. "That's right. I forgot. Yes, my boy, Arthur. Visiting his cousin in Maine."

"What's the cousin's address?"

Weldon licked his lips. "I don't exactly know," he said. "I undoubtedly have it at home. I—"

"Never mind," said Allhoff. "Battersly, take them both across the street."

Frankie Hadderman drew himself up like an indignant society dowager.

"You mean to the can?" he demanded, You can't put me in the can. I didn't do nothing. I was shot at. You can't put a guy in the can for being shot at." Allhoff looked at him. That look boded no immediate joy for Frankie Hadderman.

"You're not going to the can for being shot at," said Allhoff gently. "I can dig up a better reason than that."

He turned to me. "Simmonds, book both these guys for assaulting an officer. I don't want Weldon charged with attempted murder—yet, anyway. The story is that Battersly was walking down the street and these two guys jumped him. Fix it so they don't get a hearing. I don't want them bailed. Now get them out of here."

Weldon, maintaining his air of utter dejection and indifference, stood up without protest. Hadderman opened his mouth and objected loudly.

"You can't do it!" he yelled. "I'm clean. I'm a citizen. I know my rights. I—"

Allhoff's brows lowered and he picked up his ruler. Hadderman backed away and shut his mouth abruptly.

"One more thing," said Allhoff. "I want to see that guy, Muller, right away. You and Battersly may go home to dinner, I've kept you late enough. Have a copper bring Muller over here as soon as possible."

We took Weldon and Hadderman from the room, went across the street and booked them. I hadn't the slightest idea what was going on in Allhoff's head, but his sudden solicitude about keeping Battersly and myself overtime, had made me very, very suspicious.

CHAPTER FOUR

The 10:30 to Sing Sing

We sat in silence the next morning as Allhoff poured coffee down his blasphemous gullet. As soon as the third pint had been emptied into his stomach, he swung around abruptly in his chair and snapped: "Battersly, get me Hadderman. Spring him. Get his name off the blotter. Have them give him back his property."

Battersly got up and strode out of the room. I watched Allhoff curiously. There was something assured about his manner. From whatever evidence I had noted about this damned case, there was nothing resembling a final conclusion, but Allhoff acted for all the world as if he had the whole thing wrapped up, in the bag, and ready for delivery.

I tried to draw him out, "Well."I said, "and what do you expect to find out from your pal, Hadderman."

He snorted. "My pal," he said heavily. "That rat. Frankly, I'd rather put that guy away than Big Joe. Joe's a crook and a bum. But he's not the complete rat Hadderman is."

I agreed with him on that point, and said so. "If I had the choice," I told him. "I'd sooner see Hadderman burn than Joe, too."

He swung around in his chair and regarded me oddly. "You wouldn't care just how he died, would you? You wouldn't insist on his burning?"

"No, I wouldn't. But since you're not quite God yet, you don't control deaths, or means of dying."

His lips twisted into an odd ironic smile. "Maybe, I do," he said slowly. "Maybe I do."

I didn't know what he meant but considering his tone, I was glad it wasn't my demise he was discussing.

Battersly came back holding Hadderman's wrist, Frankie was still scared but still indignant.

"I want a lawyer," he shrilled as soon as he came in, "I insist on my rights. I—" Allhoff ignored him, He spoke to Battersly. "You saw to it that he was properly released—received his property back?"

"Yes, sir. Even the rod that he had a permit for."

"Ah," said Allhoff, "I thought as much. Take him into my bedroom there. Take his gun away and put it in the bureau drawer. Then handcuff him to the steam-pipe in the bathroom. Give him a chair to sit in. He may be there for some time."

Frankie Hadderman lifted his voice in loud and bitter protest. I raised my eyebrows. What Allhoff had up his sinister sleeve, I didn't know. However, it was clear that he was knocking a large and jagged hole in the Bill of Rights. Unless he pinned something on Hadderman, there would be a repercussion from headquarters on the extra-legal treatment he was handing out. He had as much right to hold Frankie in his bedroom as Hitler had to invade the Netherlands.

Battersly, who had learned better than to question an order, dragged the protesting Hadderman off into Allhoff's bathroom. A moment hater he emerged again, closing the door behind him.

Allhoff busied himself with the percolator and kept his mouth shut. That silence endured until a few moments before twelve. Then he looked up suddenly and said: "You two guys go to lunch. I want to be alone for a few moments. I have to think. Oh, and while you're out give Big Joe a ring at his hotel. Tell him I want to see him about two o'clock. Have Muller and Weldon here then, too."

He was so damned matter-of-fact that, for a moment, I believed he had the case all figured out. Then, considering all angles, I decided he was bluffing. On the face of things he didn't have enough evidence for a traffic rap, on Big Joe and Hadderman. Besides, it was impossible to disregard the fact that Muller was nailed dead to rights, and Weldon, too.

I decided to eat an expensive steak for lunch and forget the whole thing.

By two thirty we were all assembled. Big Joe Petroni's bulk sprawled itself in one of Allhoff's uncomfortable kitchen chairs. He looked around the room through heavy-lidded eyes. He wore, in addition to a very loud suit, an air of complete assurance. At his side Wallace Weldon provided complete contrast. He perched on the end of his seat. His attitude of beaten futility had vanished and seemed replaced by a very positive fear. His face was white and his lips twitched constantly. Muller with his pathetic blond mustache looked nervous, but far more reassured than Weldon, He was on the far side of Allhoff's desk watching Allhoff emptying his coffee cup with an incredulous expression. Whether or not Frankie Hadderman was still ensconced in Allhoff's bathroom, I hadn't any idea.

Allhoff, completing his slaking rites, slammed his chipped cup down on the desk and looked around the room. His wandering, bitter gaze came to rest on Big Joe Petroni.

"Ah," he said softly, "I understand you were in church yesterday, Joe."

Big Joe nodded gravely. "That's right, Inspector. There are sometimes things that happen in my life I like to talk over with the priest. It eases my conscience."

"I can well imagine that," said Allhoff. "Four times, during the past five months, there were certain guys, all of whom were your enemies, Joe, who had pot shots taken at them. On one occasion you were in the office of a life insurance company. On another, you were in

Bermuda. The third time you were sitting in this office and the last time you were in a church."

Big Joe Petroni smiled the smile of a guy who has just been acquitted by a blue-ribbon jury.

"Coincidental, Inspector, ain't it?"

"Too coincidental, Joe. That's what made me think you guilty."

"There ain't no one," said Joe Petroni, with a yawn, "that can be in two places at the same time. Besides, didn't you catch this monkey here right in the act." He indicated Muller with a nod.

"Sure," said Allhoff, maintaining his affable tone, which aroused all my suspicions. "Sure we did, Joe. It occurred to me that he and the other killers might have been working for you."

Big Joe laughed. "My rods are tough. I never seen that guy in my life before. You can ask him."

"What sort of copper do you think I am?" said Allhoff, "I *have* asked him."

Big Joe shrugged. "So?"

"So," said Allhoff, "I found out he was working for you. So was Weldon."

Weldon shot up from the seat of his chair as if he had been given an invisible hot foot. "No!" he yelled. "No! I wasn't working for this man. I wasn't working for anyone. I—"

Allhoff interrupted him with a roar. "Sit down! Sit down and shut up! Enough lies have been told in this case!"

Weldon swallowed something in his throat and sat down. Allhoff turned back to Big Joe.

"Just as you said, Joe, I figured the people in this case weren't typical hoods. In fact, investigation proved they weren't. But it still looked as if you were behind it all. So the question became—why do these little middle-class guys do the dirty work for Joe Petroni?"

Big Joe smiled faintly. "Why, indeed?" he echoed, "I guess there ain't no answer to a question like that, Inspector."

"There's not only an answer," snapped Allhoff. "But I know what it is."

Some of Big Joe's lethargy dropped from him. But it seemed to me that Muller in a minor way, and Weldon in a major, were far more apprehensive than Big Joe at that moment.

"Go ahead," I told Allhoff. "You've even got me interested now."

He looked over at me and achieved a magnificent sneer. "You!" he said and the contempt he put into the pronoun was worthy of a great actor. "A fine copper you are. The prime clue in the whole affair was that radio of Muller's and you missed it completely."

"Radio?" I puzzled. "Clue?"

"Clue," said Allhoff, "Radio. You'll recall when I questioned Muller here he seemed desperately anxious to provide himself with a motive for killing Wexler. He said he was a night-club habitué, said he drank and threw away his salary on women. Painted a picture of himself as a cross between Lucious Beebe and Mike Romanoff. Well, I suppose you could do those things on his salary, if you neglected your home did a lot of chiseling."

"So," I said. "I still don't know what you're talking about."

"Of course you don't! You're too damn dumb! Now get this. Here's a guy who's supposed to be a great stay-out feller. A guy who never goes home at night. And on a salary of about forty bucks a week, he spends over two hundred buying a radio! Now do you get it?"

"No," I said.

He made a gesture of complete disgust.

"All right," he said, "I'll make it clear even to you. Any guy who makes as little salary as Muller and spends two hundred bucks on a radio is a home-lover. He's a radio fan, He's spending five weeks' pay on the damned instrument. If Muller was the night-club cruiser he said he was what would he want a radio for? And if he did want one, a ten-dollar box'd be good enough for him. The expensive radio obviously wasn't for his child as the girl had one of her own in her room. It was for Muller. Two hundred bucks worth. Two hundred bucks he'd much rather spend for liquor and women if he'd been telling the truth, but he wasn't."

I rolled that over in my mind and decided with some reluctance that there was something to it. Big Joe Petroni moved in his chair and said: "So what does that prove? Only that Muller lied. I wish you'd hurry up with all this, Inspector. I got to catch a train."

"Ah," said Allhoff, "A train, I have a very nice train for you to catch, Joe. The ten-thirty. A. M."

"The ten-thirty? Where does that go?"

"To the chair, Joe. Not directly—true. You change at Ossining, Joe. For the chair."

Big Joe appealed to me. "Is he nuts, Sergeant? He ain't got anything on me."

"Look here." said Weldon. "You fellows have me dead to rights. Why all this investigation?"

Muller said nothing. His eyes were focused wonderingly on Allhoff.

Allhoff said to the room at large: "Now, not only do I suspect that these guys are working for Joe, but I find out one of them at least is lying like hell to provide a motive for his murder, Why should that be? How can Joe control these guys that much? How can he make them throw their lives away for him?"

"Maybe," I put in, nettled at his circuitous methods, "maybe he gave them radios."

Allhoff shot me a venomous glance, then continued. "The striking thing Weldon and Muller had in common was parenthood. Each of them had children. And Muller's kid was away visiting an aunt. That got me to thinking."

I exchanged a glance with Battersly. True, Allhoff had made a point with his radio theory, but I was eternally damned if I could see how the fact of a child's visit to a relative had any bearing on what Allhoff was trying to prove.

"And," went on Allhoff, "I went on thinking. Especially since I was told that Weldon had said, while in Hadderman's apartment. Why should I care about you? There are those to whom I owe protection—' I discovered afterwards, that Weldon had two children. I almost had the answer then, I asked him if one of them was away somewhere visiting a relative. He jumped at it and told me yes. Then I was sure I was right."

Big Joe was watching Allhoff keenly now and with more interest than he had evinced before.

"So?" I asked.

"So," said Allhoff, "it suddenly became very plain. Big Joe had certain enemies he wanted to get rid of. He couldn't do the job himself because the entire department would have put the finger on Joe immediately. It was well known that Davis, Rugene, Wexler and Hadderman were Joe's enemies. So Joe conceived the bright idea of having four unknowns, four little middle-class guys who'd never committed a crime in their lives do his dirty work."

"But why?" I asked. "How could he make them do it?"

"My God," said Allhoff, "Here's a blue-print. He selected men who were fathers, men who were particularly attached to their children. Then he kidnaped the children. He furnished the fathers with guns, told them where to find their victim and told them to go ahead and shoot if they ever wanted to see their children again."

I considered that a moment and decided it was one hell of a good idea—from Joe's point of view.

"*And,*" I said, "of course the fathers couldn't talk. If they ever squawked about Joe's snatching, they left themselves open to a murder rap. They *had* to keep their mouths shut."

"Right," said Allhoff. "That's why Muller was so eager to demonstrate he had a motive. He was far more worried about his daughter than about himself. That's why Weldon has tried to shut me up this afternoon."

"And the other two guys," I asked. "The guys who killed Davis and Rugene?"

Allhoff shrugged. "What's it matter? I assume they've got their kids back by now. I'm not too upset because Davis and Rugene are lying in pine boxes."

The more I thought of it the more I admired—professionally, of course—Big Joe's fool-proof scheme. While the killings were being perpetrated, Joe, of course, went out and fixed himself unbreakable alibis.

Allhoff turned to Big Joe. "You see," he said, "I don't mind you killing those guys at all. It's your method I object to. As a matter of fact, I'd rather have Hadderman dead than you, Joe."

Big Joe stood up. His eyes were bright and his jaw was set.

"You're still going to have trouble with your case, Inspector. Maybe you're right but you'll have a hell of a time proving it in court. I don't think your witnesses will be very willing to testify. Because, just in case you *are* right, maybe I still have their kids."

Allhoff looked at him oddly and there was a peculiar smile on his face which I couldn't interpret.

"Joe," said Allhoff, looking for all the world like a Nazi aviator waiting for a dropped bomb to explode, "I don't need those witnesses, I've got another piece of evidence that makes you eligible for that train I spoke of."

"Train?" said Big Joe, puzzled.

"The ten-thirty, remember?" said Allhoff. "The Death House Special. The evidence, Joe, is in my bedroom. I'm asking you to get it for me."

Joe regarded him suspiciously. "In your bedroom? Whereabouts?"

"Go right in," said Allhoff, "You can't miss it."

Big Joe stood still for a moment, then shrugging his shoulders, he spun around on his heel and strode toward the closed bedroom door. Allhoff whipped open the top drawer of his desk and withdrew his Police Special. Battersly and I, watching him, dropped our hands instinctively to our own weapons.

Big Joe opened the door, stepped across the threshold. He disappeared into the room. Then I heard three sharp epithets, only one of which was uttered in Joe's voice. There was the sound of a shot, followed by two more reports.

I sprang across the room, gun drawn, Battersly on my heels. Allhoff was grinning like an illegitimate son of Machiavelli and Satan.

Big Joe stood against the wall, his gun in his hand and blood staining the shoulder of his coat. Before him Frankie Hadderman lay on a filthy scatter rug. There were two holes in his head from which poured two tiny rivers across the dust of the bedroom floor. Battersly closed with Big Joe and wrenched the gun from him.

Then, leaving Hadderman there, the three of us returned to the other room.

Muller stared at us with eyes as wide as the Grand Canyon. Weldon was white and trembling. Allhoff sat with his gun in one hand and a raised coffee cup in the other. His grin was the epitome of all the evil gloating that has been done since the Garden of Eden.

Big Joe sank heavily into a chair. His breath came fast and blood dripped from his wound.

"That punk," he said. "I got him, though. I got him. I knew—"

"You've bought your ticket, Joe," said Allhoff.

"Ticket?"

"The ten-thirty to Sing Sing, Joe. Murder of Hadderman. Three police witnesses. You haven't a chance, Joe."

Big Joe Petroni's face contorted. "Damn you!" He yelled. "It was a frame. You can't do this, Allhoff. What about those kids? You want them innocent kids to suffer? You want—"

"Take him out," said Allhoff to Battersly. "Take 'em all out. Back across the street. I'll attend to the details later."

Weldon stood up. He glared at Allhoff and his rage seemed more intense than Joe's. "You interfering fool!" he screamed. "What about my son? What did you have to butt into this for? I'll never see him again now. I'll never—"

"Simmonds," said Allhoff wearily, "will you get them out of here? You know how I hate emotionalism."

I got up seething with anger. Two kids were in danger of their lives and he talked about emotionalism. However, I kept my mouth shut until we'd taken the trio across the street to headquarters.

When I got back to the flat, I opened up. "It would be damned difficult," I told him, "to lower my opinion of you, but you've done it. As long as you break your lousy case, as long as you put a guy in the can, what the hell do you care for anyone else? You know what Big Joe's like. God knows what his thugs'll do to those kids to get even. You're a low, crawling, arrogant—"

His fist pounded on the desk hike an anvil. "Shut up!" he howled. "You dare talk to me like that! I'm no dumb flatfoot. When I fix a case, I cover all angles. Do you think I'm a superannuated sergeant like yourself—a stupid, half-witted nincompoop—"

"Never mind what I think you are. What about those kids?"

He glared at me. "They've been home for the past three hours."

I sat down limply. "But how—how—"

"How," he mimicked in a falsetto voice. "How? Because I've got a brain, That's why. When I had the case figured, I sent for Muller. I told him what I knew, told him I could save his kid and would speak to the D. A. about *nolle prossing* his case if he'd help me. He did."

"But—how could Muller help you?"

"By doing what I told him to. He had a contact with Joe. A post-office box address. I had him write there enclosing a prescription. In the note he told Joe his kid suffered from heart trouble. If she didn't get the enclosed medicine at least three times a week, she'd probably die. Said if Joe wouldn't take the stuff to the kid, he, Muller'd talk,"

"I still don't get it."

"Of course, you don't, you muddle-minded idiot. I put a tail on that box, on Joe. Not you or Battersly, but a guy with some brains from the Detective Bureau. Joe got the note. Joe knew, as I figured, a dead kid was no good to him at all. He high-tailed it with the medicine to the hide-out where he was keeping the kids. My tail followed him, The joint was raided five hours ago."

Apologizing to Allhoff was like eating a succulent dish of fertilizer. I did it.

"But, sir," said Battersly, "I still don't understand this business about Hadderman and Petroni. About the shooting, sir, About—" He indicated the door behind which Hadderman lay growing cold in a pool of his own blood.

Allhoff filled his cup with coffee. "All right, my weak-minded aides," he said, "I'll explain it, In the first place I didn't like Frankie Hadderman. If he was dead I'd feel better. Besides, there was going to be trouble convicting Big Joe. He's got a lot of drag. The case was involved and it would drag in those little punks who did the killings for him.

"So it seemed to me that if Joe met Frankie, who already knew Joe was gunning for him, there might be a little gun play. If Frankie killed Joe, well, Joe was dead and we sent Frankie up on the ten-thirty train for the killing. If Joe killed Frankie, Frankie's dead and Joe gets the train ticket. See, I couldn't lose."

I nodded reluctantly. Once again Allhoff had come out on top. Then as I thought of something, a smile flickered about my lips. Allhoff, noting it, snarled at me: "Why the simian grin?"

"The commissioner," I reminded him. "You'll remember he's something of a stickler for civil rights and the routine method of doing things. You've stuck your neck out, Allhoff, and it makes me very, very happy. For the first time in your career the commissioner is going to fall on you like a ton of bricks. At last you've overplayed your hand."

Allhoff took his face from his coffee cup and said with wide-eyed innocence, "I don't quite understand, Sergeant."

The 'Sergeant' should have warned me. It didn't. "Why," I said confidently, "that business of a corpse in your bedroom. You know, it's illegal to arm a couple of thugs and let them shoot it out. Especially when it happens in a policeman's boudoir."

Allhoff suddenly looked like a very wise guy. "Me?" he said with phoney innocence. "I didn't do anything. Hell, I told Battersly to disarm Hadderman, to hand-cuff him to the steampipe. If he failed to lock the handcuffs properly, so that Hadderman retrieved his gun and blasted Joe when he came in, it's not my fault."

I eyed him angrily. "I know damned well what you did." I told him, "I saw that body. One handcuff, the one that'd been locked to the pipe, had been unlocked. You did it. You gave him back his gun and told him Big Joe was coming in after him."

"That's sheer speculation," snapped Allhoff. "The report will inform the commissioner of Battersly's negligence."

Battersly stared at him with morbid hating eyes. He didn't speak, but in his face there was all the concentrated bitterness of the oppressed peoples of the world. Allhoff saw it, too. For one of the few times in his life he averted his gaze.

"All right," he said briskly to cover up. "Get that corpse out of *my* bedroom. I can't go to sleep with a corpse!"

My eyes followed Battersly as he walked into the bedroom. One of those two, I reflected, would one day, go to sleep with a corpse—on his conscience.

COFFEE FOR A KILLER

CHAPTER ONE

Brains vs. Stoolies

I sat gloomily at my desk staring at the travel page of the evening paper, feeling very much like the German High Command standing at Calais gazing at the Dover cliffs across the channel. Pictorially, Miami Beach, palm lined and glistening in the sunlight was very, very attractive. The siren words strung together by the Chamber of Commerce press agent added fuel to the discontent in my breast. With a sigh I dragged my mind back from the waters of the Gulf and dumped it in the lap of reality.

I looked around the room in utter disgust. It was four o'clock of the afternoon and the lights were already lit. The chipped and soiled wood of the walls encircled the frenzied disorder of Allhoff's apartment. Dirty dishes floated in the sink like a fleet of dispirited garbage scows. Allhoff's soiled linen which had been worn at least once, lay scattered across the floor. Cigarette ash and paper which had missed the waste basket formed sporting hazards for the cockroaches in their march toward the garbage can. The general atmosphere was one of gloom, dirt, disorder and melancholy.

Directly in front of me, Battersly's blue-uniformed bent back arched over his desk as he applied every brain cell to following the adventures of his favorite comic strip detective. On my left sat Allhoff.

His swivel chair was pulled as far up to his desk as possible. His chest was pressed against its top. On his left the stained coffee pot gurgled on its electric base. Before him lay a sheet of yellow paper on which he made meaningless marks with a pencil as he stared broodingly off into space.

The feeling of depression that was upon me lifted somewhat as I watched him. After several years, I was quite fed up with Allhoff's being right, thoroughly tired of his instinctive diagnosis of whatever problem the commissioner laid in his lap. This time, however, he had established a record. For forty-eight hours he had been as completely baffled as the veriest rookie on the force. There was no sympathy in my heart.

"Perhaps," I said aloud, "you're slipping."

He made a sound like a misanthropic panther. He picked up the coffee pot and filled his cup. He ladled in sugar with a prodigal hand. He drained the cup before

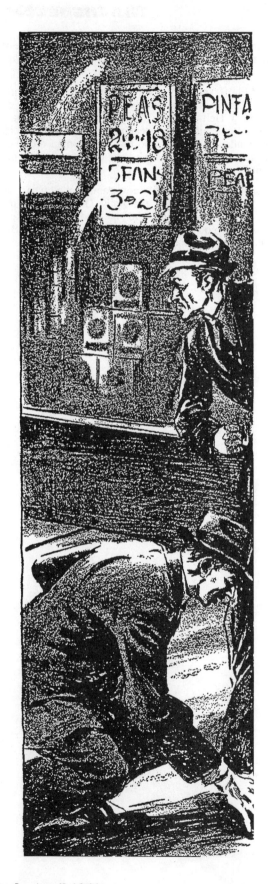

Originally Published - April 1941

he answered.

"Am I a police inspector?" He demanded. "Or a yogi? Can I solve a murder that doesn't make any sense after they've burned up all the clues? The whole thing's ridiculous. I don't see any point in anyone's killing Murdock."

"He was a banker, wasn't he? From what I hear bankers have lots of enemies. Industrial and communistic."

"Enemy or not," snapped Allhoff, "why didn't the killer take the dough? Killing a banker at his home on a night when he happens to be carrying ten grand in cash is logical enough. But why scatter the dough all over the floor and leave it there? It doesn't make any sense at all."

I lit my pipe and from sheer boredom pursued the conversation.

"Are you sure the butler was telling the truth about the money?"

"Of course. He found the body, stabbed. He saw the dough all over the floor. When he called Murdock's wife, she saw it, too. Then while they wait for the coppers to get there the mysterious fire breaks out. Burns all the dough, half the furniture, and has begun to cremate the body when the firemen arrive."

Battersly turned his attention from Dick Tracy and offered a contribution.

"Do you think the fire had anything to do with the killing? Or was it just accidental?"

"How the devil do I know?" said Allhoff testily. "The fire inspectors say there was gasoline in the room. But I don't know. Damn it, I don't know anything. I wish to God I'd never heard of the case."

He refilled his cup with coffee the color of Pluto's blood, and glowered menacingly at the far wall. I puffed at my pipe and grinned at his back.

It was not, I knew, the abstruse angles of the case that had him sore. He was nursing a personal insult. His ego, his pride, had been wounded. Heretofore, whenever the commissioner had handed a case to Allhoff, it had been all Allhoff's. No one else got a tithe of credit nor an ounce of authority.

This time, however, recognizing that there was absolutely nothing to work on, the commissioner had assigned two men to the case. He was playing two angles. Allhoff had brains and was, without doubt, a reasoning creature. Gebhart had stool-pigeons. The commissioner had assigned them both to the Murdock killing with orders to work independently. If intelligence failed to bring up the solution, perhaps the stoolies would come through, and vice versa. The commissioner, quite sensibly, was playing the percentage. But to Allhoff it was a mortal blow.

There was no living person whom Allhoff liked. There were several whom he hated. There were at least two whom he hated with every bit of the venom stored up in his twisted little soul. One of these was Gebhart. For twenty years, while both of them were rising to inspector's rank, they had fought. Allhoff detested Gebhart as a moron whose promotions depended solely on the fact of his obtaining a better class of stoolies. Gebhart hated Allhoff as a muscle man always fears the brains he cannot understand. They had double-crossed each other continually for two decades. On at least three occasions they had locked themselves in the detectives' room and proceeded to hammer each other into insensibility.

And now the commissioner had thrown a crowning insult at Allhoff by implying that Gebhart had as much chance of breaking the Murdock murder as himself. To add injury to that insult Allhoff, in some forty-eight hours had accomplished precisely nothing. I knew he was eating his miserable heart out with worry that Gebhart would get something first.

About fifteen minutes before quitting time, I heard the footsteps on the stairs. Allhoff's nose was buried in his coffee cup as a sharp rap sounded on the panels of the door, and without waiting for an answer, Gebhart walked in.

With him was a girl—a brassy blonde of indeterminate age. She was pretty as polished rock is pretty. There was nothing soft about her face and she carried her shapely body like a flag. Allhoff took the cup away from his nose and set it down clatteringly in the saucer. He glared at Gebhart who grinned back mockingly at him.

"This, baby," he said to the girl, "this slum is where the brains of the police department hangs out. Sort of needs a feminine touch don't you think?"

"Damn you," said Allhoff thickly. "What are you doing here?"

Despite the challenge in his tone, Gebhart maintained his bland amiability.

"This is Miss Whalen," he announced. "My girl friend. Had a date with her so I brought her along."

"Brought her along for what?" snarled Allhoff. "If this is official business, state it and get the hell out."

Gebhart kept his smile. He waved the girl to a chair and took one himself. He crossed his legs and lit a cigarette. Allhoff still glared at him. I knew the depth of his emotion as I watched his hand tremble when he poured more coffee.

"Say," said Gebhart, as if he'd just thought of it, "ever hear of a guy called Murdock?"

Allhoff froze with the cup lifted halfway to his lips. His eyes narrowed and his voice was taut as a spring when he spoke.

"Stop clowning, damn you! What about Murdock?"

Gebhart looked up. "Why," he said with phoney innocence, "he's dead."

The Whalen girl laughed uproariously and Gebhart joined in. Allhoff put down his cup and slopped coffee in the saucer.

"Very funny," he said with heavy sarcasm. "Very, very funny. And now that you've given us our laugh, will you kindly take your doxy and get out of here."

I wasn't quite sure what be meant by that last and Gebhart wasn't either. However since Allhoff was staring at the blonde we both gathered that it was an insult directed at Gebhart's lady friend. Gebhart stood up and now his mocking smile was gone.

"I'll get out," he said, "when I tell you what I came up here to tell you. I'm here to tell you about Murdock."

"You've told me he's dead," said Allhoff. "That I already know."

"That's all you *do* know, *I* know who killed him."

Allhoff's face became white. He said, "It's a lie," in the tone of a man who was very much afraid it wasn't.

Gebhart laughed. When he spoke his voice was high, excited and vicious.

"It's true," he said. "So true it's going to break your miserable little heart. For years you've been throwing your weight about this man's police department. For years you've been boasting that you're the only guy with an ounce of competence. Well, this time, I've licked you. You haven't even got a clue yet and I've broken the case. Maybe you'll shut up for a while now, Inspector."

"You will get out of here," said Allhoff speaking like a machine gun, "and with you, you will take your——"

This time there was no doubt he meant the blonde and there was no need of etymological research to find the definition of his word. The Whalen girl flushed and took a step toward him. Gebhart put a hand on her arm, said, "I'll handle this, baby," and towered suddenly over Allhoff's desk.

"You lousy little bum," he roared. "For years the whole damned department has hated your guts. But I've hated 'em more than all the others put together. For years I've tried to put you in your place and now, by God, I've succeeded. I've broken the Murdock case and you haven't moved an inch on it, what about the great Allhoff brain now? Sometimes I think your legs are longer than your mind."

For a moment there was a silence in the room tense as a coiled spring, vibrant as the instant before an air raid alarm, Allhoff put a hand on his desk and slowly pushed his chair back. At the edge of his chair where his knees should have been, two leather pads abruptly terminated his thighs. Battersly made a strange hissing sound as he sucked in air and broke the silence. Allhoff's voice came deeply from his chest like that of an avenging angel.

"For that," he said, "you will apologize on your knees."

The blonde laughed off key. "Apologize? To a runt like you? He could lick you with one hand."

Allhoff's right arm moved rapidly. He opened a desk drawer and closed it again. His Police Special was in his hand and its muzzle drew an accurate bead on Gebhart's heart.

"Can he lick *this*?" said Allhoff.

Gebhart looked at the gun and his jaw was set firmly. The girl's eyes were wide and worried. Battersly stared at the tableau like a peasant at a skyscraper. I put down my pipe, stood up and said sharply, "Allhoff!"

"Keep out of this, Simmonds." he said without taking his eyes from Gebhart. "You," he went on, "you and that trollop will apologize. On your knees!"

Gebhart stood uncertainly staring at the gun. The blonde put her hand on his arm.

"He wouldn't dare," she whispered. "Tell him to go to hell. He wouldn't dare."

But Gebhart knew Allhoff better than that. For that matter, so did I.

"Now listen, Inspector," said Gebhart placatingly, "maybe I said too much. Maybe I—"

"Your knees," said Allhoff. "You and your doll there."

Gebhart looked at the gun, raised his eyes and looked at Allhoff. There was maniacal purpose in Allhoff's face. His little eyes were hot and bitter, Gebhart swallowed something in his throat. He put his hand on the girl's arm, and as he sank to his knees he dragged her down with him. There was murder in his gaze as he said slowly: "I apologize, Inspector."

Allhoff nodded, transferred his glance to the Whalen girl. "And you?"

I saw Gebhart's fingers tighten on her arm. She nodded her head quickly. "Me, too." she said. "I'm sorry."

"All right," said Allhoff. "Get out!"

They rose slowly to their feet. Flushed humiliation was in Gebhart's cheeks. The girl was plainly angry but fear kept her silent. They walked slowly to the door. There, Gebhart turned around.

"I'm going to get you for this." he said in a low husky voice. "I'm going to get you if it takes the rest of *my* life."

"Get out!" Allhoff said again, and reached for the coffee pot.

I was prepared for his explosion as soon as they left the room. It was apparent that he was keeping a volcano clamped down inside him. He had been controlling himself, maintaining an icy calm before Gebhart and, knowing him as I did, I knew he couldn't keep it up much longer. He didn't.

The instant the footfalls died away on the stairs, Allhoff swung around in his swivel chair and faced Battersly. He pounded his fists on the arms of his chair and raised his voice in a surging roar.

"Curse you!" he shouted. "Because of you, because of your arrant cowardice, I'm put in a position where morons like Gebhart can insult me. I devote my brain and body to the police department and you take half the latter away from me. You—"

He pulled obscenity out of his vocabulary like a street cleaner pulling filth from a clogged sewer. His face was red as bougainvillea, his fists flailed the chair arm, his leather stumps kicked convulsively in the air.

Battersly sat with averted face before his attacker. Like a disciple of Gandhi, he bent before the onslaught meekly, without retaliation. Then, when Allhoff's profanity beat against my ears until I could stand it no longer, I took a hand myself.

"Allhoff," I said, "for God's sake, lay off. You'll drive us all crazy including yourself."

He paused for a moment to take breath. Then he turned on me. I shrugged my shoulders and went back to my desk. At least I had diverted his thunderous sentences from Battersly to myself. I went back to the travel page of the evening paper. Some seven minutes later, Allhoff, out of breath and epithet, shut up. He sipped more coffee sullenly, sibilantly.

This, I reflected on the way home in the subway, had been going on for more years then I cared to remember. It had had its genesis half a decade ago, during a raid on an upper West End Avenue rooming-house. The stool-pigeon grapevine had reported that a trio of gangsters wanted in a dozen states were hiding out at a certain address in the nineties. Allhoff had been assigned to lead the raiding squad.

Battersly, a raw rookie in those days, had been ordered to affect a rear entrance, disable the operator of the Tommy gun which, we'd been informed, commanded the stairway facing the door. Battersly got in, all right. Then, at the zero hour he developed an understandable case of stage fright, with the net result that he fled up the stairway to the roof at the precise moment Allhoff came battering through the front door.

Allhoff charged into some twenty-odd lead slugs coming with high velocity from the barrel of the Tommy gun. Most of them lodged in his legs below the

knee. A week later, gangrene set in and an hour after that came the amputation.

Of course, a legless police inspector violated every item in the civil service book. But the commissioner was of no mind to lose his best man on any technicality. He arranged that Allhoff should live in this tenement slum because of its proximity to headquarters. He arranged further that the city, through devious bookkeeping devices paid Allhoff his old salary. And with perhaps too grim a sense of justice, he had granted Allhoff's demand that Battersly be assigned as an aide. I had been thrown in the deal to keep peace between them.

Mine was a futile task. When Allhoff's legs had gone, something of his mind had gone along with them. Not that he was stupid, but there were occasions when I considered him far closer to insanity than many inmates of public institutions. Hatred and bitterness rankled in his heart and almost all of it was directed at young Battersly. He never missed a chance to extract revenge.

Personally, I would rather have walked the beat on the farthest outpost of Staten Island than loaf at a desk here. But the commissioner insisted upon this assignment and I'd spent too many years building up my pension to throw it away now.

CHAPTER TWO

Money to Burn

I arrived at the tenement the following morning as Allhoff emerged from his bedroom, unwashed and drowsy-eyed. He didn't speak. He never did until he'd absorbed at least a quart of the strong brackish brew he fondly believed was coffee. He dragged himself up into his chair, handed the coffee pot silently to me and opened the bottom desk drawer.

I filled the pot with water and returned it. Allhoff opened the can he had taken from the drawer and cursed loudly. At that moment, Battersly came in shaved and primped, his brass buttons gleaming resplendently. He saluted and headed for his desk. Allhoff's thundering voice stopped him.

"I don't ask much of you," he roared. "I do the brain work here, Simmonds handles the papers and reports. All I require from you, when you've finished keeping up with the comic strips, is that coffee and sugar be kept in the joint. You can't even do that adequately."

He held out the empty coffee can accusingly as if it were a murder weapon.

Battersly bit his lip and frowned. "It was half full yesterday, sir. I swear it was. I looked. You *couldn't* have used it all. It—"

"It's empty now," snarled Allhoff. "Get me another can. And for God's sake, hurry."

He took a worn leather purse from his pocket and extracted a quarter. Battersly put the coin in his pocket and ran down the stairs. Allhoff stared gloomily at the wall and a series of low growls came out of his dry throat. A cocaineless hophead suffered less than Allhoff minus his quota of caffeine.

His fingers drummed angrily on the desk top as time went by and Battersly did not return. A good fifteen minutes elapsed and still Allhoff had no coffee. His fingers were beating a rapid tattoo now and he was muttering to himself. Silently, I cursed Battersly. He possessed a gift for getting Allhoff in black moods. I steeled myself for the explosion which would inevitably occur when Battersly returned.

A moment later the door opened. I heard Allhoff's intake of breath as he prepared to unload a verbal barrage on Battersly's tardy head. But as he looked up he held his wrath.

Battersly stood panting in the doorway. His cap was gone. As were two buttons from his uniform. His collar was ripped and his tie askew. One eye was developing slowly but with certainty into a shiner and blood dripped from his nose on to his chest. His hair was ruffled and there were a pair of nasty scratches on his cheek.

He took a brown paper parcel from under his arm and laid it on Allhoff's desk.

"The coffee, sir," he said.

"My God," said Allhoff, "and did you go through the German lines to get it?"

"I was ganged," said Battersly. "A mob of tough guys beat me up."

"Why?" I asked.

Battersly shrugged. "I don't know. I can't figure it. Just for the hell of it, I guess."

Allhoff was staring at the wrapped-up coffee can on his desk. There was a frown upon his brow. He looked up at Battersly and said: "Exactly what happened?"

Battersly dabbed at his red nose with a handkerchief. "Well," he said, "this mob of guys—there was five of them—was hanging out a couple of doors away from the grocery store. They never paid me any attention when I passed them the first time. Then I came out of the grocer's after buying the coffee—and that's the funny part of it."

"Uproarious," said Allhoff sarcastically. "What's funny about it?"

"Well, they got me when I came *out* of the grocery store. See? They let me go when I passed right by them. Then they get me afterwards."

"What happened then?"

"They began to slug me. Two of them held my hands so I couldn't go for my gun. The others slugged me. They knocked off my cap, knocked the coffee from under my arm and proceeded to beat the hell out of me, I was half out when they quit. They was a block away when I got up. One of them had my cap. I saw him wave it at me before they scrambled around the corner of Broome Street. Souvenir, I guess."

Allhoff grunted again. I was mildly surprised that he showed no elation. The idea of Battersly's getting smacked around certainly should have appealed to him. Battersly went into the bathroom to wash his face. Allhoff remained in his brown study until Battersly reappeared, then he suddenly banged his fist hard on the desk. He opened the drawer and put away the coffee. He looked around at me and said: "Simmonds, get me a glass of water."

I stared at him. "You mean you're not going to have coffee?"

"I haven't time. I'm working now."

I went to the sink and filled a glass. "Working on what?"

"These guys that beat up Battersly." He took the water, drank it and stared thoughtfully at the door.

I watched him and felt like a guy who has seen something drop up. Allhoff, foregoing his coffee, was a phenomenon happening not more than once in a lifetime.

"Battersly," said Allhoff. "Go across the street. Look through all the pictures in the gallery. Carefully."

"Yes, sir," said Battersly. "What am I looking for, Sir?" He waited, puzzled.

"The guys that beat you up, you idiot. Get over there, see if you can pick any of them out."

Battersly went out while I stared at Allhoff in amazement for the second time in five minutes.

"I'm rather surprised," I told him, "at your zeal in wanting to put Battersly's assailants behind the bars."

"Battersly," he said, and the contempt in his voice was eloquent. "I don't give a damn about Battersly's assailants. Why should I?"

"Then what are you worrying about it for? The whole thing's obvious enough."

He swung around in his swivel chair and glared at me. "Is it?" he snapped. "Then go ahead, explain it."

"There are plenty of hooligans in this town who think it's smart to beat up coppers. It happens once a week. You know that."

Allhoff sighed the sigh of a man whose patience is sorely strained. "So that's all you get out of it."

"What else?"

He vouchsafed no answer. He stared at the wall like a professor of mathematics who in a few moments will have figured out how to square a circle.

After two hours Battersly returned. He laid a small square photograph on Allhoff's desk.

"That was one of the guys, Inspector. It was the only one I could recognize."

Allhoff picked up the photograph and examined it. "Frankie Splayton," he said. "All-around punk. Picked up four times. Robbery, D. and D., narcotics. Convicted twice on the last charge. Simmonds, what've you got on him?"

I got up, went to the filing cabinet at the side of the room. After a moment's rummaging, I told him: "Not much beside what you already know. He's a satellite of Danny Raleigh's."

"Ah," said Allhoff. "Raleigh, eh?"

Battersly and I exchanged glances. I shrugged. What was going on in Allhoff's head was utterly beyond me. And this time, I suspected it was also beyond Allhoff.

Battersly and I went back to our desks, leaving Allhoff still staring blankly into space. The three of us remained that way until my telephone rang. I picked it up and listened.

"Allhoff," I said when I had hung up, "I have some news you'll be delighted to hear."

He came out of his trance and cocked an inquiring eyebrow.

"It seems your pal, Gebhart, hasn't broken the Murdock case at all."

Allhoff uttered an oath which I decided was aimed at Gebhart rather than at me.

"That was a message from the commissioner. He wants you to bear down on the case. It seems Gebhart got some information from a stoolie which seemed to crack it open but it turned out to be phoney. Which news, I assume, fills your ears with honey."

Perhaps it did, but from his attitude it wasn't noticeable. His frown had grown more corrugated, and his register of profound thought more marked.

"Raleigh," he said suddenly. "Danny Raleigh. Counterfeiting was one of his prime activities, wasn't it?"

I nodded, "That and forgery. With perhaps a killing thrown in here and there. Why?"

"Good God, I'm beginning to see it."

"See what?"

The telephone rang again before he could answer. I listened to the message and relayed it.

"Things are happening. There was another murder,

precisely like Murdock's— except they've got the guy who did it."

"The hell they have," said Allhoff. "What's the details?"

"Guy by the name of Weldon. Stockbroker. Took some eighteen thousand dollars home with him. Shot in his study. His wife heard the shot. Rushed into the room. Saw her husband dead, dough scattered all over the floor. Went to call the coppers. While they were on the way, a fire broke out in the study. They rescued the corpse but half the house burned down before the firemen got it under control."

"Interesting," said Allhoff. "But what's this about them getting the guy who did it?"

"There was a guy who'd lost all his dough in the market. Rightly or wrongly he blamed Weldon for his losses. Swore before witnesses, he'd kill him. Was picked up near the Weldon house right after the crime. They've got him over at headquarters now. Homicide says it's cold."

"That's indicative that it isn't," said Allhoff, who had his own opinion of Homicide. "Call 'em back. Tell 'em to send that guy over. I want to see him."

I transmitted the message. At least I'd sooner having him working on the Murdock case which made some sense, rather than on the weighty problem of who beat up Battersly, which didn't.

Fifteen minutes later a burly Irish cop dragged a pale, scared little man into the office. The copper saluted Allhoff and announced: "This is Smith, sir. The prisoner in the Weldon case."

Allhoff waved Smith to a chair. Smith sat down as if he expected to be electrocuted there and then. He was a thin little guy who looked undernourished. He had a pair of wild eyes and at the moment fear had been poured into them. His fingers moved nervously at his sides.

"I didn't do it," he said to Allhoff. "I don't care what they say, I didn't."

Allhoff regarded him appraisingly and nodded his head. "I wouldn't be at all surprised if you didn't. What's your version of it all?"

Smith shifted nervously in his chair and spoke in a high-pitched voice.

"Weldon robbed me. Sold me worthless stock in enterprises controlled by him. Sure, I said I'd kill him. He took every cent I had. But I didn't do it."

"What were you doing in the neighborhood of his house?" asked Allhoff.

"I went to ask him for money. I only wanted a stake. Enough to get started again. After all he took from me, I figured maybe he had heart enough to give me that much. I was going to see him. I got in the lobby of the house and they pinched me."

"How much did Weldon leave you?"

"Three hundred bucks," said Smith bitterly. "Three hundred bucks in the bank and less than ten in my pocket. I got a wife and two kids, too. I got—"

Allhoff waved him to silence. "All right," he said to the copper, "take him away."

"Wait a minute," yelled Smith, "Aren't you going to help me? I tell you I didn't do it. I tell you—"

"Stop telling me," said Allhoff, "I know damned well you didn't do it."

"Then why—"

"You've got to go back to the can, anyway," said Allhoff, "I'm not quite ready to spring you yet."

The Irish copper dragged him away, while Smith audibly voiced his opinion of the police department.

Allhoff drank coffee morosely for the rest of the day. Basking in his silence, Battersly and I made no attempt to engage him in conversation.

The following day was Thursday and the package came. It was an oblong parcel, perhaps five by eight inches. It was wrapped securely in brown wrapping paper and bore a vast number of colored stamps. And since Allhoff had never received any mail in all my memory, I accepted it with a surprised air, from the postman.

"Have you a birthday coming up?" I said as I laid it on his desk. "Looks like a present from a wealthy pal judging by all the stamps he's plastered over it."

Allhoff looked up from his coffee. He picked up the package and turned it over slowly in his hands. He grunted, then said: "Your powers of observation are improving, Simmonds. There's a buck's worth of stamps on this. Two bits would have carried it."

He studied the exterior of the package like a philatelist, making no attempt to open it.

"Well," I said, curiosity gnawing at me, "aren't you going to see what it is? Or are you afraid it's a bomb?"

He looked at me sharply. "A bomb," he said with a sudden inhalation. "A bomb, eh?"

I was surprised at his sudden serious air.

"I have no relatives," he went on. "As you are well aware I have no friends. I can think of no one who might send me anything at all through the mails."

"So," I said, "why not dump it in a bucket of water and then open it?"

His swift glance at me held contempt.

"It's lucky you're not on the bomb squad. Water's no damned good half the time. Oil is what you use." He turned his head in Battersly's direction. "Battersly. Here, take this across the street to Sergeant Averill on the Bomb Squad. Tell him to douse it in a pail of oil, then open it. Wait there until you get his report."

I blinked at him, Allhoff was no one's sucker and he wasn't a guy with any trend toward panic. Yet here he was taking my kidding suggestion as grimly as a scary old maid. Battersly got up took the parcel, with an odd inquiring glance at me and left the room. Allhoff returned broodingly to his coffee. I shook my head and clucked at him.

"And do you look under the bed for burglars at night before retiring?" I asked solicitously.

"Idiot," he snarled, "If a man tries once to kill you and fails, it's logical he'll try again."

I opened my eyes wide at that. "Who tried to kill you? When? How?"

For reply he sucked down coffee noisily. Then after the cup had clattered back into the saucer, he said slowly: "That Danny Raleigh. His last rap, as I remember it, was counterfeiting. But he beat it in a federal court. It was bad stuff he'd been passing. Easily spotted."

"Well," I said, "what about it? What's that got to do with some guy trying to kill you?"

But now he ignored me completely. He concentrated on his coffee and pretended I wasn't there. I sighed, after a while, and went back to my desk.

Battersly returned, taking the outside stairs two at a time. He burst, flushed and breathless into the office.

"My God," he said, "what do you think, Inspector?"

Allhoff and I looked at him. I remarked that Allhoff seemed calm and in no way curious about Battersly's excitement.

"It *was* a bomb," cried Battersly. "Set to go off when that package was opened. It really was, Inspector."

"Sure." said Allhoff with the air of a man who has just been told that two and two reach a total of four.

"Good Lord," I said, "who'd be sending you a bomb? We're not even working on a case, except that screwy Murdock thing and we certainly haven't made any progress there."

Allhoff yawned. "Listen," he said, "you think you can get me some heroin from Narcotics?"

"Some *what?*"

"Heroin. It's a mixture compounded of so many parts morphine, combined with—"

"I know what it is. I just wondered if I heard you properly. What do you want heroin for?"

"Just get me some and shut up," said Allhoff, "Five or six ounces should be plenty."

"Five or six ounces," I said as I moved toward the door. "My God, the whole damned town can get high on that."

As I crossed the street to headquarters I reflected upon a very peculiar circumstance. Allhoff had appeared vastly more interested in the fact of simple assault upon Battersly than he was in an attempt upon his own life. Pondering this I was one bewildered police sergeant when I brought him back his six ounces of heroin.

Casually he tossed the drug into a desk drawer. Then turning to Battersly and myself, he said: "Tomorrow morning I want a number of people here. I want them here early. Get 'em before they've had a chance to get their breakfast, if you can. Here's the list. First, Gebhart and that blonde of his, second, Gebhart's mother and a Mrs. Charles Latrobe of Neptune Avenue, Coney Island. That's Gebhart's married sister."

"My God," I said, "what *is* this? A communion breakfast for the Gebhart clan?"

"Third," he went on, ignoring me, "I want Frankie Splayton and Danny Raleigh. I don't care how you two guys split them up—you can get more coppers or a wagon if you want to—but Battersly'd better pick up Raleigh."

"Why?" I said.

"Because he's a tough guy, Sergeant," said Allhoff mocking. "And unless I'm very, very wrong, he's not going to want to come at all."

I scratched my head. "I don't see this," I told him. "What are you going to solve? The mystery of who beat up Battersly?"

He smiled without mirth. "Among other things. I shall also solve the mystery of who killed Murdock, who killed Weldon, who tried to kill me."

He reached for the coffee pot as Battersly and I stared at him in bewilderment.

"Is that all?" I asked with heavy irony.

"No," he said over the top of his cup. "Before you go home, roll a typewriter over here where I can get at it with a modicum of effort. Thank you."

I rolled the typewriter-stand across the room and my thoughts were no more lucid after his last order. Allhoff hadn't touched a typewriter for at least a year. On the way home in the subway I decided that he had either gone utterly mad or that he expected to pull some very odd rabbits from the hat on the morrow.

CHAPTER THREE

The Affable Allhoff

It was a little after eight thirty in the morning when Battersly and I herded our motley collection into Allhoff's tenement apartment. None of them, I think, had had their breakfast and indignation hovered over their heads like a cloud. Indeed, it had taken a telephone call to the commissioner himself before Gebhart had agreed to come along with me. Gebhart's mother a plump blonde of indeterminate years, was annoyed and his sister was loudly proclaiming the fact that she, as a citizen, knew her rights under the Constitution.

Gebhart's blonde glared sullenly at Allhoff as she came in the room. It was apparent that she had neither forgiven nor forgotten the humiliation he had forced upon her during her last visit.

Battersly's customers, it seemed, were no more delighted to greet Inspector Allhoff at this hour in the morning than were mine. Splayton looked exactly what he was. A small-time punk dressed in a green suit of extreme cut. His face was pasty, his eyes shifty. He cringed as he came into the room, glanced about furtively, obviously terrified that he had been dragged here in order that Battersly could extract brutal revenge for the beating he had undergone the other day.

Danny Raleigh was a crook of vastly different caliber. His clothes were conservative and tailor made. His bearing was jaunty, though tempered with shrewd alertness. He eyed Allhoff appraisingly, then cast a swift, veiled glance at Gebhart, Battersly stood with his back to the door like a jailer as the group herded itself into the little room.

The thing that staggered me was the arrangements Allhoff had made for his involuntary guests. Chairs were grouped about his desk in a semi-circle. More amazing, they had been freshly dusted. Laid out on the desk blotter stood six coffee cups, shining and white. Obviously they had been recently washed and with soap. Obviously, too, since Battersly and I had just arrived, they had been washed by Allhoff—a fact which sent several precedents crashing into pieces upon the floor.

Six teaspoons, bright and polished, lay by the sides of the cups. Even the coffee pot, I noted, had been burnished to brightness for the first time in its venerable career. Dazed, I went over to my desk. Inspector Allhoff, apparently was entertaining at breakfast, which was rather like a professional hermit suddenly becoming an Elk.

Allhoff had been reading a sheet of typewritten paper when we had come in. Now, he placed it face down on the desk and smiled with what I'm sure he thought was beneficence. Actually he looked like a panther in need of a dentist. When he spoke there was oil, honey

and glycerine in his tone.

"I am very sorry," he said, "to disturb you all at this hour. However we all have certain duties as citizens—duties which, I'm sure, you'll be only too happy to discharge."

Mrs. Gebhart alone seemed slightly mollified by these words. Splayton, the punk, still looked as if an invisible rubber hose was suspended above his head. Danny Raleigh watched Allhoff through half closed lids as a zoo keeper might watch a dangerous animal.

Gebhart's sister and the Whalen girl retained their air of outraged dignity, while Gebhart, red-faced and angry said: "Save the editorial, Allhoff. There may be some departmental reason for you dragging me down here this morning. But, forcing my family to come also, is sheer malice. You did it to annoy me because you hate my guts."

I was watching Allhoff closely and when he didn't get angry, I came to the conclusion that he was playing a very deep game indeed.

"Now, Gebhart," he said mildly, "this is very important. It's a murder case. You as a policeman know that solving such cases is the most important thing there is to us. A little inconvenience doesn't matter. Now," he waved his hands toward the chairs, "will everyone sit down, please?"

Everyone sat down with an air of not committing themselves.

"Now," said Allhoff, "you'll remember, Gebhart, there was a case a few days ago which you announced you'd solved."

I remarked that Danny Raleigh's eyes had steel in them then. Gebhart slapped his knee angrily.

"Damn you," he said. "Must you gloat this early in the morning? I made a mistake, that's all. My information was incorrect. You know quite well, I admitted my mistake. I didn't solve the Murdock case at all."

"You're much too modest, Inspector," said Allhoff, an odd lilt in his voice. "You *did* solve it."

Gebhart's womenfolk looked at Allhoff, then back at Gebhart. Splayton, the punk, still cringed in his chair, apparently paying no attention to the conversation. I kept my eyes on Raleigh. He was always a dangerous man and at that moment he looked more dangerous than usual.

Nevertheless my ears were all for Allhoff. In our several years association, I had heard him say some crazy things. This, however, was a new high in illogic. The idea of Gebhart actually solving the Murdock murder, a feat which would have given him a splendid opportunity to crow over Allhoff, and then denying it, was utterly incredible.

Gebhart's mother voiced my thought. "Are you crazy?" she asked, "Why would my boy deny such a praiseworthy thing as that?"

"Ah," said Allhoff ministerially, "who can fathom the motives of a human heart?"

Danny Raleigh stood up. "Look here," he said briskly. "I ain't been formally arrested. Unlike Gebhart, I ain't here on the commissioner's orders. I was brought here strong-arm and it ain't right. See? I ain't going to stay."

Allhoff lifted his eyes to the door where Battersly's bulky frame still stood.

"You were brought here strong-arm," he said, "and you'll stay here strong-arm. Sit down." For an instant his air of phoney affability had left him but he turned it on again a moment later. "Of course," he went on, "I realize we're all a little out of sorts since we haven't had our breakfasts. A nice cup of coffee will fix us all up."

Now he was talking like Uncle Don and the effect was like Boris Karloff telling a bedtime story. He opened the bottom drawer of his desk. He withdrew a brown paper-wrapped parcel, tied with white string. He opened it and placed the coffee can it contained upon his desk.

"Lucky," he said, "I have enough coffee for you all. I saved this can the other day. Always like to have some in reserve in case of guests."

That, of course, was an outrageous lie. He never had any coffee in reserve. He never had any guests, either, for that matter.

He ladled coffee into the percolator with a lavish hand, never considering that his guests' taste might incline to a weaker brew than his own. He turned the electric plate on full, then turned, beaming, back to his audience. I followed his gaze in time to intercept a swift glance between Raleigh and Inspector Gebhart. Allhoff's roving eye fell upon young Splayton.

"Well. well," he said with heavy affability. "that's a nice suit you're wearing, son. Where'd you get it?"

I braced myself and wondered if my ears were playing tricks on me. Allhoff's sartorial interests were those of a nudist. Moreover, he was not in the habit of engaging guys like Splayton in polite conversation. Splayton shifted uneasily in his chair and regarded Allhoff with suspicion.

"Yes, *sir*," said Allhoff, like an insurance salesman. "It certainly looks good on you. I don't know whether I admire the cut or the fabric more. Come over here, let me feel the material."

Splayton stood up and approached Allhoff like a child who, when promised candy, expects to be struck. Allhoff swung his chair around facing him. He stretched forth his fingers and examined the cloth of Splayton's suit. He nodded his head in approval.

Gebhart's sister watched him for a moment, then blew up.

"This is a ridiculous outrage," she snapped. "Personally, Inspector, I think you're insane. You bring us here before breakfast, then force us to listen while you admire a badly-made, cheap suit. Now, tell us what you want us for immediately, or I shall leave. Coppers or no coppers."

Allhoff looked at her with a jaundiced eye. Yet his voice retained its blandness as he spoke.

"Very well," he said, feeling the side of the coffee pot to see how it was heating. "I apologize for wasting your time. I shall proceed to the point at once. It begins almost a year ago in a federal court."

He paused and drew a deep breath. I observed Raleigh and Gebhart staring at the opened coffee can on Allhoff's desk. I regarded it questioningly myself. Never since I had known him had I seen him save a can of coffee. This one certainly hadn't been bought this morning.

"Yes," went on Allhoff, "Raleigh, here, was in a little trouble with the federal boys. They claimed he'd bought a lot of counterfeit dough from someone. They claimed further that he and his henchmen were passing it at a great rate. Moreover, it wasn't very good money. It was so badly printed that even a Brooklyn delicatessen clerk would have little trouble in realizing its phoniness."

"If you're anything at all," said Raleigh, "you're a city cop. I don't see how a federal rap interests you. Besides, just for the record, I beat that rap. The jury acquitted me."

"Indeed they did," said Allhoff almost cheerfully. "They also left you with a vast number of counterfeit dollars on your hands—dollars for which you'd paid good hard cash, perhaps twenty per cent of their full face amount. That left you with the problem of cutting your losses. The stuff was so bad you didn't dare try to pass any more of it. It was too dangerous. Then you thought of an angle."

The percolator gurgled as the first spurt of coffee hit against its top. Gebhart started in his chair.

"It wasn't a direct angle," continued Allhoff. "But it was something. Instead of that counterfeit dough being a total loss you managed to devise a scheme to use it. After your flyer in the queer you went back to your usual operations of larceny and murder. Adding a crime which the records imply was novel for you."

Raleigh looked from Allhoff to the coffee pot and back again.

"What crime?"

"Arson. That, too, like your use of the phoney money was an indirect crime, though. It—"

"Inspector Allhoff," said Mrs. Gebhart, "I am an old woman. Yet no one has ever accused me of senility.

But I don't understand what you're talking about."

"Right," said Gebhart standing up.

"I've heard enough of this, Allhoff. You're a crazy old man. We're staying here no longer. Come along, all of you."

Gebhart's womenfolk stood up, relief showing on their faces. Allhoff's gaze traveled to Battersly, at the door.

"Battersly," said Allhoff, "you will draw your gun."

Battersly did so with all the enthusiasm of the Italian Army charging.

"You will permit no one to leave the room. That's an order. Gebhart, sit down."

Gebhart glared at Allhoff. His women watched him uncertainly. Then slowly he sat down. The distaff side of the family followed suit.

"I was speaking to you, Raleigh, of the Murdock and Weldon killings," Allhoff resumed conversationally. "I was about to explain the tie-tip between them, arson and counterfeit money."

The percolator was bubbling merrily now. Allhoff glanced at it once, then transferred his caustic gaze to Raleigh again.

"As I said," he went on, "you, Raleigh, returned to simple murder for a living. Somehow, through your spy system, your stool-pigeons, you found out when certain citizens were about to take large sums of cash home with them for one reason or another. Whereupon you cased the house, entered, murdered them and stole the money."

There was a moment's silence. Then Raleigh said: "It's too pat, Inspector. You may as well accuse me of being a fifth columnist. You can do it as glibly and with just as much reason."

"Now," said Allhoff, ignoring the comment, "you murder Murdock and Weldon, you steal their money. You also remove all suspicion from yourself by a judicious use of arson and your counterfeit bills."

For the first time since he had begun to talk a slow light dawned in my brain.

"You mean," I asked, "that Raleigh planted his phoney money, permitted someone to see it, then returned to the house and set it on fire? In that way he would destroy the counterfeit money so that no one would suspect it wasn't genuine. And he would also make the murder look as if it had a personal motivation."

"Precisely," said Allhoff. "Naturally when the police learned that the actual cash was not stolen they would never go looking for a professional crook such as Raleigh. On the contrary, they'd search for someone with personal motivation. As for instance that poor guy they've got in the can now for the Weldon murder. What's his name? Smith."

I thought it over for a moment and decided it sounded logical.

"Of course," said Allhoff, "Raleigh intended to commit these murders anyway. The phoney money, the arson was incidental. However, since he had the queer on hand, it was a good time to use it. In theory it was supposed to keep suspicion away from him. Actually, it pinned the whole thing right on his dapper shirt front."

"How?" said Raleigh in an expressionless tone.

"Because," said Allhoff, "it was the burnt money that set my brain cells to functioning. The second fire, under precisely the same circumstances as the first seemed something more than coincidental. If the fires were deliberate it seemed odd to me that any man would burn good money. The next thought was whether or not it *was* good money. There it lay in my mind until Splayton here attacked Battersly. Splayton was known as your man, Raleigh. You, in turn, were known to have a load of counterfeits on hand. With that tie-up, I figured it out."

Now Allhoff was going too fast for me again. True, what he had said sounded plausible. Yet, apparently he had no proof at all. Further, there was a bomb to be explained and why Battersly had been attacked at all. Danny Raleigh drew a deep breath.

"All right, Inspector," he said. "Since you know all this, since you have me dead to rights, since your evidence is—"

Gebhart swung around in his chair. His face was gray.

"Raleigh," he said, "shut up. He knows nothing. He's guessing. He can't prove anything."

Raleigh met his eyes for a long uncomfortable moment. Gebhart flushed. Raleigh said: "I thought he could prove everything. I thought he knew from—"

"He knows nothing," said Gebhart, "Nothing. Keep your mouth shut and you're clean."

"I thought—" said Raleigh again, and there was flaming rage in his eyes.

"We all make mistakes," said Allhoff and there was a suspicious oiliness in his voice.

He picked the percolator off its base and proceeded to fill all the cups in front of him.

"What we all need is a good hot cup of coffee," he said amiably. "You'll excuse me. I've already had mine."

Young Splayton stared at Allhoff, wide eyed. Gebhart bit his lip and Danny Raleigh looked around the room as if hoping reinforcements would come through the walls. No one made a move to reach for his coffee.

"Come, come," said Allhoff. "Coffee. Miss Whalen?"

The Whalen girl who hadn't spoken since she had come into the room, shook her head dully. Gebhart's sister said icily:

"I pick my company." Gebhart's mother shrugged her ample shoulders.

"Thank you, Inspector," she said. Since I've had no breakfast, I'll take it."

CHAPTER FOUR

Good to the Last Drop

Allhoff handed her the thick cup with ceremony. Danny Raleigh lit a cigarette and I remarked the shaking of his fingers. Splayton had not taken his gaze from Allhoff and was regarding Mrs. Gebhart with a glazed and horrified stare.

Mrs. Gebhart lifted the cup to her lips and I heard Splayton inhale sharply. Then Gebhart was on his feet. His right hand lashed out and slapped hard against the thick cup. Coffee spattered his mother's dress and the wall. The cup rolled to the floor.

Mrs. Gebhart stared at her son in inarticulate astonishment. Gebhart breathed hard like a man who has just run a hundred yards. Splayton slumped down in his chair. Allhoff bowed satanically.

"Thank you, Gebhart," he said mockingly. "That tells me all that I wanted to know."

Gebhart stood glaring at him. It dawned on me that I seemed to know less about what was going on than anyone else, in the room. I said so, loudly. I added: "*What* was all you wanted to know, Allhoff?"

"Who was trying to kill me. Who sent me a bomb and a pound of poisoned coffee?"

"Well, who did?"

Allhoff grinned. Now all the simulated affability had gone from his face. There was sand, not oil, in his voice as he answered me.

"Pause, Sergeant," he said. "Pause and reflect. Battersly goes out for a tin of coffee. On the way *into* the store he passes a mob of hoodlums, captained by young Splayton here. They do not molest him. On the way *out* he gets jumped on and slugged."

"All of which indicates you're about to be poisoned," I said ironically.

"Exactly," said Allhoff. "When Battersly returns here, bruised and bearing the wrapped coffee can, I observe, as you should have, that it is wrapped with white string. As far back as I can remember, that corner store has been using black string to wrap parcels with. A small thing, perhaps. But coupled with the odd circumstance of Battersly's beating, worth investigating."

"So you investigated," I said. "With what result?"

"The laboratory informed me that the coffee had been removed from the can, soaked in a cyanide solution and replaced. The attack on Battersly was to create a diversion, knock the package out of his hand and plant the other one, the poisoned one, in the street."

"Who would want to poison you?" I asked. "And why?"

"I asked myself that three days ago," said Allhoff. "Splayton might want to poison me, but he doesn't possess the nerve. Splayton ties up with Raleigh. Raleigh, who kills for money, wouldn't be murdering me free of charge, merely for the practice, would you, Danny?"

Raleigh didn't answer. He was staring at Gebhart and the expression on his face wasn't pretty.

"Gebhart," I said suddenly. "Gebhart wanted to kill you. You mean he hired Danny? You mean he—"

"No," said Allhoff. "He didn't hire Danny. I doubt that Danny would have tried it for money. He frightened Danny into it."

Raleigh wasn't the sort of guy who frightened easily and I said so.

"He's afraid of the chair," said Allhoff. "Did you ever see one of them who wasn't?"

I sighed. "Can you tell it in monosyllables?"

"Sure," said Allhoff. "You remember Gebhart came in here with his woman to sneer at me because he'd solved the Murdock case? You'll also remember that a day later it developed he'd made a mistake. To quote him his information was faulty."

"So?"

"He lied the second time. Not the first. Somehow, probably through his far flung stool-pigeon system, he learned the truth of the Murdock killing. For all I know, he had evidence to prove it, too. But after the humiliating half-hour he spent up here, he decided my death was vastly more important to him than a murder solution."

"So," I said," he told Raleigh what he had, promised to forget it if Raleigh got you."

Allhoff sighed heavily. "Simmonds," he said, "you'd make as bad a crook as you are a copper. Gebhart wouldn't tell Raleigh that. If Raleigh thought Gebhart was the sole man who knew of his guilt, Raleigh'd kill Gebhart, not me. No, Gebhart told Raleigh that I had broken the case, that I was waiting a few hours to clinch it. So Raleigh planned to kill me.

He may have planned to kill Gebhart later. I don't know. When Raleigh's coffee didn't work, he descended to the crudity of mailing a bomb."

Raleigh was standing up now. His face was turned in Gebhart's direction.

"You louse," he said. "Why don't you do your own killing? Why don't you—"

"Wait a minute," said Gebhart, grayfaced. "Wait, Danny. Don't you see it's all conjecture? He hasn't got a square inch of evidence. He can't prove a thing. If we stick together, we'll beat it. There's not one single item he can present to a Grand Jury."

There was a hollow silence in the room, broken only by the sound of Mrs. Gebhart's weeping. His sister sat staring stonily ahead, while the blond Whalen girl linked her arm through Gebhart's. Raleigh, eyelids narrowed, tapped his fingers thoughtfully on the back of his chair.

"I'll get you for this, Gebhart," he said. "I'll get you sooner or later. In the meantime, though, we'll stick together. You're right, he hasn't any evidence at all."

Allhoff grinned like a storm trooper in the Dachau camp.

"Don't bet on it," he said. "You women may go. Battersly, take Raleigh and Gebhart across the street. Book them for murder, attempted murder and anything else the desk sergeant may suggest."

"Wait a minute," said Gebhart, "you can't do this. You've no proof. We'll be sprung in an hour."

"I'll have the proof in less than that," said Allhoff. "Battersly, take 'em away."

Raleigh shrugged. "All right," he said. "Why stand there and argue? Since he has nothing, my lawyer'll have us out before lunch. We'll go quietly."

The women filed from the room. Battersly, escorting Gebhart and Raleigh, followed. Young Splayton stood up, relief on his face, and headed for the door.

"You!" said Allhoff. "Sit down."

Splayton turned around anxiously.

"You ain't finished with me yet?"

"Hell," said Allhoff. "I haven't started with *you*. Do you think I'm going to let you smack my assistant around and get away with it? Come here."

Splayton approached Allhoff's desk like a sparrow charging a rattlesnake, Allhoff turned over the typewritten sheet of paper before him.

"Now," he said, "this is a written draft of all the things I have just said. It explains everything. The Murdock and Weldon killings, the poisoned coffee, the bomb, and Gebhart's hand in this matter. Since you are as well informed of these things as I am, I must ask you to sign it."

Splayton blinked.

"You mean a confession? You mean you want me to turn rat on the boss?"

"I am uninterested in your verminous tendencies," said Allhoff. "I want you to sign this paper. It'll make you a state's witness and you won't take the rap you quite well deserve."

Splayton shook his head doggedly. "No, sir," he said emphatically. "I ain't no rat and I ain't no dope. Why, the boss just said you ain't got no proof. If I don't sign that you can't do nothing to me."

"No?" said Allhoff and he conveyed an awful lot of threat in the single word.

Splayton shuddered. "Go ahead," he said. "Beat me up. I still won't sign it. I ain't as yellow as you think. I been beat up before and I ain't talked. I can stand a beating for five, six hours, I can."

"Yes," said Allhoff slowly. "And can you take a beating for fifty years?"

"Fifty years? You can't hold me more than forty-eight hours. I know the law."

"Do you?" said Allhoff. "Do you know, then, what happens to a guy who's already carrying two convictions on a dope rap? Do you know what happens to him the third time? He never gets out, except in a hearse."

Splayton shook his head violently. "I'm clean on that, I'm taking no chances. I ain't touched any stuff since my second conviction."

Allhoff shrugged and turned to me. He said: "Arrest him, Simmonds."

I took a step forward. "For what?"

"Possession of narcotics."

"I tell you I ain't got any dope," yelled Splayton. "I ain't handled dope since—"

"Search him, Simmonds."

Something was beginning to filter into my brain. I put my hand in Splayton's right-hand coat pocket first—I found what I expected to find, I held it out to Allhoff.

"An interesting little package," he said. "What do you think's in it, Splayton?"

Splayton stared at him. His face was ashen. He knew damned well what was in the paper package.

"It's a frame," he cried. "You planted that on me when you was feeling the material of my suit. They'll send me away for life."

Allhoff picked up a fountain pen. "Not if you sign this," he said. "We'll forget what we found in your pocket."

Splayton's indecision lasted less than twenty seconds. He grabbed the pen as if it were a life preserver. He scrawled his name across the bottom of the paper.

"Can I go now?" he pleaded.

Allhoff shook his head, "You're much too valuable," he purred. "You go to the can as a material witness. And don't change your mind in the Grand Jury room. I'll just keep this junk, in case."

Battersly came back into the room as I asked Allhoff a final question.

"Why the women?" I said. "Why was, it necessary to bring Gebhart's mother, sister and mistress down here. Just to see him squirm a little more?"

Allhoff smiled happily. "In part. The most important thing was that I had to have someone Gebhart really cared for, consent to have a cup of coffee. It's quite possible that they might have refused. The more people I had here, the more chance that someone would try to drink the poison. When Gebhart knocked the cup from his mother's hand, I knew that once again I was right."

His smugness, as usual, was annoying, but there was nothing to do about it,

"Take this mug over to the D. A.," he said to Battersly. "On the way back, get me a can of coffee."

Battersly said, "Yes, sir," and stood expectantly at the side of the desk.

"Well," snarled Allhoff, "what the devil are you waiting for? A written memo?"

"No, sir. You usually give me the money first. Of course, I don't mind laying it out, though. I—"

Allhoff's fist hit the desk like Thor's hammer.

"*You* don't mind laying it out! By God, you'll pay for it yourself. Look what you brought me last time. Poison! You expect me to pay for my own poison. Get out of here and use your own money. This is the second time you've tried to murder me! You lousy yellow, low—"

Battersly scurried from the room, dragging Splayton with him. A torrent of adjectives flowed down the stairway behind him. I went back, to my desk and stared grimly out the window.

Some day, I thought, someone *will* kill him. I wondered quite seriously if it would be I.

THE CORPSE THAT WASN'T THERE

Originally Published - October 1941

CHAPTER ONE

A Corpse in My Lap

I left the house a little after eight o'clock that morning. I walked toward the subway with the taste of buttered toast and my wife's farewell kiss upon my lips. Despite the bracing autumn air there was no spring in my stride. Mentally I was grappling with what was a perennial problem, almost an obsession, with me. For possibly the thousandth time in my police career, I was frowningly engaged in figuring the angles on a transfer.

For five years I had worked with Inspector Allhoff. And in those five years I had aged ten. Fifty times I had applied for a transfer. Fifty times the commissioner had said loudly, "No!" Now, I pondered the problem again with the desperate defeatism of a convict working on an escape from Alcatraz.

As I approached the marquee of the Lafayette Hotel, I had reached the melancholy conclusion that I was licked. My only avenues of escape from Allhoff were his sudden and heartwarming demise, my own arrival at retirement age, or direct aid from heaven. Then as I passed the hotel doors heaven took a hand in the person of Ralph Bardon.

Bardon rushed suddenly out into the street. His hair was disheveled and his eyes were wide. He looked like a man who was about to begin beating his breast in public.

"There's never a copper around," he said to the ornately uniformed doorman, "when you want one. I—"

Then he swung his head around and saw me. "Simmonds," he said. "Thank God!"

I regarded him oddly. I'd known him for several years. He was part owner and manager of the hotel. He was an Elk and a solid citizen given neither to hangovers nor hysterics. But at the moment he looked very much like a man who has just seen a corpse. It developed a moment later that he had.

"Sergeant," he said to me. "Murder! And in my hotel. Not in thirty years—"

I knew that speech. I'd been hearing it from hotel men and rooming house keepers for years. I held up my hand to stop him and said: "Why don't you call Homicide? They—"

"I've called them. What am I supposed to do in the meantime? The crossword puzzle in the *Mirror?* I tell you, Sergeant, in all my thirty years, I never—"

"All right," I said wearily. "All right. Where's your corpse? I'll take a look at it."

He seized my arm and galloped me into the hotel. I accompanied him up to the twelfth floor. Bardon opened a door dramatically, flung out his hand, and said: "There! And, Sergeant, in all—"

"I know," I said. "In all your thirty years in the hotel business. Now you go down to the bar and have a drink. I'll take over here until Homicide arrives."

He left me with no reluctance whatever. I walked across the room to the bed and took a professional look at the corpse. From the point of view of a maniacal killer it was all very interesting. The face looked as if the Gestapo had handled the job on direct orders from Berchtesgaden. The skull had been smashed in as if a moderately sized building had fallen on it. The nose was neatly flattened up against the cheeks. The hair was matted with blood and the sheet on which the body lay resembled a cardinal's robe that had been dipped in cochineal.

It was a nasty mess. I sat down, my back to the corpse, and lit a cigarette. I reflected that in all my years

as a copper this was the first time a dead man had just fallen in my lap. I had often wondered about these fictional detectives and journalists who were constantly being hit on the head by corpses falling from the fourth story windows; who, through some apparently accidental inevitability, walked into murder and intrigue as an Irishman walks into a Saturday night brawl.

Well, at last it had happened to me. *Not* that I had any intention of performing some miracle of detecting— not that I intended to put my hand on the case at all. I would sit here quietly until Homicide arrived, then go downtown where Allhoff would continue his life work of driving Battersly and myself quietly crazy. I smoked my cigarette slowly and pondered the wide chasm existing between the detectives of fiction and myself.

Then I saw the fountain pen top. It was colored a rich green. It bore a gleaming gold clip on its side and it lay beneath the writing desk. I stood up. I maneuvered my way across the room with my back still to the corpse. I picked up the pen top and examined it. I glanced down at the desk. Scrawled upon a piece of the hotel writing paper was a telephone number in the Wickersham exchange. I folded the paper and put it in my pocket.

My heart was beating rapidly now. An idea, daring and radical, was gestating in my mind. A murder had been committed in this room. The commissioner, in common with most of his predecessors, didn't like murder. He was very partial to the men who solved them.

I thought for a moment of Muller. Muller, a detective-sergeant, had cleaned up a Brooklyn killing single-handed only a week ago. Muller had then drawn a month's vacation with pay, a citation, and a promotion. Now, here I stood, first man on the scene of a killing, with two clues in my hand. Suppose I held the fountain pen top, the scribbled telephone number out on Homicide? Suppose I turned up the murderer myself, alone and unaided? That certainly should be worth a transfer in any commissioner's book.

My right hand closed tightly over the pen top as the door was flung suddenly open and Lieutenant Marsden walked into the room. He looked at me in surprise not unmixed with disgust.

"Don't tell me Allhoff's on this damned case already?"

I reassured him. I told him as my pulse quickened that the case was all Homicide's. I bade him good-bye and hastened out of the room. I went downstairs and conducted the first wholly private investigation of my departmental career.

The desk informed me that the dead man was one George Green, registered from a small town in North Carolina. The switchboard told me that he had made one phone call the night before, that the number did not answer. A bellboy mentioned the fact that Green had tossed him a dollar for carrying the bags upstairs. All this was routine enough until I interviewed Room Service.

The graying clerk who handled the telephone there scratched his head.

"Green?" he said. "It's 1201, isn't it? Yeah. A bit of a nut. Eccentric, I guess. Called up late last night. Ordered two soft boiled eggs. Said they must be six minutes. Then he phoned down and squawked like hell because the eggs were hard. Who the devil ever heard of six-minute eggs, soft boiled?"

I sighed deeply, lit my pipe and went away. Perhaps, Sherlock Holmes could have gone right to work on the material I had. Frankly, none of it made any sense to me. However, I wasn't discouraged. I had a phone number to work on and I was looking for a man who'd lost the top to his fountain pen. If I found him, fine. I'd win my transfer. If I didn't, it was Homicide's rap. I was in the enviable position of a man who has something to gain and not a red cent to lose. I eschewed the subway and took a taxicab downtown.

It was twenty minutes to ten when the stairs leading to Allhoff's tenement apartment creaked beneath my foot. A moment later I entered Allhoff's combination office and living room. As always the first impression I received, crossing the threshold, was one of superlative disorder. The floor was unswept. The wastepaper baskets were overflowing. The sink was a gray mausoleum brimming with dirty dishes.

Allhoff's laundry lay piled against the west wall, climbing dispiritedly day by day. The garbage can, beneath the sink, was again yielding up free lunch to myriad cockroaches. The bedroom door was ajar, revealing an unmade bed, twisted sheets and a blanket trailing on the floor. There was an air of mustiness in the room which filled my nostrils. I sighed heavily and sat down at my desk.

Allhoff regarded me with baleful little eyes over the rim of a chipped coffee cup. On his desk the electric percolator gurgled spasmodically. Allhoff slammed the cup down in its greasy saucer. I felt his gaze on me but did not look up.

Across the room from me, young Battersly leaned against the wall and read the comic papers with the desperate boredom of a man who has absolutely nothing else to do. I shuffled papers on my desk and tensed myself for the sound of Allhoff's harsh voice against my eardrums. It came like the sound of a machine gun with laryngitis.

"I will not be put upon," he said. "I shall not have my authority flouted."

I looked at him. To someone who didn't have to spend eight hours of each day in his presence, the idea was funny. He was never put upon. He was never flouted. He was feared more than the mayor himself. He was an arrogant combination of Napoleon, Heinrich Himmler, and Donald Duck. I relit my pipe and said: "Who's flouted you?"

Allhoff picked up the coffee cup, drained it and set it down again.

"You," he snapped. "You're forty minutes late. You'd never dare pull that sort of stuff in any other department. You take advantage of me because I'm easy."

Easy? Allhoff was as easy as a problem in calculus to a Kallikak with a nervous breakdown. I took the pipe from my mouth and said as much.

"Damn you," said Allhoff. "You're insubordinate as well. You're thoroughly incompetent. So, for that matter, is Battersly. I don't know why I'm stuck with such a lousy pair of assistants. How would you like it if I sent you over to rot in Staten Island? Two hours travel a day. Decaying out there in the sticks. How would you like that?"

I met his eye squarely. "I'd love it," I said. "When do I go?"

Battersly looked up from his paper, a gleam of hope in his eyes. There was none in mine. I knew rhetoric when I heard it. Allhoff was certainly going to give me no transfer—and as for Battersly, he would work in this room until the day when either he or Allhoff died.

Allhoff opened his mouth to speak again, then closed it as we heard footfalls on the creaking stairs without. A moment later, there was a staccato rap on the door. In response to my shouted invitation, two men entered.

The first of them was stocky, well dressed, and over-groomed. He strode rather than walked and he exuded an air of authority. He stood before Allhoff's desk, regarding the gnome-like figure sitting huddled over in his chair, his chest pressed against the edge of the desk. He said, crisply: "My name's Winters. I have a note here from the commissioner. This gentleman is Robert Dawson."

Dawson who was well over six feet tall, bowed and smiled sadly. Allhoff uttered no word of greeting. He ripped open the envelope Winters had handed him, scowled and read it. He threw the note in the general direction of the wastepaper basket, looked up, and said antagonistically: "So the commissioner wants me to do a little job for his friends, eh? All right, where did you lose the dog?"

Winters blinked at him. "Dog?" he said. "What dog?"

Allhoff registered phoney surprise. "No dog?" he said. "Amazing. Don't tell me the case is more important than that. When the commissioner unloads his friends on me, I suspect political motives. The last time was a ward leader who'd lost his wallet. Having some influence, he insisted on having the best man in the department on the job."

He drank a deep draft of coffee, and added with pleasurable reminiscence: "I had him thrown out of the office."

Winters' well-manicured finger tapped Allhoff's desk irritably. "See here, Inspector," he said. "I'm a well-known man in this town. I'm here on a rather important case. I expect at least courtesy."

Allhoff waved a grimy hand in my direction. "He wants courtesy, Simmonds. Give him some. If ever, he wants some intelligence also, turn him back to me."

He buried his nose in his coffee cup and sipped noisily. Winter's face turned the color of the purple hibiscus at dawn. He opened his mouth wide and took a deep breath. I prepared to enjoy the invective he was about to hurl in Allhoff's face. Then Dawson, whose melancholy smile persisted, came into the conversation.

"Inspector," he said like a Balkan diplomat addressing Hitler, "I can well understand the impatience of a man of your talents with some of the picayune matters given you. This, however, is a rather important affair. Mr. Winters here, called his friend the commissioner only to be certain that the best brains in the entire department would be available to us."

Allhoff put down his coffee cup and grinned like a ninety-year-old ingenue who is the recipient of a pass from a football player. He bowed like an actor. He indicated two rather crummy chairs.

"Gentlemen, he said. "Sit down."

I regarded him with disgust. There were times when it seemed to me that all you had to do was tell him that he was intelligent and he'd write you a check.

Dawson and Winters sat down. The latter still appeared annoyed. Dawson, his face still wreathed in ineffable sadness, did the talking.

"I'm afraid, Inspector, we are confronted with the case of a missing man and quite possibly a murder."

"Missing Persons and Homicide." said Allhoff pleasantly. "The two most incompetent bureaus in the department. I shall be happy to show them up again. Now what's it all about?"

"The missing man," said Dawson. "is named Edwards. He is an old prospector. He was due in from Cripple Creek early yesterday morning. I was to meet him. When he failed to arrive, I got in touch with Cripple Creek. He left all right. He boarded the train. Yet he never arrived."

Allhoff took it very calmly. "Probably picked up a flat in Chicago." he said. "What about the murder?"

"A cousin of mine," said Dawson. "Killed last night in a Bronx hotel. He came up from North Carolina yesterday. I just identified the body."

I took the pipe from my mouth and blinked. My pulse picked up a beat. I said: "Bronx hotel? North Carolina? What was his name?"

"Green," said Dawson. "George Green."

Allhoff twisted his neck around and glared at me. He said through contorted lips. "Go ahead."

"Go ahead what?"

"Go ahead and tell us who killed him. Sergeant Simmonds, the great detective. Asks one single question and knows all the answers. If you're taking the case over, go right ahead. If not, shut up."

I realized I should have kept my mouth shut. I was on dangerous enough ground already, withholding evidence. Fortunately, there was a blow torch burning in Allhoff's soul at my temerity in daring to ask a question when he was handling a case. Otherwise, he would have been certain to ask my interest in the matter, to ask what the devil I cared about the corpse's name. I put my pipe back in my mouth and shut up.

Allhoff transferred his gaze from me to Dawson. "What," he asked, "is the connection, if any, between your dead cousin and this guy Edwards?"

Winters spoke impatiently as if he felt too much time was being wasted.

"Four of us were interested in a gold mine Edwards had found. Dawson here, Green, his cousin, Edwards and myself. There is no claim filed on the mine yet. Edwards is, to put it politely, not quite all there. He's a paranoiac. Delusions of persecution. Believes everyone is trying to steal his mine. He was to arrive yesterday, give us the location of the mine and collect the money for our interest. He didn't show up. In the meantime, Dawson's cousin Green, who just came in from the south to get in on the deal is killed last night in his hotel. We want you to find Edwards and Green's murderer. That's all."

"That's all!" said Allhoff. "Are you sure you don't want me to find out what became of Lord Kitchener and clean up the Elwell case for you as well?"

Winters made a gesture of annoyance and futility. "I know it's puzzling," he said. "and difficult. That's why we asked the commissioner for his top man. If there is anything either of us can do to help you, don't hesitate to call on us. During office hours you can get me at the Drovers' Bank. My home address is—"

He reached toward his vest pocket. Then he said abruptly: "I forgot. My fountain pen is broken. May I borrow a pencil?"

Allhoff handed him a pencil and my heart stood still. I had a fountain pen top in my pocket. I was looking for the murderer of a man named Green. Before me was a banker who had had business dealings with Green and he was not carrying his fountain pen!

Allhoff took the paper with Winters' address. I half stood up and craned my neck reading it over his shoulder. It was on Madison Avenue in the fifties. I recalled the exchange of the telephone number I had taken from the Lafayette Hotel was Wickersham. That fitted, too.

Allhoff said: "All right, I'll think about this. I'll get the complete report from Homicide on Green's death. Undoubtedly, I'll want information from both of you. I'll get in touch with you. Dawson, leave me your address."

Dawson handed him a card. I fought to keep my mouth shut. I didn't want to arouse Allhoff's wrath again. Nor did I want to make him suspicious of what I was doing. But I had to ask one question. No effort of will could keep my vocal chords still.

"Mr. Winters," I said, "where did you spend last night?"

Winters raised his eyebrows and Allhoff gave me his prime, Grade A nasty look.

"Home," said Winters. "With my wife. *Why?*"

"Oh, nothing," I said. Then to slant off Allhoff, I turned to Battersly. "Battersly, will you hand me those reports from the Alien Squad?"

Battersly obeyed blankly. Allhoff's eyes grew harder. He looked as if he were about to say something. But Winters spoke first.

"Battersly?" he said. "Is your name Battersly?"

Battersly admitted his identity.

"John Battersly?" persisted Winters, Battersly nodded. Winters smiled cordially for the first time since he had been in the office.

"Congratulations on your game Sunday. I enjoyed it, I'm a great fan, you know. You kicked three goals, didn't you?"

There was a sudden silence in the room broken only by the swift sibilant intake of Battersly's breath. I looked over at Allhoff. His little eyes were glowing like two coals imported on a fast plane from hell. He licked his lips slowly with a pointed tongue. He said, and his vocal chords were oiled with venom: "He kicked three *what?*"

"Goals," said Winters. "In soccer. He's the best forward in the east. Aren't you, Battersly?"

Battersly didn't answer. His face was a sickly gray and his eyes were empty. I stood up, alarmed. Allhoff opened his mouth revealing all his stained teeth. Somehow he reminded me of a crocodile about to pounce on a rabbit.

"A forward," he said and his voice rose maniacally crescendo. "He kicked three goals, eh? And what, my fine athletic friend, did you kick them with?"

Battersly moistened his dry lips. Winters exchanged a bewildered look with Dawson whose melancholy had turned to puzzlement.

"What did he kick them with?" repeated Winters. "His legs. His feet, of course. Soccer, understand? You know soccer, Inspector."

Allhoff put his right hand on the edge of his deck. He pushed with all his strength. His chair flew across the floor on its rollers. The movement revealed for the first time to Winters and Dawson the macabre fact that Allhoff's body ended where his torso did. At the juncture where his thighs should have begun, there was nothing.

Two black leather stumps protruded over the edge of his chair. At the moment they wriggled horribly, dancing a rigadoon in the empty air. His fists, clenched and taut, pounded madly on the arms of the chair. His mouth was open and his larynx rattled like hail on a drumskin.

"He kicked three goals!" he roared. "With his legs and his feet. With those legs and feet? Whose? Damn you! Tell the pretty gentleman whose feet you actually used! You cowardly, yellow dog! You—"

He dived into the depths of his vocabulary and came up again with buckets of assorted obscenity. He poured them over Battersly hysterically. Twice, I attempted to stem the evil tide that gushed from his twisted lips. My voice was drowned out in his.

Then, physically exhausted, he stopped. He turned his head toward the open mouthed Winters, the shocked and startled Dawson.

"Get out," he said. "If I want you I'll get in touch with you."

With no reluctance whatever they got out. Allhoff turned back to his desk. With a trembling hand he took the coffee pot off its base and filled his cup. He buried his nose in it and drank deep. Battersly stood cowering against the wall. His face was the color of dirty snow. His hands were tremulous, and though I could not see them I knew his knees were, too.

I breathed a deep sigh and lit my pipe. Five years of this same scene played over and over again with profane variations took almost as much out of me as Battersly. Then, I thought for a moment of the Green murder, of the fountain pen top and the telephone number in my pocket. I resolved that if I broke this case personally. I'd cut Battersly in on the credit. In the matter of a transfer, God knew, his need was greater than mine.

CHAPTER TWO

Hot and Cold Clues

Allhoff's outburst which had roared into my ears for the past five years had its genesis during a raid on a West End rooming house some time ago. In those days Battersly was a raw rookie facing danger for the first time. Allhoff was a seasoned though misanthropic campaigner.

We had it from a stoolpigeon that the two thugs we were after had rigged a Tommy gun on the stairway dominating the door. Battersly's assignment had been to affect a rear entrance, attack the gun's operator from the rear at zero hour when the raiding squad came crashing through the front door.

The first part of the assignment he had carried out. Then, inside the house, he had undergone a quite understandable case of buck fever. He became suddenly panicky. Instead of attacking, he hesitated. During that vacillating moment, Allhoff, at the head of the raiding squad, came charging through the front door.

The Tommy gun went into immediate action, sending a score of bullets through Allhoff's legs before the squad disposed of the operator. A week later gangrene set in. Twelve hours after that came amputation.

Unfortunately Allhoff's legs were not the only organs that operation cost him. Part of his brain seemed to go with them. He emerged from the hospital bitter and brooding. Within him seethed a cauldron of hate, the fires of which were never low.

The commissioner was of no mind to lose one of his best men, legs or no legs. So he had arranged that Allhoff rent this tenement slum opposite headquarters and remain a member of the department *ex officio*. Allhoff had acceded to this request, but had laid down one adamant condition. Battersly was to be his assistant.

This, then, had been the setup for the past five years. Allhoff devoted his life to extracting his revenge, losing no opportunity to make young Battersly pay for that one weak moment which had cost Allhoff his legs. I had been tossed into the combination, ostensibly to take care of the paper work, actually to lend a hand when Allhoff became too violent.

All in all, the three of us led a miserable life. I was thoroughly sick of it. That was the prime reason that I deliberately had jeopardized a clean career by withholding evidence in a murder case. There was nothing I would not do to insure a transfer from this desk and miserable slum apartment where Allhoff dwelt with hate and venom in his twisted heart.

It was a little after four o'clock in the afternoon when the complete report on the Green murder came in from Homicide. I glanced over the single-spaced typing on the onionskin sheets of paper and noted with marked satisfaction that Homicide was baffled

With the two purloined clues in my own pocket, with the fact of Winters' broken fountain pen, plus the check I had done at lunch and discovered that the Wickersham telephone number was listed as Winters' residence, I figured I'd have little trouble breaking the case before Homicide had even evolved a tenable theory. Even better, before Allhoff had got his stained teeth into the case at all.

Allhoff watched me as I scanned the report. He removed his coffee cup from his mouth. "All right," he said. "Give."

I took a deep breath, I quoted and summarized. Almost everything contained in the paper I already knew. At the bottom of the final page I came across a fresh fact which set my heart to beating wildly.

"They found fingerprints." I told Allhoff, "on the bathroom faucets. They didn't belong to the dead man. They belonged to none of the hotel employees. They belonged undoubtedly to the murderer."

"So what?" said Allhoff. "If the killer has no record that means nothing. We can't go around printing every guy in town."

"There's something else," I said. "Though it's equally unimportant."

"Give me a fact," said Allhoff. "It's more valuable than your opinion."

"The bathroom faucets were reversed. The hot tap was fixed to the cold water and vice versa. Bardon, the manager, says he can't understand it."

Allhoff wrinkled up his brow and poured himself another cup of coffee. The fact that he was registering deep thought with absolutely nothing to work on, rather amused me. I was pretty sure, by now, that I had almost the entire answer to Green's death. For the first time in my life I was entering the stretch some eight lengths in front of Inspector Allhoff.

I looked across the room toward Battersly. He sat, the newspaper open to the comic page on his knees, staring broodingly out the window. There was something shocking about the expression of utter despair and futility upon so youthful a face. His eyes were blank and though he sat upright I had a distinct impression that his back was bowed.

I smiled at him and felt a warm glow inside me. Battersly didn't know it yet but he was going to get half credit in the solution of a murder case which had baffled Homicide, ala ordinary enough occurrence, and defeated the great Inspector Allhoff, which wasn't.

Allhoff poured two more minims of caffeine into his system. He said abruptly: "What about those faucets? Does the report mention what kind of faucets they are?"

I picked up the onionskin again. Homicide wasn't

very efficient, true. But they were damned thorough. They even mentioned the color of the dead man's shirt.

"Sure," I said. "It's all here. But I could have told you that. They use those bar-shaped modernistic faucets at the Lafayette. Those single lever affairs. Why?"

Allhoff grunted and returned to his coffee. He was silent for a long moment.

"It's damned funny," he said at last. "There are a number of angles I can see in this damned case. On the other hand, there are at least an equal number that I can't."

He drew a deep sigh up from his intestines and shook his head. I grinned happily. There were a number of angles I could see, too. Only one that I couldn't. And I knew where to look for that.

"After all," I said pleasantly, "no one's infallible."

He spun around in his chair and glared at me. He said, "I am." He reached for the telephone, picked it up and said: "Get me Cripple Creek, Colorado. Chief of police, if they have one." He hung on to the wire and stared at Battersly and myself, "You two, get out," he snapped. "Go home. The atmosphere is more conducive to clear thinking without the presence of a pair of nitwits like you guys. Lam."

Nothing loath we lammed. Downstairs, I steered Battersly into Noonan's for a drink. He sat staring moodily into his beer. I drained my rye, set down the glass, and tossed the panacea for all his troubles in his lap.

"Listen," I said, "how would you like to be a hero?"

"At what?" he said bitterly. "Soccer?"

I shook my head. "A police hero. A headline copper. With the newspapers showering praises on you. With the commissioner handing you a bow. With yourself in so solid that you could probably wangle a transfer into any precinct, any department you wanted."

He hooked up, a faint glimmer of interest in his eyes.

"Are you kidding?"

"I'm not kidding. I walked into a murder today. That Green murder that they've saddled Allhoff with. I believe I've got it tied up and in the bag. I'm certain I know whose fingerprints those are. Homicide and Allhoff will never figure it. All that's lacking is a motivation, and unless I'm badly mistaken we can dig that up at this guy Winters' house. I'll cut you in."

Battersly's beer was forgotten now. The dull weariness that constantly glazed his eyes was gone. For the first time in years, he was eager and alert.

"Sergeant," he said, "God knows I'm grateful. This is the greatest break anyone ever gave me. What are the details?"

Benignly, like a scoutmaster who has bestowed another Eagle badge on a promising lad, I told him what I had.

"You see," I concluded, "everything points to Winters. There's the fountain pen angle. There's the fact of that phone number. I'm certain those are his fingerprints. We need motive. We're going to his house now to look for it."

Battersly ordered another beer. He looked suddenly thoughtful.

"But," he objected, "Winters apparently has an alibi. You asked him what he did last night. He said that he stayed home with his wife."

"Wives don't furnish very good alibis," told him. "We can probably break that down. It's bound to fall anyway if the fingerprint angle holds up."

Battersly lifted his beer. I raised my rye. Our eyes met. We spoke no word.

Yet I knew that each of us in his heart as drinking to the downfall of Inspector Allhoff.

I felt the nervousness of a playwright on the eve of an opening as I rang the bell of Winters' Madison Avenue apartment. A rigid butler opened the door. He informed us that Mr. Winters was not in. Mrs. Winters was. Since that was the way I preferred to play it, I considered this an omen.

Janet Winters received us in the drawing room. She was a tall, dark girl with provocative black eyes. There was, rather to my concern, a great deal of poise about her. I made my identity known. She took that calmly enough. I wracked my brains trying to remember the Allhoff technique of breaking down self-possessed young women. I achieved no good result. Battersly, I observed, wasn't going to be much help either.

He stood, hat in hand, eyes fixed on Janet Winters. He rather resembled a shy freshman calling on the campus belle. I sighed, cleared my throat and plunged in.

"Mrs. Winters," I said. "There is no reason for alarm."

She raised two delicate eyebrows. "Do I give the impression of being alarmed, Sergeant?"

She most certainly didn't.

"I called to see your husband," I went on. "With your permission, I'll wait for him. In the meantime I'd like to ask you a question or two."

She lit a cigarette with long slim fingers. "All right, go ahead."

"Your husband, I understand, spent last night at home?" I asked without much hope.

Janet Winters took the cigarette from her mouth. "As a matter of fact, Sergeant, he didn't. Why do you ask?"

In that moment I felt like a guy who has picked the daily double three days in a row. For once in my life, I felt shot with luck. Far from having the difficult task of breaking down Winters' alibi, his wife had calmly done it for me and tossed the fragments in my lap.

"Oh," I said, suppressing my excitement, "Can you tell me what time he went out? What time he returned?"

"He left a little after nine. He came in quite late. I was in bed at the time. It must have been well after midnight."

I exchanged a glance with Battersly. At that moment we both saw the same vision. An eight-hour tour of duty in a precinct as far removed from Allhoff's tenement as departmental geography would allow.

I thanked Janet Winters profusely for her help. I asked her again if she minded our waiting for her husband. She rose to her feet. She said, graciously: "Not at all, Sergeant. Perhaps you'd be more comfortable waiting in his study. If you'll follow me—"

I followed her, elation soaring in my heart. Battersly, his eyes shining, closed fast on my heels,

The first thing I saw on the study desk, after the door had closed was the cigarette holder. Exultantly, I picked it up with my handkerchief. Battersly watched me with a conspiratorial air.

"Undoubtedly," I told him, "Winters' prints are on this. We can compare them with those prints Homicide took off the faucets in the Lafayette bathroom."

Battersly nodded. He turned to a steel filing cabinet against the east wall. He said, a touch of grimness in his tone: "We need a motive, don't we, Sergeant? Perhaps, we can find it here."

I stowed the cigarette holder away carefully in my pocket. A sudden hunch struck me.

"Look in the G file," I said. "See if there's any correspondence there."

"G?"

"For Green. George Green."

Battersly went through the files like a pirate digging for buried treasure. He extracted a sheaf of letters. He held them with trembling fingers as he ran his eyes across the page. Then he uttered an oath that was more a prayer of thanksgiving than blasphemy.

"Sergeant." he said excitedly. "It's here. He's been fighting with this guy Green about who should have control of that gold mine. Here, read some of this."

I pored over the correspondence. I gathered from the earlier letters that Green and Winters had never met—that Green had an out-of-town investor's suspicion of Winters, a baron of Wall Street. As the dates on the letters grew more recent, the context grew more acrimonious.

Green accused Winters of attempting to get control

of Edwards' mine, whereas, he, Green, had been promised majority stock several months ago for lesser money. Green pointed out that since he had grubstaked the prospector, Edwards, though with no written contract, he was entitled to control.

Winters had replied to him angrily. Green retaliated by hinting there was a scandal somewhere in Winters' life, and threatening to expose him when they met in New York.

Then in a letter written less than two weeks ago. Winters angrily denied the scandal charge and threatened to thrash Green if he tried any blackmail. There was more in the same key.

I stuffed the letters in my pocket. "We're in," I announced gleefully. "We have our motive. Winters meets Green when he gets to town. They quarrel. Winters kills him. If the prints on this cigarette holder check with the ones Homicide already has, we've a case as cold as any Allhoff ever solved himself. Come on."

"Aren't we going to wait for Winters?"

"Why? We have everything we need. We're going down to headquarters now. Fingerprint division. Tomorrow morning, unless I'm badly mistaken, we'll have Allhoff's back against the wall."

At nine thirty the following morning, the telephone on my desk jangled. It was Fingerprints.

"Simmonds," said Dutch Slagle, "the marks on the cigarette holder you left here check with those hotel faucets. Homicide wants to know what the hell Allhoff's got. They're scared to ask him."

I said in an unnecessarily loud voice: "Allhoff's got nothing. Battersly and I have it. We'll present the whole case wrapped up and tied with a neat pink ribbon to the D. A. before lunch."

I hung up. I looked around to see Battersly grinning at me, and Allhoff glaring over the chipped rim of his coffee cup.

"Did I understand you to say that you were solving a murder case?"

"Battersly and I. The Green case."

He looked at me as if I had announced I had just squared the circle. Then he threw back his head and laughed. The laugh nettled me.

"Go ahead," I said. "Have a jolly time. Your ego won't take it so well when we break the case before you've even got around to a theory."

"A theory." he said. "I have a theory. It's a cast-iron theory. But there's a missing piece. There's one angle I simply can't figure."

I gave him my smuggest expression.

"We have all the angles figured," I told him. "We're ready to turn the Green killer in now."

"Green?" he said. "What about this guy Edwards?"

"What about him? That's for Missing Persons. Battersly and I've been working on a murder case."

He regarded me strangely. He ran his fingers through his hair. "You have the confidence of a man who knows nothing."

"On the contrary, I have the confidence of a man who knows everything."

He filled his coffee cup. Oddly enough he remained calm. The explosion I had anticipated wasn't forthcoming. He emptied the cup and said: "What do you propose doing about it?"

"With your permission, Battersly and I will go out. We will bring Winters, his wife and Dawson down here. Then I'll solve your murder for you."

He lit a cigarette and looked at me for a long time.

"Go ahead," he said. "I haven't been amazed in years. Perhaps it's a pleasant sensation. But if you two guys, with your limited minds can solve a case I can't figure, I'll stop being a copper and go in for crossword puzzles in the tabloids. All right, go ahead. Send out your invitations."

Battersly and I marched from the room as if each of us carried a royal flush in his hip pocket.

CHAPTER THREE

A Rude Awakening

I felt like an actor on a first night who is certain he is starring in a hit play. I was exultantly nervous. I believed that I held in my hand the key which would release me from the handcuffs chaining me to Allhoff's side. Across the room Battersly watched me with shining eyes. I was glad I had cut him in. I had never, in five years, seen him look so alive.

Allhoff sat crouched over his desk, his face expressionless. He poured coffee incessantly and drank it with an ugly gurgling noise. Winters, smoking an expensive cigar whose fumes gave fragrant battle to the normal mustiness of Allhoff's apartment, sat upright in a battered Windsor chair. He appeared, I observed, magnificently unworried.

Dawson, gaunt and melancholy, lounged back on our decrepit sofa. His fingers intertwined themselves nervously. He watched Allhoff drinking coffee much in the manner of Emily Post regarding a shoat toying with the day's garbage.

Between them, silken knees crossed, was Winters' wife. Even in the murky atmosphere which framed her, she remained beautiful. Her face was serious enough

but there was an ineffable mockery in her black eyes which seemed to laugh at us all.

Allhoff suddenly slammed down his cup. He said, rather like Pontius Pilate washing his hands of the whole business:

"There was some loose talk, Simmonds, about your solving a murder case. Go ahead."

"Battersly is on this."

Battersly flashed me a glance of gratitude and I felt, for a moment, like Sam Rover of the Eagle Patrol who has just done his good deed for the day.

"You mean," asked Winters, "that you've discovered who killed Green? That you've found Edwards?"

I met his eyes squarely. "I know who killed Green," I said evenly. "I don't know anything about Edwards."

Allhoff clucked with phoney sympathy. "An oversight, undoubtedly," he purred. "After cleaning up a murder case, Simmonds can handle a missing person in stride. He'll probably take ten minutes off this afternoon and dig up Edwards for you."

I held my tongue. At the moment I could afford to be magnanimous. I cleared my throat and stepped into the center of the room. I had seen Allhoff play this scene a hundred times. I intended to play it along his pattern.

"Now," I said, "let's begin at the beginning."

Allhoff's eyebrows lifted themselves in the general direction of the ceiling. "It's customary," he murmured *sotto voce*.

I summoned all my dignity as I ignored him, "George Green," I began, "comes to town from North Carolina. He is interested in a mining deal. He's invested money through his cousin in this guy Edwards' mine."

Allhoff filled his cup. "By the way," he said and the mockery was thick in his tone, "whatever *became* of Edwards?"

I gave him my most freezing look which had no effect at all.

"Green," I continued, "registers at the Lafayette Hotel. While there he is visited by someone who is also interested in the mine. Someone who has quarreled with him about who owns how many shares of it."

Still playing it according to Allhoff's technique, I glanced about the room, then brought my eyes to bear upon my suspect. Winters was watching me, a frown upon his brow. The man, I decided, had nerves. He evinced neither nervousness nor guilt.

I continued: "I have in my possession letters proving motive absolutely. The fingerprints Homicide discovered on the bathroom faucets, I have checked. Homicide couldn't find out to who those fingerprints belonged. Battersly and I did."

I looked over at Battersly, and in retrospect I must admit we bowed like two ham actors before the exit. Winters' brow was screwed up like the plans of the Italian General Staff. Dawson was regarding me intently. Janet Winters' eyes were still mocking. She possessed an odd quality of making a man feel like a fool even when he was quite sure of himself.

Allhoff registered mild boredom. He embraced Battersly and myself with his gaze and muttered: "Battersly and Simmonds, the bloodhounds of the law! The underworld trembles! Go on, Sergeant."

"All right," I said. "We have the motive. We have, in the hotel bathroom, the fingerprints of a man who denies he was ever in the room. Which is evidence enough to convict even a man of your standing, Mr. Winters."

I stood there like a lawyer who has just produced evidence which the Supreme Court is eating out of his hand. I turned my face in Allhoff's direction and gloated silently. Winters got up out of his chair and looked at me as if I were a congenital idiot.

"Do I understand that you are accusing me of killing Green?"

"Exactly,"I said. "We have the motive. We have your fingerprints."

Allhoff swallowed a cup of coffee with the sound of a plugged sewer during a heavy rain.

"Hasn't Winters an alibi?" he asked. "Didn't he spend the evening of the murder at home with his wife?"

"Of course," snapped Winters. "Thank God there's someone around here with an iota of intelligence."

I cleared my throat and spoke very much like Ely Culbertson playing the thirteenth trump.

"Winters was not a home that night. Was he, Mrs. Winters?"

Janet Winters drew a deep breath. Her face was most serious, yet the odd mocking glint remained in her deep black eyes.

"No," she said softly. "He was not."

Winters stared at her as if someone had hit him on the head with an invisible club. His mouth was open and his eyes gaping.

Janet Winters met his eye. She shook her head almost imperceptibly.

"I do not consider that my conjugal duties demand I lie to the law," she said evenly. "When murder is involved my conscience insists upon the truth."

Winters expelled air from his lungs with the sound of a deflating tire. He turned to Allhoff, wide-eyed.

"Inspector," he said. "I don't understand this? Am I being framed?"

Allhoff shrugged his shoulders. "I haven't the slightest idea," he said amiably. Then to me: "Simmonds, is the gentleman being framed?"

"The Grand Jury won't think so," I said. "Battersly and I have a case as solid as any you ever solved."

"Look here," said Winters desperately. "This is insane. Now think, Janet. You remember that night. You must—"

"Yes." said Allhoff quietly. "Think, Mrs. Winters. Are you sure you're not making a mistake? Your husband's life may well be at stake."

"Are you prompting her?" I asked indignantly. "Because we've broken this case under your very nose, are you trying to get Mrs. Winters to lie?"

Janet Winters shook her head, "I won't lie," she said evenly. "This is a murder case. I have been brought up to believe that murder is a hideous crime. Not even to save my husband would I lie."

"All right," I said. "Battersly, take Winters downstairs and book him. I'll take my evidence over to the D.A."

Allhoff emptied his coffee cup. "Just a minute," he said. "There's one thing I'd like to know, Simmonds."

"What?"

"Those fingerprints which were in Green's bathroom. Homicide found them. They couldn't find out to whom they belonged. Winters has no criminal record. How did you happen to get a sample of Winters' prints and compare them?"

To answer that question truthfully was to get myself into one hell of a lot of trouble. I said: "I worked on some private clues which apparently escaped Homicide."

"Apparently," said Allhoff dryly. He lifted his head and stared for a moment at Dawson. Dawson had sat silent throughout the entire proceedings. He smiled sadly and shook his head as if commiserating with Winters.

Allhoff spoke commandingly. "Dawson, come here!"

Dawson raised first his eyebrows, then his gaunt body. He walked across the room and stood at Allhoff's side.

"Bend down," said Allhoff.

Dawson stooped over until his face was within six inches of Allhoff's. Allhoff's voice, suddenly savage and crescendo, filled the room.

"I don't like you," he screamed. "You and your damned smug smile. Are you pitying me because I'm a cripple? Do you consider me an inferior object because I have no legs? I can't stand your damned attitude any longer. I won't. I won't!"

Without warning he lifted both his hands. His left curled around the back of Dawson's neck. His right clenched into a fist and smashed twice into Dawson's face. Blood and two teeth fell down upon the floor.

I took a step across the room as Janet Winters' voice rang out.

"You dirty sadistic little beast! I'll report you for this. I—"

"Allhoff," I said, seizing his arm. "For God's sake!"

Dawson backed away. He dabbed at his face with a handkerchief. He wiped off some of the blood but none of the astonishment and rage.

"Are you crazy?" he demanded thickly. "By God, if it weren't for the fact—"

"Sure," said Allhoff with amazing calm. "If I had my legs you'd beat me up. Isn't that it?"

"My God," said Winters querulously, "is everyone insane?"

I didn't answer. I was still regarding Allhoff. There was a bland smugness about him I didn't quite like. The only explanation for his outburst that I could evolve was the fact that he was so enraged at his own case being broken under his nose that he had gone suddenly amuck.

"Well," I said again. "Book Winters, Battersly, I'll—"

Allhoff ladled sugar into his coffee with a prodigal hand. "Just one more minute," he said with strange quietness. "I discovered this morning, Simmonds that you were in Green's hotel room when Homicide arrived."

"Right." I gave him the details.

"So you went to work independently on this case, eh?"

"I had Battersly's help."

"You figured that if you two solved it you could gloat over me. Is that it?"

"It is not. I like you so little I don't even want to gloat. I want a transfer. So does Battersly. Perhaps, with this murder case wrapped up and in the bag the commissioner might see it our way."

"A transfer," said Allhoff slowly. "A transfer. And you were the first copper at the scene of the crime. And you solved it. Always, of course, with Battersly's aid." He was silent for a moment. Then an expression of demoniac glee distorted his features. He lifted his fist and brought it smashing down on the desk top. He opened his mouth and peals of gargantuan laughter resounded through the room. "Click!" he roared. "Click! That's the missing piece."

Bewildered I shook my head and looked around the room. Janet Winters regarded Allhoff as if he were something that had just crawled out of a swamp. Dawson holding his handkerchief to his face blinked dazedly. Winters held his hand to his temple as if he were desperately trying to understand what was going on. Battersly asked me for his cue with his eyes.

"Allhoff," I said politely, "have you gone mad?"

His laughter ceased abruptly. "Wait a minute," he said and there was an unholy glint in his eyes. "I am fighting an internal battle."

"Go ahead and fight it." I said. "In the meantime, Battersly, take Winters—"

"No!" roared Allhoff. "No one is to leave this room until I say so. I've got to make a decision."

There was something so completely dominant in his tone that no one moved. He sat, hunched over his desk, the center of a great silence. His brow was corrugated and his stubby forefinger beat a thoughtful tattoo on the desk top. Finally he unleashed a sigh that came from the very bottom of his being. "No," he said, "I won't do it. There's a lot of copper in me after all. A sort of a compulsion to make a criminal pay for his crime no matter how satisfactory it would be the other way."

"Allhoff," I said, "you're talking Choctaw."

"I'll put it into English. I'll tell you who killed Green. I'll tell you what became of Edwards from Cripple Creek. I have solved the case, Sergeant. Without, I may add, Battersly's help."

I shook my head: "I know what you're doing. You're putting up a desperate fight to save your face. You can't go behind my case. You can't go behind my evidence. It's sure-fire."

"I can go so far behind it," he said viciously, "that you'll find yourself facing charges, Sergeant. That odd cloud you may notice hovering over your head is the endangering of your pension rights."

I felt a slight quiver at the pit of my stomach. Allhoff was rarely wrong. And I *had* withheld vital evidence. But how, I asked myself, could he possibly know that? How could he conceivably crack the case I'd built up against Winters?

He filled his coffee cup. He emptied it. He took a deep breath. He said: "To quote yourself, Sergeant, let's begin at the beginning."

"You mean the night Green was murdered?"

"I mean the moment Edwards stepped off the train from Colorado."

"But he didn't," said Dawson.

"The hell he didn't," said Allhoff. "He arrived on schedule."

"Then where is he?" asked Winters excitedly. "Perhaps he can throw some light on all this. Where is he?"

"In Woodlawn Cemetery," said Allhoff, "lying in a coffin with a ton of earth over him."

I gaped at him. How he'd found this out, I had no idea. "You mean," I asked, "that it was a double murder? Green and Edwards?"

"No, Dick Tracy. I don't mean any such thing. Since you were at the hotel before I got any information, I guess you had the same clues to work on that I did. More, as a matter of fact. But with your customary stupidity, you blew them."

"What clues?" I was frankly nervous now. "How did I blow them?"

"You found a corpse registered as George Green from North Carolina, didn't you?"

I nodded.

"You probably found out that he ordered soft boiled six-minute eggs for breakfast. Moreover, it's quite likely that a bellboy told you Green tossed him a dollar tip."

This was all true enough and I said so. Allhoff refilled his coffee cup. He sighed as if exasperated with the utter stupidity of the world.

"Well," he said, "Green wasn't Green. He was Edwards."

Winters gasped. Battersly glanced at me but I did not meet his eye. The hollow sensation at the pit of my stomach spread to the lower intestines.

"How could Green be Edwards?" said Dawson through his bleeding mouth. "That's ridiculous."

"No more ridiculous than a six-minute soft boiled egg," snapped Allhoff.

"Look," I said, "would you kindly take a moment to tell what in the name of God eggs have to do with it?"

"Sure," said Allhoff. "Edwards came from Cripple Creek. That's about ten thousand feet high. The boiling point of water is much lower than it is at sea level. It would take six minutes to cook a soft boiled egg in Cripple Creek."

I blinked and digested this information. Allhoff grinned at me happily.

"Then there's the dollar," he said. "No one apparently thought to ask that bellboy how a flimsy dollar bill could be tossed at him. Yet Homicide assures me 'tossed' was the word he used. Obviously it was a silver dollar. There are more silver dollars in use around Denver than anywhere else. I immediately arrived at the conclusion that Edwards was Green."

I thought it over and took heart. I nodded reassuringly in Battersly's direction.

"That doesn't touch our case," I said. "Edwards or Green. He was murdered, wasn't he? So my cast-iron evidence makes Winters the killer of Edwards instead. In effect, it's still the same case."

"In effect," said Allhoff, "you're a blundering slow-witted lout whose screwing around has almost sent an innocent man to the chair, made a fortune for a murderer and dragged yourself and Battersly into the stinkingest departmental trial that ever gave off an odor."

I didn't know precisely what he was driving at. But somehow I wished I was a long way from here. There was a certain gloating assurance about him. I remembered his reputation for being right, my own for being wrong. I bit my lip. I said: "Will you explain all this?"

"Willingly and loudly. Since Sherlock Simmonds and Doctor Watson Battersly have stepped down, Inspector Allhoff will take over. Hold on to your hats everybody, here we go!"

CHAPTER FOUR

Prof. Allhoff's Murder

There was a breezy confidence about him that I didn't like at all. He tilted his coffee cup, spilling the last three drops upon his chin. He leaned back in his chair and began to talk with all the apodictic authority of an isolationist senator.

"This guy, Edwards, apparently finds a gold mine. He is, as Dawson has told us, as Cripple Creek has wired us, a bit of a nut. He'd been gypped out of mines before this and now he's panicky about city slickers. He doesn't even file his claim. He comes to New York to sell part of it for a lot of cash. Dawson, who knows him, is supposed to meet him at the station."

"And," I murmured, taking heart, "today is Tuesday. We know all these facts."

"Thus far you do," said Allhoff. "Now I'll give you some more facts. Facts which completely escaped you. Edwards does arrive on that train. Dawson does meet him. Dawson takes him to the Lafayette Hotel. But before doing so he pours a lot of slime in the old guy's ear. He plays on the old man's delusion of persecution. He tells him that big operators from Wall Street are out to steal his mine. That extreme caution is called for."

Dawson took the crimson handkerchief from his lips. He said: "This is ridiculous."

Allhoff ignored him. He continued.

"To this end Dawson persuades Edwards to mask his identity. This, says Dawson, will fool the crooks who are after the mine's location. Dawson, his old pal, has it all fixed. Edwards is to assume the person of one George Green, Dawson's cousin from Carolina. Edwards, who apparently trusts Dawson, agrees. Dawson loads Edwards with papers and stuff which will identify him as Green and takes away everything which might identify him as Edwards. Then he registers him as Green at the Lafayette Hotel and tells Winters that Edwards never arrived."

I considered this. It sounded all right, but for the life of me, I didn't see that it interfered with my case against Winters.

"What about the fingerprints?" I said. "What about Winters' prints on the bathroom faucets?"

"Ah," said Allhoff, "you mean those very odd faucets? The one marked hot on the cold water tap and vice versa?"

"What's so significant about that? It often happens."

"Not in first-class hotels," said Allhoff. He leaned across the desk and fixed Winters with his index finger. "Now, 'Winters, it is true, isn't it, that recently your wife decided to change your bathroom fixtures? She brought home samples for you to examine?"

Winters blinked. "My God," he said, glancing at his wife. "Yes, yes, Inspector. That's true. I—"

Allhoff's upheld hand silenced him. "The fact of those faucets being reversed started me thinking that perhaps the fingerprints had been planted on them *before* they were taken into the hotel. That's exactly what happened. Our killer in his haste accidentally reverses them when he screws them into the water pipe."

"You mean," I asked, "someone was trying to frame Winters?"

"With your help," said Allhoff, "yes. We have these bitter letters about the mine between Green and Winters. That makes a motive. The theory is that Winters called on Green to straighten things out, they had a fight and in a rage Winters killed him. The fingerprints in the bathroom prove it. Hell, you figured that all out yourself, Simmonds. That was exactly what the killer wanted you to do."

"I still don't get it," I said. "What's the murderer's motive?" Allhoff cocked an eyebrow in Dawson's direction, "Do you care to tell him, Dawson, or shall I?"

Dawson took the handkerchief away from his mouth. He said again, "Ridiculous." I noted, with a sinking heart, that he didn't say it with a great deal of conviction.

"Edwards is dead," said Allhoff. "Only Dawson now knows the location of the mine. Moreover, Dawson has the dough that Winters put up. He's already claimed he forwarded it to Edwards in Cripple Creek. He also has something else."

Winters glared at Dawson. Then he turned his head and regarded his wife with an odd mixture of fear and wrath.

"What else has he?" he asked and he was obviously fearful of the answer.

"Mrs. Winters," said Allhoff.

There was a hush in the room broken only by the swift intake of Janet Winters' breath.

"It had to be." said Allhoff. "If a man is using his wife to front for him on a phoney alibi, he certainly has it fixed with her first. Winters told us at once that he spent the night of the murder at home with his wife. His wife denied it. Then when I checked on those faucets it was clear her hand was in it, too. Why?"

"Why?" I echoed weakly.

"Because she's been having an affair with Dawson. Because if Winter burns for murder she and her lover get the money. This figured obviously. A few moments ago I proved it."

"How could you prove such a charge as that?" snapped Janet Winters.

Allhoff grinned satanically. "With Dawson's teeth. You sat quiet and still while your husband was being railroaded to the electric chair. You made not the slightest protest. Yet when I smacked Dawson, you unleashed a howl. Obvious, wasn't it?"

Janet Winters bit her lip. I focused my eyes on the far wall and called every brain cell into action. If Allhoff was right and I was wrong, I was going to find myself in more trouble than a rugged individualist at Camp Dix.

"Wait a minute," I said. "What about this Green? Where is he? And why should Dawson have gone through that business of switching Edwards' identity? Couldn't he have framed Winters for killing Edwards with the same result? Why all this business of substituting the identity of the two men?"

"A fair question," said Allhoff. "Green exists only in Dawson's mind and on the police blotter. That switch was done for reasons of motive. Dawson couldn't possibly cook up a motive for Winters' murdering Edwards. Edwards demanded a certain price for an interest in his mine. Winters was prepared to pay it. Edwards, who I gather was rather illiterate, would not engage in any angry correspondence. No, Dawson needed this Green whom he invented. Green, a supposed business man, ostensibly gets into this bitter financial controversy with Winters. Dawson, of course, is actually writing these Green letters, having them forwarded by some stooge of his in Carolina.

"I've been in touch by phone with the coppers in that Carolina town Green was supposed to come from. They found out from the post office that letters addressed to Green were being picked up from a certain box. They got the guy who was picking them. They found the original of Winters' letters in his possession. He talked at the drop of a rubber hose."

Winters sighed heavily.

"What I fail to understand," he said, "is if those fingerprints of mine were planted in the hotel, how did Dawson figure they'd be traced to me? After all, the police can't go around checking prints with every person in New York City."

I exchanged a glance with Battersly.

There was something cold and unpleasant at the pit of my stomach. Allhoff drained his cup again and looked at me like the devil about to light a particularly hot fire in Hades.

"The Sergeant wanted a transfer, didn't you, Sergeant?" he said mockingly. "The point Winters just made had me troubled for a while. If the killer left Winters' prints, it was obvious he must also leave some clues which would lead Homicide to Winters. I'm quite sure he did. What did you do with them, Sergeant?"

I sat down, feeling as if there were water instead of blood in my knees. I saw Allhoff's unholy grin through a haze. He had me cold and completely. If I got out of this with less than a fine of two months' pay, I'd consider myself lucky.

I took a deep breath. I murmured a silent prayer to the patron saint of dumb police sergeants. I took the pipe from my mouth with a trembling hand and told him everything. As I spoke I was aware of Battersly's eyes upon me. He looked rather like a little boy who has discovered that his father has lied to him.

Allhoff heard my recital, his face twisted up, and gleaming mockery in his eyes.

"So." he said as I finished, "you withheld evidence, eh, Sergeant? And Battersly was in this, too."

"No," I said. "He really wasn't. He—"

"You said he was," said Allhoff mercilessly. "You said it three times before witnesses. Of course, the matter will be reported. It'll probably cost you both a degree of seniority and a month's pay."

I did not meet Battersly's eye. Yesterday I had lifted him up beautifully. Today, I had dropped him with a thud.

"You see," Allhoff went on, "Dawson figures it simply. As a relative, he identifies Green. The body is buried and no questions asked."

Across the room, Dawson cleared his throat. "Inspector," he said, "you're a master of conjecture. You'll need more than conjecture in a jury room."

"I have a witness," said Allhoff. "Haven't I, Mrs. Winters?"

For the first time since I had known her, Janet Winters revealed a measure of uncertainty. She glanced quickly toward Dawson, then back at Allhoff.

"You see," said Allhoff, "when I figured this plumbing business, I had a couple of boys from the detective bureau— not my own assistants here, of course; they were too busy working out the case for themselves—canvass the hardware shops in your neighbor-

hood. It was simple since the faucets you bought had to be the same type as those used in the Hotel Lafayette. I discovered the store where you purchased those faucets, Mrs. Winters. I discovered further that the hardware dealer has an identifying mark on all his merchandise. That's enough, with the rest of the evidence to make a very tight case against you, Mrs. Winters. If you can explain it all without involving Dawson, you're most ingenious. If you can't, you'd better involve him now. Being a woman and a witness for the state, you'll probably save your life."

Dawson leaned forward on the couch. Janet Winters avoided her husband's eye and looked squarely at Allhoff.

"I've always been a realist," she said evenly. "So I see your point, Inspector. I do involve Dawson. And right now."

Dawson said, "Janet!" But she didn't look at him. She regarded Allhoff with her deep black eyes and it seemed to me there was some hatred in them—some hatred and a great deal of respect. "Maybe," she said, "I should have married a man like you."

"In my day—" said Allhoff, so softly, so reminiscently, that for an instant I was shocked. Then he broke off abruptly. He snapped: "Battersly, get me a copper. Take Mrs. Winters and Dawson out of here. Book them across the street."

Battersly moved dully toward the door. All the hope he had glowed with yesterday was gone. He moved like a beaten man. I felt like a louse. Allhoff drank coffee noisily like Goering toasting the fall of Paris.

The three of us sat alone in the office. Allhoff chuckled without turning around.

"Why don't you boys get in touch with Eddie Hoover?" he said mockingly. "I understand he needs men badly."

I didn't answer him directly. I mentioned something that had been on my mind for the past few minutes.

"About that hardware store—" I said. "Isn't it odd that each dealer should carry identifying marks on every piece of material?"

"Odd?" said Allhoff. "It's impossible. But what woman would ever know that?"

I shook my head. Whenever he tried a bluff it seemed to work. When I tried one, I invariably fell on my face.

"There's one more thing," I said. "Do you recall before you began your explanation you announced you were conducting an internal struggle? After that you said that there was a lot of copper in you after all. What was it all about?"

Allhoff spun around in his chair. He balanced his coffee cup delicately on the stub of his right thigh.

"Oh, that," he said. "I was wondering if I ought to teach you guys a lesson. I was considering letting you get away with your case. Letting Winters burn. Then I would produce my own evidence. You certainly would've looked like a couple of first-rate idiots then."

"You actually considered that?"

He grinned. "Why not? I think it would have been damned funny."

"Allhoff," I said very seriously. "Why don't you see a psychiatrist? Consider, for God's sake, your mental health, You don't think it's normal, do you?"

His eyes lit up. His twisted smile spread over his face. "How's my mental health?" he said, and there was a hysterical note in his voice. "Oh, I can't kick, Simmonds." His voice rose like a siren blown by a maniac. His fist beat furiously on the desk top. "I can't kick, damn you! *I can't kick!*"

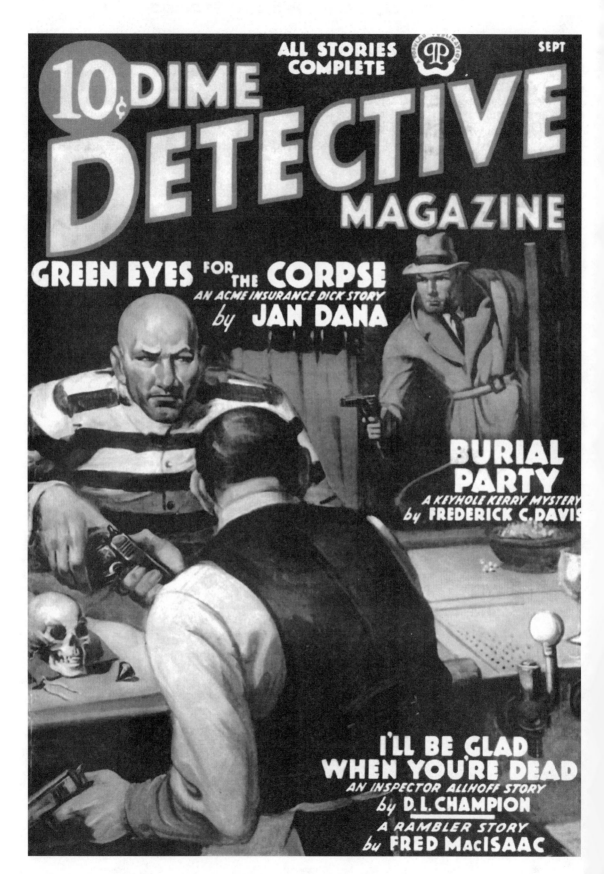

ALL STORIES COMPLETE

SEPT

10¢ DIME DETECTIVE MAGAZINE

GREEN EYES FOR THE CORPSE
AN ACME INSURANCE DICK STORY
by JAN DANA

BURIAL PARTY
A KEYHOLE KERRY MYSTERY
by FREDERICK C. DAVIS

I'LL BE GLAD WHEN YOU'RE DEAD
AN INSPECTOR ALLHOFF STORY
by D.L. CHAMPION
A RAMBLER STORY
by FRED MacISAAC

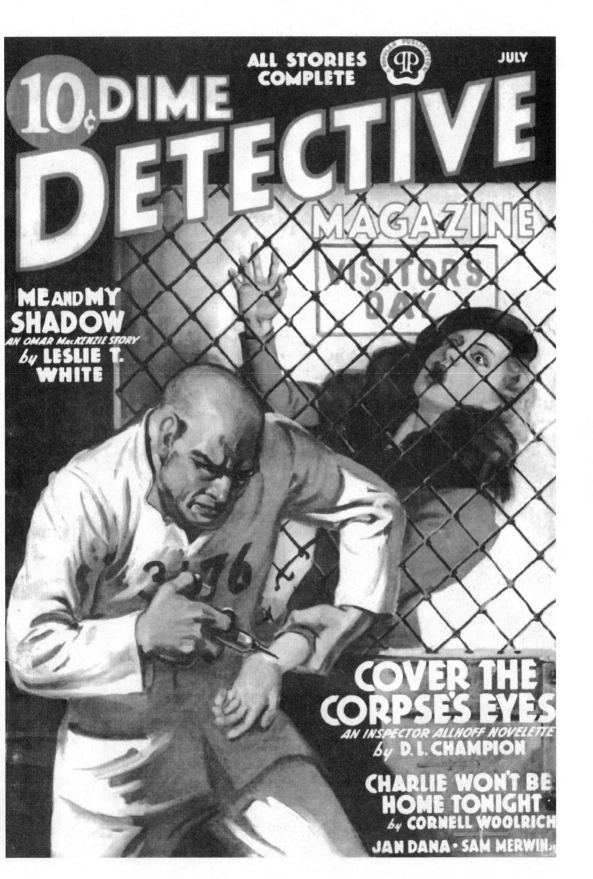

10¢ ALL STORIES COMPLETE OCTOBER

DIME DETECTIVE MAGAZINE

DEAD AND DUMB
AN INSPECTOR ALLHOFF NOVELETTE
by D. L. CHAMPION

MAN HUNT
A MARQUIS OF BROADWAY STORY
by JOHN LAWRENCE

MURDER MARCH OF THE TOY SOLDIERS
by SAM MERWIN JR.

ALL STORIES COMPLETE

MARCH

10¢ DIME DETECTIVE MAGAZINE

THE BOSS SAYS KILL
A MURDER MYSTERY
by T. T. FLYNN

INSPECTOR'S FUNERAL
A MARQUIS OF BROADWAY STORY
by JOHN LAWRENCE

AN INSPECTOR ALLHOFF NOVELETTE
by D. L. CHAMPION

204

ALL STORIES COMPLETE

JANUARY

10¢ DIME DETECTIVE MAGAZINE

THE 10:30 TO
SING SING
AN INSPECTOR ALLHOFF STORY
by D. L. CHAMPION
THE SAINT IN
SILVER
A STEVE MIDNIGHT NOVELETTE
by JOHN K. BUTLER
A MATTER OF
POLICY
A NOVEL-LENGTH MURDER MYSTERY
by SAM MERWIN JR.

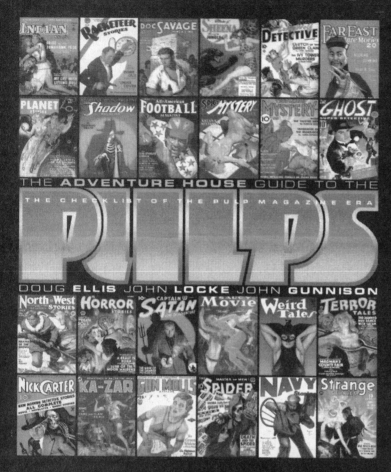